THE AMERICAS
IN TRANSITION

THE AMERICAS IN TRANSITION

The Contours of Regionalism

Gordon Mace, Louis Bélanger,
and contributors

LYNNE
RIENNER
PUBLISHERS

BOULDER
LONDON

Published in the United States of America in 1999 by
Lynne Rienner Publishers, Inc.
1800 30th Street, Boulder, Colorado 80301

and in the United Kingdom by
Lynne Rienner Publishers, Inc.
3 Henrietta Street, Covent Garden, London WC2E 8LU

Library of Congress Cataloging-in-Publication Data
Mace, Gordon.
    The Americas in transition : the contours of regionalism / Gordon
Mace, Louis Bélanger, and contributors.
        p.   cm.
    Includes bibliographical references and index.
    ISBN 1-55587-717-6
    1. America—Relations—20th century. 2. Regionalism—America—
History—20th century. 3. Pan-Americanism—History—20th century.
4. North America—Economic integration. 5. South America—Economic
integration. I. Bélanger, Louis, 1930–   . II. Title.
E18.85.M27   1999
327'.098'09045—dc21   99-10363
                                                              CIP

British Cataloguing in Publication Data
A Cataloguing in Publication record for this book
is available from the British Library.

Printed and bound in the United States of America

        The paper used in this publication meets the requirements
 ∞ of the American National Standard for Permanence of
        Paper for Printed Library Materials Z39.48-1984.

    5 4 3 2 1

To the victims of Hurricane Mitch,
November 1998

Contents

Acknowledgments

This book is the product of a team effort. We want first of all to convey to all of our colleagues involved in the project our deepest appreciation for their cooperation and commitment throughout the endeavor.

We would also like to express our gratitude to the staff and members of the Research Group on International Relations. Many thanks to Élise Lapalme, who, again and as always, worked diligently on the various drafts and on the final version of the manuscript. Thank you also to our research associate Martin Roy for helping us coordinate the whole project, and to our various research assistants whose work, at one time or another, in collecting information and assembling and analyzing data was particularly helpful. Thanks also to David Hagen, Mary Richardson, and Maureen Magee for translating some of the chapters and editing others.

We also deeply appreciate the help and support of the people at Lynne Rienner Publishers. We would like to acknowledge first of all the encouragement of Lynne Rienner herself. And we want to express our gratitude to Sally Glover; to Laurie Rogers, who did a superb job of copyediting; and to Lesli Brooks Athanasoulis, who, as project editor, supervised the production of this book. Special thanks also to the anonymous reviewer, whose comments were extremely useful in preparing the final draft of the manuscript.

Financial support for our research was provided by the Social Sciences and Humanities Research Council of Canada and the Fonds FCAR of the Government of Québec. We also want to express our gratitude to the Department of Political Science at Laval University, and especially to its chair, Guy Laforest, for having supported in many ways our efforts, and to the Graduate Institute of International Studies at Laval, which generously provides office space and other material support.

Gordon Mace
Louis Bélanger

1

Hemispheric Regionalism in Perspective

Gordon Mace & Louis Bélanger

Regionalism, as we understand it, is a multidimensional political process of integration occurring between two or more countries in a given geographical region. In the long term, such a process seldom leads to the creation of a new political unit, but it should result in a higher level of cohesion between the countries involved in the process and some form of joint management of regional problems. Regionalism is a social construct devoid of automaticity in the sense that it is a product of human agency, not of some sort of natural evolution. In other words, regionalism is a response to economic, geographic, and other conditions without any deterministic force behind it.

This absence of automaticity means that progress in one area of a regional process of integration will not necessarily entail progress in another area and that progression in a particular dimension may be halted and reversed. All is well and integration can take place when, in a particular regional scheme, major actors share similar perceptions, attitudes, and behavior. However, integration can be halted or reversed when actors have opposing points of view and adopt confrontational policies or behavior. Like any other social and political construct, regionalism is determined by the behavior of the multiple actors involved in the process and by the way regionalism converges with their different interests and strategies. Once launched, regionalism itself becomes part of the strategic environment of these actors, as well as others. This interplay of actors' strategic behavior and the processes of regionalism is what this book proposes to study.

Having made some conceptual clarifications, we certainly agree with Andrew Hurrell's comment that the words "region" and "regionalism" are "ambiguous terms" (Hurrell 1995b: 38). That ambiguity, understandable given the complexity of the subject matter, appears in the way various authors over the past forty years have used almost interchangeably the terms "political integration," "regional integration," "regionalism," "regionalization," "regionness," and "new regionalism" to identify a phenomenon that may have taken different forms along the years, but that in essence remained the same. This ambiguity also appears in definitions found in the literature throughout the years.[1] This listing of definitions makes two points: (1) it underlines the literature's difficulty in arriving at conceptual clarity when trying to circumscribe a phenomenon as complex as regionalism; and (2) it shows that, nevertheless, some recurrent themes or characterizations do emerge such as the idea that (i) regionalism is a process; (ii) the phenomenon is multidimensional; and (iii) it is constructed by actors involved in the process, most particularly state actors. Our conceptual definition tries to stay as close as possible to these basic characterizations.

That being said, the phenomenon of regionalism is not something new. Its rediscovery should not conceal the fact that it has been one of the main structuring forces of the international system over the past forty years. Indeed, since the 1950s, the tension between the global and multilateral and the regional levels of governance has always been present, particularly in trade and commerce (Anderson and Blackburst 1993), but also in general economic activity (Oman 1994) and in broader strategic terms. Some scholars even view the region as the most significant future matrix for the regulation of political and economic activity and the central strategic space in the global system (Badie 1995; Laïdi 1994: 217). Although this view may be an exaggeration, the fact remains that regionalism became a significant feature of the international system with the thrust toward European unification in the 1950s. In this introductory chapter, we survey these early manifestations of regionalism in the Americas and elsewhere in order to situate the phenomenon within a historical context. We then review the pertinent theoretical literature addressing regionalism and propose our own actor-focused perspective. Finally, we briefly explain the outline of this book.

Regionalism Since 1945

The creation of the European Coal and Steel Community (ECSC) in 1952 and the establishment of the European Economic Community (EEC) by the Treaty of Rome in 1957 were fundamental manifestations of strategic regionalism. Although its security aspect was often overlooked later on, one of the main achievements of the ECSC was preventing further European wars between France and Germany (Axline 1995: 2) and transforming a historically confrontational relationship into a cooperative one to create the core area around which European unification could develop. The

EEC, for its part, enabled the Western European countries to foster a political space of their own between the all-pervasive superpowers of the Cold War era. Finally, the progressive transformation of the EEC into the European Union resulted in the creation of a new global actor (Piening 1997; Rhodes 1998), confirming the wisdom of David Mitrany's precepts and reestablishing some of the legitimacy of the neofunctionalist approach to regional integration, at least for the analysis of that particular phenomenon (Mutimer 1989).

Experiences at regional integration were not limited to the European continent, however. The EEC soon became a model or a goal for other countries, particularly in what was then called the Third World. In Asia, the Association of Southeast Asian Nations (ASEAN) was established in 1967 primarily as a response to a perceived communist threat coming from China, Vietnam, Laos, and Cambodia. Like the EEC, ASEAN was an example of strategic regionalism and resulted in a loose political and economic arrangement whose objective was to develop free trade among member countries, but also to establish a forum for political consultation in the event of a reduced U.S. presence in Asia as a result of the Vietnam War. In Africa, in the meantime, regional integration was also very much on the agenda as one of the instruments to help African countries get a better deal in the anticipated new international economic order. The Customs and Economic Union of Central Africa,[2] the East African Common Market, and the West African Economic Community,[3] to name a few, were economically oriented, whereas groupings such as the Community of West Africa's States[4] had more political objectives in mind.

Apart from Europe, however, the thrust toward regionalism was most profound and diverse in the Americas during the 1960s and 1970s. The push toward integration in the hemisphere was influenced by two contending paradigms. In the first, the main emphasis of Latin American integration went from political unity to economic integration under the influence of what could be called the developmental philosophy of the recently created Economic Commission for Latin America (ECLA, later to become ECLAC after the inclusion of the Caribbean and better known by its Spanish abbreviation CEPAL). In the second, the Pan-American paradigm sought to revive the "Western Hemisphere idea" leading to continental integration.

The ECLA doctrine was based on the ideas of its first secretary-general and respected Argentinian economist Raùl Prebisch. What became known as the Latin American structuralist school of development theory sought to explain underdevelopment in Latin America essentially as the result of an international system composed of a center and a periphery. This underlying international structure was the cause as well as the result of an international division of labor wherein the center produced and exported manufactured goods while the countries of the periphery produced and exported raw materials and commodities. The fact that historically the price of manufactured goods has risen faster than the price of raw materials created a situation of deteriorating terms of trade as the basis of the "unequal exchange" between North and South. Unequal exchange was the main cause of Latin American underdevelopment, a situation that could be overcome only by industrialization based on import substitution. But national markets were too small and the strategy of industrialization by import substitution at the local level had reached its limits. Only regional integration schemes could provide the larger markets and the accompanying economies of scale necessary for industrialization. Industrialization would then take place in an economic environment constrained by state regulation, and when necessary, state intervention would lead to the modernization of Latin American societies and, eventually, their inclusion in the First World (W. Baer 1962; ECLA 1950).

On the basis of these precepts, in the 1950s and early 1960s ECLA became extremely active in supporting efforts at regional integration (Mitchell 1967), most notably in Central America, where such efforts led to the establishment of the Central American Common Market (CACM). ECLA ideas were also influential to a certain extent in the discussions leading to the creation of the Andean Group and the Caribbean Community and Common Market (CARICOM). However, both integration schemes, particularly the Andean Group, went much further than what was presented in the ECLA doctrine (Axline 1979; Fontaine 1977; Mace 1981).

Consequently, by the first half of the 1970s, the Latin American and Caribbean landscape was covered with integration schemes varying in both form and content. In addition to the CACM, the Andean Group, and CARICOM, there was also the Latin American Free Trade Association (LAFTA)[5] and the Latin American Economic System (SELA).[6] Although SELA was more a forum supporting economic integration than a real integration scheme, LAFTA was an integration process that had little to do with the ECLA doctrine. An extension of a Southern Cone project devised by governments opposed to ECLA's intervention and supported by the United States, LAFTA was essentially a loose free trade arrangement based on two limited mechanisms: annual negotiated tariff reductions and industrial complementary agreements. The region hosted all three types of integration schemes identified by Lynn K. Mytelka (Mytelka 1979: 10–21) in the developing world: laissez-faire integrative systems (LAFTA), laissez-faire with elements of compensation through planning (CACM and CARICOM), and interventionist integrative systems (the Andean Group).

At the end of the 1970s, however, regional integration in Latin America and elsewhere in the developing world was in a state of crisis. A combination of factors contributed to the situation, including specific events related to each integration scheme, for example, Chile's withdrawal from the Andean Group and the refusal of LAFTA's larger member countries to adopt compensation mechanisms favorable to the less developed members of the integration process. But without a doubt, what most affected regionalism in the 1970s was the oil crisis of 1973–1974 and the resulting economic stagnation worldwide. This new turn of events had a negative impact on regional integration in developing countries in two major ways. The recession in industrialized countries increased protectionism, making access to their markets more difficult for developing countries. At the same time, the North-South dialogue came to an end, the 1981 Cancún conference being the last of its kind. The oil crisis also created severe budget deficits for most oil-importing developing countries, which in a matter of months had to face huge increases in the price of oil products and derivatives. The resulting fiscal deficits required huge loans from international money markets, directly causing the debt crisis of the early 1980s. Moreover, the economic downturn reinforced inward-looking attitudes and put an end to the spirit of cooperation needed for the give-and-take approach that could ensure the success of regional integration.

Hemispheric regionalism, the other integration paradigm in the Americas, was reactivated in 1948 at the Bogotá conference. With the signing of the charter establishing the Organization of American States (OAS), the new inter-American system experienced a promising debut. It was hoped that the OAS, with its network of specialized conferences and agencies, later complemented by the Inter-American Development Bank, would become the main diplomatic forum for inter-American affairs as well as the major regional institution for cooperation in areas such as health, education, and culture. In matters of security, the contours of a regional system were established with the signing in 1947 of the Rio Treaty, providing for collective defense against aggression either from outside or from within the region. The major drawback, however, concerned economic affairs; the failure to ratify the economic agreement signed at the Bogotá conference brought the dream of a free trade area in the Americas to a standstill.

But on balance, there might have been enough support for continental integration in the early 1950s if U.S. attention had not been concentrated in other regions of the world and if positive gestures had been made, such as the adoption of an aid package similar to the Marshall Plan. Such aid was what Latin American governments were hoping for, but it never materialized. On the contrary, when U.S. attention was diverted back to the Americas, it resulted essentially in unilateral interventions or ill-fated policies such as the 1954 Guatemalan episode, the Bay of Pigs episode and the embargo against Cuba, and the 1965 intervention in the Dominican Republic. Even the 1961 Alliance for Progress failed to repair the damage, and by the mid-1960s, hemispheric regionalism had become an agonizing process.

For the Johnson administration, the Meeting of American Chiefs of State at Punta del Este, Uruguay, in April 1967 was supposed to encourage Latin American integration, revitalize the Alliance for Progress, and improve inter-American relations generally (Connell-Smith 1974: 248). Instead, it proved to be the last meeting of its kind for many years to come. As it turned out, a combination of factors pushed inter-American relations into a period of decline lasting almost twenty years. The war in Vietnam had the effect of diverting U.S. attention away from Latin America for several years. Subsequently, the U.S. government and its Latin American counterparts had very divergent views on issues such as control over natural resources, treatment of foreign investments, the external debt, and the crisis in Central America, to name but a few.

Consequently, both paths toward regionalism (the Latin American and the Pan-American) had come to a dead end by the early 1980s. As was the case with regionalism elsewhere in the Third World, Latin American and Caribbean integration schemes had become empty shells, barely surviving. Hemispheric regionalism, for its part, was almost nonexistent, as Latin American governments had lost all faith in the OAS. How is it, then, that at the end of that same decade, regionalism had made a stunning comeback not only in the Americas but in Europe and Asia as well, again becoming a central feature of contemporary international relations?

Of course, this evolution cannot be explained by any single factor, and in the Americas the combinations of factors vary from country to country.[7] However, three elements seem to have played a central role in the analysis put forward by decisionmakers throughout the region. The collapse of the Soviet empire and the implosion of the Soviet Union meant an important victory for the Western-based model of democracy and economic development. These events also confirmed the status of the United States as the only remaining superpower. The modernization of the former Eastern bloc countries also meant that Latin America as a whole would have to compete with Eastern Europe for development funds. A second reason had to do with the perception that the world economy was in the process of being reorganized around three major economic blocs: Western Europe, North America, and Asia (Belous and Hartley 1990; Brand 1992; Buelens 1992). Latin America could not afford to be excluded from the principal axes of economic transactions. Finally, the effects of the external debt crisis on the psyche of Latin American elites must not be underestimated. The results of the crisis led to an important change in their values and perceptions with regard to the traditional economic development model, the role of the state in the economy, political behavior, and the nature of their relationship with the United States (ECLAC 1992, 1994).

These factors are at the root of the significant reemergence of basic patterns of regionalism in the Americas, the subregional Latin American and Caribbean integration schemes, and the U.S.-led thrust at continental integration. In the case of Latin America and the Caribbean, the adoption of new forms of regional integration throughout the subregion, starting in the second half of the 1980s, can be explained by the combination of fundamental attitudinal changes resulting from the debt crisis and the perception of an emerging world order dominated by three blocs of mostly industrialized countries, which generated an acute fear of marginalization. The Southern Cone Common Market (Mercosur), the Group of Three (Mexico, Colombia, and Venezuela), the Andean Community (reformed Andean Group), and, moving in the same direction, the CACM and CARICOM now represent what Klaus Peter Fischer has called in Chapter 10 the "integrationist/competitive" model of integration. Supported by liberal democracy and market economics, this new form of integration favors elements such as financial liberalization, limited protection for local industries, and a weak presence of the state in the economy, among other things. It is what ECLAC has called "open regionalism" and it represents a fundamental shift in the way Latin America and the Caribbean address regionalism.

In the case of U.S.-led hemispheric regionalism, this third attempt at continental integration was launched by Washington as one of the measures to strengthen the United States' global influence in the context of the new post–Cold War international order. It was also a response to a very strong belief in Washington's administrative branch that the changes in political behavior and economic policies throughout Latin America during the 1980s created a historic moment of a convergence of values and a window of opportunity that had to be seized. With the North American Free Trade Agreement (NAFTA) in the background, the building blocks of continental integration were the Enterprise for the Americas Initiative, announced by President George Bush on June 27, 1990, and the Summit of the Americas, attended by thirty-four countries of the hemisphere in Miami in December 1994. The documents produced in the context of these two major diplomatic initiatives trace the contours of a hemisphere-wide integration process whose highlight is the proposal to establish a Free Trade Area of the Americas (FTAA). But as we will see in Chapter 2, what is involved in the so-called Miami process goes beyond free trade; it is really a multidimensional integration process involving issues in many areas of hemispheric cooperation.

This book is essentially a study of the contours of hemispheric regionalism as it shapes the future of the Americas. The literature on the subject has been growing steadily over the past few years (Grugel 1996; Hurrell 1995a; Mace and Thérien 1996b; Muñoz and Rosenberg 1993; Nishijima and Smith 1996; Payne 1996; P. Smith 1993a; Weintraub 1994a). However, a considerable portion of this literature has focused on trade and the FTAA, whereas other contributions deal with specific issues without attempting a general examination of the whole process. This book is an attempt to assess the hemispheric integration project by trying to understand its specific nature, by locating it in its immediate environment, and by examining the strategies of the actors involved in the process.

Analyzing Hemispheric Regionalism

How should one analyze contemporary regionalism as applied to the Americas? The first wave of theoretical studies on regional integration was centered more or less on three analytical frameworks that were strongly influenced by the European unification process. The neofunctionalist school (Haas 1958, 1964; Haas and Schmitter 1964; Nye 1968a, 1970) basically understood integration as a process leading to the formation of a new political unit superseding the nation-states participating in it. The creation of a new political unit resulted from a shift in loyalties and expectations from the national to the supranational level, along a continuum from economic to political integration through a movement of spillover. Analytically, the research strategy involved examining and measuring background conditions and process mechanisms in order to explain the evolution of integration and to arrive at projections concerning the future state of the integration process.

The transactionalist/communications approach (Deutsch 1954, 1964; Deutsch et al. 1957; W. Fischer 1969; Puchala 1970) constructed a logic of integration that in essence was not very different from that of the neofunctionalist school. Integration was conceived as a process leading to the establishment of a security community, be it pluralistic or amalgamated. Provided that certain essential background conditions are present, takeoff can occur and integration will move forward on the basis of shared values and transactions among the communities being integrated. In this conception, increased transactions and growing value compatibility reinforce each other, contributing to the development of mutual trust, which generates support for economic integration, which in turn builds support for political integration. The research strategy of this approach consists of measuring flows of transactions and value compatibility in order to arrive at conclusions on the evolution of the integration process. Compared with the other theoretical perspectives, the transactionalist/communications approach places less emphasis on institutions and on the political aspects of the integration process.

The third theoretical framework, particularly attuned to the realities of the European integration process, could be called the decisionmaking perspective (Lindberg 1963, 1967, 1970; Lindberg and Scheingold 1970). In a way, it is an expanded adaptation of David Easton's input-output model for the analysis of regional integration. Integration is conceived as a process in which actors of national systems are progressively led to redirect their demands and support to a higher-level political system that will transform these demands into decisions whose binding character is accepted by the communities participating in the process. The ultimate test for regional integration therefore consists in its collective decisionmaking capacity, that is, its ability to process more and more decisions. The research strategy is centered on the analysis of the collective decision-making apparatus in relation to which three groups of properties (level, animators, consequences) are measured and conclusions are drawn concerning the progress of integration or lack thereof.

By the early 1970s, these first attempts at theory building in the field of regional integration were rejected by those who had originally proposed the theoretical constructs (Haas 1975b)[8] as well as by the larger scientific community. First, these original theoretical perspectives were believed to be inadequate for the study of regionalism mainly because the dependent variable had never been adequately conceptualized. Second, the assumption of automaticity in the continuum from economic to political integration was also proved false by the observation of the actual functioning of regional integration schemes. Third, a close examination of the analytical frameworks and their empirical applications revealed problems associated with conceptualization, operationalization, and measurement (De Vree 1972; Pentland 1973). Finally, the fact that these theoretical constructs did not easily adapt to the realities of regionalism outside Europe, particularly in the Third World, also constituted a major handicap.

The more recent literature on regionalism contrasts dramatically with earlier writings on regional integration. In general, it appears less preoccupied with problems related to conceptualization, theory formation, and the empirical investigation of regionalism.

There are, however, some exceptions in which analysts have tried to provide insights for a theoretical understanding of regionalism. Björn Hettne, for one, has tried to construct a structural explanation of what he calls the "new regionalism" (Hettne 1994). Essentially, he seeks to understand the relationship between regionalism and world order and, more precisely, how the world order is being shaped by a process of regionalization. To understand this relationship, he starts by identifying two processes or levels of regionalism: macroregionalism (transnational or supranational) and microregionalism (subnational). There are three types of macroregionalism: trading blocs, power blocs, and "transnational formations," the last being a process of regional integration and the new regionalism on which Hettne focuses. Regionalism or regional integration is therefore viewed as a process with a variety of dimensions, "the most important being culture, security, economic policies, development, and political regime" (Hettne 1994: 8). Finally, regionalism is animated by a dynamics whose central element is the "dialectical relationship between the two logics, the forces of market expansion and the need for political control" (Hettne 1994: 3).

Little more is said on how to carry out a structured observation of the dynamics of regionalism. It is also unclear how dynamics relate to the dimensions identified or, for that matter, how dynamics of the new regionalism differ from the dynamics of, let's say, trading blocs. But Hettne's theoretical reflections do constitute an interesting starting point for a structural analysis of contemporary regionalism, particularly as it relates to hegemony and world order.

In the same line of thought, but focused more specifically on the relationship between regionalism and globalization, James Mittelman proposes analytical parameters for the understanding of regionalism and eventually for the comparison of regionalist experiences (Mittelman 1996b). These parameters are the pattern of production and how it is related to the international division of labor; the way neoliberalism is ingrained in a particular regional context; the configuration of power relations; the social-cultural networks being developed in the regional framework; and the actors, institutions, and the nature of global governance involved in an integration process.

These variables cover many aspects of the dynamics of regionalism. They lay the foundation for the comparative analysis of regionalism and for the examination of how regionalism both participates in and is influenced by globalization. However, Mittelman's analytical categories appear more useful for telling us where to look than how to observe. More theoretical refinements are needed to determine how each analytical category is related to regionalism. For instance, how are power relations connected to regionalism? What should we analyze and how? What does a particular configuration of power relations mean for the evolution of regionalism? In order for the analytical framework to be used to provide explanations, such questions need to be answered.

Working from another angle and recognizing, as does Peter Robson (1993: 330), that theoretical and conceptual work on regionalism since the late 1980s "has been relatively modest," Andrew Hurrell attempts an examination of how sets of international relations (IR) theories could be used to explain the dynamics of regionalism (Hurrell 1995b). He starts by looking at systemic theories that offer an outside-in perspective for the study of regionalism. Included here are what Hurrell calls structural theories, which he divides into two sets: neorealism, with its significant variant hegemony, and the approaches related to structural interdependence and globalization. These systemic or structural theories are said to have an outside-in perspective because they seek essentially to analyze and understand regionalism in relation to the broader international system. Theories of hegemony, for example, may help explain how regionalism can act as a response to a perceived threat from a hegemonic power or as an attempt to restrict the power of a hegemony through the creation of regional institutions. They could also be useful in analyzing situations in which a hegemony is pushing regionalism as a way to enhance its global influence. Approaches to globalization may help explain better the interrelations between the regional and global spaces. However, as Hurrell himself emphasizes, the link between regionalism and globalization is often quite complex and ambiguous (Hurrell 1995b: 55).

The second cluster of theories identified by Hurrell are those that concentrate on the link between regionalism and interdependence at the regional level. Included here are neofunctionalism, neoliberal institutionalism, and constructivism. This set of theories is different from the previous set in that it focuses essentially on the regional construct itself. Neofunctionalism and neoliberal institutionalism could be used to examine the way states and regional institutions move toward interdependence by fostering and developing regional cohesion. Hurrell admits, however, that the relevance of neofunctionalism to the analysis of regionalism outside Europe is not clear (Hurrell 1995b: 60). He maintains that, for its part, constructivism could be useful in examining how regional identity and community building are developed.

Finally, domestic-level theories form a third group of theoretical frameworks that can provide tools for the analysis of domestic attributes or characteristics. According to Hurrell, theories dealing with state coherence, types of political regimes and democratization, and convergence in relation to domestic policy preferences could all provide interesting insights to the analysis of regionalism at the level of national or domestic policies and strategies.

Hurrell's presentation is certainly interesting and thought provoking. The problem, however, is that apart from neofunctionalism, which may not apply to regionalism outside Europe, none of these theoretical frameworks have been constructed for the analysis of regionalism or regional integration. It would be a demanding enterprise to make these frameworks operational, thus facilitating the systematic analysis of regional integration processes and generating significant findings. Another problem is the difficulty of approaching a relatively specific subject matter (regionalism) from such a vast array of theoretical angles.

This general and brief examination of the theoretical literature on regionalism and regional integration points to two basic conclusions. First, in the case of the first wave of theoretical frameworks proposed for the study of regional integration, the literature contains many basic concepts, central ideas, and insights that are fundamental to the explanation of regionalism today. However, as analytical models per se, early theoretical proposals have proved problematic in terms of both operationalization and measurement. Furthermore, the usefulness of these models for the analysis of regional experiences outside Europe remains unclear.

Second, the contemporary literature on regionalism, as noted by Hurrell and others, remains relatively weak on the conceptual and theoretical levels. The rare attempts at theory building do point in some interesting directions, but it is clear that they need further conceptual refinements. The work of Hettne and Mittelman has demonstrated that the literature emphasizes a structural explanation of regionalism by seeking essentially to understand it in relation to larger structures or phenomena such as world order or globalization. This theoretical perspective is in line with current trends in IR studies that seek to move away from statist or national-level explanations, focusing instead on transnational or subnational forces (Badie and Smouts 1992; Keohane and Nye 1971; Risse-Kapen 1995; Taylor 1984) and larger structures such as world systems, regimes, production systems, hegemony, interdependence, and globalization (Chase-Dunn 1989; Cox 1987; Gill and Law 1988; Keohane 1984; Keohane and Nye 1977; Krasner 1983a; Mittelman 1996a; Rittberger 1993; Rosenau 1990; Rupert 1995; Wallerstein 1974). Still, the structural explanation, however necessary for the understanding of human activity and international events, is by itself incomplete as an explanatory construction.

An Actor's Perspective

The outside-in or top-down perspective implicit in the structural explanation must be complemented by an inside-out or bottom-up perspective that focuses attention on how international phenomena are dependent on the way they are used by actors. An analysis based on an actor's perspective is therefore an appropriate complement. Since the advent of behaviorism, the social sciences, and IR studies in particular, have increasingly focused on actors. This focus has always been one of two basic approaches to the study of international relations used to construct explanations (Hollis and Smith 1992: 1–12). It is still central to the discipline in regard to theory building, as evidenced by discussions on the agent-structure problem (Buzan, Jones, and Little 1993; Carlsnaes 1992; Wendt 1987).

In this book we propose a study of regionalism and an examination of hemispheric regionalism based on an actor's perspective. We identify three main categories of actors—states, regional organizations, and civil society actors—and try to analyze their strategies, policies, and behavior. Our decision to focus on actors to observe and study hemispheric regionalism is based on the belief that it is not possible to understand regionalism (or any other international phenomenon, for that matter) if we do not start by examining the actions of the actors involved in the process and their motivations or calculus. It is the actors who, by their respective appropriation of regionalism, essentially determine the evolution of the integration process. It is only when we have an understanding of this perspective that we can carry out a broader examination of how regionalism is related to larger phenomena. In other words, we think that the best way of analyzing how regionalism interacts with other structuring features of the world system is to look at how actors use these different realities simultaneously.

Naturally, our first category of actors is states. Nation-states have always been recognized as the central political actors of regional integration processes in first-generation analytical models on integration, particularly the neofunctionalist school and Leon Lindberg's model. This category also features prominently in the most recent definitions of regionalism, which is still considered essentially a states-led project. Normally, the literature refers to state actors in general without introducing distinctions between categories of states.

We feel that the state actor in an integration process must be conceptualized differently, more precisely. Depending on their size, weight, and capacity, states behave differently and do not have the same impact on the evolution of the integration process. As W. Andrew Axline has pointed out, there are at least two categories of states in a regionalist project: the large states (the "makers") and the small states (the "takers"). In general, the small states, precisely because of their limited resources, cannot hope to have a significant impact on the integration process, and their options are limited. Sometimes their only choice is whether or not to participate in the process, as illustrated by the case of Paraguay and Uruguay in the Mercosur project. Although the analysis of the strategies of small states in relation to hemispheric regionalism is far from uninteresting, space limits have precluded us from examining their behavior in this book.

Our focus is on large states, particularly the United States and Brazil, whose strategies and actions reflect the power relationship in the context of continental integration. As an American and world hegemony, the United States is central to the success or failure of hemispheric regionalism, so much so that we felt it necessary to dedicate two chapters of the book to the United States. Chapter 5 focuses on Washington's foreign policy toward the Americas, and Chapter 6 examines the role of Congress, which is significant in the formulation of foreign policy, particularly foreign economic policy (Brewer and Teitelbaum 1997: 115–137; Mastanduno et al. 1988). The role of Brazil is examined in Chapter 7.

But large and small states are not the only categories of state actors, either in general or in the specific context of inter-American affairs. There are medium-sized states whose power base and diplomatic skills give them greater room to maneuver than smaller states may have. These states are an interesting study because the options available to them are more diverse and because they have the potential, individually or collectively, to influence regional outcomes. Chapter 8 takes a closer look at these states through a comparative analysis of Argentina, Canada, and Mexico.

Alongside the nation-states is a second category of actors: regional institutions. They are at the heart of Lindberg's model as applied to the European integration process in which both the Commission of the European Communities and the European Parliament are strategic in policy formulation and as a regional decisionmaking apparatus. But policy formulation and decisionmaking are carried out by regional organizations only in the more structured or advanced integration processes such as the European Union or the former Andean Group. In most regionalist projects, regional institutions essentially play two roles. They serve as a forum wherein issues are raised and discussed by states in order to arrive at a consensus on which collective action can develop. Regional institutions can also intervene as active participants in their own right when proposing courses of action, defining norms, or implementing collective decisions. In both instances, their role is complex because they are often subjected to opposing points of view and divergent demands. How they cope with the situation may significantly influence the evolution of the integration process, because whether or not support is given to other categories of actors may determine specific outcomes and, more generally, the regional project itself. An examination of the role of regional institutions is therefore an important part of the study of regionalism. In the context of hemispheric regionalism, the Organization of American States is a central regional institution and the subject of Chapter 9.

The third important category of actors in the context of regionalism is what is now called civil society. This term refers to the myriad of subnational actors who, from corporate businesses to labor unions to women's associations, form an extremely diverse collectivity. Quite different in nature, organization, and objectives, these actors can influence the evolution of the integration process as they support or oppose the ideas, proposals, and actions of the other two categories of actors. They do so by acting individually or collectively and by selecting channels of intervention in national settings or at the regional level. For example, they may include an Argentinian business firm that pressures its government to approve or oppose a specific proposal related to continental free trade or a loose regional grouping of aboriginal associations supporting or opposing OAS behavior in the area of human rights or health programs.

Among the many subnational actors involved in hemispheric regionalism, the decision to focus on Latin American businesses in Chapter 10 and new social movements in Chapter 11 seemed particularly appropriate in the sense that both subjects are on opposite ends of a continuum: Business is among the oldest and best-organized subnational actors in the context of integration in the Americas, whereas new social movements represent a more recent and, up to now, less structured type of interlocutor.

The first part of this book traces the contours of hemispheric regionalism as it is currently unfolding and situates the project in its immediate environment, in a sense, the situation within which actors must operate. After a presentation of the nature and scope of existing initiatives of hemispheric regionalism in Chapter 2, the focus of Chapter 3 turns toward the structural contexts conditioning the integration process. Then Chapter 4 presents a comparative analysis of integration models as represented by NAFTA and Mercosur. This is a logical end point for the first part of the book, since our observations lead us to the conclusion that hemispheric regionalism, in its current form, rests on two nuclei: NAFTA and Mercosur. Whether they come together or move apart will determine the future of continental integration.

In the second part of the book, attention is drawn to the strategies and actions of our three categories of actors. On the basis of the analyses conducted on our selection of actors, we draw conclusions regarding the current state of hemispheric regionalism and its prospects for the near future.

Notes

1. A sample would include the following:

The process whereby political actors in several distinct national settings are persuaded to shift their loyalties, expectations and political activities toward a new centre, whose institutions possess or demand jurisdiction over the pre-existing national states. The end-result of a process of political integration is a new political community, superimposed over the pre-existing ones. (Haas 1958: 16)

By integration we mean the attainment within a territory of a "sense of community" and of institutions and practices strong enough and widespread enough to assure, for a "a long time," dependable expectations of "peaceful change" among its populations. (Deutsch et al. 1957: 5)

Political integration will be defined as a process, but without reference to an end point. In specific terms, political integration is (1) the process whereby nations forgo the desire and ability to conduct foreign and key domestic policies independently of each other, seeking instead to make *joint decisions* or to *delegate* the decision-making process to new central organs; and (2) the process whereby political actors in several distinct settings are persuaded to shift their expectations and political activities to a new center. (Lindberg 1963: 6)

I will use "regionalism" . . . to mean a set of policies by one or more states designed to promote the emergence of a cohesive regional unit, which dominates the pattern of relations between the states of that region and the rest of the world, and which forms the organizing basis for policy within the region across a range of issues. (Hurrell 1992: 123)

There are four levels of political integration. . . . Institutional integration occurs when states agree to engage in collective decision-making and develop institutions which formulate and implement the required rules and regulations. . . . Policy integration concerns the transfer of policy to a higher level of government onto a jointly-managed or coordinated level of policymaking and implementation. . . . Attitudinal integration assesses public support for integration at the state level. . . . Security integration is evident when there is a commitment and expectation among states of nonviolent relations. (Rogers 1995: 17–18)

The new regionalism can be defined as a multidimensional process of regional integration which includes economic, political, social and cultural aspects. It is a package rather than a single policy. Whether concerned with economics or foreign policy. (Hettne 1994: 11)

Formally speaking, we define economic integration as a series of voluntary decisions by previously sovereign states to remove barriers to the mutual exchange of goods, services, capital, or persons. . . . Integration is not the same as intergovernmental cooperation. . . . Integration entails the creation of a new entity . . . that provides a recognized framework for accommodation among member states on issues relating to the mutual exchange of goods, services, capital, or persons. . . . Intergovernmental cooperation, on the other hand, results from ad hoc bargaining between sovereign states; it does not necessarily occur within a framework of long-term expectations, convergent interests, and shared benefits. (P. Smith 1993b: 4–5)

The authors of this book . . . adopt an approach which . . . conceives of regionalism as a state-led or states-led project designed to reorganise a particular regional space along defined economic and political lines. (Payne and Gamble 1996: 2)

2. Union Douanière et Économique de l'Afrique Centrale.

3. Communauté Économique de l'Afrique de l'Ouest.

4. Communauté des États de l'Afrique de l'Ouest.

5. Modified in 1980 to become the Asociación Latinoamericana de Integración.

6. Sistema Económico Latinoamericano.

7. For an overview of these factors as they relate to the major American countries, see the contributions in Mace and Thérien (1996b).

8. See also the Fall 1970 special issue of *International Organization*, considered by many as the testament of this special group of dynamic and dedicated regional integration scholars who then moved on to other fields of inquiry.

Part 1

The Regionalist Project
and Its Environment

2

The Origins, Nature, and Scope of the Hemispheric Project

Gordon Mace

After fifteen-odd years in relative oblivion everywhere but in Western Europe, regionalism returned to global prominence in a variety of guises at the end of the 1980s. Like the first wave of regional integration in the 1960s, current manifestations of regionalism span many continents and involve numerous actors. This phenomenon has also attracted renewed scientific interest (Fawcett and Hurrell 1995; Gamble and Payne 1996; Hettne 1994), although, for reasons of complexity, it remains poorly conceptualized and understood.

As Andrew Hurrell (1995b: 250) has accurately pointed out, regionalism in the Americas has basically adopted two forms or levels: hemispheric-wide regionalism and what could be called subregional integration. These two forms reflect two competing visions that have constantly vied for prominence in the history of inter-American relations. Hemispheric-wide regionalism is rooted in the Western Hemisphere Idea long promoted by U.S. statespeople. It has historically centered on multilateral fora such as the Pan-American conferences and the Organization of American States (OAS), which have provided a loose cooperative framework for addressing a wide array of issues in areas like security affairs, democracy, health, human rights, and trade and development. Subregional integration, which has evolved from the Bolivarian dream of Latin American unity, has essentially taken the form of regional integration schemes featuring more or less binding institutional structures and dealing mostly with economic cooperation, but also, in some cases, social and cultural cooperation as well.

The central focus of this book is the current U.S. project for hemispheric regionalism, the Enterprise for the Americas Initiative (EAI) launched by President George Bush in June 1990.[1] The main elements of this project were laid out in the Declaration of Principles and the Plan of Action signed by thirty-four heads of state at the Miami summit of December 1994. The Miami process is the third major attempt by the United States to establish a framework for inter-American cooperation after the relative failures of 1889 and 1948.

The success of the current proposal for hemispheric integration, essentially a U.S. initiative, largely depends on Washington's involvement in the process. Although the Miami summit Plan of Action makes it clear that the project for continental integration centers on the establishment of a free trade area in the Americas, the project under discussion goes much further than that. As we shall see in the coming pages, it is also a political project for the management of hemispheric affairs involving cooperation in numerous areas, including democracy, illegal drugs, and the environment.

At the same time, the current U.S. initiative for hemispheric integration is not a well-structured policy that Washington is absolutely determined to impose on the rest of the hemisphere; witness President Bill Clinton's difficulties in obtaining congressional fast-track authority to negotiate free trade agreements. Instead, the initiative pertains to the realm of expectations and to the vision that U.S. policymakers have for the future of the Americas (Aronson 1996). From the U.S. perspective, inter-American relations at the start of the 1990s offered a window of opportunity, a unique occasion to propose a "new architecture" for the Americas based on what U.S. business and political circles perceived as a new convergence of intents between the United States and her neighbors (Watson 1995: 3, 5). In other words, there is no carefully constructed master plan or grand design. The initiative is essentially a U.S. option made possible by circumstances and will be pursued only if it is accepted by the rest of the Americas.

This chapter has four objectives. In the first section, I return to the historical roots of the project in an attempt to circumscribe the original vision of the Americas held by U.S. policymakers, as well as Washington's role therein. My intention is to demonstrate how the current hemispheric project is part (and the result) of a U.S. vision that has existed for almost as long as the country itself. In the second section, I deal with previous attempts to promote hemispheric regionalism in order to show how the outcomes of 1889 and 1948 have affected the current situation. In the third part, which focuses on the 1980s, I seek to identify and understand the significant changes underlying the strategic reorientations that occurred in the Americas at the end of the 1980s and continued into the 1990s. Finally, the last part of the chapter traces the outlines of the current hemispheric project and identifies its main components.

The Original U.S. Vision for the Americas

As Anthony J. Payne (1996: 94) has rightly remarked, most accounts of inter-American relations start with an almost inevitable reference to the Monroe Doctrine, whereas in actual fact, the president's message to the U.S. Congress of December 1823 had little to do with inter-American affairs. Not only were the two sole passages dealing with the subject essentially directed at the Holy Alliance, but it has also been shown that James Monroe and his secretary of state, John Quincy Adams, had no interest in Spanish America prior to 1822 (Connell-Smith 1974: 49). Furthermore, the United States did not at the time have the naval power capable of protecting the Americas against incursions by the countries of the Holy Alliance—it was the British fleet that actually enforced this aspect of the U.S. declaration. The importance of President Monroe's message to Congress only came later when U.S. policymakers transformed it into the Monroe Doctrine (G. Smith 1994). It was then used by Washington in conjunction with the Roosevelt Corollary to legitimize U.S. policy and intervention in Latin America and the Caribbean.

Although various segments of Washington's political elite saw no advantage in a closer relationship with the new Spanish republics—which, in Adams's words, did not "have the first elements of good and free government" (Connell-Smith 1974: 53)—important political figures were already offering a vision of the future state of the Western Hemisphere and of Washington's place in that system. From the start, this early vision emphasized two distinct aspects: one political, the other largely economic.

The political vision of the future configuration of inter-American affairs first appeared in the writings of Alexander Hamilton and Thomas Jefferson, who as early as 1786 foresaw a system of the Americas centered on the United States (Aguilar 1968: 25). But the main propagandist for the idea was Henry Clay. Clay, a speaker of the U.S. House of Representatives and Adams's rival to succeed Monroe, submitted a motion in 1820 proposing the creation of a "system of which we shall be the centre, and in which all South America will act with us" (Connell-Smith 1974: 52).

For most of the nineteenth century, however, events in the United States and in Central and South America prevented any form of rapprochement between Washington and its Latin American neighbors. In the South, border conflicts, coups d'état, and chronic instability caused by warring political factions and caudillos made governing almost impossible and prevented serious foreign policy making. In the North, the war with Mexico, the Civil War, the Reconstruction of the South, and the settlement of the West either impeded progress in inter-American relations or diverted Washington's attention elsewhere. However, the Western Hemisphere Idea was launched anew during the subsequent age of empire through the declarations of President Grover Cleveland and, more important, through what was to become the Roosevelt Corollary to the Monroe Doctrine. Theodore Roosevelt's self-assigned role of regional policeman and his "big stick" reference, although unpopular with many in the region, reaffirmed the idea of the United States as a nucleus of the Americas and sustained the political vision of a regional system dominated by the United States (G. Smith 1994: 25).

As for the economic component of the U.S. hemispheric vision, it was essentially trade oriented. The genesis of what is today called the Free Trade Area of the Americas was an idea already present in the thinking of Henry Clay in the 1820s. However, its main advocate in the nineteenth century was Secretary of State James G. Blaine, whose Latin American policy in the 1880s involved two central objectives: the establishment of a customs union among the countries of the Americas and the adoption of a mechanism for the peaceful settlement of disputes. As we shall see in the next section, these objectives were at the heart of Washington's strategy when it convened the First International Conference of American States in Washington on October 2, 1889.

Historically, then, the U.S. vision of the regional system of the Americas—what Molineu (1986: 13–19) and others have termed the Western Hemisphere Idea—consists of a project built upon three pillars: (1) the political primacy of the United States in the inter-American system, (2) an exclusively American institutional framework for the settlement of disputes, and (3) a free trade area of the Americas. And although, for a number of reasons, the development of this regional system has been anything but constant, it is also accurate, as Gordon Connell-Smith (1974: 121) has pointed out, to speak of "logical growth" from the original vision of Jefferson and Clay, through the attempts by Blaine and Franklin D. Roosevelt, and right up to the current project developed under George Bush. In spite of historical ups and downs, some of them a direct result of U.S. policy itself, the present hemispheric project is in many ways a contemporary manifestation of a U.S. vision kept alive for almost two hundred years.

Attempts at Region Building

Objective conditions throughout most of the nineteenth century were unfavorable to the implementation of the U.S. vision for the Americas. Only in the final decades of the century did the situation change, essentially because of the improved economic and political situation in Latin America and the position of the United States in the world system. By the 1880s, Washington had established effective control over the entire continental

United States. The economic outlook was extremely promising, so much so that U.S. business expanded decisively outside U.S. borders in a spirit magnificently rendered in Gore Vidal's *Empire*. During the next sixty years or so, the U.S. rise to superpower status led Washington to make two attempts to develop a regional system of the Americas.

The first attempt came in 1889 with the convening in Washington of the First International Conference of American States. In hosting the conference, the U.S. government, led by its most ardent advocate for inter-American cooperation, Secretary of State James G. Blaine, had two specific objectives: the establishment of a customs union to foster inter-American commerce and the adoption of arbitration as a mechanism for the settlement of disputes.

The objectives were related in the sense that both would contribute to creating an environment favorable to the conduct of economic relations in the hemisphere. However, the Latin American governments, under Argentina's leadership, rejected both proposals out of fear that they would add economic domination to what was already seen as U.S. political hegemony in inter-American relations (Connell-Smith 1974: 110). The only tangible result of this first inter-American conference was the creation of the International Union of American Republics, which ended up essentially collecting and disseminating commercial information, and its agency, the Commercial Bureau. The bureau was renamed the Pan-American Union in 1910 (Connell-Smith 1974: 110–126).

All in all, there were nine Pan-American conferences, the last of which, in 1948, established the OAS as the main institutional structure of the nascent inter-American system. These conferences, understandably, generated limited concrete results because the majority of them were held at a time when Washington's Latin American policy was dominated by Theodore Roosevelt's "big stick" policy, William Taft's dollar diplomacy, and the missionary diplomacy of Woodrow Wilson. The numerous U.S. interventions in Central America and the Caribbean resulting from these policies fostered widespread suspicions and deep distrust of U.S. attitudes and behavior throughout Latin America. This mistrust, in turn, made progress almost impossible in the Pan-American context.

Nevertheless, the first U.S. initiative in favor of Pan-Americanism generated three advantages for Washington, which, although less tangible than a customs union or an arbitration treaty, were nonetheless significant in the long term. First, Pan-Americanism served as a framework to legitimize U.S. involvement and intervention in Latin American and Caribbean affairs. Second, by maintaining the Pan-American conferences as an exclusive dialogue between Washington and the Latin American governments, the U.S. government succeeded in excluding European nations from participating in the management of inter-American relations. Third,

Pan-Americanism was extremely helpful in preventing the creation of a Latin American bloc, which Simón Bolívar had seen as essential to balancing U.S. predominance in the region. All of these advantages left the United States in a position of hemispheric hegemony that was virtually unassailable at the outbreak of World War II.

The other significant U.S. initiative in region building in the Americas prior to the 1990s occurred in 1947–1948 and dealt with issues of political, economic, and military cooperation. This initiative complemented Washington's overall strategy to structure the post–World War II international system and was made possible by two sets of events that laid the groundwork for this second major attempt at inter-American cooperation.

The first set of events was initiated by the announcement by Franklin D. Roosevelt in April 1933 of a new U.S. policy toward Latin America. Subsequently referred to as the good neighbor policy, it had three main elements: the abandonment of intervention, the return to a just and objective policy of recognition, and the establishment of a new Pan-Americanism based on mutual understanding (Molineu 1986: 23). The new policy was ambiguous. On the one hand, its contribution to hemispheric unity was problematic because, as the Cuban episode of May 1933 quickly proved, it did not completely eliminate the threat of unilateral intervention. On the other hand, the policy did reduce some of the apprehensions of Latin American governments regarding larger issues such as sovereign rights. For instance, it established the framework for U.S. acceptance of the Convention on the Rights and Duties of States, which was a major Latin American proposal at the International Conference of American States at Montevideo, Uruguay, in December 1933.

The other set of events that paved the way for the restructuring of the inter-American system was linked to World War II itself. Among the various meetings and conferences held throughout the Americas during the course of the war, three played a significant role in creating what Payne (1996: 96) has called an emergent security community in the Western Hemisphere. The Havana conference of July 1940 was the starting point; Washington was able to persuade the participating governments to sign the Act of Havana. One of the main elements of this agreement was the acceptance of the principle of collective security in the Americas, which meant that an act of aggression against an American state originating from outside the region would be considered an act of aggression against all the states of the region. Eighteen months later, in January 1942, the Third Meeting of Consultation of American Foreign Ministers in Rio de Janeiro established two mechanisms for consultation and coordination related to the conduct of the war effort: the Inter-American Defense Board and the Emergency Advisory Committee for Political Defense. Finally, the Inter-American Conference on Problems of War and Peace, held in Mexico City in February–March 1945, was also important because of the adoption of the Act of Chapultepec. This resolution extended the notion of collective security as applied to the Americas to include not only aggression from outside the region but also aggression from a member state, as well as provisions for sanctions (Connell-Smith 1974: 189). The regional security complex that emerged from the war-related conferences and the improved overall climate resulting from the good neighbor policy played a role in transforming Pan-Americanism into the inter-American system.

This transformation occurred in 1947–1948 with the adoption of four important international documents at two regional conferences. At the Inter-American Conference for the Maintenance of Continental Peace and Security held in Rio de Janeiro in August–September 1947, two issues were on the minds of the participants. Latin American delegates were preoccupied with the postwar economic situation in their respective countries. The U.S. demand for Latin American products and resources was down, and access to U.S. products had been made more difficult by the demands of European reconstruction. For its part, Washington was preoccupied with the emerging Cold War and the containment of the communist threat. The main U.S. objective at Rio was therefore to reinforce the principle of collective security agreed upon in 1940 through mechanisms such as a joint command for U.S. and Latin American military forces in the region similar to that later adopted by the North Atlantic Treaty Organization.

Latin America's preoccupation with economic development received short shrift at the Rio conference, where U.S. representatives rejected the idea of a Marshall Plan for the Americas. At the same time, Washington was only partially successful in its efforts to establish a security complex for the region. Latin American governments refused to accept the joint command of military forces and also limited the binding character of the U.S.-backed principle of collective security with a provision (article 20) stating that "no state shall be required to use armed force without its consent" (Atkins 1977: 530). However, the region covered by the Inter-American Treaty of Reciprocal Assistance (also called the Rio Treaty), which went into effect in December 1948, now extended to all of the Americas. Even more important, the notion of aggression was widened to cover not only military action originating outside the region but also "an aggression which is not an armed attack" and which may come from within the region (Connell-Smith 1974: 196–197).

Although an incomplete success for Washington, the Rio Treaty did provide a more solid foundation for the notion of collective security in the region. More significantly, by extending the notion of aggression, it legitimized to some extent U.S. actions and interventions against communist and other forces of subversion. This was an important feature of U.S.–Latin American relations in the Cold War years because, as Anthony J. Payne

(1996: 97) has remarked, it was vital for a nascent hegemony to show its control over its sphere of influence.

The other important conference was the Ninth International Conference of American States held in Bogotá in April–May 1948. The most significant achievement of this conference was the adoption of the charter of the OAS, which gave the new inter-American system its basic legal foundation. Essentially, the charter reaffirmed the principles and ideals that had governed the inter-American system since 1889 and described the principal organs of the OAS: the secretariat; the Council of the OAS, with its specialized conferences and subsidiary organs; and the Inter-American Conference, which was transformed into the General Assembly in 1967 (Atkins 1977: 317–320; Connell-Smith 1974: 200–204).

The delegates at the 1948 conference also signed the American Treaty on Pacific Settlement, or Pact of Bogotá, a U.S. government objective dating back to the first Pan-American conference in 1889. All regional governments agreed in principle with the notion of a peaceful settlement of disputes, but, as had been the case in 1889, there were serious divergencies regarding its implementation. As a result, the Pact of Bogotá was signed with so many restrictions that it was for all intents and purposes stillborn. The Economic Agreement of Bogotá, under which Washington hoped to make progress toward a free trade area, met a similar fate. Although complemented by rules concerning the protection of investments and the difficult issue of expropriation, the agreement was not even ratified.

These failures aside, a historical examination of inter-American affairs reveals a remarkable common thread linking Washington's proposals of 1889 and 1948. What emerges is an almost perennial vision for the future of the Western Hemisphere built around certain key elements. Historically, the U.S. vision of an architecture of the Americas has been focused first and foremost on the establishment of a political regional system, a fact often overlooked, given the emphasis on economics and trade issues in contemporary literature. The most important tangible results of U.S. attempts at hemispheric region building in the Americas have been the regional institutions: the Pan-American Union and the OAS. These institutions, which, given U.S. attitudes toward its sovereignty and role, are expressions of intergovernmentalism rather than supranationalism, have been important for Washington. They have provided the necessary structure for dealing with the problems involved in managing inter-American affairs, they have played a significant role in impeding the creation of a Latin American bloc, and they have been useful, if not always adequate, channels or instruments for the subtle legitimization of U.S. political supremacy in the Americas.

Along with a political regional system for the Western Hemisphere, the U.S. vision of the Americas also foresaw the establishment of a security complex to create an environment favorable for the conduct of business and other types of relations throughout the region. The Rio Treaty contributed to the acceptance of the idea that aggression—and later subversion under the Kennan Corollary to the Monroe Doctrine (G. Smith 1994: 68–73)—had to be resisted by all and that the United States had a certain legitimate role to play in this respect.

Finally, the third element consistently present in the U.S. vision of an architecture of the Americas was the idea of an economic area centered on the notion of free trade and characterized by free movement of capital and limited state intervention in the economy.

In the forty years that followed the Bogotá conference in 1948, the United States was largely unsuccessful in having its vision accepted by other countries in the Americas. One of the main reasons for this failure was the Cold War and its influence on Washington's behavior toward Latin America, behavior marked by a series of unilateral interventions often followed by what Latin American governments perceived as benign neglect. U.S. interventions in Guatemala and in the Dominican Republic and Washington's involvement in the overthrow of Salvador Allende in Chile served to demonstrate that the spirit underlying the good neighbor policy had been short-lived and did not fit in the regular pattern of U.S.–Latin American relations.

As a result of this pattern of successive intervention and disinterest, the attitudes of Latin American governments toward the United States were constantly moving from deep mistrust most of the time to cautious optimism at best, and to vocal opposition on occasion. From the mid-1960s until the end of the 1970s, Latin America's active participation in the North-South confrontation provided the channel for this vocal opposition and acted as both a catalyst and a structure for the profound divergencies between the U.S. and Latin American visions of the world system and inter-American affairs.

It therefore comes as no surprise that the inter-American system went into a steady decline during the twenty years after the Bogotá conference of 1948. The Alliance for Progress, which, as Peter H. Smith (1996a: 149) rightly points out, was essentially a response to the Cuban threat rather than an attempt at region building, slowly faded away without any significant success. This dissipation is understandable because the Alliance for Progress, like the subsequent Caribbean Basin Initiative, was a context-specific response to a perceived communist threat: Cuba in 1959; Cuba, Nicaragua, and Grenada in 1981. Interest in both initiatives naturally disappeared as the threat itself diminished or was eliminated. As for the Punta del Este Conference of Inter-American Heads of State in 1967, it was supposed to give a new impetus to the regional system, but in fact it served only to confirm the inter-American stalemate.

During the twenty years following Punta del Este, the inter-American system fell into a period of almost complete obsolescence characterized by the declining significance of the OAS, alternately viewed by most members of the Latin American political elite as an empty shell or a U.S.-dominated instrument.

This obsolescence had much to do with U.S. attitudes and behavior toward Latin America from the mid-1960s to the end of the 1980s and with the impact of world events on the countries of the Americas during this period. During the 1960s, the Alliance for Progress was quickly shuffled to the back burner of U.S. foreign policy as the war in Vietnam became the central focus of policymaking in Washington. For most of the 1970s, with the exception of President Jimmy Carter's efforts to establish better relations with the region, inter-American affairs were deeply influenced by the difficulties and, ultimately, the failure of the North-South dialogue. The adoption of confrontational strategies by Latin American countries such as Chile, Peru, and Bolivia antagonized the United States and created a stalemate in the inter-American agenda. The situation was made even more difficult in the 1980s by President Ronald Reagan's use of the Central American crisis to reintroduce Cold War attitudes and policies in the conduct of U.S. relations with Latin America and the Caribbean.

A Completely New Environment

With the future of the inter-American system looking bleak at the start of the 1980s, what happened in the course of the decade to modify the situation so significantly? Which events and factors explain the U.S. initiative in favor of hemispheric regionalism at the start of the 1990s and the nature of the response from the other governments of the Americas?

In the literature focusing on the resurgence of regionalism, there is a strong tendency to establish a relationship between globalization and the rise of what is called the "new regionalism" (Axline 1995: 12–17; Gamble and Payne 1996: 247–251; Holm and Sorensen 1995: 3–7; Mittelman 1996b). There are at least three problems associated with this interpretation. First, despite certain attempts to clarify "new regionalism" (Axline 1995: 18–22; Hettne 1994: 1–11; Oman 1994; Robson 1993) and "globalization" (Holm and Sorensen 1995: 4–6; R. Robertson 1990; Stark 1996: 4), both terms still lack conceptual clarity, making it almost impossible to determine specifically how globalization has influenced governments in relation to their regional strategies. Second, as it has been pointed out (Hirst and Thompson 1992), globalization may not be such a global phenomenon after all. It is still essentially related to financial flows and rarely extends beyond the borders of the industrialized world. Finally, although globalization may constitute an attractive scheme of reference for understanding contemporary world society, it is far from certain that this pervasive phenomenon has directly influenced governmental behavior toward regionalism in Washington or Tokyo, let alone La Paz, Tegucigalpa, or Roseau.

Consequently, although globalization may have had a certain influence on shaping strategies for regional integration in the Americas, it has not been the sole and probably not the most significant influence. More appropriately, both the U.S. initiative for hemispheric integration and the ensuing response from Washington's neighbors in the Americas are the result of events unfolding within the region and in the rest of the world during the 1980s. It is these events, as factored in by states and other actors, that are primarily responsible for the changing environment of the 1980s in the Americas and that explain the thrust toward hemispheric regionalism.

In the case of the United States, it would probably be fair to say that the two main outside influences on U.S. policy on regionalism in the Americas have been economics, particularly trade, and the end of the Cold War. In the case of the former, despite ongoing debate on the "relative decline" of U.S. hegemony (Kennedy 1989; Nye 1990), in the early 1980s many U.S. policymakers felt that U.S. economic supremacy should be based on increased competitiveness and that a more open trade environment would be instrumental in achieving this goal. The main objective was therefore an improved multilateral trade regime. However, the rejection by the other members of the General Agreement on Tariffs and Trade (GATT) of a 1982 U.S. initiative in this direction followed by the slow progress of the Uruguay Round that got under way in 1986 left Washington with the impression that other countries, notably those in Europe, were not prepared to follow the multilateral trade route. As a result, a fallback strategy—regional free trade—was deemed necessary as an alternative solution or as a negotiating device in the GATT framework (Gamble and Payne 1996: 102).

The difficulties in concluding the Uruguay Round and the perception that increased protectionism in Europe and Asia could potentially lead to the creation of trading blocs (fortress Europe) all led to the idea of a free trade area of the Americas. In this sense, the regional trade option was a bargaining chip in broader trade negotiations with Europe and Asia. A successful outcome to these negotiations, something partially achieved with the conclusion of the Uruguay Round, implied, of course, that Washington's commitment to regional free trade could eventually diminish, particularly in the face of strong domestic opposition.

The other main systemic influence on U.S. attitudes toward the Americas was the end of the Cold War, along with the demise of Third Worldism (Fawcett 1995: 17–27). This earthshaking transformation left the United States as the world's only superpower and restored its status as hegemon on the American continent in the second half of the 1980s (P. Smith 1996a: 224, 1996b: 30–35). With the retreat of extrahemispheric powers from the Americas, Washington once again felt it could impose its will in the region and that it could do so through cooperation rather than intervention (P. Smith 1996a: 233).

Probably more significant in shaping Washington's views of the hemisphere throughout the 1980s were the events unfolding in the Americas themselves. One such event, albeit not the most important, was Canada's decision to enter into the negotiations that led to the January 1988 agreement establishing a free trade area between Canada and the United States. The agreement sent the message that if a country like Canada, historically opposed to continentalism and free trade with the United States, could radically change its position, then the same could apply to the rest of the Americas.

Soon after, Mexico's offer to negotiate a free trade agreement further reinforced U.S. perceptions that new proposals for hemispheric integration would probably meet with a positive response in many parts of the region. Giving weight to this belief was the fact that the Mexican initiative, contrary to the Canadian one, came from a Latin American country with characteristics different from those of the United States and Canada. Mexico's attitude could also be interpreted as a major breach within the Latin American family of nations, one that opened the door for accommodation between the United States and Latin America.

From the U.S. point of view, however, the most important regional influence and the leading factor behind the decision to launch a new hemispheric initiative was probably the political and economic changes occurring in Latin America and the Caribbean in the 1980s. These changes were a direct result of the debt crisis affecting most of Latin America and the Caribbean that was made official in 1982 with Mexico's announcement that it was suspending repayments. The debt crisis created an economic and psychological shock whose effects were felt in the region for most of the decade.

This made it clear that drastic changes were required to both the prevailing economic development model and the political landscape, still characterized by military dictatorships and closed political systems. It sparked a region-wide movement toward various forms of economic liberalization and political democratization during the 1980s.

Although the real significance of these changes and the true depth of elite commitment to political and economic liberalization are still questioned by some observers (Wiarda 1997), the U.S. government has viewed these developments in a positive light since the end of the 1980s. U.S. decisionmakers feel that there has been a "convergence of values" between the United States and Latin America. They see this convergence as a "window of opportunity," a "turning point" representing a "historic" moment that should be seized upon (Aronson 1996: 184; Bush 1989: 505; Christopher

1993: 625, 1995a: 417; Gore 1994: 785; Watson 1995). This reaction to regional dynamics has been the most significant influence in Washington's decision to make a new attempt at hemispheric integration.

For the other actors in the Americas,[2] developments in the world at large have been more significant than regional events in explaining the response to the U.S. initiative. Canada and Mexico had similar reasons for seeking a free trade agreement with the United States (Barry 1995: 5–11): Both countries were heavily dependent economically on the United States. The eventual emergence of trading blocs in Europe and Asia, combined with what was perceived as increasing protectionism in the United States, would have left Canada and Mexico facing increasingly difficult access to their traditional markets. This factor was the most salient in the decision by both governments to secure access to their major U.S. market through a free trade agreement. Once that decision was made and the agreements signed, the only remaining alternative was to participate in the building of the hemispheric community, a counterweight to the limits on the room to maneuver resulting from membership in the North American system. Mexico's position in this sense was more ambiguous, but Canada's participation in hemispheric fora increased dramatically in the 1990s.

The factors influencing the other countries of Latin America and the Caribbean have been somewhat different. In these countries, the end of the Cold War was a key factor for two reasons. First, the implosion of the Soviet Union eliminated the most important extrahemispheric actor, thereby preventing certain Latin American governments from using the threat of rapprochement with Moscow to obtain concessions from the United States as they had in the past. They were now left with the United States as the only valuable interlocutor.

The second reason concerned the reconstruction of the former communist countries of Eastern Europe in a post–Cold War context. Many Latin American governments feared that lending agencies would divert funds previously reserved for the Latin American and Caribbean region to Eastern and Central Europe. Combined with the fiasco of the debt crisis, this anxiety engendered an "acute fear of marginalization" (Hurrell 1994: 170) and grave concerns about the "Africanization" of the American subcontinent.

Along with these perceptions of a newly hostile world environment, many Latin American governments were concerned about regional developments. Mexico's decision to begin free trade negotiations with Washington was seen as a defection, if not a betrayal, of the Latin American family that left the rest of the hemisphere still more isolated. This sentiment of isolation and exclusion only became more acute after the successful conclusion of the North American Free Trade Agreement (NAFTA).

Of course, there were specific combinations of factors at work in almost every country involved in the process. Nonetheless, the factors mentioned here sum up the most significant influences bearing on the U.S. government's decision to launch a new initiative for hemispheric regionalism and the subsequent reactions of the other governments of the region. Together, these elements account for an environment that profoundly modified the traditional context of inter-American relations. Were it not for this completely new landscape, no one would be discussing a new architecture of the Americas.

The Contours of the Hemispheric Integration Project

The Declaration of Principles and the Plan of Action adopted by the thirty-four states attending the December 1994 Summit of the Americas contain the essential elements of the hemispheric integration project initiated by the United States (Rosenberg and Stein 1995: 9–27). By no means did this project materialize instantaneously, and it must be emphasized that what has been called the "Miami process" in some U.S. circles is still just a project with an uncertain future, particularly in light of the Clinton administration's difficulties in securing fast-track approval from the U.S. Congress. This hemispheric project has been in the making since the mid-1980s and was the result of a process whose main building blocks were the 1988 Canada-U.S. Free Trade Agreement (FTA), the 1990 Enterprise for the Americas Initiative, and the 1994 North American Free Trade Agreement.

As mentioned earlier, the FTA may not have marked a turning point in inter-American relations, but it was significant for the evolution of things to come. It was a trade agreement between two industrialized countries, but two countries that were dissimilar in terms of overall economic weight. Furthermore, the agreement involved a country that had always been extremely vulnerable to U.S. domination and influence, a vulnerability that explains Ottawa's historical rejection of continentalism as a policy option. That such a country decided to reverse course was a clear message to Washington as well as to other governments of the region. If Ottawa felt that it had to establish a more secure relationship with the United States in the face of a hostile world environment, then this became a possible course of action for the other countries of the region.

Shortly after the implementation of the FTA came the Enterprise for the Americas Initiative, built around three elements of an essentially economic nature: the proposal for a hemispheric free trade zone, debt reduction measures, and an investment package primarily channeled through a fund administered by the Inter-American Development Bank (IDB). Announced on June 27, 1990, the EAI came only four months after the Cartagena drug summit, where the presidents of the Andean countries had apparently managed to convince President Bush that sweeping changes were occurring in Latin America and that the United States had to become more involved in sustaining the reform process (Bush 1991: 1733). The measures included in the EAI translated U.S. willingness to do just that and also gave a clear signal to governments of the region that NAFTA negotiations with Mexico would not jeopardize U.S. commitments to the region. They also conveyed the idea that the economic dimensions of the hemispheric integration project would rest solidly on the foundations of free market economic liberalism.

The negotiations that would eventually lead to NAFTA ratification in 1994 got under way in 1991. In one sense, NAFTA had little to do with hemispheric integration. From Washington's point of view, it was not only a trade deal but also a mechanism that could be used to manage problems affecting North America as a whole (such as the environment and human migration). In security matters, NAFTA would in some ways extend U.S. borders to the very fringes of North America. And by establishing a truly North American economy and the potential for a truly North American community, NAFTA would provide the United States with a "continental base, economically and politically," to promote "U.S. global influence" (Zoellik 1992: 290). In another sense, however, NAFTA was also a link in the chain leading to hemispheric integration. It represented both an example of what could be done between North and South America and a base on which to build hemispheric regionalism. Like the EAI, but even more so, NAFTA was a clear indication that hemispheric integration would be based on market capitalism yet would also take into account environmental and labor issues.

In many ways, the FTA, the EAI, and NAFTA were building blocks in the process leading to the first Summit of the Americas in Miami in 1994. The hemispheric integration project that emerged from the summit is a multidimensional project encompassing measures related to the economic, political, military-strategic, environmental, and social-cultural spheres of human activity.

It is the economic dimension of the hemispheric project that has been most widely discussed. Economics are the material foundation in the architecture of hemispheric regionalism. The main pillar of the proposed economic integration project is a Free Trade Area of the Americas, negotiations for which should be completed by 2005 if government commitments are met. Normally, a free trade area is the lowest level of economic integration, one whose main purpose is to open the markets of participating countries essentially through the elimination of tariff barriers. This hemispheric integration project goes much further. Working groups have been established to examine such matters as market access, customs procedures and rules of origin, investment, technical and sanitary barriers to trade, subsidies, antidumping and countervailing duties, government procurement, intellectual property rights, services, competition policy, and dispute settlement. Other issues being examined include the development and liberalization of capital markets, cooperation in energy, science, and technology, and the development of hemispheric infrastructure in such fields as telecommunications and information (Rosenberg and Stein 1995: 18–20).

Given the items being examined by the working groups and Washington's insistence on incorporating private sector perspectives into the process (Davidow 1997), current talks go far beyond the relatively technical and neutral issue of establishing a free trade area. The proposed free trade area will be established within the framework of an economic development model characterized by open markets, deregulation, and limited state intervention in the economy. Aside from technical assistance, no provisions have been made for the adjustment problems of smaller economies, and from the U.S. point of view, NAFTA requirements should apply in all areas, though not everyone agrees with this perspective.

Economically, then, the hemispheric project centers on the establishment of a free trade area but has implications that are much more far-reaching than that. The project involves an economic development model within which protectionist policies are replaced by open markets, the private sector is the main economic actor, and growth comes from trade and investment rather than foreign assistance.

The political dimension is also a significant component of the hemispheric project. Political integration is mentioned at the very beginning of the Declaration of Principles, with two central means identified for achieving this goal: the promotion of democratic institutions and the protection of human rights. The former, which Bloomfield has called the "OAS-Defense-of-Democracy Regime" (Bloomfield 1994), is part of a broader plan to reinforce throughout the region institutions and practices associated with Western liberal democracies and pluralist political systems. Essential features of liberal democracies are access to power through regular and fair elections, separation of executive, legislative, and judiciary powers, protection of human and minority rights, fair and equal access to state structures by citizens and groups, and transparency and honesty on the part of state representatives. In seeking to strengthen and generalize this model of democratic governance, the hemispheric project relies heavily on government initiatives but also encourages extensive OAS involvement in promoting and protecting democratic institutions, particularly through the organization's Unit for the Promotion of Democracy.

Even though it is not mentioned specifically, the OAS is also viewed as a regional political structure and forum for the management of region-wide problems whose solutions can come only from concerted governmental actions. The OAS and the IDB have a significant role to play in the hemispheric project (Christopher 1995b); however, this role does not entail the supranationalism that characterizes certain aspects of the European Commission's responsibilities. American states are not yet prepared to go that far, and the essential feature of regional decisionmaking will be intergovernmentalism.

As for the security dimension of hemispheric regionalism, participating governments have so far agreed to deal with issues such as drug production and trafficking, prevention of international terrorism, and confidence-building measures (Rosenberg and Stein 1995: 16). However, Washington will clearly try to take further measures to achieve its ultimate objective— the establishment of a true security complex throughout the Americas. To this end, the United States would certainly be supportive of such intermediary steps as the clarification of the role of the Inter-American Defense Board (IADB). The IADB could serve as a "matrix for inter-military cooperation throughout the hemisphere" (Gelbard 1992: 810–811) to provide regional solutions not only to problems already on the hemispheric agenda, but also to other matters such as insurgencies and nonproliferation.

Hemispheric integration also has an important environmental dimension. Participating states have agreed to implement commitments made at the UN Rio Conference on Environment and Development while creating "cooperative partnerships" on issues related to sustainable development, the protection of biodiversity, and pollution prevention. Here again, a good part of the effort will depend on intergovernmental cooperation, but OAS specialized agencies and the IDB will also play an important role.

Another important element of hemispheric regionalism is the sociocultural dimension. It includes the promotion of cultural values and the development of exchange programs, universal access to education, equitable access to basic health services, the strengthening of the role of women in society, hemispheric cooperation in science and technology, and the creation of an Emergency and Development Corps to assist governments of the hemisphere in dealing with development problems and situations of natural disasters.

These additional dimensions aside, however, the fact remains that the free trade area and the related economic proposals form the backbone of the hemispheric integration project. If they fail, it is doubtful that the rest of the integration project can be salvaged. But it is clear that the current hemispheric regionalism project is also a political, strategic, and sociocultural process. It is far from a unidimensional endeavor, and in the long run, its noneconomic dimensions may have a far greater impact on the future architecture of the Americas.

What will ultimately be the fate of the current attempt at hemispheric regionalism? Since the Summit of the Americas in 1994, the mood of both observers and actors in the process has fluctuated wildly as events have unfolded. But if the European integration process has taught a lesson, it is that regional integration is a long-term enterprise marked by waves and undercurrents. Although scholars of regionalism take notice of the waves, those high-profile official gestures or proclamations like the EAI or the Summit of the Americas, often ignored are the undercurrents, the daily actions of the countless smaller actors who keep the project moving forward in response to the waves.

It is still too early to determine the fate of the hemispheric project in any definite way. Only provisional assessments can be made at this time. The only certainty scholars have is that the future of the hemispheric integration process will be determined largely by the responses of the actors involved, namely the national governments, the regional institutions, and the social actors examined in the second part of this book. These actors do not all necessarily share the same vision of the future architecture of the Americas, as reactions to U.S. proposals so clearly indicate. The future of inter-American affairs may also be influenced by the behavior of extrahemispheric actors such as the members of the European Union, which are strengthening their relationship with the Mercosur countries, or by events outside the American continent, such as developments with Asia-Pacific Economic Cooperation.

Finally, as we shall see in Chapter 3, the shape of hemispheric integration—if it does occur—will be strongly influenced by such structural constraints as the relative power of the actors involved in the process, basic economic trends, levels of economic development, and the weight of past U.S.–Latin American relations. It will also have to take into consideration the different integration models represented by NAFTA and Mercosur, as we shall see in Chapter 4.

We must therefore keep in mind that when it comes to regional integration in the Americas, nothing is settled. There is a world of difference between the U.S. initiative as incorporated in the Miami process and the result of hemispheric integration. The scope and direction of the process are still uncertain and the final outcome will depend heavily on how the various actors position themselves with respect to continental integration.

Notes

1. By selecting such a focus, the authors of this book by no means seek to negate the very rich history of Bolivarian or Latin American experiences with political unity and regional economic integration. We merely want to underline the fact that the current attempt at continental integration in the Americas was a U.S. initiative. The result of this endeavor, should it be successful, will certainly be quite different from what was imagined at the start.

2. This is only a sketchy presentation of the factors taken into consideration by the other governments of the Americas when they decided in the 1980s to reconsider regionalism as a policy alternative. For a more extensive treatment, see the contributions in Mace and Thérien (1996b).

3

The Structural Contexts of Hemispheric Regionalism: Power, Trade, Political Culture, and Economic Development

Gordon Mace & Louis Bélanger

Regional integration, like any other social construct, is a process embedded in and in constant interaction with a specific environment. It evolves in a context defined by events and material realities as well as ideational structures that are preexistent or that develop inside and outside the region. More specifically, the individual and collective actors involved in a regional integration process find themselves already positioned in relation to these events or structures, a situation that both constrains and empowers them when it comes to designing strategies and organizing their behavior so as to orient the integration process.

The original theoretical literature on regional integration paid a good deal of attention to certain sets of circumstances considered important for the success of the integration process. Both the neofunctionalist and pluralist/communications schools identified a number of conditions, including the existence of an external threat (Haas 1961: 376; Haas and Schmitter 1964: 730), unbroken social communication links, and the compatibility of main values held by political elites (Deutsch et al. 1957: 46–57), as well as linkage and coalition formation, unit symmetry, pluralism, and an increase in transactions (Nye 1970: 821). The presence of these and other elements was seen as a prerequisite for launching and achieving the integration process. And logically, the absence of these conditions or contrary sets of circumstances were seen as impediments to the development of integration schemes.

It is impossible to discuss here all the conditions related to the success of the integration process referred to in the theoretical literature—all the more so since some of these conditions have been criticized by scholars

(De Vree 1972; Galtung 1968; Hansen 1969; Inglehart 1967; Puchala 1972) and may not apply in every case. Instead, this chapter deals with four structural features that seem to bear heavily on the future of hemi spheric integration in the Americas. In one way or another, these elements are all related to what we believe are the most salient prerequisites for integration identified in the theoretical literature. These four structural elements are the distribution of power among the countries of the Americas, the pattern of trade relations in the region, similarities and differences in political culture and, finally, symmetry or asymmetry in levels of economic development.

The Distribution of Power

The distribution of power or capabilities among political units participating in an integration process is an important structural condition for the future of any integration scheme. This fact was recognized early on in the theoretical literature with the reference to the presence of "cores of strength," or core areas having a positive impact on the evolution of the integration process (Deutsch et al. 1957: 38, 72–73).

For Deutsch and his colleagues of the pluralist school, the fact that Germany and France, the two most powerful European countries of their day, saw eye to eye and agreed to act as leaders within the framework of the European Economic Community constituted a significant positive influence for the development of European integration. Similarly, the success of a region-wide integration process in Asia or the Americas today is unthinkable without the active participation of either Japan (and probably China) or the United States. At the same time, difficulties in the process could be expected if the major powers of either region did not share the same vision of integration and adopted opposing strategies. Students of cooperation—realists and liberals alike—also agree that both the relative power of a state vis-à-vis other states and the evolution of its position will affect its interest in cross-border cooperation (Keohane 1993: 282–283; Grieco 1990: 46).

Consequently, the evolution of the hierarchy of power in a given geographical region is a highly salient structural constraint for the evolution of an integration process. The location of each state in the hierarchy will greatly influence its regional strategy and determine, in W. Andrew Axline's words, who will be the "makers," who will be the "takers" (Axline 1996: 214), and who will be the cooperators.

In order to examine the particular structural context of hemispheric regionalism in the Americas, we have updated a previous analysis of the hierarchy of power in the Western Hemisphere (Mace, Bélanger, and

Thérien 1993).[1] The procedure for establishing the ranking is quite conventional and in accordance with what is found in the literature (Cline 1980; Doran 1991; W. Ferris 1973; Stoll and Ward 1988; Wallace 1973). It also recognizes the arbitrary nature of any attempt to objectively measure the distribution of power (Doran 1991: 49). We have measured national capabilities using seven indicators regrouped along five dimensions. Size was measured by population and gross domestic product (GDP). Development was measured by GDP per capita. Defense spending was used to measure military strength, and diplomatic missions served as an indicator for political prestige. Finally, trading power was established on the basis of total exports.

On this basis, and in a manner similar to that of Charles F. Doran (1991: 49–54), we have constructed an aggregate index giving equal weight to each indicator. We calculated the index by assigning each country a value for the selected indicators, with each value a function of that country's relative status compared to the country with the highest score and to which 1,000 points were assigned. Recorded values were then averaged to give us the aggregate index for each country's capacity. From the index, we established the rank ordering of the countries. The main innovation in relation to our previous analysis was the introduction of a fourth time period (1991–1994) to provide us with a portrait of the situation in the 1990s.

The main findings are as follows. First of all, Figures 3.1a and 3.1b reveal that the distribution of power among the countries of the Americas has remained relatively stable over the past thirty years. There is no major shift on the power scale from one period to the other, although there are some interesting changes. Note, for example, Guatemala's and Nicaragua's relative decline in power from the 1960s through the 1990s, the inversion of Chile's and Peru's positions, and the trajectory of Argentina, which started off in fourth place in 1966–1969, lost ground in the 1970s and 1980s, and is making a comeback in the 1990s. Table 3.1 also shows that among the largest countries of the region, only Mexico managed to improve its position in relation to the United States from one period to the next. Finally, it is worth pointing out that during the last period, which corresponds with the launch of regional initiatives by the United States, the large Hispanic countries have recovered the economic ground they lost during the 1980s. Canada and Brazil seemed unable to recover at the same rate, despite the fact that the U.S. economy was booming.

Another significant finding is that only six countries in the region carry enough weight to have any real potential impact on the future of continental integration. In addition to the United States, these are Argentina, Brazil, Canada, Mexico, and Venezuela, the only other nations with decile rankings above 1.00. The rest of the countries in the hemisphere are too far

Figure 3.1a   Dispersion of Power in the Americas

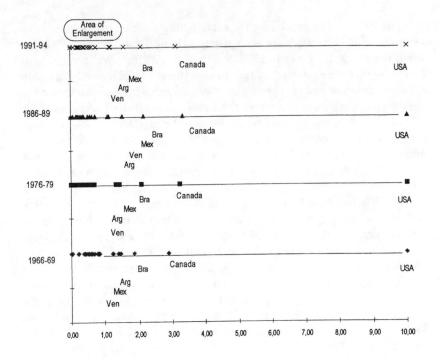

Figure 3.1b   Enlargement of 0.0 to 1.0

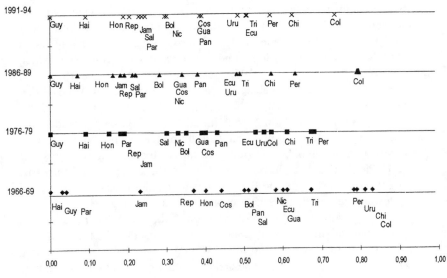

Note: See the chapter Appendix for a key to the abbreviaitons used in this figure.

Table 3.1 Aggregate Index of National Capabilities

	1966–1969			1976–1979			1986–1989			1991–1994		
	Country	Index	Decile	Country	Index	Decile	Country	Index	Decile	Country	Index	Decile
1.	United States	1,000.00	10.00	United States	1,000.00	10.00	United States	1,000.00	10.00	United States	1,000.00	10.00
2.	Canada	294.31	2.89	Canada	342.31	3.23	Canada	348.35	3.32	Canada	326.01	3.13
3.	Brazil	191.97	1.86	Brazil	230.35	2.08	Brazil	233.71	2.15	Brazil	223.15	2.08
4.	Argentina	151.19	1.45	Mexico	165.94	1.42	Mexico	170.99	1.51	Mexico	173.69	1.57
5.	Mexico	144.88	1.38	Argentina	162.62	1.38	Venezuela	132.67	1.11	Argentina	135.63	1.18
6.	Venezuela	131.76	1.25	Venezuela	156.45	1.32	Argentina	129.55	1.08	Venezuela	130.52	1.13
7.	Colombia	90.60	0.83	Peru	93.78	0.68	Colombia	94.02	0.72	Colombia	91.51	0.73
8.	Chile	88.14	0.81	Trinidad and Tobago	93.04	0.67	Peru	85.90	0.63	Chile	80.54	0.62
9.	Uruguay	86.55	0.79	Chile	87.75	0.61	Chile	79.76	0.57	Peru	75.20	0.57
10.	Peru	85.00	0.78	Colombia	83.62	0.57	Trinidad and Tobago	71.81	0.49	Ecuador	69.26	0.51
11.	Trinidad and Tobago	74.63	0.67	Uruguay	81.72	0.55	Uruguay	71.08	0.48	Trinidad and Tobago	69.19	0.51
12.	Guatemala	67.79	0.61	Ecuador	79.85	0.53	Ecuador	70.84	0.48	Uruguay	66.98	0.48
13.	Ecuador	67.23	0.60	Panama	69.86	0.43	Panama	61.15	0.38	Panama	57.85	0.39
14.	Nicaragua	65.11	0.58	Costa Rica	66.84	0.40	Nicaragua	57.64	0.34	Guatemala	57.78	0.39
15.	El Salvador	60.01	0.53	Guatemala	66.42	0.39	Costa Rica	57.27	0.34	Costa Rica	57.33	0.39
16.	Panama	58.76	0.51	Bolivia	61.99	0.35	Guatemala	56.99	0.34	Nicaragua	48.95	0.30
17.	Bolivia	57.84	0.50	Nicaragua	60.63	0.33	Bolivia	51.36	0.28	Bolivia	48.48	0.29
18.	Costa Rica	51.40	0.44	El Salvador	57.10	0.30	Paraguay	45.08	0.22	Paraguay	43.37	0.24
19.	Honduras	47.43	0.40	Jamaica	46.54	0.19	El Salvador	44.27	0.21	El Salvador	42.68	0.24
20.	Dominican Republic	44.78	0.37	Dominican Republic	46.16	0.19	Dominican Republic	43.02	0.19	Jamaica	41.85	0.23
21.	Jamaica	30.57	0.23	Paraguay	45.75	0.18	Jamaica	41.11	0.18	Dominican Republic	39.55	0.20
22.	Paraguay	11.90	0.04	Honduras	42.92	0.15	Honduras	39.70	0.16	Honduras	37.85	0.19
23.	Guyana	10.66	0.03	Haiti	36.75	0.09	Haiti	31.09	0.07	Haiti	28.51	0.09
24.	Haiti	7.74	0.00	Guyana	28.14	0.00	Guyana	24.02	0.00	Guyana	19.58	0.00

back on the power scale to have serious hope for any significant role in the evolution of hemispheric integration. On the strict basis of power distribution, these countries will almost inevitably be the "takers" of the integration process.

A last finding points to the extremely dominant position of the United States in the Americas over the years. Not only is the United States the only remaining superpower in the world system, but it has also maintained the existing power gap between itself and the other countries in the region over a thirty-year period.

What does this mean for the dynamics of hemispheric regionalism? First, U.S. dominance means that hemispheric regionalism makes very little sense without U.S. involvement. Second, it means that the United States is the only country in the region with the capacity to push and mold continental integration the way it wants, provided that it has the political will to do so and the necessary domestic support. Third, no other country can hope to challenge the hegemonic role of the United States on an individual basis.[2] Although Washington's leadership appears to have faded somewhat since 1995, all other major countries in the hemisphere except Mexico and Argentina have also lost ground on the power scale in relation to the United States.[3] This means that the only significant counterweight to U.S. dominance in the framework of continental integration is collective action. And with Canada, Mexico, and, to a lesser extent, Venezuela handicapped by their economic dependence on the United States, the Brazil-Argentina pole offers the only viable alternative.

On the sole basis of distribution of power, the future of hemispheric integration should therefore be highly dependent on the interplay between the United States and the Brazil-Argentina pole, which draws much of its power from a strong Southern Cone Common Market (Mercosur). Brazil's position as the leader of the Southern Cone is less solidly rooted than that of the U.S. because it depends heavily on Mercosur's good health and on the reaction of its neighbors, particularly Argentina and Chile.[4]

The distribution of power among the countries of the Americas over the last thirty years is therefore an important structural constraint for the future of hemispheric integration. As things now stand, the shape of future continental integration will be determined fundamentally by the basic relationship between the United States and Brazil. And if we look at regionalism as a problem of cooperation, the power structure in the Americas again has implications. The relative position of the United States leads us to expect that cooperation, should it occur, will be hegemonical in form, based on the capacity of the United States to essentially ensure compliance and assume costs. Is the United States ready for this when it is already in a position of unilaterally exercising pressure on every regional power?

This is highly problematic in a context of nonhegemonic global and subregional cooperation. Why would other states accept regional hegemonic rules when, to a large extent, they can achieve similar gains through a combination of nonhegemonic mechanisms of cooperation at the global and subregional levels? Unless there is a significant payoff linked to the regional option, they are unlikely to do so. Inversely, hegemonic cooperation would require that the United States be willing to pay the price for a hegemonic relationship in the region at the very moment it is in the process of disentangling itself from similar relations elsewhere and looking for greater reciprocity.

Major inequalities in the distribution of power can also have positive effects on cooperation. According to neorealist theory, these inequalities reduce state sensitivity to possible inequalities in the distribution of gains produced by cooperation. The theory holds that states in close competition for positions in the hierarchy of power are less likely to cooperate for fear that the benefits of cooperation would be greater for their competitors than for themselves, thereby negatively affecting their power relationship (Grieco 1990). Inversely, states separated by very high gaps of relative capability, which cannot be significantly affected by cooperation payoffs, may satisfy themselves with absolute anticipated gains and simply forget about problems of relative distribution.

Authors theorizing about the importance of relative gains generally limit their comments to relationships with the dominant powers. The focus on dominant powers overshadows competition between second-range states, which can be crucial for regional cooperation.

For instance, sensitivity to expected gains by Latin American competitors may help explain Mexican attitudes toward the expansion of NAFTA and the regionalist agenda in general. Since the 1950s, Mexico has managed to distance itself from Argentina and Venezuela, the two other countries maintaining a decile ranking between 1 and 2 in the hierarchy of power. Mexico seems unwilling to compromise its rising position by sharing the comparative advantage it has gained from NAFTA with others. This question of second-range states' sensitivity to each other's gains will be discussed in more depth in Chapter 8.

Looking at the regional distribution of power, therefore, not only allows us to identify the poles likely to structure hemispheric regionalism but also helps us understand how key actors in the process evaluate the benefits of Pan-American cooperation.

The Pattern of Trade Relations

As mentioned earlier in this chapter, the theoretical literature on regional integration identified an increase in transactions either as a condition for the success of an integration process (Deutsch 1952: 358; Deutsch et al. 1957: 46–57) or as a process mechanism (Nye 1970: 805, 821).

Among these transactions trade occupies an important place, particularly because of its link with another essential condition for the success of integration, namely, the expectation of rewards for the participating units.[5] Changes in the volume and the pattern of regional trade can therefore constitute another important structural pillar for the future of an integration process.

This section seeks to offer a comprehensive view of the evolution of trade patterns in the Western Hemisphere by presenting a comparative analysis of the periods 1975–1979, 1985–1989, and 1990–1994. By examining the pattern of trade flows during these three periods, we hope to be able to draw conclusions about the structure of regionalism in the Americas in the years to come.

For our calculations, average annual trade between twenty-seven American countries was measured for three periods, 1975–1979, 1985–1989, and 1990–1994.[6] We chose four-year periods to reduce the volatility of the data, the last four-year period ending with the last year for which data were available at the time of collection. The 1980–1984 period was skipped because of the difficulty of establishing reliable U.S. dollar equivalencies for this period.

The data show that the share of foreign goods exported by all economies in the Americas to other countries within the hemisphere rose from 47.3 percent in 1975–1979 to 48.4 percent in 1985–1989, and to 49.5 percent in 1990–1994, indicating a slight but regular increase in the relative importance of intraregional over extraregional hemispheric trade. It remains to be seen, however, whether these figures provide us with any information about the presence or absence of true regional cohesion. The results could be attributed to a few strong bilateral relationships, which may well prove insignificant in the context of regional reality taken as a whole. In other words, are the Americas an arbitrary creation? Are we speaking of one region or many regions? What is the structure of intraregional trade? These are questions for which answers cannot be obtained by using simple measures.

Correspondence analysis, a technique that offers the advantage of situating each trading partner with respect to every other, is the measurement strategy adopted here to answer these questions (see Figures 3.2–3.4). Often utilized as a preliminary step in classification exercises where data must be regrouped on the basis of a large number of variables, this automatic data assortment technique allows us to represent trade affinities between countries and to assess similarities in their trade profiles. By using a table representing each country as both an exporter and an importer, we projected a three-dimensional cloud of points in which each country's profile is represented by one point, the location of which is a function of its relative importance for its trading partners.[7] The distance of each point

Figure 3.2 Commercial Trade Between American Countries (1975–1979)

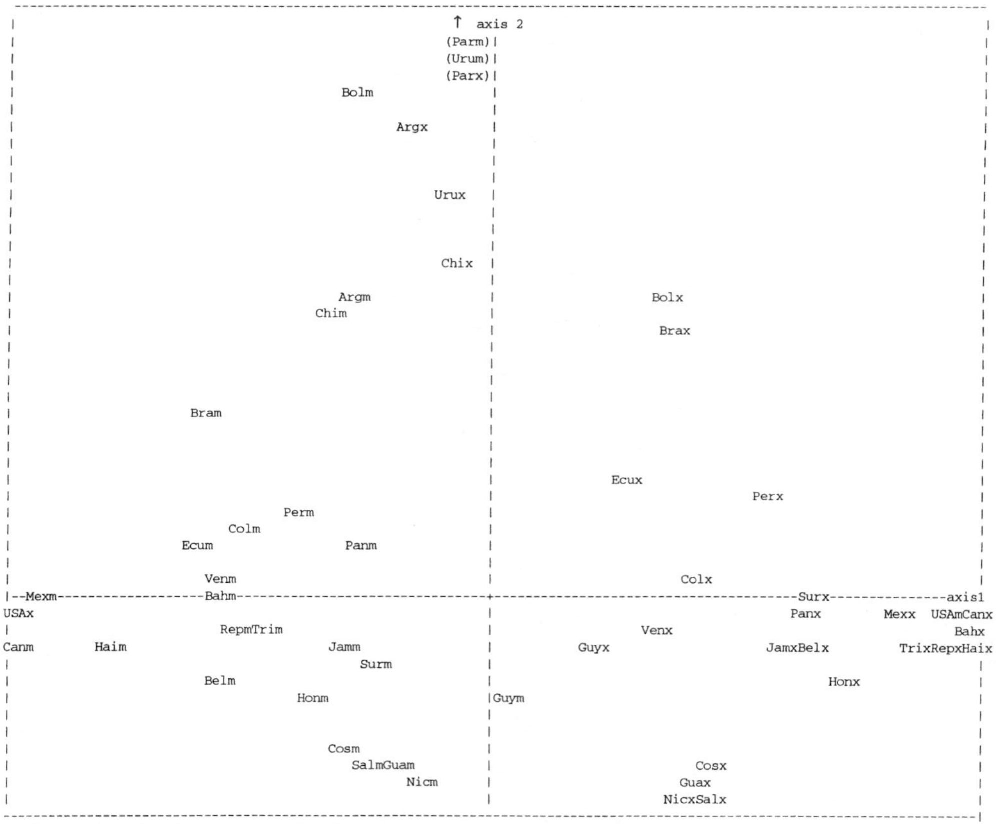

```
                                                            ↑ axis 2
                                                          (Parm)|
                                                          (Urum)|
                                                          (Parx)|
                                        Bolm              |
                                    Argx                  |
                          Bram                            |
                                 Argm                     |
                                 Chim                     |
                         Colm          Urux               |
                 Ecum    Perm                   Chix      |
                 Venm    Parm                             |
USAx ---Mexm----------Bahm-------------------------------------Surx--------axis1
Canm        RepmTrim  Jamm                          Guym  |
       Haim           Surm                                |
            Belm                                          |
                  Honm                                    |
                 Cosm                           Ecux      |
                 SalmGuam                 Colx            |
                       Nicm                               |
                                                          | Guyx
                                              Venx        |
                                                          |     Bolx
                                                          |     Brax
                                                          |          Perx
                                                     Colx |
                                               Panx  Surx-----axis1
                                      JamxBelx   Panx  Mexx  USAmCanx
                                                      Bahx
                                         Honx   TrixRepxBalx
```

Notes: See the chapter Appendix for a key to the abbreviations used in this figure.
Axis 1, horizontal: proper value = 0.77; rate (part of total inertia) = 61 percent.
Axis 2, vertical: proper value = 0.14; rate = 11 percent.

Figure 3.3 Commercial Trade Between American Countries (1985–1989)

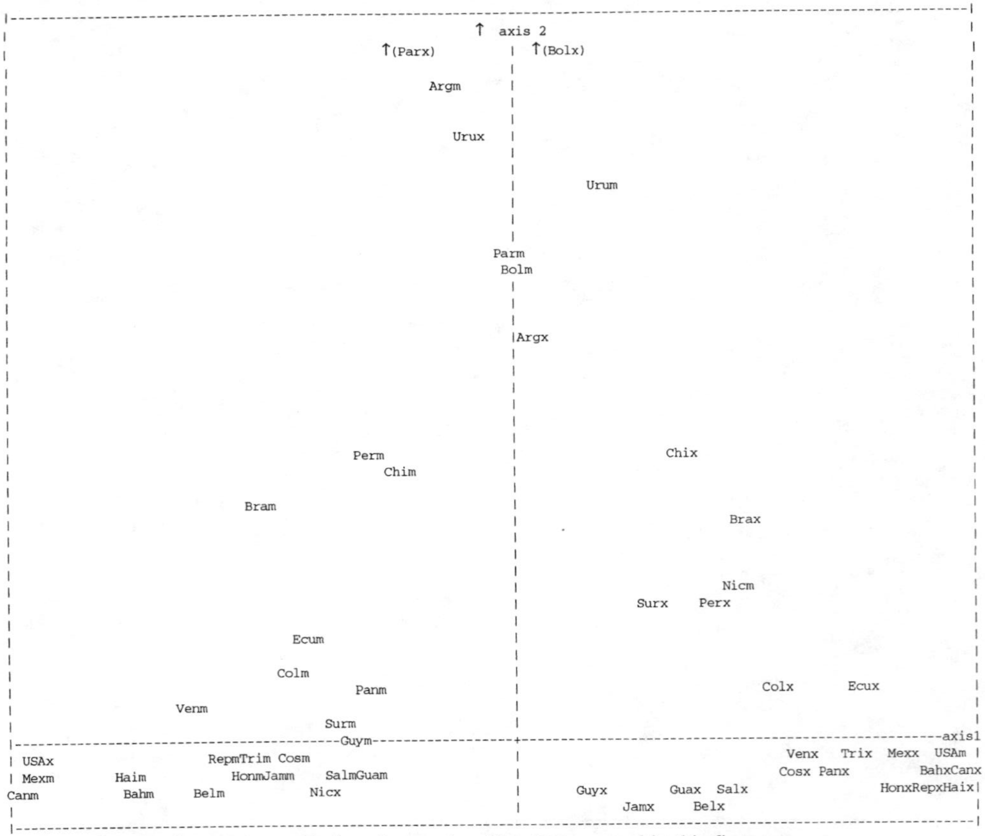

Notes: See the chapter Appendix for a key to the abbreviations used in this figure.
Axis 1, horizontal: proper value = 0.85; rate (part of total inertia) = 71 percent.
Axis 2, vertical: proper value = 0.13; rate = 11 percent.

Figure 3.4 Commercial Trade Between American Countries (1990–1994)

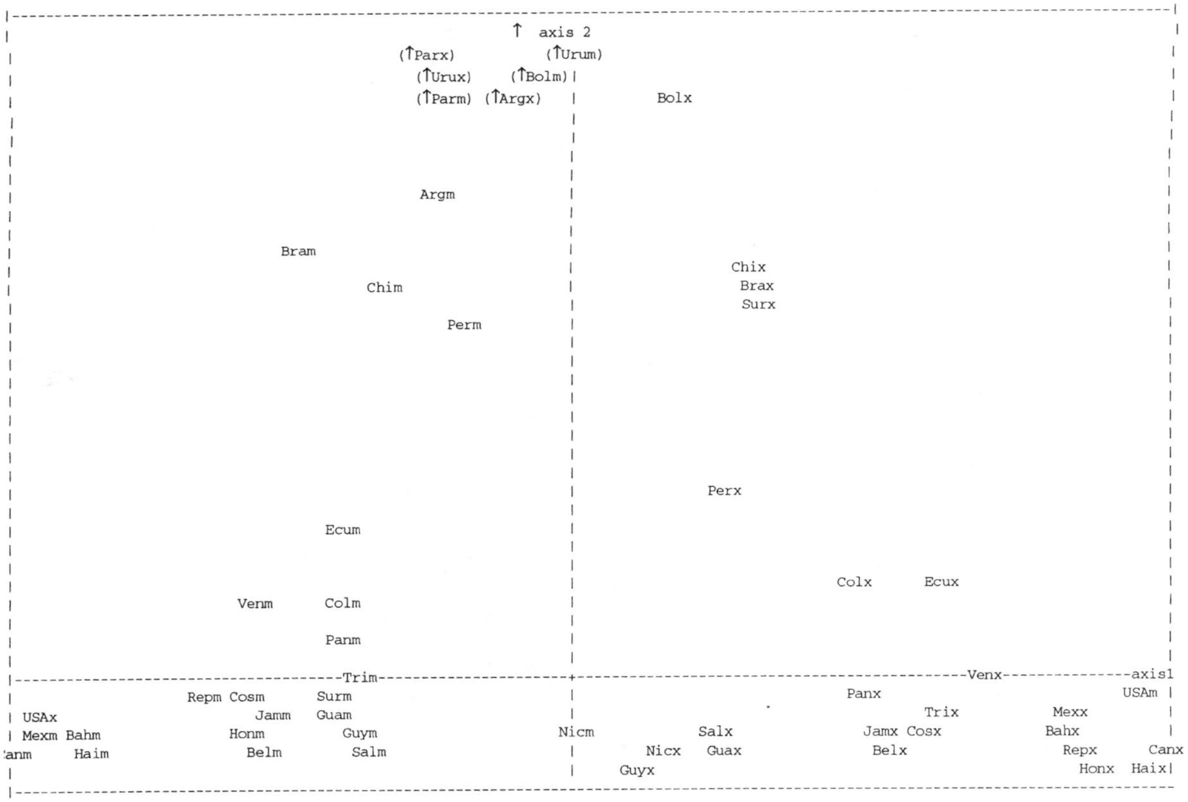

Notes: See the chapter Appendix for a key to the abbreviations used in this figure. Axis 1, horizontal: proper value = 0.84; rate (part of total inertia) = 66 percent. Axis 2, vertical: proper value = 0.19; rate = 15 percent.

from the intersection of the two axes is a function of its degree of deviation from what would be considered average trade behavior or structure. The proximity of two points therefore indicates that the two corresponding countries share, either as exporters or importers, a common trade profile or, in other words, that their trade is distributed among regional partners in a similar way. This is a very important point because we are primarily interested in homogeneity of profile instead of strength. Weight is important as well, of course, but principally as it affects the trade patterns of others.

To understand the significance of the position of a single point in the clouds, it is essential to take into account the general pattern of cloud distribution revealed in Figures 3.2–3.4. The general patterns of distribution will help answer the following simple questions: In what respect do clusters form and deviate from the average situation represented by the center of gravity? How do groups of countries with similar trade profiles distinguish themselves from each other?

The displays of cloud point dispersions presented here are divided by two inertia axes crossing the clouds' center of gravity: axis 1 (horizontal) and axis 2 (vertical). Among several possibilities, these are, respectively, the first and second axes on which the dot clouds are projected with a maximum of dispersion. This analysis compares three data sets, Figure 3.2 representing the 1975–1979 period, Figure 3.3 the 1985–1989 period, and Figure 3.4 the 1990–1994 period. Data used are those of the International Monetary Fund. Our discussion of findings centers on two major subregions: North America and the Southern Cone, which together account for 90 percent of intraregional trade.

General View: The Dominance of the North

A certain number of conclusions can be drawn from preliminary general observation of the figures. First of all, in all cases, axis 1 shows opposition between the United States and Canada, both as suppliers (USAx and CANx) to which are attached their principal clients and as clients (USAm and CANm) with which are associated their main suppliers.[8] Given the weight of the U.S. economy, the distribution on this axis is essentially a function of the relative power of attraction exercised by the United States in its capacity as the main regional client and supplier in opposition to other regional economic powers. Canada is the most important of these other powers and is the most integrated into the U.S. economy. Because the U.S. situation is unique, other countries will have their positions on axis 1 determined by their proximity to the Canadian situation. This tension is quite apparent in the case of Mexico. Like Canada, Mexico is strongly integrated into the U.S. economy. However, as is also the case with Canada, it does not maintain bilateral ties with other economies strong enough to counterweigh this attraction. Because of this similarity in profile, Mexico is situated in close proximity to Canada in the figures as both an exporter and a supplier.

The figures also show that the power of attraction exercised by the United States is stronger as a client than as a supplier; dots are more closely clustered around USAm than around USAx. More precisely, more countries share similarities of profile with the Canadian position in relation to the United States in their capacity as exporters than in their capacity as importers.

Axis 2 is dominated by the presence of a strong counterweight to the North American center of gravity: the nations of the Southern Cone. The relative cohesion and autonomy of the Southern Cone countries is quite noticeable at the top of the axis. In the middle, between the Southern Cone and the other nations, are most of the Andean countries. At the bottom of the axis stands Central America. Between 1975 and 1979, the region displays a clear profile of cohesion and relative autonomy, particularly with regard to South America. However, South America's position is more consistent with that of its northern neighbors for the 1985–1989 and 1990–1994 periods.

North America and Its Immediate Zone of Influence

Let us begin by observing the countries that are the most dependent on the United States for their exports, grouped at the right end of axis 1 in Figure 3.2. A cluster of exporting countries that is virtually glued to the U.S. market (USAm) forms the core of this group. More than 85 percent of the regional exports from these nations are directed toward the United States. A second sphere of U.S. influence made up of countries dependent on the U.S. market for more than 70 percent of their regional exports is clearly identifiable for 1975–1979 on the periphery of the core group of suppliers. It includes Surinam, Panama, Jamaica, Belize, and Honduras. However, by 1985–1989 this second circle of influence has largely dissipated to be replaced in the 1990–1994 period by another cluster composed of Venezuela, Panama, Trinidad and Tobago, Jamaica, Costa Rica, and Belize, countries that are dependent on the U.S. market for 65 percent to 77 percent of their exports. Guyana and the other Central American countries now form a third cluster.

As we observed previously, the zone of influence of the United States is more diffuse when its exports are considered. During the three periods studied, the United States imported more than it exported in the region. However, the data also indicate that the U.S. position as supplier tended to gain in importance during the last period (from 44 percent to 46 percent of all exports), and its relative position as a buyer declined (from 50 to 46 percent of all imports). Canada's and Mexico's alignment with the United States also became stronger.

It is no surprise, then, that the United States is the foremost trading partner in the Americas. Its presence structures the web of trade relations in the region.

The Southern Cone

As Figures 3.2–3.4 show, the Southern Cone constitutes the main counterweight to North American trading power in the region. The countries most integrated into this subregion are located at the upper end of axis 2. This pattern clearly reveals the relative weakness of the Southern Cone's relationship with North America, as well as its remarkable lack of economic ties with Central America and the Caribbean.

Brazil, for which the United States represents a more important economic partner, occupies a median position that varies little from the first to the second period but changes significantly during 1990–1994, when Brazil became more entrenched in the Southern Cone. There is a fundamental shift here: As the proportion of Brazil's regional exports going to the United States dropped significantly between the second and third periods (from 65.5 percent to 49.2 percent), Brazil became more dependent on its neighbors' markets. Argentina, for example, which accounted for 6.6 percent of Brazilian regional exports in the second period, received 17 percent of them in 1990–1994.

Modifications in the export profile of Argentina and Chile created a certain disturbance in the group's trade structure. The position of the two exporters on the left side of axis 1 for 1975–1979 reveals their relative autonomy in relation to the U.S. market and the relative importance of neighboring states as customers. However, the situation changes radically during the 1985–1989 period. Argentina and especially Chile now appear on the right side of axis 1, which means that they are aligning themselves on North American patterns of trade with the United States. The situation changes again in the 1990–1994 period as Argentina moves back to the left side of axis 1, joining Paraguay and Uruguay in a closer relationship with Brazil as importers.

Figure 3.4 is extremely interesting because it reveals that the Southern Cone is developing a distinct regional trading structure. Axis 2, representing the Southern Cone counterweight, shows a significant rise in importance for 1990–1994, jumping to 19 percent in terms of its general dispersion value and lining up more strongly than previously along the dual

Brazil-Argentina pole. The Southern Cone's integration into the region as a whole is relatively weak, especially in the case of the smaller economies (Paraguay, Uruguay) strongly dependent on middle powers such as Brazil and Argentina. The countries of the subregion also maintain relatively strong trade links among themselves. This structure nevertheless underwent significant changes over the three periods under study. Relations between the middle powers and the United States grew closer, and the smaller economies grew more dependent on the middle powers for their regional external trade. However, the positive effects of Mercosur are clearly revealed by the increased clustering of the Southern Cone countries in the 1990–1994 period. In fact, Figure 3.4 is an eloquent illustration of the fact that the Americas of the 1990s are now composed of two main trade subregions.

Trade Patterns and Regionalism

Traditional literature on regional integration, particularly works from the transactionalist school (Deutsch 1954; Deutsch et al. 1957), assumed a close relationship between certain types of transactions, notably trade, and the success or failure of integration schemes. Combined with other indices, variations in the level of regional trade and the distribution of trade flows between neighboring countries were seen as advance indicators of the future state of integration processes. Although the main idea behind such reasoning—that trade influences political cooperation—has inspired important works informed by classical liberal theses, even after the golden age of transactionalism (Polachek 1980), a growing body of literature emerging from public choice and neorealist approaches to international political economy is providing evidence of the opposite—that it is good political relations that have a positive impact on trade (Pollins 1989a, 1989b; Dixon and Moon 1993; Gowa 1994). All these studies converge in one sense by clearly demonstrating that political cooperation and trade are inextricably linked. States are less inclined to abandon political partnership if they expect it to have a negative effect on trade, and states are more inclined to develop trade relations with political allies they can trust.

Our analysis of trade ties in the Americas in the 1970s, 1980s, and 1990s follows this reasoning. We believe that a structured observation of trade flows over a certain period of time will give us an idea of the strength and geographical configuration of regionalism in a given geographical region. The regional structure of exports and imports becomes the key to determining whether a region is organized around "industrial centers of gravity" (Peschel 1990: 71) or whether it grows out of a logic of "hegemonic power relations" (Fishlow and Haggard 1992: 13). It then permits us to identify the specific economic-political relationships on which regionalism can be built. In this perspective, the results of our factor analysis demonstrate that the countries of the Western Hemisphere possess widely variable leadership capacities in relation to the regional environment.

These capacities point to two possible scenarios—both found in the literature—for the eventual configuration of a regional system in the Americas (Fishlow and Haggard 1992: 26–27). In the first scenario, inspired by the "hub-and-spoke" model, the United States would become the center of a network of bilateral agreements signed by a number of countries in the region. This situation would evolve and eventually give way to the creation of a regional system of the Americas dominated by the hegemonic power of the United States. In contrast, a second scenario, inspired by the "hub-hub" model, suggests that regional transactions would follow another pattern of agglutination around two groups of countries. This would eventually lead to the creation of two regional systems within the Western Hemisphere.

The results of our analysis of trade patterns in the Americas provide evidence that would seem to support the latter scenario, at least regarding trade relations. A comparison of data for the three time periods reveals the increasingly powerful attraction of the U.S. market, as well as the structuring effect of the Brazil-Argentina pole.

The U.S. market has effectively grown in importance, not only for its immediate Canadian and Mexican neighbors but also for many countries in Central America and the Caribbean, and Venezuela as well. Should this trend continue in upcoming years, it could jeopardize the future of the Caribbean Community and Common Market, the Central American Common Market, and the so-called Group of Three (Mexico, Venezuela, and Colombia). These integration or cooperation schemes could well fall into disarray as more and more of their members became attracted to or even engulfed by a North American regional system.

For the southern half of the hemisphere, the data analysis for the three time periods also reveals the growing importance of Brazil and Argentina as poles of attraction. The trend here is not as clear as it is in the North American case, but in the 1990s the Southern Cone trading zone has become increasingly structured compared with the North American trading system.

The major casualty of this development will probably be the Andean integration scheme. Indeed, the Andean nations seem to be increasingly affected by conflicting centrifugal forces. Venezuela and, to a lesser extent, Colombia look northward; Bolivia appears to be increasingly linked to the Southern Cone; and Peru and Ecuador are exporting more to the United States but importing more from the countries of the Southern Cone. For these countries, there is also a political appeal in having stronger links with the Mercosur countries. With Mexico increasingly integrated into the North American environment, the center of Latin American political and diplomatic activity and leadership has shifted more to the Brazil-Argentina axis dominating Mercosur.

Consequently, the slow but progressive emergence of two subregional trading systems in the Americas constitutes a significant structural feature that cannot be ignored in negotiations leading to a free trade area of the Americas. Combined with the trends in the distribution of power discussed previously, the evolution in the pattern of trade relations in the Western Hemisphere suggests that initial U.S. plans to extend the North American Free Trade Agreement (NAFTA) to the rest of the region have little chance of success if they imply some kind of dissolution of the politico-economic alliance represented by Mercosur. And success appears even less likely in light of the recent failures to implement the fast-track procedure in the United States. In the current context, it therefore appears that continental integration is more likely to proceed on the basis of accommodation between the NAFTA and Mercosur economic development models.

Still a Political Cultural Divide[9]

Regional integration theory recognizes that integration processes can develop initially to a certain point provided that the participating units receive some economic benefits or at least expect economic benefits to materialize from their participation in the integration scheme. In the long term, however, economic gains are not enough to sustain and deepen the integration process. For this to happen, certain sociocultural conditions are deemed necessary, including compatibility of main values (Deutsch et al. 1957: 46–57; Nye 1970: 821), unbroken social communications links (Deutsch et al. 1957: 46–57), common aspirations and mutual identification (Lindberg and Scheingold 1970: 26, 39, 98–94), and consensus (Etzioni 1968: 167, 469). Here again, we know that these political links and similarities can be fostered, especially in light of the relative success of European Community expansion.

These and other similar elements mentioned in the literature all fall more or less under the general heading of differences and similarities in political culture. Analysts have used political culture to explain why Latin America followed a path so different from that of the United States and Canada in terms of political institutions. In one of the most fascinating interpretations in the literature, Stanley and Barbara Stein identified the political culture of Britain, Spain, and Portugal at the time of New World colonization as the main explanation for the diverging paths of political and economic development in North and South-Central America during the last three hundred years (Stein and Stein 1970). In essence, the Steins argue that colonial-era Britain was a society in the process of modernization, with an economy that was starting to industrialize, a political system in transformation, and a general openness toward scientific ideas. In contrast, Spain and Portugal were still preindustrial commodity producers characterized by extreme centralization of political authority, tightly closed political systems, excessively rigid social hierarchies, and strict adherence to traditional values enforced by tight Catholic church control. It was this preindustrialized social model with its antiquated political and economic system that was imposed on the Ibero-American colonies and is primarily responsible for Latin America's evolution since the period of independence. This interpretation is also shared by Abel, Taras, and Cochrane (1991: 27–28).

According to another view of political culture, the Americas are home to three very different types of countries: premodern, modern, and postmodern. According to Robert Cooper (1996), premodern states are countries like Haiti, Surinam, and Paraguay, where the legitimate monopoly on the use of force is still not accepted by all. Modern states, found throughout most of Latin America and the Caribbean, are those still functioning on the basis of a nineteenth-century European system in which belief in state sovereignty remains strong and international relations are governed by the balance of power. Finally, the postmoderns—namely, Canada and the United States—are those states where sovereignty is less important and governments and citizens are more open to intrusions into domestic affairs by global forces and international or regional institutions. Clearly, the integration process in the Americas will have to accommodate these three categories of states.

Numerous commentators from academic and political circles have stated that one of the main explanations for the present-day momentum in favor of regionalism in the Americas is found in the rapid shrinking of those differences in political culture. Sudden democratization during the 1980s in Latin American countries has been seen as both the removal of a major obstacle to political cooperation and a positive movement that should be encouraged and sanctioned through cooperation. The question, then, is how much of the gap in political culture between North America and Latin America has been closed and how solid this progression toward democratization really is.

Howard Wiarda recently noted how great a distance still separates the United States and Canada from Latin American countries in the areas of democracy and human rights despite representative democracy's strong comeback throughout Latin America during the 1980s and 1990s (Wiarda 1997). Although military regimes were all replaced and regular elections are now held virtually everywhere, problems persist between elections. Pluralism remains limited and corporatism is apparently making a comeback in many countries (Wiarda 1997: 18).

Political reforms, albeit still incomplete, are progressing normally in two important countries, Argentina and Chile, as well as in others, such as Nicaragua and El Salvador. In contrast, the situation in the two principal regional powers appears to be essentially blocked. In Brazil, reforms have been left hanging and have produced chronic failure at the government level. As for Mexico, change appears imperceptible, particularly with regard to the question of free and fair elections and the alternation of power, as the Zapatista National Liberation Army (EZLN) rebellion so clearly indicated. Although Brazil, in 1992, and Venezuela, in 1993, were able to replace presidents accused of corruption without placing their democratic regimes in jeopardy, both regimes were shaken by the bids for consolidation of power (*autogolpe*) undertaken by Presidents Alberto Fujimori in Peru and Jorge Serrano Elías in Guatemala during the same period (1992–1993). Serious problems thus remain within countries of pivotal importance to the regional equilibrium.

An examination of the particular issue of human rights completes this general overview of the evolution of political reforms. A democratic regime does not necessarily guarantee complete respect of human rights, but the human rights situation is a good indicator of democratic health. On the one hand, several countries in the region were obliged to assume the legacy of massive human rights violations attributed to former military regimes in pursuing the transition to democracy. In most instances, to use Manuel Antonio Garreton's terms (Garreton 1994), a policy of amnesty and impunity prevailed, accompanied by occasional efforts to establish guilt and administer justice for appearance's sake. This was the case, for example, in Argentina, Brazil, Chile, Guatemala, Nicaragua, and El Salvador.

On the other hand, Table 3.2 indicates that whereas the overall human rights situation in Latin America has improved over the longer term (1975–1990), the assessment is much less conclusive in the specific area of civil rights.[10] In the 1990–1993 period, respect for civil rights effectively deteriorated in several important countries, particularly those that face ongoing guerrilla and terrorist activities, such as Colombia and Peru. As for Mexico, where guerrilla activity is recent, it is the lack of progress that stands out. In addition, the civil rights situation also deteriorated or stagnated in several other nations, most notably in Brazil, Venezuela, and Argentina.

In sum, the consolidation of democratic regimes generally appears to be an arduous task. Although the situation varies from one country to another, certain states, including Brazil and Mexico, the two most important nations, still face grave problems. Rights violations are of major significance in Mexico and notable in Brazil. Corruption is widespread and institutional reforms unsatisfactory in both countries. The situation prevailing in these two nations exercises an important influence on regional stability.

Table 3.2   Civil and Political Rights in the Americas[a]

	1980		1985		1990		1993	
	PR[b]	CR[c]	PR	CR	PR	CR	PR	CR
Argentina	6	5	2	2	1	2	2	3
Bolivia	7	5	2	3	2	3	2	3
Brazil	4	3	3	2	2	3	2	3
Canada	1	1	1	1	1	1	1	1
Chile	6	5	6	5	4	3	2(1991)	2(1991)
Colombia	2	3	2	3	3	4	2	4
Costa Rica	1	1	1	1	1	1	1	1
Cuba	6	6	6	6	7	7	7	7
Dominican Republic	2	3	1	3	1	3	2	3
Ecuador	2	2	2	3	2	2	2	3
El Salvador	6	4	2	4	3	4	3	3
Guatemala	5	6	4	4	3	3	4	5
Haiti	6	6	7	6	7	5	7	7
Honduras	4	3	2	3	2	3	2	3
Mexico	3	4	4	4	4	3	4	3
Nicaragua	5	5	5	5	5	5	4	3
Panama	4	4	6	3	7	6	4	3
Paraguay	5	5	5	5	4	3	3	3
Peru	2	3	2	3	2	4	6	5
United States	1	1	1	1	1	1	1	1
Uruguay	5	5	2	2	1	2	1	2
Venezuela	1	2	1	2	1	3	3	3

Source: Committee on Latin American Studies (1996), *Statistical Abstract of Latin America* (Los Angeles: Latin American Center, University of California), p. 274

Notes: a. On a scale of 1 to 7, 1 corresponds to a situation where rights are most respected, and 7 to a situation where they are least respected.

b. The score for political rights is determined by the degree to which a given country satisfies the following requirements: (1) leaders are chosen in decisions made on the basis of an open voting process; (2) significant opposition is allowed to compete in this process; (3) there are multiple political parties and candidates not selected by the government; (4) polling and counting of votes are conducted without coercion or fraud; (5) a significant share of political power is exercised by elected representatives; (6) all regions, even the most remote, are included in the political process; and (7) the country is free of foreign or military control or influence. Countries assigned a rank of 1 most closely satisfy these requirements and those assigned a rank of 7 most seriously violate them.

c. The score for civil rights is determined by the degree of liberty a given country grants its news media and individual citizens, primarily as it applies to political expression. The survey looks at censorship applied to the press or radio. It also assesses the rights granted any individual to openly express ideas and to belong to an organization free of government supervision and the individual's right to a free trial, that is, the degree to which the judiciary is independent of administrative control. Also important is the number of political prisoners held in a country, the use of torture or brutality, and the degree to which the state security forces respect individual rights. Countries assigned the rank of 1 grant the greatest degree of civil liberties, and those assigned the rank of 7 most seriously violate them.

On the regional level, the failure of OAS attempts to restore democracy in Haiti has revealed how difficult it will be to establish a hemispheric regime for democracy in the face of strongly opposing points of view.

The areas of civil rights, human rights, and democratization are only three examples of how culture and history have nurtured conflicting ideas and fundamental differences. These differences are structural realities that will influence continental integration.

Worlds Apart: Levels of Economic Development

Scholars studying regional integration schemes involving developing countries quickly became aware of the significant structural constraints created by uneven levels of economic development among participating countries (Axline 1977; Mytelka 1979: 10–15). In almost all cases, the establishment and eventual success of these integration processes required the adoption of compensatory or redistributive measures in support of their less developed members. Such measures were often an important condition for the inclusion of these countries at the start of the integration process; even the European Community had to address the problem. In the rare cases where the larger and more developed countries refused or were reluctant to establish measures in support of less developed members—as in the Latin American Free Trade Association, for example—integration schemes faltered after only a few years of existence.

In the Americas, economic development has been extremely diverse. When GDP per capita is used as a measure of economic development (see Table 3.6 in the chapter Appendix), there are significant variations among the twenty-four countries for which information was available. Alongside countries such as the United States and Canada, which have a GDP per capita of over $14,000, are a good number of countries whose GDP per capita is less than $2,000. Furthermore, although the GDP per capita of many countries did grow over the time period studied, in the 1990s most lost ground in relation to the United States. In fact, only Canada improved its position significantly in relation to the United States, with a gain of more than 1.00 (from 6.6 in 1966–1969 to 7.7 in 1991–1994).

Given the huge disparities in economic development levels throughout the Americas, this means that it is almost impossible to envisage the establishment of an integration process that does not include some form of special treatment for the less developed countries of the region. In particular, an early U.S. idea of extending NAFTA to the rest of the hemisphere appears extremely unrealistic, because only a few countries of the region are able to comply with such a model of economic integration.

In fact, strict application of a rigorous free trade agreement to the whole hemisphere would seriously harm Caribbean and Central American countries as well as certain South American countries, such as Bolivia, Ecuador, Paraguay, and Peru, which would require important structural adjustment in order to comply with such a treaty. The problem of taking account of the differences in level of development has already emerged as a major challenge during the prenegotiations on the Free Trade Area of the Americas. Although NAFTA's and Mercosur's larger countries recognize the need to take appropriate measures in order to facilitate small economies' integration to the future zone, they rejected a proposal by the Economic Commission for Latin America and the Caribbean to create a Regional Integration Fund to finance programs of adjustment, saying that existing institutions should be able to support transition costs ("Caricom" 1997). However, they ultimately accepted the idea of accommodating small economies by agreeing to consider "on a case by case basis" "measures such as technical assistance in specific areas and longer periods for implementing the obligations" (*San José* 1998).

Of course, the need to accommodate smaller economies will be the subject of hard negotiations, and it shows the immediate relevance of the disparities in levels of development to the development of hemispheric regionalism. It is a key structural constraint that will have to be addressed if integration is to involve countries other than the NAFTA and Mercosur member states.

Conclusion

In this chapter we have examined four main areas of structural constraint and opportunity that will necessarily influence the evolution of continental integration in the Americas. Distribution of power and patterns of trade relations over the past thirty years constitute structural realities pointing to two possible scenarios for the future of hemispheric integration. In the first case, integration would proceed along an integration framework based on NAFTA and the U.S. agenda for inter-American affairs, with the United States as the major center of gravity. In the second, hemispheric integration would develop on the basis of two core areas—the U.S.-NAFTA subregion and the Brazil-Mercosur subregion—and proceed more slowly because of the need to accommodate the interests of both areas. If only the first two structural constraints are considered, then the current situation favors the second scenario: Washington's bargaining position has been weakened by the administration's incapacity to secure fast-track authority and the concurrent strengthening of the Mercosur subregion. But we must always keep in mind that this particular situation can change rapidly and again modify the dynamics of integration in the Americas.

When the two other structural parameters—political culture and levels of development—are taken into consideration, however, the situation becomes much more complex and leaves the very future of hemispheric integration open to question. Differences and disparities are so important that it is difficult to imagine the success of a hemisphere-wide integration scheme based essentially on North American views or even negotiated by the major countries of the region without concern for the smaller ones. It seems clear that the only way for hemispheric integration to succeed is through practicality, open-mindedness, and genuine compromise. That means compromise by the United States and Canada with regard to the interests and points of view of the rest of the region, as well as compromise by larger, more developed countries regarding the situation of their smaller, less developed counterparts.

This may seem a Herculean task, but as the forty-year European integration process reminds us, regional integration is a long-term enterprise. The window of opportunity for hemispheric integration opened at the end of the 1980s was only a starting point. A learning process is now in progress and its ultimate results will depend a great deal on the attitudes and the behavior of the actors setting the stage for continental integration in the Americas.

Appendix

Abbreviations used in Figures 3.1–3.4

Argentina	Arg
Bahamas	Bah
Belize	Bel
Bolivia	Bol
Brazil	Bra
Canada	Can
Chile	Chi
Colombia	Col
Costa Rica	Cos
Dominican Republic	Rep
Ecuador	Ecu
El Salvador	Sal
Guatemala	Gua
Guyana	Guy
Haiti	Hai
Honduras	Hon
Jamaïca	Jam
Mexico	Mex
Nicaragua	Nic
Panama	Pan

Abbreviations continued

Paraguay	Par
Peru	Per
Surinam	Sur
Trinidad and Tobago	Tri
United States	USA
Uruguay	Uru
Venezuela	Ven

*   *   *

Table 3.3 Military Expenditures (1988 U.S.$ millions)

Country	1966–1969 Average	Decile	1976–1979 Average	Decile	1986–1989 Average	Decile	1991–1994[a] Average	Decile
Argentina	3,777	0.15	5,520	0.28	3,096	0.10	2,070	0.09
Bolivia	74	0.00	199	0.01	171	0.00	232	0.01
Brazil	3,647	0.14	4,818	0.25	4,034	0.13	1,803	0.08
Canada	5,911	0.23	7,033	0.36	9,756	0.33	8,788	0.37
Chile	231	0.01	1,074	0.05	1,470	0.05	1,639	0.07
Colombia	542	0.02	431	0.02	855	0.03	1,455	0.06
Costa Rica	14	0.00	23	0.00	23	0.00	19	0.00
Dominican Republic	19	0.00	23	0.00	51	0.00	35	0.00
Ecuador	52	0.00	139	0.01	174	0.01	189	0.01
El Salvador	94	0.00	164	0.01	198	0.01	97	0.00
Guatemala	42	0.00	101	0.00	199	0.01	115	0.00
Guyana	9	0.00	39	0.00	32	0.00	73	0.00
Haiti	27	0.00	21	0.00	28	0.00	89	0.00
Honduras	18	0.00	43	0.00	235	0.01	69	0.00
Jamaica	22	0.00	54	0.00	26	0.00	89	0.00
Mexico	531	0.02	982	0.05	782	0.03	468	0.02
Nicaragua	52	0.00	138	0.01	351	0.01	38	0.00
Panama	17	0.00	40	0.00	104	0.00	69	0.00
Paraguay	29	0.00	68	0.00	65	0.00	115	0.00
Peru	187	0.01	490	0.02	620	0.02	334	0.01
Trinidad and Tobago	68	0.00	136	0.01	144	0.00	132	0.00
United States	258,649	10.00	195,651	10.00	297,739	10.00	235,252	10.00
Uruguay	125	0.00	203	0.01	167	0.00	123	0.00
Venezuela	856	0.03	1,471	0.07	1,244	0.04	1,508	0.06

Source: Compiled by authors from Stockholm International Peace Research Institute (1991, 1992, 1993, 1994, 1995) and International Institute of Strategic Studies (1995: 267).

Note: a. Period data for Guyana, Haiti, Jamaica, Nicaragua, and Trinidad and Tobago are from the IISS. Data for Nicaragua are in 1993 dollars rather than 1988 dollars like all the others.

Table 3.4 Exports (U.S.$ millions)

Country	1966–1969 Average	1966–1969 Decile	1976–1979 Average	1976–1979 Decile	1986–1989 Average	1986–1989 Decile	1991–1994 Average	1991–1994 Decile
Argentina	1,510	0.44	6,028	0.42	7,977	0.27	13,109	0.28
Bolivia	160	0.04	672	0.04	658	0.02	844	0.01
Brazil	1,897	0.55	12,486	0.88	28,768	0.99	37,995	0.82
Canada	11,754	3.48	47,615	3.38	106,225	3.68	140,406	3.04
Chile	945	0.27	2,608	0.17	6,145	0.21	10,094	0.21
Colombia	546	0.15	2,759	0.18	5,224	0.17	7,667	0.16
Costa Rica	162	0.04	819	0.05	1,218	0.04	2,390	0.05
Dominican Republic	160	0.04	762	0.04	814	0.02	619	0.01
Ecuador	215	0.05	1,465	0.09	2,179	0.07	3,226	0.07
El Salvador	203	0.05	941	0.05	623	0.02	802	0.01
Guatemala	225	0.06	1,075	0.06	1,100	0.03	1,402	0.03
Guyana	114	0.02	278	0.01	228	0.00	380	0.00
Haiti	40	0.00	177	0.00	187	0.00	176	0.00
Honduras	184	0.04	571	0.03	857	0.02	1,076	0.02
Jamaica	237	0.06	730	0.04	784	0.02	1,412	0.03
Mexico	1,262	0.36	5,543	0.38	20,097	0.69	39,545	0.85
Nicaragua	154	0.03	627	0.03	278	0.00	274	0.00
Panama	91	0.02	362	0.01	313	0.00	559	0.01
Paraguay	49	0.00	255	0.01	541	0.01	763	0.01
Peru	817	0.23	1,946	0.13	2,830	0.09	3,696	0.08
Trinidad and Tobago	450	0.12	2,247	0.15	1,443	0.04	1,910	0.04
United States	33,684	10.00	140,423	10.00	288,449	10.00	461,715	10.00
Uruguay	181	0.04	656	0.03	1,317	0.04	1,695	0.03
Venezuela	2,833	0.83	10,224	0.72	30,264	1.04	16,677	0.36

Source: Compiled by authors from International Monetary Fund (1995a).

Table 3.5 GDP (1985 U.S.$ billions)

Country	1966–1969 Average	1966–1969 Decile	1976–1979 Average	1976–1979 Decile	1986–1989 Average	1986–1989 Decile	1991–1994 Average	1991–1994 Decile
Argentina	53	0.20	69	0.20	69	0.16	109	0.23
Bolivia	4	0.01	7	0.02	7	0.01	8	0.01
Brazil	80	0.31	179	0.53	248	0.57	256	0.54
Canada	177	0.69	316	0.94	385	0.88	408	0.86
Chile	12	0.04	13	0.04	19	0.04	26	0.05
Colombia	16	0.06	27	0.08	39	0.09	47	0.10
Costa Rica	2	0.01	4	0.01	4	0.01	6	0.01
Dominican Republic	2	0.01	4	0.01	5	0.01	5	0.01
Ecuador	5	0.02	13	0.04	17	0.04	19	0.04
El Salvador	4	0.01	7	0.02	6	0.01	7	0.01
Guatemala	6	0.02	11	0.03	12	0.03	14	0.03
Guyana	0	0.00	1	0.00	0	0.00	0	0.00
Haiti	1	0.00	2	0.00	2	0.00	2	0.00
Honduras	2	0.01	3	0.01	4	0.01	5	0.01
Jamaica	2	0.01	2	0.00	2	0.00	2	0.00
Mexico	73	0.28	135	0.40	175	0.40	209	0.44
Nicaragua	4	0.01	5	0.01	4	0.01	4	0.01
Panama	2	0.01	3	0.01	5	0.01	6	0.01
Paraguay	2	0.00	3	0.01	5	0.01	6	0.01
Peru	11	0.04	16	0.05	19	0.04	16	0.03
Trinidad and Tobago	5	0.02	7	0.02	7	0.01	7	0.01
United States	2,571	10.00	3,354	10.00	4,356	10.00	4,743	10.00
Uruguay	4	0.01	5	0.01	6	0.01	6	0.01
Venezuela	37	0.14	62	0.18	66	0.15	80	0.17

Source: Compiled by authors from International Monetary Fund (1990, 1995c).

Table 3.6 GDP per Capita (1985 U.S.$ thousands)

Country	1966–1969 Average	Decile	1976–1979 Average	Decile	1986–1989 Average	Decile	1991–1994 Average	Decile
Argentina	2,312	1.59	2,540	1.46	2,205	1.07	3,241	1.64
Bolivia	915	0.48	1,368	0.67	951	0.35	972	0.40
Brazil	924	0.49	1,602	0.83	1,736	0.80	1,607	0.74
Canada	8,601	6.60	12,161	7.98	14,960	8.35	14,206	7.66
Chile	1,341	0.82	1,257	0.59	1,482	0.66	1,875	0.89
Colombia	819	0.40	1,111	0.50	1,300	0.55	1,394	0.63
Costa Rica	1,174	0.69	1,683	0.88	1,564	0.70	1,860	0.88
Dominican Republic	469	0.12	728	0.24	729	0.23	707	0.25
Ecuador	993	0.54	1,661	0.87	1,648	0.75	1,763	0.83
El Salvador	1,316	0.80	1,556	0.80	1,168	0.48	1,268	0.56
Guatemala	1,244	0.74	1,636	0.85	1,383	0.60	1,439	0.65
Guyana	715	0.32	749	0.25	573	0.14	587	0.18
Haiti	313	0.00	380	0.00	332	0.00	250	0.00
Honduras	814	0.40	869	0.33	817	0.28	843	0.33
Jamaica	1,025	0.57	1,034	0.44	926	0.34	1,040	0.43
Mexico	1,576	1.01	2,089	1.16	2,130	1.03	2,335	1.14
Nicaragua	2,052	1.38	2,166	1.21	1,110	0.44	848	0.33
Panama	1,564	1.00	1,908	1.04	2,068	0.99	2,222	1.08
Paraguay	752	0.35	1,071	0.47	1,234	0.51	1,300	0.58
Peru	869	0.44	999	0.42	884	0.32	724	0.26
Trinidad and Tobago	4,497	3.33	6,558	4.19	5,372	2.88	5,327	2.79
United States	12,872	10.00	15,138	10.00	17,848	10.00	18,470	10.00
Uruguay	1,510	0.95	1,853	1.00	1,926	0.91	2,009	0.97
Venezuela	3,855	2.82	4,495	2.79	3,592	1.86	3,916	2.01

Source: Compiled by authors from International Monetary Fund (1990, 1995c).

Table 3.7 Population (in millions)

Country	1966–1969 Average	1966–1969 Decile	1976–1979 Average	1976–1979 Decile	1986–1989 Average	1986–1989 Decile	1991–1994 Average	1991–1994 Decile
Argentina	23	1.12	27	1.19	31	1.26	34	1.28
Bolivia	4	0.19	5	0.20	7	0.25	8	0.27
Brazil	86	4.31	112	5.02	143	5.85	156	6.08
Canada	21	1.00	23	1.02	26	1.03	29	1.09
Chile	9	0.42	11	0.45	13	0.49	14	0.50
Colombia	19	0.93	25	1.08	30	1.22	34	1.28
Costa Rica	2	0.05	2	0.06	3	0.08	3	0.08
Dominican Republic	4	0.16	5	0.19	7	0.25	7	0.26
Ecuador	5	0.24	8	0.31	10	0.38	11	0.39
El Salvador	3	0.13	4	0.16	5	0.18	5	0.18
Guatemala	5	0.21	6	0.26	9	0.32	10	0.35
Guyana	1	0.00	1	0.00	1	0.00		0.00
Haiti	4	0.17	5	0.18	6	0.22	7	0.24
Honduras	2	0.08	3	0.12	5	0.16	6	0.18
Jamaica	2	0.06	2	0.06	2	0.06	2	0.06
Mexico	47	2.30	65	2.90	82	3.34	90	3.50
Nicaragua	2	0.05	2	0.07	4	0.11	4	0.13
Panama	1	0.03	2	0.04	2	0.06	3	0.07
Paraguay	2	0.07	3	0.09	4	0.13	5	0.14
Peru	13	0.59	16	0.70	21	0.83	23	0.85
Trinidad and Tobago	1	0.02	1	0.01	1	0.02	1	0.02
United States	200	10.00	221	10.00	244	10.00	257	10.00
Uruguay	3	0.10	3	0.09	3	0.09	3	0.09
Venezuela	9	0.44	14	0.59	19	0.73	20	0.77

Source: Compiled by authors from International Monetary Fund (1995b).

Table 3.8 Diplomatic Missions

Country	1966–1969 Average	1966–1969 Decile	1976–1979 Average	1976–1979 Decile	1986–1989 Average	1986–1989 Decile	1991–1994 Average	1991–1994 Decile
Argentina	62	5.07	76	5.48	70	4.08	72	3.99
Bolivia	29	2.05	32	1.65	33	1.28	33	1.33
Brazil	63	5.21	78	5.61	82	4.94	80	4.55
Canada	64	5.30	87	6.39	98	6.15	104	6.17
Chile	40	3.11	47	2.96	47	2.30	47	2.32
Colombia	42	3.24	50	3.17	50	2.57	50	2.49
Costa Rica	24	1.60	35	1.91	36	1.47	36	1.57
Dominican Republic	24	1.64	26	1.09	28	0.87	27	0.94
Ecuador	34	2.51	41	2.43	42	1.92	43	2.01
El Salvador	27	1.92	27	1.22	26	0.75	26	0.89
Guatemala	32	2.37	32	1.65	33	1.28	36	1.55
Guyana	6	0.00	15	0.13	16	0.00	13	0.00
Haiti	n.a.	—	22	0.78	21	0.38	21	0.53
Honduras	24	1.60	23	0.87	25	0.68	25	0.82
Jamaica	10	0.37	25	1.04	27	0.83	29	1.09
Mexico	52	4.16	62	4.22	68	3.92	69	3.82
Nicaragua	25	1.74	26	1.13	40	1.77	37	1.62
Panama	26	1.78	36	2.00	36	1.47	34	1.45
Paraguay	n.a.	—	24	0.96	27	0.83	27	0.95
Peru	41	3.15	52	3.35	54	2.87	50	2.50
Trinidad and Tobago	9	0.27	13	0.00	18	0.11	19	0.37
United States	116	10.00	128	10.00	149	10.00	160	10.00
Uruguay	44	3.47	45	2.74	45	2.15	44	2.11
Venezuela	40	3.06	62	4.22	69	4.00	69	3.82

Source: Compiled by authors from *The Europa World Yearbook (1966–1995).*

Notes

1. Space restrictions preclude an extensive discussion of the methodological prerequisites underlying the construction of the indexes and the resulting analysis. For a more elaborate explanation, please see the original article (Mace, Bélanger, and Thérien 1993).
2. Not even Brazil. See remarks in this sense by Maria Regina Soares de Lima in Chapter 7.
3. From the 1980s to the 1990s, Brazil's overall decline relative to the United States was caused by a weakening of its position in terms of exports, GDP per capita, military spending, and the presence of diplomatic missions. With the exception of military spending, these same indicators explain Venezuela's relative decline in the 1990s as compared with the 1970s, whereas Canada's decline from the 1980s to the 1990s is mainly attributable to a relative loss in terms of GDP per capita, GDP, and exports.
4. This is why Chile was asked to coordinate its position with Mercosur members in the talks on Pan-American free trade held at the Mercosur presidential meeting in mid-December 1997 (*Economist* 1997: 33), a request to which it agreed.
5. "By economic ties, we mean primarily close relations of trade permitting large-scale division of labor and almost always giving rise to vested interests" (Deutsch et al. 1957: 29).
6. Some countries have been excluded because of insufficient data. We have attempted to control this factor in our analysis by comparing the totals in our tables with the data on total regional trade available from IMF yearbooks.
7. In general and statistical terms,

we attempt to group points representative of features in mutual proximity in order to delimit some areas of the factorial space where individuals will be of similar profile. Data will then be composed of the totality of points representing individual descriptive characters (in the statistical sense) defined by their factorial coordinates and their weight (or frequency of appearance). . . . It is important to note that the number of classes to be defined is not fixed a priori, nor is it a matter of chance. It is the structure of the data that helps to determine it. (Bordet and Kokosowski 1982: 198) (our translation)

For a more detailed account of the calculus required for this type of analysis that is accessible to the layman, see F. Benzécri (1986). For a comprehensive account in English, see J.-P. Benzécri (1992).
8. Such a configuration on the first axis, a result provoked by the unit with the greatest weight, is inevitable in the case of tables with a null diagonal (Gmardellis 1986: 287).
9. The expression "cultural divide" is borrowed from Lawrence Harrison (Harrison 1997: 5).
10. Data for this section are drawn for the most part from Freedom House (1991); Human Rights Watch (1994); Observatoire de l'information (1989); Reporters sans frontières (1994).

4

NAFTA and Mercosur: Two Competing Models?

Ivan Bernier & Martin Roy

During his visit to South America in October 1997, President Bill Clinton categorically stated that the Southern Cone Common Market (Mercosur) could very well survive in a future Free Trade Area of the Americas (FTAA) ("Washington apoya" 1997). Clinton was more than likely feeling the need to reassure Argentina and Brazil about U.S. support for the South American economic bloc—the world's fourth largest—given the avowed skepticism of the U.S. government toward Mercosur. First attacked in 1991 for its credibility and internal cohesion, Mercosur was subsequently depicted as a threat to hemispheric regionalism.[1] In contrast, the North American Free Trade Agreement (NAFTA) was portrayed as the model of reference for such a project (Feinberg 1997: 66; Watson 1994a: 22, 1994b: 155–156). With time, however, Mercosur has successfully established its international credibility,[2] thereby raising the question of whether the two regional groupings can coexist within a future FTAA.

Despite meetings in Denver (1995), Cartagena (1996), Belo Horizonte (1997), and San José (1998) between trade and economic ministers involved in the FTAA negotiations, the issue is still unresolved. So far, participating nations have agreed on a relatively uncompromising formula "for constructing the FTAA which will build on existing subregional and bilateral arrangements in order to broaden and deepen hemispheric economic integration and to bring the agreements together" (Summit of the Americas Trade Ministerial 1995). However, the formula remains ambiguous in several respects. It is vague about the place of NAFTA and Mercosur in the FTAA, as well as about their roles in the different phases of the negotiation process. Even more important, it is rooted in the still highly controversial notion that subregional integration agreements are initiatives

69

converging toward the creation of the FTAA (Nofal 1995: 215). In fact, nothing is less certain. Although the countries involved in the FTAA negotiations are strongly committed to market liberalization and internal economic reforms, the shape of the hemispheric integration regime has yet to be determined. And even though NAFTA and Mercosur are, generally speaking, compatible with the legal framework of the World Trade Organization (WTO), they do not necessarily endorse the same concept of regional economic integration.

It is therefore vital to conduct an in-depth comparative analysis of NAFTA and Mercosur to assess the extent to which they represent compatible or competing models of economic integration. Few studies have looked directly at the two regional groupings from a comparative perspective. Instead, debate has centered on the conditions likely to favor a rapprochement between the two agreements. In particular, attention has been focused on the workings and stability of the agreements (Di Marco 1995: 19); the asymmetries between trading partners (Petrash 1997; Di Marco 1995: 20); anticipated effects on trade, both static and dynamic (Bouzas 1992: 188–192; Buxedas 1994: 24–26); and the structure of trade and U.S. involvement in the external trade of the countries concerned (Bouzas 1992: 173–188; Di Marco 1995: 18; Foweraker 1996: 159). The few comparative studies that do exist are partial and fragmented. At best, they highlight the differences related to integration objectives (i.e., free trade area versus common market), tariff and nontariff barriers, trade liberalization timetables, and the openness of the agreements to the multilateral system (Buxedas 1994: 23–24; Nofal 1995: 215–216).

But beyond these general observations, one can ask what truly characterizes NAFTA and Mercosur. In reality, if we are to speak of distinct models of regional economic integration, the arrangements must be clearly distinguishable in terms of their formal and material characteristics, their dynamics of integration, and the requirements they impose on member states. Such arrangements will attract other participants or be reproduced by other countries. The Treaty of Rome, for example, became a reference for common markets. In our view, the same can be said of NAFTA for free trade areas. Somewhere in between the two lies another model in the making: Mercosur. As Canada's former minister of international trade Art Eggleton pointed out at the second meeting of Western Hemisphere trade ministers in Cartagena in March 1996:

> Mercosur is a bold undertaking to create a common market in the southern part of our Hemisphere and continues to deepen its obligations towards achieving that objective. NAFTA is a very advanced model of a free trade agreement. These two agreements have fundamentally different objectives and could not be merged without one or the other dispensing with its core objectives. (Eggleton 1996)

This remark, made in anticipation of the creation of the FTAA by 2005, needs to be examined more closely. Although the two arrangements are often said to represent different models for regional economic integration, their fundamental differences remain to be demonstrated.

NAFTA and Mercosur as
Distinct Models for Regional Economic Integration

Various criteria can be used to compare regional economic integration agreements. If the goal is simply to distinguish between them in terms of their fields of application, a horizontal approach stressing the sectors and types of intervention covered (goods, services, investments, government procurement, intellectual property) is used. If the goal is to distinguish them in terms of their envisaged levels of integration, institutional characteristics are examined, with a particular accent placed on the relative autonomy of common institutions vis-à-vis the member states—arrangements classified as simple free trade zones, customs unions, common markets, or economic unions (Soldatos 1989; Organisation de coopération et de développement economiques 1993). Finally, to situate regional economic integration agreements in relation to the multilateral framework of trade liberalization, the emphasis is placed on aspects such as their compatibility with the multilateral system, their protectionist features, and their openness to new members (De la Torre and Kelly 1992: 41–49).

Although these criteria are well established in the literature, they tend to neglect other fundamental characteristics of regional economic integration agreements that could eventually influence the choice of an integration model for the Americas. Thus it might be more relevant to examine how member states formulate commitments than to simply determine areas of application, more useful to assess the particular dynamics of each of these regional economic integration models than to ascertain their levels of institutional development, and more revealing to measure the extent to which these agreements constrain economic management by member states than to judge their compatibility with the multilateral system or their degree of openness. In our view, these elements reveal more about the substance and particular rationality of such agreements.

The Scope and Language of the Agreements

The scope and language of economic integration agreements give at the outset a good indication of how they will evolve in the future. The more comprehensive and detailed they are in their scope and normative approach, the less they leave for further negotiations. Conversely, if their reach is defined in broad and general terms, and if the obligations of the parties are simply sketched out, further discussions and negotiations will be needed to make the agreements truly operational.

NAFTA: A comprehensive and detailed agreement with precise undertakings. Anyone reading the text of NAFTA for the first time is immediately struck by its length and extreme detail. At some 700 pages, it is longer than the original General Agreement on Tariffs and Trade (GATT) document of 1947 (Winham and Grant 1995: 26) or the 1958 Treaty of Rome establishing the European Common Market. We know of no other free trade agreement of NAFTA's magnitude.[3] In fact, very little was excluded from the negotiation of this agreement, which contains some 295 articles and 90 annexes (often themselves supplemented with appendices), as well as explanatory notes. It is indeed exhaustive: In addition to the chapters on trade of goods, which cover access to markets, rules of origin, customs procedures, energy and petrochemical products, agricultural products, and emergency measures, there are sixteen chapters covering such matters as technical barriers to trade, government procurement, investment, cross-border trade in services, telecommunications, financial services, temporary entry for businesspeople, intellectual property rights, dispute settlement in cases of antidumping or countervailing duties, and dispute settlement.

NAFTA is not limited to the actual text of the agreement. At the request of the United States, two parallel agreements were negotiated and signed at the same time, one concerning employment and the other the environment. Although they constitute separate documents, they are considered indissociable at the policy level.

Not only is NAFTA very broad in scope, which accounts in part for its length, it is also extremely precise and comprehensive. In addition to a chapter titled "General Definitions," each chapter of NAFTA contains one or more articles (where annexes are included) providing definitions specific to the chapter in question. In all, some three hundred definitions are spread throughout the agreement in an effort to dispel any ambiguity as to the meaning of the terms and expressions used. Several of these definitions—including those for "investment" and "cultural industries"—were intended to be truly exhaustive and cover almost an entire page. This same degree of precision is demonstrated in the repeated use of often long and technical annexes and appendices. Of these annexes, special note must be taken of Annex 401, concerning rules of origin. To avoid disputes, it sets out in detail the type of processing a foreign product must undergo to be considered a product of origin. This alone takes up close to 175 pages.

One might justifiably question the need for such efforts at precision and thoroughness. The most plausible explanation is that in the absence of common institutions like those of the European Union—institutions

NAFTA members obviously did not want—such precision obviates the need to return to the table to clarify members' commitments or to settle disputes caused by misinterpretations. In this light, NAFTA is a comprehensive and technical agreement, and its enforcement leaves little leeway for politics.

Mercosur: A simple and evolving agreement with ambitious goals. In contrast to NAFTA, whose detailed legal framework leaves little room for political debate, Mercosur more closely resembles a loose structure that is evolving to meet the needs of its members and that remains in part to be determined (Arocena 1997: 155). Mercosur was built on fragile footing: With its twenty-four articles covering only twelve pages and its five brief annexes, the Treaty of Asunción set out what are at best a simple series of flexible principles establishing relations between member states, an institutional body with limited powers, and minimal rules concerning the liberalization of trade and the establishment of a customs union. This apparent laxity in the legal structure of Mercosur was identified early on as a major obstacle to creating a common market (Gamio 1995: 75; Halperin 1992). Marcelo Halperin observes that the goals of the Treaty of Asunción contrast "with the lack of precepts for the identification of legal sources, the prescriptive value given decisions and rules, and the avenues for future institutional development" (Halperin 1992: 33).

Mercosur has now attained a certain maturity thanks to a series of developments over the past six years. The Brasília (1991), Colonia (1993), and Ouro Prêto (1994) protocols served to define key elements of the agreement left unresolved in 1991, including the final operating mode for its institutional bodies, common tariff nomenclature, the dispute settlement mechanism, and reciprocal investment protection codes. Further decisions by the Common Market Council (CMC), resolutions by the Common Market Group (CMG), and Trade Commission (TC) directives periodically add to the legal foundations of the association while clarifying certain points of law necessary for day-to-day operations. From 1991 to 1997, there were no fewer than 97 decisions (CMC) and 501 resolutions (CMG), not to mention 43 directives on the development and implementation of a common external tariff issued by the Trade Commission since 1995 (Laird 1997: 5, note 8). As a result, the scope of the agreement has broadened over time to include customs procedures, rules of origin, and rules for dispute settlement, as well as emergency measures, investments, energy, and agriculture.

Despite the progress of recent years, Mercosur has yet to address key issues such as intellectual property rights, trade in services, fair competition and consumer protection standards, adjustment of the customs practices of national institutions, the effective coordination of exchange policies, government procurement, and the free movement of workers. NAFTA covers many of these sectors in detail, whereas Mercosur has barely touched on them.

The same can be said regarding the precision of the standards and rules governing relations between members. The difference between NAFTA and Mercosur is significant: The language of the latter is more ambiguous and there are fewer definitions.

Mercosur also differs substantially from NAFTA both in its legal corpus and in the clear definition of terms. As a result, one would expect Mercosur institutions, which appear to be more developed than those of their North American counterpart, to step in to fill the apparent legal vacuum in a number of sectors still under negotiation. The complexity of the Mercosur organization chart belies the fact that neither the CMC, the CMG, the TC, nor any of the other bodies[4] constitute supranational entities. In this regard, the relative success Mercosur has had in each of its development phases is no guarantor of its future. Even though its members were able to make do with the rule of consensus in the negative phases of integration—the removal of tariff and nontariff barriers—this does not mean that the positive stages, which involve a greater degree of policy harmonization and coordination, will be as successful (Gamio 1995; Laird 1997: 5). The adoption of a common external tariff (CET) was a difficult hurdle. With a number of disputes still unsettled, notably between Brazil and Argentina, the creation of a true common market will probably prove more difficult.[5]

The Dynamics of Integration

To the extent that agreements such as NAFTA and Mercosur involve fundamental changes in the economic relations of their member states, it is essential to understand what causes such changes. As we shall see, NAFTA differs fundamentally from Mercosur in this respect.

NAFTA: A legal dynamic. For an agreement as complex as NAFTA, its implementation has been remarkably smooth to date, as if everything had happened automatically without political intervention. For example, January 1, 1996, ushered in a new phase of the agreement with the liberalization of goods traded among NAFTA partners and the reduction of customs duties still applicable on products of origin (a 20 percent, 10 percent, or 6.6 percent reduction, depending on the country and the product). On the same day, provisions of Article 303 concerning the elimination of existing drawback and duty deferral programs went into effect between Canada and the United States. These provisions provide for the elimination of existing programs and their replacement by new measures allowing manufacturers to collect reimbursements, a refund equal to the lesser of the duties paid on imported inputs or the duties assessed on exports of finished products. January 1, 1996, was also the deadline for the inclusion in Annex I of existing nonconforming measures maintained by a province or state concerning investments (Chapter 11) and services (Chapter 12). As these few examples show, NAFTA appears to be proceeding systematically and inexorably along its set course.

The only possible exception to the process is provided in Article 801, which allows members, during the transition period only, to counteract serious damage the agreement's lowered trade barriers cause to their producers by suspending duty reductions for a specified period or by reinstating most-favored-nation rates.[6] These measures cannot extend beyond three years, nor can they remain in effect after the transition period, except by the consent of the member whose product is affected by them. Surprisingly, especially in the wake of the Mexican peso crisis, the bilateral emergency measures authorized in Article 801 have hardly been used to date. Whether the reason is that the conditions are too onerous or that recourse to such measures would discourage investors, they appear unlikely to affect the automatic nature of the NAFTA implementation process. After the transition period, no measures aside from tariff commitments may be taken to counter sudden increases resulting from the application of the agreement except by the mutual consent of interested parties.

To the extent that political decisions are requested for the implementation of the agreement, the Free Trade Commission could have been expected to play an increasing role in the development of NAFTA. Under Article 2001 of the agreement, the commission supervises NAFTA implementation, oversees its further development, resolves disputes that may arise regarding its interpretation or application, supervises the work of all committees and working groups, and considers any other matter that may affect the operation of the agreement. However, outside of Chapter 20, there is barely any reference to the commission. Furthermore, the commission is requested to meet "at least once a year in regular session" (Article 2001.4), which gives a good idea of the role it is expected to play. Not surprisingly, the commission, outside of its judicial role, has not shown any great desire to become actively involved in the further development of NAFTA.

An important aspect to consider in the dynamics of economic integration is the procedure for dispute settlement. Setting aside the mechanisms contained in Chapters 11 (arbitration in areas of investment) and 13 (special provisions concerning financial services), NAFTA dispute settlement is essentially covered in Chapters 19 and 20. Chapter 19, reproducing Chapter 19 of the Free Trade Agreement (FTA), provides for the replacement of judicial review by national courts of final determinations in countervailing duty or antidumping duty investigations with binding binational panel reviews. Before the introduction of the FTA and, later, NAFTA, appeals were heard before national courts, with final rulings by one or another of the governments. Under NAFTA, Article 1904 defines the mechanism by which special bilateral panels take the place of the judicial review process within these jurisdictions, thereby ensuring objective and impartial rulings by the administrative bodies concerned.

Chapter 20, reproducing with a few modifications Chapter 18 of the FTA, contains provisions that aim to avoid or settle disputes over interpretation or enforcement of the agreement. Under Article 2008, should a dispute involving NAFTA remain unresolved after talks over a prescribed period, one of the members may request that it be referred to a special panel whose rulings are nonbinding. This procedure is very similar to dispute settlement within the WTO.

From January 1, 1989, to July 1, 1997, eighty-eight cases were settled through the FTA and NAFTA dispute settlement system. The great majority, eighty-one in all, concerned antidumping and countervailing duties. Of these, nine were still under review on July 1, 1997. Of the seventy-two resolved cases on antidumping and countervailing duties, the majority came under FTA jurisdiction; twenty-two were governed by NAFTA provisions. The United States also requested that three extraordinary challenge committees be formed under FTA Article 1904.13 to revise panel decisions. For cases involving the interpretation and enforcement of FTA and NAFTA, five special arbitration panels were formed under the provisions of Chapter 18 of FTA, and two more were formed under Chapter 20 of NAFTA, for a total of seven.

Although they are slightly less frequently used than the corresponding provisions of the FTA, there is no doubt that the provisions of Chapter 19 of NAFTA still play an important role in the overall economy of the agreement. Their relative success may be explained by the fact that they are limited in their objective to making sure that national antidumping and countervailing duties legislations have been correctly applied and by the fact that they have offered in practice a much faster relief than the appeal process of the members. Chapter 19 of NAFTA, in that respect, is typical of the technical and legalist approach of the agreement. By contrast, the limited number of decisions in cases involving the interpretation and application of NAFTA (Chapter 20) may reflect the fact that these cases are somewhat more political in nature and follow a judicial process that is closer to the dispute settlement mechanism of the World Trade Organization.

Mercosur: A political dynamic. Mercosur implementation cannot be evaluated strictly on the basis of the formal time frame contained in the Treaty of Asunción and related agreements. An important aspect of the agreement lies in the ongoing process of adjustment, in which a number of parameters develop gradually through direct negotiations. Another factor that must be taken into account is the gap between the stated objectives and the situation prevailing in member countries, which must maintain a balance between commitments to their partners and the need to bring about economic changes without causing undue social unrest. For the four countries involved—Argentina, Brazil, Uruguay, and Paraguay—this dilemma represents an integral part of progress toward assuming their place on the global scene and colors the process on several levels: It paves the way for a flexible system, a less stringent application of restrictions, and relatively frequent recourse to safeguard measures and exceptions.

One of the main ways that Mercosur differs from NAFTA is in its sequence of integration. It defines automatic criteria for applying certain provisions of the agreement but leaves other issues to future talks. The introduction of a trade liberalization program and the common external tariff typifies the situation that prevails within Mercosur. Defined as cornerstones of the Treaty of Asunción, these two mechanisms have not proceeded according to the same timetable. The first was drawn up back in 1991 as an automatic, linear program meant to completely eliminate tariff and nontariff barriers within four years (Treaty of Asunción, Annex I), whereas the second was the subject of talks right up to the close of the transition period. In addition, although the decisions, resolutions, and directives adopted by Mercosur institutions were ratified by member parliaments, they were not immediately applicable by member states. Whereas NAFTA members ratified their agreement as a whole and even adopted implementation measures prior to its effective date, Mercosur members must integrate various measures progressively approved at the regional level according to a graduated process. Such delays occasionally complicate organization operations and relations between partners.[7]

Furthermore, exceptions appear to be more prevalent in Mercosur than in NAFTA. Even though most exceptions apply only temporarily and have a limited impact on intraregional trade,[8] for certain countries they affect a number of product categories,[9] including key economic sectors such as the textile industry, the steel industry, agriculture, and the lumber industry. By virtue of the *régimen de adecuación,* areas deemed sensitive for national economies are temporarily excluded from the free trade area to allow sectoral industries to adapt to the new conditions of the subregional market. Deadlines for the total elimination of tariff barriers vary from five years (Argentina, Brazil) to six years (Uruguay, Paraguay). However, the convergence schema includes neither sugar nor automobiles, two sectors on which member states have not come to an agreement. There are also exceptions to the common tariff nomenclature: Along with those products for which tariffs will be gradually adjusted,[10] members have the right to exclude up to 300 products from the CET.[11]

On a more general level, these exceptions reveal a commercial approach that allows authorities considerable leeway in the application of selective protectionist measures. Roberto Bouzas explains that sectoral pressures and the discretionary power of governments result in "the use of *ad hoc* means of protection such as anti-dumping duties, nontariff barriers, recourse to safeguard clauses,[12] and/or recourse to orderly marketing arrangements (OMAs) by the private sector" (Bouzas 1996: 69). Such practices were widespread between 1991 and 1994 in the paper, steel, and textile industries. Several such measures—some unilateral—caused major conflicts between member nations, at times jeopardizing the process of integration. This was the case in 1992, when Argentina decided to apply a statistical tax on imports at the same time that Brazil was buying agricultural by-products in extraregional markets (Fernández 1997: 7). Certain initiatives contravened Mercosur legal provisions, as was the case for Measure 1569 passed by the Brazilian government in March 1997, which limited the financing of imports.[13] Though its legitimacy cannot be argued, the measure has no grounding in the exceptions provided for within the common market (Instituto de Relaciones Europeo-Latinoamericanas 1997: 7).

Ultimately, however, it is the manner in which conflict has been reduced more than arbitrary recourse to protectionist measures that characterizes Mercosur. Formally, at least, members have access to a dispute settlement mechanism similar to the type found in free trade zones. The procedure defined by the Brasília and Ouro Prêto protocols is based on an arbitration approach inspired by WTO provisions (Haines-Ferrari 1998). Parties are first invited to negotiate directly. If they fail to negotiate a solution, their case is submitted to a consultative body[14] charged with making recommendations. In the absence of consensus, an ad hoc tribunal of international experts decides the issue. If the party or parties refuse to accept the decision rendered, the tribunal may initiate compulsory enforcement procedures under which the aggrieved party is authorized to respond with appropriate measures of reprisal.

Given the objectives of the member states, these measures appear modest, falling well short of comparable mechanisms within the European Union, which are backed by a veritable court of international justice. In some ways, these measures are even more limited than NAFTA mechanisms, which provide for distinct procedures and sanctions depending on whether disputes involve antidumping and countervailing duties or more general issues. But the fundamental distinction lies in the practices of the different states. Until now, conflicts within Mercosur have been resolved primarily through direct talks involving leaders from each country rather than through the use of a dispute settlement mechanism (Haines-Ferrari 1998: 284). As indicated in a WTO working paper, "by the beginning of 1997 only one dispute had been sent to a specially constituted tribunal or expert panel under the Brasília Protocol, and this was settled bilaterally (i.e. 'out of court') in April 1997" (Laird 1997: 5).

In short, to judge the current Mercosur dynamic, it is essential to take into account the organization's general approach regarding the type of relations deemed appropriate between partners. Respect for standards and established deadlines seems to be sacrificed on occasion for the sake of national interest and short-term constraints, as a result modifying the relationship with the legal order and Mercosur standards. Mercosur, in its various phases of implementation, leaves room for backtracking and negotiation (Fernández 1997: 7). Sanction and enforcement of the law spring more from the socialization process among member states than from existing institutional mechanisms.

The Degree of Constraint on State Intervention in Economic Affairs

Ultimately, the success of economic integration agreements such as NAFTA and Mercosur depends to a large extent on the existence of a shared view among their members of the role of the state in economic affairs. From this point of view, NAFTA and Mercosur represent two different conceptions, one much more constraining than the other.

NAFTA: A constraining free trade zone. A closer look at the contents of the NAFTA agreement reveals a striking level of state disengagement. By "state disengagement" we mean the state's gradual withdrawal from areas of intervention that have a distorting effect on production or trade. A number of authors have remarked upon NAFTA requirements in this regard, particularly in relation to the accession of Mexico. Gustavo del Castillo V. has described the requirements of free trade for Mexico in the following terms:

> It is important to note that liberalization was not just a question of removing tariffs, but also of eliminating the econo-political system that had imposed them. These changes have implied three things: redefinition of the state as a social actor; application of self-imposed and exogenously imposed limits on the intervention of the state in economic affairs; and the crafting of the necessary economic and social conditions for putting the redefinition into practice. (Del Castillo V. 1995: 113, 115)

In a similar vein, Canadian observer Ann Weston has pointed out that by joining NAFTA, Mexico "is agreeing to abide by the same rules as Canada and the U.S., severely limiting the government's freedom to intervene in the economy" (Weston 1995: 145, 150). And more generally, Delal Baer has stated: "By definition, NAFTA embodies a set of trinational rules governing economic behavior. Acceptance of these rules has required fundamental modifications of traditional notions of sovereignty" (Baer 1994: 183, 188). However, these claims are not backed by any articulate demonstration, which makes it difficult to develop a clear idea of NAFTA's significance as a model for economic integration from this perspective.

To provide a better idea of NAFTA requirements in this area, we will successively outline the disciplines governing state intervention with regard to goods, services, public markets, and investment.

Goods. The state's ability to intervene in the circulation of goods is directly affected by several NAFTA requirements. Apart from the gradual elimination of customs duties on products of origin, the basic requirements, which have been taken directly from the 1947 GATT agreement, concern the equal treatment of foreign and domestic products (national treatment, Article 301) and the ban on quantitative restrictions (Article 309). The only exceptions to these requirements are those explicitly listed in Annex 301.3, which are very limited in scope.[15]

But NAFTA requirements regarding the circulation of goods are not just limited to these commitments. Although NAFTA, as a free trade agreement, leaves member states free to set customs duties for third countries as they see fit, members cannot act in such a way as to cause intrazone distortions in trade and investment. Under the terms of Article 303, both the drawback and duty deferral programs governing foreign trade zones, temporary importations under bond, and "maquiladoras" must be altered so that they no longer apply to products of origin by the end of the transition period. There are very few exceptions to these measures. As mentioned previously, the implementation date for changes in Canada and the United States was January 1, 1996. Mexico must follow suit by January 1, 2001.

A number of other NAFTA provisions clearly reveal the orientation of the agreement with respect to state interventions likely to cause trade distortions. These include the ban on export taxes if products intended for domestic consumption are not equally taxed (Article 314), the ban on agricultural export subsidies between Canada and the United States (Article 702[1]), and the special provisions on these subsidies that apply between Mexico and the other parties (Article 705).

Services. Three chapters in NAFTA deal specifically with services: Chapter 12 covers measures relative to cross-border trade in all but financial, air, social, and maritime services; Chapter 13 specifies member commitments with regard to telecommunications; and Chapter 14 deals exclusively with financial services. As a whole, the legal framework for services in NAFTA appears to be more precise, more transparent, and more restrictive than that of either the FTA or GATT.

Chapter 12 applies to all measures related to (1) the production, distribution, marketing, sale, or delivery of services; (2) the purchase, payment, or use of services; (3) the access and use of distribution and transportation systems in connection with the provision of a service; (4) the presence of third-party service providers on member state territory; and (5) the provision of a bond or any other form of financial security as a condition for the provision of a service. The main commitments by members cover the granting of national treatment and most-favored-nation status, including the obligation, when appropriate, to accord the better of the two. The parties have renounced the right to require service providers to establish or maintain representative offices or other forms of business or to be residents in order to provide a service (Article 1205). Finally, NAFTA contains a number of provisions regarding professional recognition and the right to practice that are intended to help avoid unnecessary trade barriers (Article 1210).

Chapter 12 of NAFTA is based on the principle that all services are covered except for reservations and exceptions. The majority of reservations in the services field are found in Annex I (existing nonconforming measures), with the Mexican list by far the longest (thirty measures), followed by the Canadian list (thirteen measures) and the U.S. list (seven measures). The reservations in Annex II (areas of reserved activity) are much fewer in number: seven for Canada, ten for Mexico, and five for the United States. Last, Appendix V, which covers quantitative restrictions, lists six measures for Canada, three for Mexico, and five for the United States.

Chapter 13, which covers telecommunications, sets the common rules for computer and telecommunications service providers and users in North America. The main obligations are the following: Conditions of access to public networks and services must be reasonable and nondiscriminatory; no conditions may be imposed on access to and use of public networks other than those required to safeguard the public service responsibilities of network providers or to protect networks' technical integrity; all licensing procedures must be open and nondiscriminatory; and member states must see to it that service providers that are granted a monopoly on telecommunications services not take advantage of the situation to implement anticompetitive business practices. All of these requirements are clearly intended to keep member states away from any intervention that distorts access to their basic communications networks. Not surprisingly, as a number of observers have pointed out, most of the adjustments to meet these requirements have been made by Mexico (Lipsey, Schwanen, and Wonnacott 1994: 80).

The same holds true for Chapter 14, which addresses financial services. One of the primary Canadian and U.S. goals during NAFTA negotiations was to obtain access to the Mexican financial market. Now banks, insurance companies, and brokerage firms can set up wholly owned subsidiaries in Mexico and acquire companies there (Appleton 1994: 110–112). Another major goal was to go beyond the ad-hoc U.S. and Canadian commitments contained in the FTA to establish an all-encompassing, comprehensive regime with market access based on national treatment, most-favored-nation status, the consumer's right to purchase out-of-country financial services, and the right to market access through the establishment of sales offices. NAFTA effectively contains specific operational principles covering these areas.

Even more interesting is Article 1403, which establishes what Jon R. Johnson calls "the prospective principles" (Johnson 1994: 360–361) of the envisaged regime, that is, the basic philosophy of NAFTA on this issue. In this article, NAFTA members recognize that trade is encouraged when investors can choose the legal form of their investments, when financial institutions can establish subsidiaries where they wish, and when no restrictive conditions prevent them from offering a range of financial services through distinct financial institutions. Implementing these prospective principles will involve considerable state disengagement from the financial sector.

Investments.   NAFTA Chapter 11, on investment, borrows extensively from the FTA and, through it, from U.S. bilateral agreements on investment (Johnson 1994: 277–278). However, it goes even further by increasing the range of obligations, tightening the links between them, and providing for a conflict resolution mechanism intended to settle disputes between investors and NAFTA member states. Upon examination, it quickly becomes evident that this chapter lays out a comprehensive set of standards that has no equivalent within the WTO system.

The regime covers intra-NAFTA investments by investors from NAFTA countries. The definition of "investment" includes all forms of property or ownership, including minority ownership, portfolio investments, and fixed assets. Each member country must treat NAFTA investors no less favorably than they treat domestic or third-country investors (national treatment or most-favored-nation status).

Apart from these obligations of nondiscrimination, Chapter 11 also includes commitments that limit even further member countries' leeway with regard to foreign investment. No party can impose performance requirements for investments on its territory—including those from third country investors—whether for set export levels, minimum national content, preference for domestic producers, a balance in technology transfer, or the obligation to supply a given product (Article 1106). Each party must also allow free and unhindered movement of all investment-related transfers (profits, loan repayments, liquidations, etc.); complementary to this commitment, no government can force repatriation of capital (Article 1109). Last, no NAFTA country can expropriate an investment belonging to an investor from another member state unless the public interest is at stake. Any such expropriation must be nondiscriminatory, follow normal legal standards, and include compensation equivalent to fair market value for the investment. Several observers have perceived this last condition as a rejection of the Calvo doctrine Mexico had subscribed to prior to joining NAFTA (Daby 1994: 1147).

In some respects, the most important NAFTA innovation in the investment field was the establishment of the detailed dispute resolution mechanism designed to take effect when host countries violate NAFTA investment rules. In such cases, NAFTA investors can either claim damages with interest through a binding arbitration procedure between the investor and the state or seek redress through the courts in the host country. An important point to emphasize is that member states agree in advance to follow up on investor requests for arbitration to the extent that the procedure provided for is followed (Article 1122).

As in Chapter 12, the chapter on investment allows member states to formulate reservations and exceptions. In fact, a substantial number of the reservations contained in Annexes I and II of NAFTA have to do with investment. As for Annex III, it focuses primarily on Mexican exceptions, that is, the right to exclude all foreign investment in the sectors identified (energy, communications, railways). Overall, however, these reservations are sufficiently limited and visible to leave Chapter 11 with considerable scope.

NAFTA investment provisions have drawn severe criticism from a number of observers who see them as a dangerous attack on the sovereignty and economic management capacity of member states. Such is the position of Thea Lee of the Economic Policy Institute in Washington, D.C., who has described NAFTA investment rules as follows:

> The text is designed to foster corporate mobility, to make it as easy for a U.S. company to operate in Mataramos, Mexico, as in Milwaukee. In the process, the pact invades territory traditionally reserved for domestic policy in order to promote and protect the interests of investors. All three countries would sign away important tools of economic policy. (Lee 1993: 70, 75)

The customary response to comments like these is that if states wish to attract foreign investment, they must avoid any unnecessary restrictions on investor activity. Yet in a way, this very answer confirms the chapter's essential objective: to restrict member state interventions intended to control foreign investment.

Government procurement. Chapter 10 of NAFTA, on government procurement, considerably extends existing obligations contained in the WTO's Agreement on Government Procurement and the FTA. Among other things, it broadens the scope of liberalized procurement practices with a view to including construction services and markets, a major advance in international agreements on government procurement. In addition to requirements for national treatment and most-favored-nation status, NAFTA imposes procedural requirements on covered markets to foster openness and predictability through the establishment of rules governing technical specifications, supplier qualifications, the setting of deadlines, and other aspects of government contracting mechanisms. Furthermore, each member country is required to set up a claims system if it has not already done so to allow suppliers to contest contract procedures and awards. All of these requirements once again clearly illustrate the extent to which NAFTA imposes extensive state disengagement in the economic sphere.

At the end of his book on NAFTA, Barry Appleton writes: "Throughout its provisions, the NAFTA displays a classical liberal non-interventionist view on what constitutes an appropriate role for government" (Appleton 1994: 205). Referring to S. M. Lipset, he goes on to suggest that this view is in keeping with the dominant U.S. political culture, which is fundamentally antistatist, individualistic, and classically liberal, as opposed to Canada's and Mexico's more statist and communitarian tradition. This in turn leads him to conclude: "NAFTA will mark the transformation of the predominantly American view into the North American view" (Appleton 1994: 207). If this is true for North America, chances are that it is also true for the hemisphere.

This conclusion suggests a further question: whether the agreement, despite its apparent openness to new members (Article 2204), is in fact closed. For the majority of observers, the basic content of NAFTA is non-negotiable to the extent that it conveys a relatively homogenous vision of the state's role in managing the economy. NAFTA requirements in that respect are such that it is doubtful whether the states of Mercosur could join NAFTA without being forced to make internal changes even more significant than those they have undertaken thus far. Because the great majority of Latin American states are even further away from being in a position to join NAFTA, the possibility of NAFTA's becoming the model for the FTAA can only be envisaged in a long-term perspective.

Mercosur: A flexible common market. The exact degree of government disengagement in the Southern Cone remains difficult to determine given that commitments have yet to be defined in a number of sectors. This is the case for services, government procurement, and intellectual property, areas that are incompletely dealt with. However, in areas already consolidated within Mercosur, the level of constraint imposed on member states appears to be lower than that of NAFTA.

Goods. The creation of Mercosur has had important consequences for the commercial activities of member states. Not only did member countries by and large respect the 1991–1994 program of trade liberalization, but they also managed to agree on the thorny issue of a common external tariff, which covered more than 85 percent of tariff positions in January 1995.[16] These two aspects of the integration program have substantially limited member countries' maneuvering room in trade policy.

Aside from these changes, which have been widely discussed (Bouzas 1996; Nofal 1995), a more detailed account of the prescriptive provisions governing market access is called for. Once again, the Mercosur regime appears to offer greater latitude to members in formulating their economic and trade policies. In addition to sectors that are excluded from the free trade area[17] and exceptions allowed for key industries in certain countries,[18] many uncertainties remain about the scope of regulations aimed at reducing distortions and restrictive trade practices. National treatment is a good example: In Mercosur it applies to tax regulations but not to national laws and regulations applying to trade in general, as is the case with NAFTA (Treaty of Asunción, Article 7).

The matter of national treatment falls within the larger question of restrictions on imports and exports inside the free trade area. Mercosur countries committed early on to eliminating completely nontariff barriers,[19] a goal that has been only partially met. One difficulty is the success of the trade liberalization program, which produced pressure at the national level to erect nontariff barriers (Bouzas 1996: 71). Another difficulty lies in the identification of trade restrictions that hide under a number of guises and are difficult to control because of the complex questions they raise. The problem is also political and calls into question the will of the respective governments to abolish such restrictive measures. The creation of a Nontariff Barrier Committee (CMG, 123/94), mandated to analyze the various national approaches, is a step in the right direction but may not be enough.

Other important measures that could influence the trade of goods include provisions concerning foreign trade zones, export processing zones, and special customs zones. Mercosur does not specifically prohibit them but allows countries faced with unforeseen increases in imports that harm or threaten local production to use safeguard measures as defined in GATT and the WTO. Of final note, the Manaus and Tierra del Fuego customs zones created because of their geographical location may continue to operate under present conditions until the year 2013.

Investment. Investment is one of the rare areas where NAFTA and Mercosur have a great number of points in common. The definition of investment in the Protocol of Colonia (CMC, 11/93: Article 1) is in almost every respect identical to that found in NAFTA. The parties also agreed to confer national treatment and most-favored-nation status on each other (CMC, 11/93: Article 3). In addition, Mercosur allows unrestricted repatriation of profits, dividends, and the whole of investment realizations. The same applies to bans on expropriation or any similar act, which are covered on the same basis as in NAFTA (CMC, 11/93: Article 9). With specific regard to the dispute settlement mechanism, Mercosur also defines two areas of application for arbitration, one concerning litigation between states (CMC, 11/93: Article 8) and the other between investor and state (CMC, 11/93: Article 9).

A comparison of these formal elements must allow for investment practices and opting-out agreements that limit the scope of the above measures. In Brazil, for example, national treatment and most-favored-nation status are restricted by certain constitutional clauses stipulating, among other things, that certain investments are reserved for enterprises with "national capital" (C. Robinson 1995: 31). To this add sectoral restrictions in mining, hydroelectricity, health care, rural property, telecommunications, banking, insurance, social security, and coasting trade. Argentina also imposes limits, specifically on real estate investment along borders, air transport, shipbuilding, nuclear power plants, uranium mining, insurance, and fisheries (C. Robinson 1995: 31). Even though many of these restrictions will eventually be phased out, they remain, for now, major restraints that hamper the integration of the four countries' economies.

Services and government procurement. In contrast to NAFTA, these two sectors have received only superficial attention in Mercosur and are the subject of exploratory talks on future regulations. In the service sector, the four member countries have yet to negotiate the liberalization of financial and telecommunications services. All they have done is partially open up land-based and maritime transport along with transportation of hazardous goods and multimodal transport (CMC, 14/94, 15/94). Brazilian and Argentine legislation in these areas differ: In Brazil the service sector continues to be subject to tremendous constitutional restraints, whereas in Argentina it has been increasingly deregulated in recent years. The Brazilian system specifically restricts the banking industry through provisions of the 1988 constitution limiting the number of foreign institutions that may operate in the country (Bouzas 1997: 80). In the insurance industry, state-owned monopolies in reinsurance have insulated Brazil from international competition (Bouzas 1997: 80).

In the area of government procurement, the situation remains largely unchanged. A technical committee was set up in December 1994 to make recommendations on government procurement (Organization of American States 1997b: 95, 120). In 1988 the presidents of the Mercosur countries met in Ushuaia, where Argentina defined general guidelines for the establishment of a government procurement regime, but no concrete measures have yet been implemented. Once again, Brazilian legislation in this area differs from that adopted by the other partners, particularly Argentina, which applies a national treatment clause in government when calling for government tenders. Brazil's specificity in the area of procurement is linked to the same constitutional provision mentioned earlier. As the economist Roberto Bouzas has pointed out:

> In Brazil preferences for domestic suppliers prevail. Article 171 of the Constitution authorizes preferential treatment for Brazilian firms of "national" capital. Executive Order No. 2300 regulating state procurement establishes that domestic producers will have preference whenever price, quality and time conditions are comparable to those of foreign suppliers. (Bouzas 1997: 81)

This last point concerning the distinctive features of the Brazilian economic system explains why Mercosur is and must be a flexible agreement. Mercosur is a work in progress and does not claim to offer a concrete vision of the government's role in the economy as does NAFTA. Such relative flexibility allows the coexistence of somewhat different political and economic systems. Without such flexibility, it is unlikely that Brazil and Argentina would have ever agreed upon a joint cooperative project. It is equally unlikely that Mercosur would have attracted countries such as Chile and Bolivia, which have signed bilateral trade agreements with the group.

Conclusion:
NAFTA and Mercosur, Two Competing Models?

Comparative analysis shows that NAFTA and Mercosur are different enough to be considered distinct models for integration. Our comparison centers on two broad concepts that best characterize the regional associations. In our view, NAFTA represents a mostly contractual approach based on legal dynamics, and Mercosur represents a participatory approach based on political dynamics. The contractual approach focuses primarily on rules that place rigid controls on the behavior of members. Goals for cooperation, the rights and obligations of the contracting parties, and contract enforcement mechanisms are strictly defined and leave little leeway for negotiation, bargaining, or altering the stated goals. This type of arrangement essentially works by restricting government powers and is usually effective provided the parties respect their commitments. The participatory approach, though not radically different, focuses on a process of political cooperation working within broad goals and flexible guidelines. In this type of cooperation, restrictions on government are often offset by efforts at compromise in the interest of all the parties. The participatory approach can be used for more than achieving formal goals of cooperation provided it defines a space of socialization for the players involved. Institutions are harnessed and restructured to meet the evolving needs of players that have to adapt to a new international environment.

Beyond the purely formal differences that such a comparison highlights, the existence of two fundamental approaches to integration is revealed. NAFTA and Mercosur are options between which regional players will have to choose. They define restraints on government management and state sovereignty, generate perceptions, bring values into focus, and ultimately help define the regional economic entity. More than a customs union or a future common market, Mercosur provides a political voice for countries with economies in transition, whose governments are still fragile and whose international legitimacy is still to be constructed. NAFTA, in contrast, reflects the concerns and the level of development of its two main architects, the United States and Canada. More rigid in the standards and restrictions it imposes on member states, NAFTA tends to favor a certain legalism in relations between member states, thereby limiting its political expression to the express contents of the contracted agreement.

In this context, the remark by Art Eggleton that the two agreements cannot be combined without sacrificing their fundamental objectives rings true. NAFTA and Mercosur will probably never become one. The question is not so much which agreement will supplant the other, but rather how they will influence the creation of the FTAA and the overall structure of economic cooperation on the continents. In this light, NAFTA and Mercosur are clearly opposing integration approaches.

This is particularly apparent when the logic of the models is transposed to hemispheric free trade negotiation. The positions put forward by the protagonists at the conference of trade and economic ministers in Belo Horizonte in May 1997 seem to point in that direction. From the outset, the U.S. text was "'more precise' and contained 'more deadlines' that could be 'monitored and judged'" than the Mercosur draft ("U.S. Drops" 1997). The content of the different proposals would serve to highlight a number of areas of dispute. For instance, the United States supported simultaneous negotiations on all sectors, whereas Mercosur proposed a three-phase process starting with business facilitation (1998–1999), followed by the harmonization of technical standards (2001–2002), and, finally, the lowering of trade barriers (2003–2005) ("Matrix Comparing" 1997: 8–12). Differences also arose on the more basic questions of the level of commitment and the legal scope of the proposed FTAA. U.S. intentions in this respect were clear: "high levels of disciplines using as a

base the WTO agreements, and even better, incorporating the best appropriate disciplines of existing sub-regional agreements" ("Matrix Comparing" 1997: 8).
     The United States also insisted that all areas of economic activity be
put on the table, including new sectors such as services, intellectual property rights, investments, and government procurement. The Mercosur delegation took a different line: The new sectors could be included "only if
their direct relation to trade is demonstrated and their treatment has ma-
tured sufficiently at the multilateral level" ("Matrix Comparing" 1997: 9).
Although some of these issues were settled at the trade ministerial in San
José in 1998, two competing views still prevail. Clearly, the United States
is pushing for a hemispheric integration model that is based on the highest common denominator and would essentially include the rights and
obligations conferred by NAFTA. In the face of this expansionist logic,
Mercosur has offered a zone of resistance that has, until now, effectively
delayed deadlines, lessened the scope of commitments, fostered local par-
ticularities, and politicized certain issues on which disagreement persists.
     The future FTAA will no doubt bear more resemblance to the contrac-
tual model favored by the United States, but not without a nod to the interests of influential Latin American states such as Brazil and Argentina.
This was made clear during President Clinton's recent visit to South America, when Brazil president Fernando Henrique Cardoso declared that the
FTAA should represent "a space for our individual and legitimate interests" ("Brasil defendió" 1997). It remains to be seen how far the United
States is prepared to go to seek compromise with Latin America. Clinton's
difficulties in obtaining fast-track approval from Congress greatly limit the
United States' ability to impose its vision of regional economic integration
on the continents.

Notes

     1. The attacks on Mercosur originated in the U.S. State Department and were
subsequently taken up by the U.S. trade representative Charlene Barshefsky and
the office of Secretary of State Madeleine Albright. Implicit to the U.S. offensive
was the belief that progress by Mercosur was harmful to the FTAA ("Clinton-
MERCOSUR" 1997). There was even criticism from World Bank representatives.
Guillermo Perry, the organization's chief economist, highlighted Mercosur weak-
nesses in coordinating the macroeconomic policies of member states ("El Banco
Mundial" 1997), and Allan Winters accused Mercosur of protectionism and caus-
ing trade diversion (World Bank 1997). On this subject, see also Yeats (1997).
     2. Various attempts to sign economic cooperation agreements with the bloc by
Latin American countries such as Chile and Bolivia, as well as by the European
Union and even Canada, bear out Mercosur's success in this regard. Speaking in
Asunción, the director-general of the WTO described the bloc as "one of the most

dynamic and imaginative initiatives on the world stage today" (Ruggiero 1997; see also Instituto de Relationes Europeo-Latinoamericanas 1997: 1).

3. If not the Canada-Chile Free Trade Agreement, which is essentially a replica of NAFTA negotiated in the perspective of Chile's eventual adhesion to the North American agreement.

4. Joint Parliamentary Committee, Economic and Social Advisory Forum, and Administrative Secretariat.

5. Since January 1997, for example, no fewer than four disputes have erupted between Argentina and Brazil. Argentina is contesting the Brazilian government's subsidized investments in the Nordeste automobile sector, controls on imported foodstuffs, and restrictions on imports following deterioration in Brazil's balance of trade. Brazil is unhappy with Argentina, where the Senate recently approved restrictions on refined sugar imports from Brazil ("Campbell" 1997).

6. In the case of Canada and the United States, the bilateral emergency measures that apply are the provisions of Article 1101 of the Canada-U.S. Free Trade Agreement (NAFTA Appendix 801.1). Article 1101 of the FTA has largely the same effect, the main differences being at the level of conditions and limits.

7. In a working paper of the WTO, Sam Laird mentioned that "[l]egislative ratification and national implementation sometimes lag behind the commonly agreed measures." Argentina and Brazil would have apparently ratified around 50 percent of the current decisions, resolutions, and directives (Laird 1997: 5, note 8).

8. A recent study by the Inter-American Development Bank reveals that the weight of these exceptions on intraregional imports stood at 13.3 percent for Uruguay, 6.8 percent for Argentina, 3.1 percent for Paraguay and 0.2 percent for Brazil. As cited in Arocena (1997: 157).

9. The number of categories is 1,018 for Uruguay, 427 for Paraguay, 221 for Argentina, and only 29 for Brazil.

10. Tariffs on capital goods and computer and telecommunications products will gradually adjust to the CET. A 14 percent tariff on capital goods will come into effect in 2001 for Argentina and Brazil, and in 2006 for Paraguay and Uruguay (CMC, 7/94: Section 3a). As for computer and telecommunications products, national tariffs will be gradually adjusted to reach 16 percent by 2006 (CMC, 7/94: Section 3b).

11. The Paraguayan list includes 399 products.

12. With regard to safeguard clauses, member countries that met at the Fortaleza summit in December 1996 agreed to the creation of a regional safeguard clause plan, the components of which will be determined sometime in the future. In the meantime, member states can temporarily impose import restrictions on the basis of safeguard clauses in their respective national legislations.

13. Officially, provisional measure 1569 is intended to contain Brazil's increasingly negative balance of trade and, according to the Brazilian Central Bank, put a halt to financial speculation. Brazil is asking its importers to pay in full within 360 days for all foreign products worth over U.S.$10,000. For other Mercosur countries (as well as Chile and Bolivia), the period is 89 days for goods worth over U.S.$40,000 (Instituto de Relaciones Europeo-Latinoamericanas 1997: 7). See also "Se complica" (1997), and "Al final" (1997).

14. In the case of disputes between states, or between individuals and the state, the Common Market Group, with the possible assistance of a group of experts, is required to make recommendations to the concerned parties. If such disputes are related to common external tariffs, a Mercosur Trade Commission committee of experts is called upon to hear the complaint. If the experts fail to reach a consensus, the TC is required to rule on the issue within thirty days.

15. These limited exceptions apply to the export of logs, unprocessed fish exports, exports of alcoholic beverages to countries where alcohol is banned, imported perfume, and coasting trade, as well as certain other imports banned on moral, security, and health grounds.

16. Member states finally agreed on a common external tariff divided into eleven different levels that vary between 0 percent and 20 percent depending on the product category. However, the CET is still incomplete because it covers 85 percent of total tariff headings, that is, some 8,000 products (C. Robinson 1995: 15).

17. Trade in vehicles, automotive parts, and sugar is still excluded from the free trade zone. In the automotive sector, the different parties appear incapable of reaching a compromise. This issue was supposed to be resolved in 1997.

18. Steel products in Argentina (57 percent), textiles (57 percent in Paraguay and 22 percent in Uruguay), agricultural products, etc.

19. Article 5 of the Treaty of Asunción.

Part 2

Actors' Strategies

5

U.S. Foreign Policy and the Regionalist Option in the Americas

Louis Bélanger

It might be tempting to see in the sequence of post–Cold War events that have advanced the idea of regionalism in the Americas the manifestation of a triumphant, unilateral, and virtually unrivaled U.S. leadership on the North American continent. However, such an impression would be wrong. First, it rests on an exaggeration of the extent to which the Eastern bloc was previously able to act as a counterweight in the region and the current dependence of Latin American states on the United States. Second, although the U.S. administration has played the central and indispensable role in the recent process of reactivating and redefining Pan-American cooperation—from President George Bush's Enterprise for the Americas Initiative (EAI) to President Bill Clinton's first Summit of the Americas—when all is said and done, the United States has so far failed to provide strong leadership or a clear vision in its policy on hemispheric regionalism. It is clear, however, that every overture made by Washington, especially in the area of trade liberalization, has greatly raised expectations among the other states in the region, which have seized the opportunity given to them to successfully advance their own regionalist agenda.

It it is important to remember that Mexico, not the United States, took the first steps toward negotiating the North American Free Trade Agreement (NAFTA) in 1990, opening the "hemispheric floodgates" of regional trade liberalization (Pastor 1992: 96). That same year, George Bush presented his EAI, which, in addition to bilateral economic measures that had little impact, contained a vague statement of intent regarding the possible negotiation of a hemisphere-wide agreement on trade liberalization. This proposal, which was obviously made without much evaluation of its impact, generated immediate enthusiasm among the Latin American states, which were not about to pass up such an opportunity. This attitude was illustrated by the reaction of Luis Lacalle, who was then president of Uruguay: "When, after years of our complaining of neglect, the most important man in the world offers his hand, then, I think we should grab it—and the arm and the elbow and the shoulder, too" (Pastor 1992: 97).

On the basis of a vague U.S. proposal, Latin American political elites set out to build a genuine regional agenda. However, while these states were taking unilateral measures to lower their tariff barriers and liberalize their economies, as well as forging subregional alliances in preparation for the approaching negotiations, the U.S. leadership was showing signs of weakness: Bill Clinton did not seem to share his predecessor's enthusiasm for bold foreign policy initiatives; NAFTA's adoption by Congress was difficult and exposed the ferocious resistance to free trade that existed in the political class and U.S. society; and the administration was unable to obtain a renewal of fast-track authority from Congress allowing it to undertake new trade negotiations. When, in another example of policy improvisation, the United States finally proposed that a Summit of the Americas be held in Miami, the other states in the hemisphere were surprised to find that they had to insist that their host put trade at the top of the agenda (Wiarda 1995a). A commitment was made in Miami to have a hemispheric free trade agreement signed by 2005, but the Clinton administration has still not obtained fast-track authority from Congress and had to water down its own commitment at the second Summit of the Americas held in 1998 in Santiago, Chile, putting education on the front burner instead.

While the United States hesitates, other governments are forging ahead: The Southern Cone Common Market (Mercosur) countries have consolidated their own common market; Chile has both moved closer to Mercosur and signed free trade agreements with Canada and Mexico; Mexico and Mercosur have started free trade negotiations with the European Union; and all of these countries are participating actively within the technical groups preparing for the negotiations that were launched officially in Santiago. Indeed, as Sidney Weintraub points out, the United States has now lost by default its de facto leadership position within the process of regionalization, which it possessed during the Bush era (Weintraub 1997: 64). As a result, instead of the preferred U.S. scenario of a progressive and selective enlargement of NAFTA, the ongoing FTAA negotiations are based on the principles of hemispheric inclusiveness and single undertaking. The FTAA principles form a much heavier and more multilateral institutionalized path toward regional economic liberalization than the one initially foreseen by Washington.

Thus, since 1990, U.S. foreign policy on hemispheric regionalism has been both tentative and ambiguous. In fact, the U.S. position could probably best be characterized as maintaining a regionalist option rather than following a clear regionalist policy. It is therefore just as important to understand why the U.S. position represents a mere option as it is to understand what exactly that option is.

This chapter attempts to answer these questions by examining how the regionalist option for the Americas fits within the general framework of U.S. foreign policy. Commentators and scholars have often invoked the combination of two features of the domestic political climate to explain why Washington is reluctant to move from a regionalist option to a regionalist policy in the Americas: namely, the lack of bipartisan consensus in Congress and the influence of organized groups—mainly labor unions and environmentalists—traditionally opposed to free trade and close to the Democrats. Although these are undoubtedly important factors, their importance in the political process determining U.S. regional policy is precisely due to the fact that the administration has been unable to propose a regionalist policy that is sufficiently consistent and integrated into its world foreign policy for it to generate the necessary support (Pastor 1997: 121). Referring to the general inability of the current administration to build up public support in favor of foreign policy initiatives, Fareed Zakaria notes: "The public was, after all, initially against American involvement in World War II, the Marshall Plan, the Gulf War and almost all free trade agreements" (Zakaria 1998: 80). For this reason, the present chapter examines how the international environment, as opposed to internal political processes, affects the definition of U.S. interests and preferences toward the region.

Beyond Hegemony and Harmony: Security and Existing Institutions

International relations theorists have long maintained that although at any particular point in time the international social order reflects the underlying structural distribution of power in the system, there also exist a number of forces of inertia that help prevent this social order from being immediately affected by each disturbance to the distribution of power. The institutional and normative order that organizes international relationships is adjusted only at dramatic points, when some states have enough power to provoke a change and an interest in doing so (Gilpin 1981; Krasner 1983b). The end of the Cold War certainly represented such a dramatic moment, but with the defeat of its main rival for international influence, the dominant power was left in place, its dominance strengthened but facing a completely new strategic situation. This allowed institutions and ideas forged in the Cold War period to survive at the global and regional levels and continue to shape an international order, which nevertheless needed readjustment. Moreover, it allowed them to continue to shape U.S. foreign policy, both globally and regionally.

This state of inertia raises the question of what might provoke a change in the U.S. attitude in the current international context of opportunities brought about by the end of the Cold War. What would cause the United States to change established institutional arrangements or create new ones? After all, this is precisely the focus of the hemispheric regionalist project. In this regard, both neorealism and neoliberal institutionalism can help us better define the area of investigation. To a certain extent, since the early 1990s, relations between the United States and the other states in the hemisphere could be described as both hegemonic and harmonious. However, although hegemony and harmony may contribute to establishing regimes of institutionalized cooperation, by themselves they do not constitute sufficient reasons for initiating such a form of cooperation.

Looking first at hegemony, classic realist theories point to the distribution of power as the ultimate explanatory factor of institutional arrangements. From the point of view of hegemonic stability, for example (Gilpin 1981; Kindleberger 1973), it would be in the interest of the United States, as the regional hegemonic power, to use the existing power relationship to institutionalize the regional economic and political order to its advantage. This is in fact the interpretation frequently put forward by authors who are surprised by the lack of eagerness on the part of the United States to espouse the regionalist cause in the Americas, prompting some to ask whether this lack of leadership is indicative of a relative decline in U.S. hegemonic power in the region (Atkins 1992).

Indeed, since the early 1980s, Latin American countries have acted more independently of the United States at the diplomatic level than they had previously, particularly in the management of regional affairs (e.g., in the area of conflict resolution in Central America), but should this be interpreted as a sign of growing U.S. incapacity? It certainly suggests that Washington's current attitude toward the regionalist project should probably be situated within a long-term historical perspective (Atkins 1992: 6). However, it would be difficult to argue that the United States has declined as a hegemonic power. As Peter Smith (1996a: 223ff) has pointed out, and as Gordon Mace and Louis Bélanger have demonstrated in Chapter 3 of this volume in their analysis of the distribution of power in the hemisphere and the structure of trade relations, the United States continues to enjoy unquestionable economic and military supremacy on the continent. Moreover, there is no source of countervailing power outside the hemisphere that can challenge this supremacy. Expressed in structural terms, regional hegemony in itself does not seem sufficient to give rise to a U.S. regionalist policy: It didn't have this effect in the past, and it doesn't today.

This circumstance, in fact, is perfectly understandable. Institutionalization doesn't necessarily follow hegemony because, for a hegemonic actor, an institutionalist strategy has some serious disadvantages (Keohane 1984; Grieco 1990). First, institutions limit its room to maneuver. If the hegemonic power is not dependent on the collaboration of other members of the international system to achieve its goals, if it can act unilaterally through the sole exercise of its power, it is unlikely to allow itself to be constrained by an institutional framework. Second, in cooperative regimes founded on a hegemonic relationship, the hegemon generally assumes a large part of the costs of cooperation by being ultimately responsible for ensuring that rules are respected in the regime, by being the main source of benefits to its partners—which are, of course, primarily interested in its market and resources—and by ensuring that its partners are protected against intraregional and extraregional instabilities. Thus, hegemons do not automatically seek to project their domination into institutions.

Like hegemony, harmony is often seen as favoring the emergence of regional institutions. A classic liberal conception of international relations would lead us to expect that, given the benefits to the United States of increased trade between it and the other countries in the region and the growing convergence of Latin American political systems with the U.S. system, the United States should seek to institutionalize the present state of affairs. Once again, this discourse is often heard from those who are surprised by Washington's demonstrated lack of regionalist conviction in the hemisphere. Relations between the states of the Americas have never been so harmonious, scholars and politicians say. Almost all of the states share the same commitment to democracy (see Chapter 3 of this volume for data). They are all working toward liberalizing their economies and opening them to foreign capital and products. The United States should leap at this opportunity to consolidate and perpetuate these conditions by setting up common institutions (Feinberg 1997: 40, 46).

What these authors and decisionmakers overlook is that although harmony provides a context that encourages cooperation, it is not in itself a motive for cooperation. In *After Hegemony,* Robert Keohane demonstrates convincingly that cooperation is a response to a problem of adjusting behavior to obtain a common benefit. If this adjustment takes place on its own, the institutionalization of mechanisms of cooperation loses its raison d'être (Keohane 1984: 51–55). Obviously, in the area of trade, as in other fields, complete harmony is rare. Thus, what must be determined in each case is whether the gains to be made from regional cooperation in terms of adjusting behavior are worth the investment. From the U.S. point of view, even if the regionalist option was more advantageous, for example, in terms of trade relations in the region, it would still have to be enough of a gain to compensate for the loss of autonomy implied by such an option.

Hegemony and harmony may lead the United States to consider the regionalist option, but it is unlikely that in and of themselves they will be sufficient to give rise to the change of attitude needed for Washington to make a firm commitment to a regionalist policy that would overthrow the status quo. The literature on institutionalized forms of cooperation reveals that, in similar contexts, the presence of two factors—a strategic issue and already existing institutions—may prove to be decisive. As I discuss later in the chapter, the two are not unconnected.

A great power would be ready to accept such a loss of autonomy implied by regional institutions in order to counter a threat. In Europe, for example, the United States used an institutional strategy and encouraged regionalism after World War II because they were the best ways to include Germany in the West's defense system. However, the United States resisted using such a strategy in Asia, for example, where it would have been counterproductive from a strategic point of view (Grieco 1996). This argument is of interest here because it helps illustrate the point that if regionalism in the Americas is not linked to a strategic issue, it is unlikely to be sufficiently attractive for the United States to consider sacrificing the enormous maneuvering room that it enjoys in the hemisphere. Thus, if we want to understand U.S. policy on regionalism in the Americas, we need to determine the global strategic vision animating the U.S. government and how this vision is connected to its attitude toward the institutionalization of foreign relations.

Another factor that appears to determine the decision to pursue a regionalist strategy is the presence of already existing regional institutions. Because the initial costs associated with the creation of international institutions are high, it is easier to carry on a regionalist policy based on existing institutions. Students of European regionalism, for example, wondered if the end of the Soviet threat in Europe would provoke a collapse of the institutions created in the Cold War era. In fact, they realized that these institutions had acquired a structuring effect on the cooperative behavior of states (Keohane, Nye, and Hoffmann 1993). Conversely, the weak development of institutional ties among the states of East Asia, a situation fostered by the manner in which the region's actors and the United States reacted to the strategic context of the Cold War, continues to be detrimental to the development of an East Asian regionalism: The lack of development "surely reduces sharply the frameworks, and the possibilities for the 'nesting' of new arrangements in more established frameworks, and the possibilities for the development of the habits of trust and cooperation— that is, international 'social capital'—needed to pursue such arrangements" (Grieco 1996: 13). Regional institutions conceived to cope with a particular strategic situation at a given moment therefore continue to influence the attitudes of actors regarding the construction of a region even after the strategic situation has changed dramatically.

Thus, if the current U.S. position on hemispheric regionalism is to be understood, two elements of its general foreign policy attitudes and preferences require particular attention. First, it is important to look at how the region fits into the U.S. evaluation of its global strategic situation in the region and what strategies it is most likely to deploy in response to that evaluation. Second, it seems equally important to situate the regionalist option within the present U.S. attitude toward institution building as a suitable strategy of action.

The Missing Strategic Link

The further away we get from the Cold War period, the more we realize how important the conflict with the USSR was for mobilization and as a source of popular support for the conduct of U.S. foreign policy. Among other things, the Truman Doctrine allowed the United States to get involved in regions of the world where, had it not been for the alleged goal of halting the advance of communism, very few U.S. interests were involved. Thus, what is commonly called the periphery of the international system—regions such as Latin America where there are neither major strategic issues nor a great power—became linked to U.S. interests (Mandelbaum 1996: 19–20). Moreover, in the specific case of Latin America, it seems that historically the perception of an external threat and foreign intrusion, rather than the search for economic advantages, has been the deciding factor in U.S. foreign policy in the region (Atkins 1992). Whether the impact on Pan-American cooperation has been positive (the Alliance for Progress of the 1960s) or negative (the Central American policy of the 1980s), the perception of an external threat has functioned as a catalyst for U.S. interest in a region that in itself has always been the object of a "strategic denial" by Washington (Atkins 1992).

This strategic denial has an important cognitive corollary that affects the manner in which U.S. leaders perceive and describe the region's states and peoples. Martha Cottam accurately describes how U.S. decisionmakers, by reducing their interest in the region to a question of allegiance of countries to an external power, construct an image of Latin American elites and peoples as essentially "dependent" (Cottam 1994: 25–26). Unlike other countries that occupy more central positions in the international system and that the United States is prepared to recognize as having a certain degree of autonomy, the countries that it sees as dependent are considered to be incapable of independence. A show of autonomy is immediately perceived as a real, or at least a potential, switch in allegiance. Above all, relations founded on a relationship of equality are unthinkable with dependant countries:

Latin American countries are the prototypical example of the U.S. dependant image: weak, childlike, inferior, inept, and led by a small and often corrupt elite. This type of country is viewed with contempt, and its society and polities are seen in very simple terms; they are not treated as equals because they are not seen as equals. (Cottam 1994: 25)

The Cold War linkage between U.S. national interests and Latin America no longer exists today. The question is thus whether the U.S. tradition of strategic denial regarding the region will reassert itself or whether a new conceptualization of the relationship between the United States and the periphery will emerge to take its place. Immediately following the end of the Cold War, during the final years that Bush was in power and the early years of Clinton's presidency, the U.S. administration behaved as if foreign policy resources, having been freed from the burden of containment, could be reallocated to a periphery that, if not neglected, had at least been mistreated during the forty years of the Cold War. However, in the absence of a coherent view of the world and a doctrine that could link U.S. national interests to these peripheral zones, it quickly became obvious that Washington could not sustain such a project. For example, after its involvement in Bosnia, Somalia, and Haiti, guided by bold and generous intentions—what Michael Mandelbaum (1996) refers to as "foreign policy as social work"—the United States was obliged to withdraw because it could not generate the necessary support.

Nearly a year after the 1992 presidential election, the Clinton administration finally got down to the work of devising a new foreign policy doctrine that could replace containment and provide an instrumental rationality for its ambitions. What resulted was the "enlargement" doctrine, which was introduced by National Security Adviser Anthony Lake: "The successor to a doctrine of containment must be a strategy of enlargement, the enlargement of the world's free community of market democracies" (Haass 1995: 44). In fact, this approach meant a reduction of the U.S. ambition to play the role of global crusader and the delimitation of an order of priority for action from center to periphery. At the center, the new doctrine called for a strengthening of the community of market democracies, and on the periphery, U.S. foreign policy would seek to "foster and consolidate new democracies and market economies where possible" (Lake cited in Brinkley 1997: 116). The key words here are "where possible." The Clinton administration decided to focus its efforts on countries where it considered the chances of democratization and liberalization were good and no longer to make commitments to countries where aid seemed unproductive and involvement could lead to risky and unsustainable promises. It was hoped that encouraging the success of some countries would create a domino effect for others, drawing them into the family of market democracies through example and competition (Lake cited in Brinkley 1997: 116).

In this strategy, trade is not considered in primarily economic terms, but as both a means of global action and a way of linking foreign involvement to the U.S. national interest. First, entering into free trade with certain countries is seen as the best way to give rise to political, social, and economic structural changes in those countries, making them better partners for the United States. Moreover, this strategy can be pursued with minimum commitment but carries the possibility of an economic benefit. It is expected that trade liberalization will favor the development in certain countries of a middle class, which will become the engine of change toward greater political openness, meaning, in turn, greater stability and prosperity for the United States. Second, by focusing its attention on countries that are already significant, though perhaps modest, trading partners or that have the potential to become so, Washington gives itself the ability to invoke the economic argument to justify to Congress and to the U.S. people a deeper political or financial involvement should circumstances require it.

However, enlargement does not offer peripheral regions a genuine strategic substitute for containment, because it only situates within a conceptual framework the recognition that these regions no longer represent strategic interests for the United States. The enlargement doctrine proposes that in regions where there are no major powers, the United States should limit its action by carefully selecting partners and focusing on trade. This course has already given rise to a significant strategic shift in Africa, where Washington has decided to distance itself from turbulent spots and to focus on countries that, apart from South Africa, have no strategic leverage but nonetheless make respectable prospective trade partners, such as Uganda, Ghana, and Botswana. In the Western Hemisphere, such a strategy helps explain the United States' resistance to carrying through the regionalist project that it initiated before it started to think in terms of enlargement theory.

Since the Enterprise for the Americas Initiative was launched, the United States has clearly reevaluated its strategic interests in the hemisphere. There is no longer a power outside the region whose influence could constitute a threat to U.S. security, and there is no power in Latin America or the Caribbean that the United States would want to neutralize.

Other endogenous dangers exist, but they do not significantly threaten U.S. national interests. One by one, drug production and trafficking, violations of democratic and human rights, and uncontrolled immigration have been invoked by the U.S. administration, but these threats have not generated support for costly involvement in the region. For example, neither the possibility of a massive influx of refugees nor the evocation of the risk that the new hemispheric standards of democracy would be undermined was enough for the Clinton administration to win the support of

Congress and the U.S. people for its decision to use force to restore democracy to Haiti in 1994 (Mandelbaum 1996: 20–22).

The emergence of the enlargement theory within the U.S. administration signaled its renouncement of extensive involvement in regions where there is no traditional strategic issue. Accordingly, it follows that the administration now has a more limited and selective conception of where its interests lie in the hemisphere. The United States wants to be able to develop certain special partnerships (for instance, with Argentina, which has proved to be an important ally since its conversion to democracy and the market economy) while limiting its commitments to less stable countries that do not affect its interests.

Another important change is the role accorded to trade policy in U.S. foreign policy. Bush's initiative included non-trade issues and was not as closely integrated into U.S. global strategy as it is now. However, now that trade policy is a central policy lever, it is no longer certain that the current regionalist project, which foresees the negotiation in one fell swoop of a free trade zone embracing all of the states in the region, will satisfy Washington. In light of U.S. behavior in other peripheral zones, it might in fact be concluded that the United States would prefer to use the leverage flowing from its trade power in a more selective manner, that is, by granting selective trade advantages to those countries that are undertaking the economic and political reforms that Washington believes are necessary. If the United States had to apply its trade policy consistently or if it lost control over the phasing-in of the free trade zone, this would amount to, in Washington's view, giving a free ride to a large number of states. That is, those states would benefit from free trade without having to implement the economic and political reforms that Washington could otherwise require them to adopt if trade negotiations remained on a bilateral basis.

Another reason for U.S. reticence regarding a rapid implementation of free trade is that if such an implementation were to occur, the United States might have to assume financial and security obligations on behalf of a significant number of states that are not seen as important in terms of U.S. interests. A selective, gradual, and modulated enlargement of a core trade pact zone like NAFTA would undoubtedly be easier to sell to a skittish Congress.

Perhaps the most dramatic consequence of current strategic thinking in Washington is that it perpetuates the U.S. attitude of strategic denial toward Latin America and the Caribbean. Thus, the image that the United States constructed of the region and its relationship with the southern part of the hemisphere during the Cold War survives even after the end of that era. As Cottam shows in her analysis of the behavior of the Bush administration in the region, and particularly the war on drugs in the Andean countries, U.S. foreign policy may have abandoned the containment script regarding the strategic situation on the ground, but the image of dependence still strongly shapes how policies are conceived and implemented (Cottam 1994: 162–177). Cottam demonstrates how Washington, informed by a dependent image of the Andean countries, refused to incorporate the ideas and expertise of states from the region into the establishment and implementation of the Andean Initiative, relying instead on its superiority to impose an essentially military solution to the problem. This analysis may be extended to include the unilateral and profoundly paternalist nature of Washington's annual practice of certifying those Latin American nations that in its view have made a demonstrably conscientious effort to eradicate the production and trafficking of drugs. The dependent image is clearly deeply rooted.

This brings us to the democratic dimension of the U.S. regionalist project. The econocentrism that has taken shape within the foreign policy of the Clinton era has resulted in democracy being given a lower priority. Elsewhere, notably in Asia and Africa, it has become obvious that, although democratization is always a stated goal of U.S. action, it is not always an immediate objective. An emphasis is placed, first and foremost, on economic stability and development, which, it is assumed, will lead more or less naturally to democracy (Brinkley 1997: 116). This has two implications for the U.S. attitude toward the regionalist project.

First, the progress of democracy in Latin America and the Caribbean cannot be considered by the United States as a strategic objective to which other objectives should be subordinated. That is, the promotion of democracy does not in itself constitute a sufficient reason for the United States to adopt a regionalist policy.

Second, and conversely, "promoting democracy" will continue to be a stated objective of U.S. policy in the hemisphere, but the significance of this objective will vary, as it has in the past, as a function of more immediate U.S. interests (Volk 1997). If free trade is thought to be in U.S. interests, then free trade will come first. This suggests that if the United States opts for regionalism, it will not be because U.S. leaders have adopted a new attitude toward democracy in the region (Martz 1992; Volk 1997). Perhaps the most striking example of this phenomenon may be found in the United States' attitude toward Mexico since the signature of NAFTA. Clearly, in this case Washington shows remarkable confidence about the long-term effects of free trade on democratization.

Institutional Strategies

Since the end of the Cold War, the United States has not developed a firm institutional strategy in its international relations. Of course, the Clinton administration extended the spirit of Bush's "new international order" with a commitment to "assertive multilateralism," that is, by encouraging the development of the capacities and legitimacy of international organizations and formal alliance systems (Haass 1995: 51). However, this commitment has not prevented the United States from resorting to unilateral action when it was considered necessary, often, as in the Haitian crisis, under the cloak of legitimacy provided by the National Security Council. In fact, several constants in the U.S. attitude toward institutions can be identified from its recent actions.

First, the United States appears to have made a deliberate choice to build on existing institutions instead of creating new ones. The most striking example of this decision was the strategy of enlargement of the North Atlantic Treaty Organization (NATO) and the Partnership for Peace, which uses NATO as the basis for formalizing security relations with countries of the Commonwealth of Independent States. Such a development confirms the views of those who predicted that the end of the Cold War would not result in the disappearance of the institutions created to respond to the strategic context of the era and believed that it was more rational to adapt and broaden their mandate.

Second, the further the United States moves away from the area of security and the core of relations between the powers that form the heart of the current international system (the United States, Russia, China, Japan, the European Union), the less it tends to favor institutional strategies and the more it resorts to unilateralism. For example, in the area of trade or even in narcotics, Washington does not hesitate to use unilateral strategies—the threat of sanctions in the former case and its certification policy in the latter. Similarly, in relations with Cuba and Iraq, the United States has demonstrated that it is ready to take action despite the disapproval of its allies.

Finally, when the collaboration of other states is needed to accomplish U.S. objectives in a situation where already existing institutions are not available, the United States favors the building of informal coalitions rather than the creation of new formal organizations—what Haass refers to as the "leadership approach" (Haass 1995: 52). A case in point is summitry in the Americas, an approach that has also been proposed more recently to the African nations. However, contact groups and other configurations have been instituted to deal with a number of specific situations in, for example, the Middle East, the Balkans, and Northern Ireland.

Thus, the general attitude reflects a concern for minimalism consistent with an enlargement strategy: Do not invest in new structures in which there is a danger of getting entangled; work from existing institutions; and, above all, retain as much maneuvering room as possible in regions where U.S. strategic imperatives so allow. This general approach also entails the use of socialization as a means to get states to adopt certain domestic or foreign policy behaviors rather than their integration into an institutionalized framework of formal commitments. Thus, U.S. action—whether unilateral or coalition based—remains regulative in the sense that it establishes a set of standards of behavior that are enforced through rewards and sanctions.

In this context, the combination of existing institutions and strategic imperatives is fundamental. How, then, does this combination work in the regional context of the Americas? The region has inherited the institutionalized Inter-American System (IAS), which, contrary to the system that exists in Europe and Asia, predates the Cold War, its principal components being the Organization of American States (OAS) (founded in 1890 as the International Union of American Republics), the Inter-American Treaty of Reciprocal Assistance (Rio Treaty) of 1947, and the Inter-American Development Bank (IDB). This system has suffered rather than benefited from the strategic context that has existed since the late 1950s. At the height of the Cold War, after U.S. intervention in the Dominican Republic, the Latin American states abandoned the system. Whereas the United States increasingly resorted to unilateral action, the Latin American countries developed their own multilateral subregional mechanisms to solve conflicts in the region, in particular in Central America (Atkins 1992: 14). Thus, at the end of the Cold War, the hemisphere possessed an institutional system, but one that was fragile.

Given the absence of strategic issues that would justify using the IAS, the United States will develop its regionalist option outside these institutions, except perhaps in the field of human rights and democracy, in which the OAS has acquired a solid reputation and expertise during the 1970s and 1980s. The U.S. strategy favors the combination of maintaining existing multilateral fora such as the OAS and the less formal coalition building represented by the current trend toward summitry that was initiated by Washington in Miami in 1994.

The only significant regional institution building in which the United States has been engaged is NAFTA. In order to appreciate the significance of this move, we should keep in mind that NAFTA is much more than a trade agreement (see Chapter 4 in this volume). The NAFTA zone has no political institutions, but NAFTA has highly institutionalized norms. Plus, the agreement established a series of common institutions, from the Free Trade Commission to various working groups, and it opened the way for the future creation of additional coordination mechanisms (Weintraub 1997: 64ff). The U.S. decision to opt for the creation of new institutions in this case may be explained by the fact that the integration of Mexico into a common institutional structure was fundamentally motivated by a security, not a trade, objective. The strategic impulse was rooted in the imperative to shore up its immediate neighbor's political stability and to guarantee U.S. access to Mexican petroleum resources (P. Smith 1996a: 246–247).

Strategic issues of this kind do not exist elsewhere in the hemisphere. This leads Peter Smith, for example, to conclude that the main obstacle to creating a Free Trade Area of the Americas (FTAA) is probably the absence of clear political motivation on the part of the United States: "Geopolitical motivation could come about in response to major events, realignments, or developments in the international arena, but it was not apparent by the mid-1990s" (P. Smith 1996a: 251). At the end of the 1990s, this lack of motivation is still keeping the issue on hold. Without an issue of this kind, the idea of an FTAA does not fit into the institutional strategy supported by enlargement thinking. Much closer to the enlargement strategy is the idea of gradually widening the NAFTA zone, a proposal that has not been abandoned by Washington, even though it is having difficulty gaining congressional approval to move forward on the promise to make Chile a partner in NAFTA. A trade-based enlargement strategy in the Western Hemisphere could also make room for IAS institutions. Sidney Weintraub has already proposed such a solution, which would combine the gradual and prudent extension of the NAFTA zone and the use of the IDB, the Economic Commission for Latin America and the Caribbean, and the OAS, for example, as intermediate institutional bases in order to advance the regional agenda (Weintraub 1994b: 101–102).

But the widening of NAFTA will inevitably raise the problem of its articulation with the Mercosur zone. The creation of Mercosur has not escaped the kind of political imperatives that were at play in the case of NAFTA. Indeed, Argentina and Brazil became involved in this undertaking above all to stabilize their political relations (Sánchez Bajo 1992). Beyond the questions raised in Chapter 4 of this volume related to the economic and technical linkages between the two zones, it appears that the problem of the political connection will need to be resolved before the United States could envisage such an association. If a NAFTA-Mercosur merger were to take place, it would have enormous strategic implications for Washington, which would find itself directly linked to the political situation of the Southern Cone countries.

Conclusion

Regionalism, as an instrument of foreign policy, has never been an automatic response by the United States to either harmony or hegemony. As a superpower, the United States has developed regional institutional strategies and has thus relinquished part of its autonomy in cases where it was justified by a serious security issue. With the end of the Cold War, after a period of juggling the different versions of neo-Wilsonian multilateralism, the United States renounced a wider definition of its national interests as a basis for the redeployment of its engagement in the periphery of the international system. In the meantime, however, heightened expectations were created, and Washington must now inevitably deal with these expectations. This situation explains the hesitancy and apparent inconsistency of current U.S. diplomacy with regard to regional construction in the hemisphere.

Current U.S. foreign policy has made trade the central instrument of geopolitical action. A project such as the FTAA is therefore not seen simply in terms of economic rationality. Paradoxically, this means that perhaps the FTAA is no longer as attractive to the United States as it used to be. Because it now intends to use the leverage of its powerful trade position to regulate the international order, the United States would probably prefer to use this instrument in a more targeted way with the region's countries rather than get involved in an already inclusive project.

Note

I would like to thank Alexandre Brassard-Desjardins and M. S. Baruti for valuable research assistance, Martin Roy for having read and commented on a first version of the text, and the Center for North American Studies at Duke University for its hospitality during the research.

6

From Warmth to Coolness: The U.S. Congress and the Free Trade Issue in the Americas, 1988–1996

Bernard Lemelin

November 20, 1993, was a day of rejoicing for the Clinton administration: By a vote of 61 to 38, the Senate passed bill H.R. 3450 implementing the North American Free Trade Agreement (NAFTA), just three days after the House of Representatives endorsed the same proposal (*Congressional Quarterly Almanac* 1994: 171). NAFTA took effect on January 1, 1994. This historic trade pact, which called for among other things the total elimination of tariffs between the United States, Mexico, and Canada over a fifteen-year period, was an example of a genuine trend toward economic regionalism in the Western Hemisphere. Also representative of this trend was the Canada-U.S. Free Trade Agreement (FTA) signed in January 1988. The FTA's key provisions phased out tariffs between the two nations over a ten-year period.

This chapter seeks to examine and analyze the attitude of the U.S. Congress toward the free trade issue in the Americas during the period between the 1988 debate over FTA and the presidential election of 1996. This was not only a period of rapid economic transformation but also one that seemed to mark an interesting evolution in congressional behavior: Capitol Hill's initial support for economic regionalism in the Americas, which was obvious in the debates of 1988 and 1993, waned perceptibly between 1994 and 1996, as exemplified by the stalemate on free trade negotiations with Chile. Furthermore, the U.S. Congress, to which the U.S. Constitution ascribed a key role for regulating commerce with foreign nations (Destler 1986: 3), played an influential role in the evolution of regionalism in the Americas—the same Congress that political scientist Jerel Rosati has characterized as "a significant actor in foreign economic

111

policy" (Rosati 1984: 326)[1] and whose involvement in overall foreign policy making has increased since the end of the Vietnam War and the Watergate affair.[2] For example, the successful negotiation of the NAFTA side agreements on labor and the environment was linked to the willingness of the Clinton administration to please many Democratic members of Congress (Wiarda 1994: 133). In fact, the legislative branch has become much more active and visible on trade issues since the 1960s (Destler 1994: 245). Equally illustrative of the substantial increase in the congressional role regarding trade policy was the Omnibus Trade and Competitiveness Act, authorizing U.S. participation in the multilateral Uruguay Round of the General Agreement on Tariffs and Trade (GATT). As I. M. Destler has noted: "It was the product primarily of congressional initiative. Not only was its initiation shaped by congressional more than executive priorities, but a considerable portion of its 467 pages addressed issues where members of Congress wanted legislation and the administration (for the most part) did not" (Destler 1994: 228).

More specifically, in this chapter I will attempt to address the following questions: Why is it that the protectionist sentiment so acute on Capitol Hill during the 1980s[3] did not prevail in the debates of 1988 and 1993? Who were the supporters and the opponents of FTA and NAFTA in Congress? Did NAFTA critics deserve the label of "neo-isolationists"? Did the endorsement of regional initiatives such as FTA and NAFTA signal decreased support for multilateralism in the legislative branch? Why did the post-NAFTA period see a strong resurgence in congressional opposition to the idea of economic regionalism in the Americas?

The literature relating to congressional attitudes on this issue is surprisingly limited. For instance, on the Free Trade Agreement of 1988, historians John Thompson and Stephen Randall devoted only a few words to this particular aspect in their 1994 volume on Canadian-U.S. relations (Thompson and Randall 1994: 288). Likewise, Howard Wiarda's recent article on U.S. domestic politics and NAFTA, although it contains relevant information concerning congressional attitudes in 1993, neglects a rich primary source for determining the views of Capitol Hill politicians on legislation, the *Congressional Record* (Wiarda 1994: 141–143). As I have already implied, a thorough examination of the U.S. Congress's stance is therefore highly relevant considering the key role played by domestic actors in the integration process. This is what prompted political scientist Andrew Hurrell to declare that "domestic policy convergence has undoubtedly been an important factor in the resurgence of regionalism" (Hurrell 1995b: 71).

This chapter, which is chronological and topical in its approach, has three sections. In the first section, which deals with the debate of 1988, I present and then analyze the views of FTA supporters and opponents in the legislative branch. I also make some general observations on the congressional vote on the issue. In the second part of this chapter I do roughly the same thing for the 1993 debate on NAFTA. Finally, in the last section I aim primarily to demonstrate that the post-NAFTA period was not an auspicious one for Capitol Hill supporters of economic regionalism in the Americas.

"The Most Ambitious Bilateral Trade Agreement in History"

Hailed by Ronald Reagan as "an historic agreement for both sides" (*Public Papers of the Presidents of the United States* 1990: 4), the January 2, 1988, accord between Canada and the United States generated numerous reactions on Capitol Hill before both houses voted on the issue at the end of the summer. Some of these reactions were frankly harsh, and others were unequivocally approving.

First and foremost, the defenders of the Free Trade Agreement in Congress emphasized the special relationship that existed between the two nations. The views of Oregon senator Bob Packwood were a good illustration of this position. Packwood, a Republican, affirmed that Canada and the United States were "two major industrial countries with an immense border, common interests, common language" (U.S. Senate 1988: 3). According to the senator, a refusal to ratify such a landmark agreement would constitute nothing less than an "absolute crime" (U.S. Senate 1988: 3). His colleague John Chafee of Rhode Island declared that "Canada is our largest export market" (U.S. Senate 1988: 4), and Republican representative Philip Crane of Illinois resorted to citing statistics to make the point: "In 1987 . . . total bilateral trade in goods and services between the United States and Canada exceeded $166 billion, making these two countries the largest trading partners in the world. . . . The United States purchases 76 percent of Canada's exported goods, and the United States supplies 68 percent of Canadian imports" (*Congressional Record* 1988: 21311).

Moreover, several members of Congress asserted that the Free Trade Agreement held out specific economic advantages for their constituencies. For instance, Democratic representative David Skaggs of Colorado emphasized the positive impact the FTA would have on high-tech industries in the Rocky Mountain region: "More than 41,000 Coloradans are employed in the electronic and electric equipment and machinery industries. . . . In 1986, Colorado companies exported $49 million worth of electronic computers to Canada. . . . The . . . liberalization in service and investment industries will translate into many new export opportunities to the state's technology-based sectors" (U.S. House 1988a: 760). Still others suggested that the agreement of January 1988 would stimulate tourism from Canada (*Congressional Record* 1988: 24427).

Although the FTA aroused greater political opposition in Canada than in the United States (McGaughey Jr. 1992: 49), several opposing voices were also heard south of the forty-ninth parallel, particularly on Capitol Hill. Indeed, some members of Congress castigated the FTA, which was little known to the U.S. people (Thompson and Randall 1994: 283).

Senator Pete Domenici, a Republican from New Mexico, was among the critics. His fears included concerns over the FTA's impact on the U.S. uranium industry: "A reading of the agreement would wipe out the Atomic Energy Act provision that requires that America have a viable uranium industry. Under the agreement the case would be mooted" (U.S. House 1988a: 262). As Domenici admitted, he was primarily motivated by a desire to preserve the struggling uranium industry in his own state (*Congressional Record* 1988: 24406).

For his part, Senator Carl Levin, a Michigan Democrat, was especially resentful of the FTA's reaffirmation of the 1965 U.S.-Canada Auto Pact, under which, as he specified, "automotive manufacturers are required to produce at least one car in Canada for every car they sell there, and to maintain at least a 60 percent Canadian content in the cars they build in Canada" (*Congressional Record* 1988: 24391). Levin deplored the absence of similar protection for U.S. auto production (*Congressional Record* 1988: 24391).

However, it was the detrimental effects of the Canadian subsidy system that rallied the largest contingent of congressional opponents to the agreement signed by Ronald Reagan and Canadian prime minister Brian Mulrooney. As Republican representative Larry Craig of Idaho explained, the prevalence of this system gave Canadian products "an advantage over the nonsubsidized American products that compete directly with them" (*Congressional Record* 1988: 21338). Certain members of Congress felt Canadian federal and provincial subsidy practices were particularly harmful to specific U.S. agricultural commodities.

Wheat was a good example. As Senator Kent Conrad, a Democrat from North Dakota, pointed out, the U.S. farm program, which was designed to store surplus grain during bountiful years and sell it to the world in times of shortage, differed drastically from the Canadian farm program:

> In contrast to the United States farm program, the Canadian farm program is designed to move Canadian grain to export terminals and to obtain the best possible price for their farmers in the world market. To do this, Canada heavily subsidizes rail transport from the grain producing areas of Canada to port cities. In addition, the Canadian Wheat Board acts as an agent for export sales of all Canadian wheat as well as other products. (*Congressional Record* 1988: 24388)

In the same vein, Democratic senator George Mitchell of Maine argued that the Free Trade Agreement was unfair for the potato industry in

his own state: "Canada now subsidizes its potato industry. The United
States does not. This agreement doesn't change that. Canada has laws
which effectively prohibit Maine potatoes from being shipping [*sic*] into
Canada. The United States has no comparable laws. This agreement does-
n't change that" (U.S. Senate 1988: 5).

Interestingly, several FTA supporters openly shared some of their adversaries' anxieties. Representative Rod Chandler, a Washington Republican who had expressed his excitement about the prospects of creating what
he called "the most ambitious bilateral trade agreement in history" (U.S.
House 1988b: 117), feared the impact of the FTA on the plywood industry:
"Under the agreement, U.S. plywood producers would continue to be de-
nied access to 90 percent of the Canadian market, while Canadian producers would have free access to our market" (U.S. House 1988b: 118).[4]

On August 9, 1988, the House of Representatives passed the bill implementing the FTA by a 366 to 40 margin (H.R. 5090); the Senate did the
same on September 19 by a vote of 83 to 9 (*Congressional Quarterly Almanac* 1989: 228). Such "overwhelming approval by both Houses" (*Public Papers of the Presidents of the United States* 1991: 1232), to use
Ronald Reagan's words, was not really surprising.

In fact, aside from the merits of the agreement itself and the helpful
fast-track procedure that accompanied its consideration in Congress, the
FTA also received strong backing from some very influential quarters.
Business groups such as the National Association of Manufacturers and
the American Business Conference unhesitatingly endorsed the deal (*Congressional Quarterly Almanac* 1989: 223). In addition, the nation's governors voted 30 to 5 in favor of the FTA as early as late February 1988 (*Congressional Quarterly Almanac* 1989: 223). And the Reagan administration
spared no effort in promoting the agreement with the backing of organizations like the 500-member American Coalition for Trade Expansion with
Canada, a pro-FTA business lobby (*Congressional Quarterly Almanac*
1989: 223). The administration's "broad-scale educational effort on Capitol Hill" (Aho 1988: 182) certainly helped convince some members of
Congress that failure to implement the Free Trade Agreement would have
pernicious effects on both nations. John Thompson and Stephen Randall
went so far as to declare that "the easy success of the FTA in Congress
owed everything to the pressure and support by Reagan and his officials"
(Thompson and Randall 1994: 288). Be this as it may, Reagan's attitude
must essentially be viewed within the context of the transformations occurring in the world system during the 1980s: His fears of U.S. decline in
the face of resurgent Japan and Europe spurred the president even further
in his determination to build bridges with his northern neighbor (Thompson and Randall 1994: 287).

These elements help us understand what led an FTA opponent like
New Mexico's Pete Domenici to predict prior to the Senate vote that "[the

Free Trade Agreement] will pass and that it will pass overwhelmingly" (*Congressional Record* 1988: 24406). In short, the 1988 decrease in protectionist sentiment in the Democrat-controlled 100th Congress appeared unavoidable.

An examination of the 1988 congressional vote on the FTA shows three things. First, the agreement received extensive bipartisan support: of the 83 FTA supporters in the Senate, 43 were Democrats and 40 Republicans (*Congressional Record* 1988: 24444–24445). Second, many Capitol Hill opponents to the pact were from the states along the Canadian border, a phenomenon linked to expectations that the FTA would have a severe impact in this area. Of the nine FTA dissenters in the Senate, six were from the states of Maine (William Cohen and George Mitchell), Michigan (Carl Levin), North Dakota (Kent Conrad and Quentin Burdick), and Montana (John Melcher) (*Congressional Record* 1988: 24445). Third, the vote shows that the Western states also accounted for a good number of free trade adversaries: five of the nine opponents in the Senate—namely, Jeff Bingaman (New Mexico), Quentin Burdick (North Dakota), Kent Conrad (North Dakota), Pete Domenici (New Mexico), and John Melcher (Montana)—were from states west of the Mississippi River (*Congressional Record* 1988: 24445). Naturally, this situation was linked to the fact that some of these states depended heavily on agriculture and that many of their inhabitants believed that the FTA would lead to increased problems with their subsidized Canadian competitors. Indeed, in North Dakota, spokesmen from organizations such as the Wheat Commission and the Barley Council (U.S. House 1988a: 446–449, 481–484) made sure they voiced their "agricultural concerns" in public during the free trade debate.

However, such dissatisfaction was not enough to stop the U.S.-Canada Free Trade Agreement, "one of the more enlightened trade initiatives of the postwar period" (Nivola 1990: 253), from taking effect on January 1, 1989, several days after winning approval from the Canadian House of Commons (*Congressional Quarterly Almanac* 1989: 228).

"One of the Biggest Triumphs of [the Clinton] Presidency"

Although the 1988 debate provoked strong reactions on Capitol Hill, the 1993 debate on the North American Free Trade Agreement was even more emotional. Democrat Claiborne Pell of Rhode Island, who was first elected in 1961, claimed that the agreement had "sparked the largest and most comprehensive public debate on international trade that I have witnessed in all my years in the Senate" (*Congressional Record* 1993: S15536). His words highlight the importance of examining what Democratic representative Rosa DeLauro of Connecticut called "this tumultuous debate" (*Congressional*

Record 1993: H7335)—a debate that clearly reflected Congress's particular sensitivity on "intermestic" issues.[5]

The employment issue was central to the arguments of the congressional supporters of the historic trade agreement signed by the United States, Canada, and Mexico on December 17, 1992. As one senator explained, "At the heart of the debate is whether NAFTA will mean job creation or job loss" (*Congressional Record* 1993: S16974). Republican representative David Dreier of California was among those who believed that "the job creating aspects of free trade are one of the most important reasons to support NAFTA" (*Congressional Record* 1993: H4855). Dreier, who was commended by President Clinton for his pro-NAFTA efforts (*Public Papers of the Presidents of the United States* 1994: 2139), argued that the positive impact of the agreement on employment was easy to understand: "NAFTA will create jobs here because high Mexican barriers to our exports will be reduced (*Congressional Record* 1993: H4855). Dreier's optimism was shared by many of his colleagues in the House, including Michigan Republican Peter Hoekstra, who found fault with the job loss argument: "The argument that we will lost [*sic*] jobs because of NAFTA ignores reality. The ability to move jobs out of the United States exists today. By approving NAFTA, we will reduce the incentive to move jobs to Mexico by lowering and eliminating tariffs on United States goods" (*Congressional Record* 1993: H9911). For his part, Californian Steve Horn deplored the malevolence of certain NAFTA opponents: "Those who exaggerate potential job losses do not discuss American job gains from NAFTA. . . . 283 top economists of all political views—including 12 winners of the Nobel Prize in economics—signed a statement supporting NAFTA. They agreed that America will gain many more jobs than we might lose" (*Congressional Record* 1993: H7343).

According to some Capitol Hill politicians, the agreement was also favorable to agriculture. Senator David Pryor, a Democrat from Arkansas, noted the benefits that NAFTA would bring to the rice farmers of his state. As he explained, "Rice exports to Mexico . . . are hit by a 20–percent tariff on milled rice and a 10-percent tariff on rough rice. With NAFTA, these tariffs will be phased out over a 10-year period" (*Congressional Record* 1993: S14584).

Still others stressed that the December 1992 agreement would not be harmful to the U.S. environment. In fact, Senator Max Baucus, a Democrat from Montana who has been described as "one of the leading environmentalists in the whole Congress" (*Congressional Record* 1993: S12058), agreed that NAFTA was "the greenest trade agreement in history" (U.S. Senate 1993: 1). However, he was also conscious of the gap existing between the United States and its southern neighbor in the area of environmental enforcement (U.S. Senate 1993: 2). For his part, Republican John

Chafee asserted that NAFTA contained several provisions on the environment and that it had been endorsed by spokespeople from organizations such as the National Wildlife Federation (*Congressional Record* 1993: S12058).

Moreover, many members of Congress felt that NAFTA would contribute to reducing illegal immigration from Mexico. Democratic senator Bill Bradley of New Jersey explained his conviction that this would be the case on the grounds that NAFTA would boost the economy south of the Rio Grande (*Congressional Record* 1993: S12058).

For a good number of Washington-based politicians, NAFTA was good news from a foreign policy standpoint. Republican representative Jim Kolbe of Arizona, for example, viewed NAFTA as a "very important initiative to improve our relationships with Mexico and the rest of Latin America" (*Congressional Record* 1993: H5445), and Bill Bradley underscored that NAFTA would ensure a secure oil supply for the nation (*Congressional Record* 1993: S15530). For his part, Democratic senator John Kerry of Massachusetts judged that the creation of such a powerful trading bloc was vital "as we watch China and Asia, the Asian tigers, emerge with even greater power today" (*Congressional Record* 1993: S16603). According to Democratic representative Mike Kopetski of Oregon, one of these "Asian tigers" was particularly eager to make a move in the event that NAFTA was rejected: "If not this NAFTA, the probability is that Mexico and Japan—Japan, our major competitor—will attempt to negotiate a bilateral trade agreement. If that happens, Japan will use Mexico as an even greater staging area to ship their goods into the United States" (*Congressional Record* 1993: H8802). Of course, NAFTA, by enhancing U.S. competitiveness, was also perceived by people like Republican representative Ron Packard of California (*Congressional Record* 1993: H9864) to be an effective means of competing with another strong regional trading bloc, the European Community.

Finally, some members of Congress resorted to the lessons of history to condemn protectionism and promote NAFTA ratification. Republican representative Herbert Bateman of Virginia provided a good example: "For 50 years, American leaders have supported the systemic expansion of global free trade. Within this framework, the United States has prospered enormously. However, the opposite occurred when Congress enacted the Smoot-Hawley Tariff Act of 1930, short-sighted . . . legislation that raised barriers to trade" (*Congressional Record* 1993: E2884).

NAFTA opponents on Capitol Hill also resorted to an imposing range of arguments to justify their position. Scholar Howard Wiarda has identified twenty-two different arguments used by NAFTA critics both inside and outside Congress (Wiarda 1994: 135–136). "A product of corporate America" (*Congressional Record* 1993: S11752), "a destructive agreement"

(*Congressional Record* 1993: H9876), "a jobs program for Mexico" (*Congressional Record* 1993: S16013)—these were among the strongest denunciations from NAFTA detractors criticizing the deal in Congress.

Not surprisingly, most opponents emphasized that ratification of such a regional initiative would mean job losses for U.S. workers or, as Democratic representative George Miller of California called them, "these people who helped us to win the Cold War" (*Congressional Record* 1993: H9878). Democratic representative and majority whip David Bonior of Michigan was convinced that job losses were inevitable:

> American workers are the best in the world and . . . they can win in the new global marketplace if . . . the playing field is fair . . . ; but NAFTA threatens to . . . put us at a tremendous disadvantage. Why? Because primarily there is a systematic policy in Mexico to keep wages low. . . . Even in the highest paying jobs, Mexican workers earn less in a day than American workers earn in an hour. . . . If . . . wages are so low, and the Government rolls out the red carpet called NAFTA, the big multinationals would be crazy not to use that red carpet to close up shop here and move south of the border. (*Congressional Record* 1993: H4670)

In fact, Bonior considered that the huge wage disparities between the two countries would hurt countless people in the United States: "If NAFTA passes, Henry Kissinger will not be put out of work, . . . Lee Iacocca will not lose his job, but 500,000 Americans will. . . . There is not a single word [in this agreement] . . . that says anything or that does anything to raise Mexican wages . . . or to ensure that Mexican workers earn enough to buy our products" (*Congressional Record* 1993: H9858). In the same vein, Democratic senator Donald Riegle of Michigan expressed his concern about integration with a nation that "has a Third World economy . . . in terms of its wage structure" (*Congressional Record* 1993: S5861), and Democratic representative Marcy Kaptur of Ohio argued that approval of NAFTA would be particularly harmful to women because so many of them worked in the textile industry (*Congressional Record* 1993: H4674–H4675). For her part, Barbara-Rose Collins, a Democratic representative from Michigan, argued that NAFTA would hurt African Americans: "NAFTA will liberalize access to Mexico manufacturing. This . . . will cause the number of jobs traditionally held by blue-collar workers . . . to evaporate. Because minorities are concentrated disproportionately in these jobs, we will see unemployment among minorities shoot up. At 14.6 percent, unemployment among African-Americans is already more than double that of other Americans" (*Congressional Record* 1993: H8336).

Some Capitol Hill politicians also thought that NAFTA would have detrimental effects on agricultural jobs. Democratic representative Patsy Mink of Hawaii was particularly concerned about the impact of NAFTA "sugar provisions" on 17,000 Hawaiian sugar plantation workers. The provisions stipulated that there would be no limit on Mexican sugar exported north of the Rio Grande after fifteen years (*Congressional Record* 1993: E905–E906).

Naturally, the issue of NAFTA's environmental impact was raised by many members of Congress. Democratic senator Howard Metzenbaum of Ohio, for instance, stated that although Mexico's environmental standards were strict on paper, they had a notoriously bad enforcement record. The senator contended that such a situation might have deleterious effects on public health (U.S. Senate 1993: 9). Furthermore, the argument that NAFTA would contribute to reducing illegal immigration from Mexico was also assailed by certain Capitol Hill politicians. Dianne Feinstein, a Democratic senator from California, said that there were no provisions in NAFTA requiring Mexico to control its own borders (*Congressional Record* 1993: S16067). She also quoted a study by NAFTA supporter Philip Martin of the Institute of International Economics that predicted an increase in illegal immigration into the United States "as the Mexican economy turns to manufacturing and displaces those Mexican agricultural workers whose crops are inefficiently grown" (*Congressional Record* 1993: S16068).

A number of NAFTA opponents also declared that the "dictatorial" nature of the Mexican political system and the issue of human rights south of the Rio Grande constituted another impediment to NAFTA ratification. In the words of Independent representative Bernard Sanders of Vermont: "The [Institutional Revolutionary Party] has been in complete control of the Government since 1929, never having lost an election. Workers in Mexico today are not allowed to organize free trade unions, state and federal elections are rigged, . . . and dissidents have been jailed and killed. How do you have a free trade agreement with a country that is not free?" (*Congressional Record* 1993: E2353).

Although the arguments summarized here were the most prominent in the anti-NAFTA discourse, several other issues were raised by members of Congress, including claims that the agreement would create new bureaucracies[6] and threaten U.S. motorists.[7]

In retrospect, however, most NAFTA opponents on Capitol Hill did not deserve the label of "neo-isolationists" since many of them seemed receptive to the free trade idea[8] and privately recognized that more U.S. jobs would be created than lost in the long run (Wiarda 1994: 140). Thus, politicians like Ohio's Howard Metzenbaum (*Congressional Record* 1993: S11074) and California's Dianne Feinstein (*Congressional Record* 1993: S16068) publicly rejected protectionism and voiced their support of free trade principles. Above all, it is important to remember that several NAFTA opponents, including Michigan's David Bonior (*Congressional*

Record 1988: 21351) and Donald Riegle (*Congressional Record* 1988: 24444), voted in favor of the 1988 Free Trade Agreement with Canada. However, the enormous differences between the U.S. and Mexican economies, as well as pressures from interest groups and constituents, prompted many members of Congress to back away from their pro–free trade position.

As mentioned earlier, the bill to implement NAFTA (H.R. 3450) was passed in the Senate by a vote of 61 to 38 on November 20, 1993. Three days earlier, the House had approved the same piece of legislation by a majority of 234 to 200 (*Congressional Quarterly Almanac* 1994: 171), a vote that David Rosenbaum of the *New York Times* qualified as "one of the biggest triumphs of [the Clinton] Presidency" (*New York Times* 1993a). As with the 1988 vote, this congressional endorsement was not altogether surprising, although the prospects of a free trade victory had appeared somewhat doubtful as late as September 1993 (*Congressional Quarterly Almanac* 1994: 172). Although NAFTA had generated considerable criticism outside Congress (from Ross Perot, Pat Buchanan, organized labor, etc.) (*Congressional Quarterly Almanac* 1994: 172), it was supported not only by prominent economists and certain environmental groups but also by two former U.S. presidents,[9] a large majority of governors,[10] numerous newspapers (*Congressional Record* 1993: S12070), most major business groups, and the greater part of the Hispanic community (Wiarda 1994: 121–123). Support from this last group was by no means trivial; Hispanics are well on their way to becoming the largest minority in the United States by the year 2000 (Wiarda 1994: 123).

Furthermore, the growth of U.S. exports as a result of Mexico's adhesion to the General Agreement on Tariffs and Trade in 1986 was another reason that several senators and representatives saw NAFTA in an auspicious light; many felt that the 1992 accord would intensify such a trend by eliminating remaining tariff barriers (*Congressional Record* 1993: H9879). Quite a few legislators were aware that public opinion, in spite of its negative perception of the measure, was not intensely opposed to NAFTA. This sentiment, among other things, was evident in a poll taken just a few days before the congressional vote: "It found that of the respondents who were opposed to NAFTA, a reassuring 75 percent said that how their members of Congress voted on the NAFTA issue would not alone determine whether or not they would vote to reelect their representative or senator" (Rourke, Carter, and Boyer 1996: 396).

Another similarity with 1988 was the bipartisan nature of the NAFTA vote: In the House 102 Democrats and 132 Republicans supported the agreement (*New York Times* 1993a: A1), whereas 27 Democrats and 34 Republicans did the same in the Senate (*New York Times* 1993b). Representative Newt Gingrich of Georgia contended that the NAFTA debate was "in the past traditions of historic bipartisanship, the tradition of the . . . Truman doctrine, and the vote on Desert Storm" (*Congressional Record* 1993: H9876). However, the Democrats, who controlled the 103rd Congress, were much more divided on the issue than the Republicans. This was especially true in the House, where 156 Democrats voted against NAFTA, compared with only 43 Republicans (*New York Times* 1993a: A20). These results can be explained by the fact that many Democratic representatives wanted to retain the backing of organized labor, which remained "a potent force at local, state, and regional levels" despite its declining influence in national politics (Wiarda 1994: 132). As for the stronger support NAFTA enjoyed in the Senate, it was due in part to the fact that senators, because of their six-year terms in office, were less susceptible to the pressures that led many representatives to vote against the measure (*Congressional Quarterly Almanac* 1994: 179).

An examination of the November 1993 vote also reveals that politicians from the four Mexican border states (California, Arizona, New Mexico, and Texas) tended to be strong NAFTA supporters. New Mexico senators Pete Domenici and Jeff Bingaman, who had both opposed the FTA in 1988, voted in favor of the deal (*New York Times* 1993b), and no less than twenty-four of the thirty-member Texan delegation in the House of Representatives did the same (*New York Times* 1993a: A20).[11] In fact, politicians from states west of the Mississippi River, most of them probably reassured by the positive impact of the 1988 Canada-U.S. agreement, seemed receptive to the free trade idea. Only 29 percent of NAFTA opponents in the Senate were from the West, compared with 56 percent of those who had voted against the FTA five years earlier (*New York Times* 1993b).[12] Also different from 1988 was the strong legislative opposition to NAFTA coming from older industrial states of the Northeast, such as Michigan, Ohio, Pennsylvania, and New York. The region accounted for 55 of the votes cast against NAFTA in the House of Representatives, but only 9 of the votes against the FTA.[13]

There are a number of reasons for this opposition. On the one hand, siding against organized labor in these and certain other states would have appeared suicidal for a member of Congress seeking reelection—something akin to a political "kiss of death" (Wiarda 1994: 132). Indeed, several Democratic members of Congress from the region were heavily dependent on the American Federation of Labor and Congress of Industrial Organizations, the dominant labor organization, for campaign contributions (Wiarda 1994: 132). On the other hand, the old northeastern "manufacturing belt," which includes these states,[14] has experienced economic stagnation since the 1960s while the "sunbelt" has grown and prospered.[15] Naturally, the economic situation in the Northeast has had an impact in the area of foreign economic policy. As scholar Peter Trubowitz has pointed out, the growing vulnerability of many key industrial sectors (automobiles, steel, etc.) to global competition in the 1960s and 1970s gradually eroded support for free trade in the manufacturing belt as protectionism grew increasingly attractive (Wiarda 1994: 186).[16] This would certainly explain why the most outspoken critics of NAFTA in Congress—people such as Donald Riegle, David Bonior (who was called "the real leader in the House in opposition to [the agreement]") (*Congressional Record* 1993: H6966), and Marcy Kaptur—were from these states.

Although the U.S. Congress supported the free trade agreements of 1988 and 1993, the endorsement of such regional initiatives did not mean that support for multilateralism[17] had declined in the legislative branch. On the contrary, many indicators of congressional attitudes for the years 1988–1993 seem to confirm, as French scholars Bertrand Badie and Marie-Claude Smouts have argued, that regionalization and globalization are not antinomic notions (Badie and Smouts 1992: 203).

Of course, both FTA and NAFTA stimulated the trend toward regionalism. During the debate of 1993, for instance, several Capitol Hill politicians convinced of the merits of trade liberalization advocated similar initiatives elsewhere in the Western Hemisphere. For example, Minnesota senator Dave Durenberger argued that the extension of NAFTA to countries in the Caribbean and in Central and South America was highly desirable (*Congressional Record* 1993: S16605).

Congress's commitment to multilateralism, however, remained strong during both the 1988 and 1993 debates. Although agreements like FTA and NAFTA essentially resemble what Badie and Smouts have called "une stratégie de défense contre l'extérieur" (Badie and Smouts 1992: 198), Capitol Hill's willingness to eliminate obstacles to international trade and build bridges to countries outside the Western Hemisphere had not faded. Oregon representative Bob Smith, for example, viewed the Canada-U.S. rapprochement of 1988 as "a chance for America to begin an agreement which will expand possibly to . . . Japan, Taiwan, Singapore, and South Korea" (*Congressional Record* 1988: 21331). Even more important, several members of Congress expressed considerable interest in the GATT Uruguay Round negotiations. President Reagan had authorized U.S. participation in these important talks when he signed the Omnibus Trade and Competitiveness Act on August 23, 1988 (Destler 1994: 228), and Republican senator James Jeffords of Vermont, for one, maintained that refusal to approve NAFTA would jeopardize the successful completion of the negotiations (*Congressional Record* 1993: S16013).

Thus, as Gary Hufbauer and Jeffrey Schott have affirmed, regional initiatives such as NAFTA must not be regarded "as a shift in U.S. policy away from its central focus on multilateralism" (Hufbauer and Schott 1993: 116).

"We Need a Cooling-off Period"

At first glance, U.S. congressional support for free trade appeared to remain strong during the post-NAFTA period. Congressional endorsement of U.S. participation in GATT at the end of 1994 seemed to exemplify this continued commitment to multilateralism. The vote ratifying "the most ambitious global trade accord reached in four decades" (*New York Times* 1994c), a 124–nation pact that slashed tariffs by one-third and created a new international body designed to police trade between countries (the World Trade Organization), was unequivocal: The House of Representatives approved the deal by a vote of 288 to 146 (*New York Times* 1994b) and the Senate by a tally of 76 to 24 (*New York Times* 1994c). And as had been the case with the previous free trade agreements, congressional support was bipartisan in nature: In the House, for example, 121 Republicans and 167 Democrats voted in favor of GATT (*New York Times* 1994b).

Congressional supporters of economic regionalism in the Americas were also quick to voice their praises after NAFTA took effect. As early as June 1994, Representatives David Dreier and Jay Dickey (an Arkansas Republican) weighed in with positive assessments of the first six months of NAFTA. Dreier underscored the fact that U.S. exports to Mexico had increased to $11.8 billion between January and March, and Dickey emphasized the various benefits for Arkansas (*Congressional Record* 1994: H5451–H5452). A few months later, Democratic senator Dennis DeConcini of Arizona expressed a similar opinion for his home state: "Almost 1 year after NAFTA went into effect . . . the facts paint a much different picture than the alarmist concerns raised by some opponents of NAFTA. For example, in . . . Arizona, it is estimated that our state's exports to Mexico in the first half of 1994 were up almost 25 percent" (*Congressional Record* 1994: S14959).

These considerations probably explain why members of Congress such as Representative Doug Bereuter of Nebraska spoke out in 1995 to advocate NAFTA expansion. The Republican expressed his strong support for Chile's accession to NAFTA in light of its success in economic liberalization (*Congressional Record* 1995: H10811). In Bereuter's view, however, the benefits of the 1992 trade pact were not the only factor justifying NAFTA expansion: "The simple truth is that the United States, and the American people, have no good economic choice but to push for expansion of NAFTA gradually . . . to the entire Western Hemisphere or risk being excluded from a rapidly liberalizing world economy. Economic integration and trade liberalization is occurring in nearly every part of the world including Europe, Asia, and South America" (*Congressional Record* 1995: H10811).

For his part, Republican senator Richard Lugar of Indiana advocated Trinidad and Tobago's admission to NAFTA on several grounds: "As one of the most advanced economies in the Caribbean, the island nation has successfully implemented economic reforms that have deregulated industry, lowered tariff barriers. . . . Trinidad and Tobago and the United States have long enjoyed cordial diplomatic relations as well as strong economic ties arising from the investment of United States companies in the energy sector of [this country]" (*Congressional Record* 1995: S18921).

Interestingly, 1995 even saw the introduction of several bills promoting economic regionalism in the Western Hemisphere. For instance, bill H.R. 465 introduced by Democratic representative Sam Gibbons of Florida aimed to authorize "entry into free-trade agreements between the United States and certain Caribbean Basin countries" (*Congressional Record* 1995: H229).

Despite these free trade bills and strong statements by certain members of Congress about NAFTA's alleged benefits, the 1994–1996 period was not auspicious for Capitol Hill supporters of economic regionalism in the Americas. Their efforts to pass new legislation were unsuccessful and they obtained little congressional support for either the December 1994 Summit of the Americas held in Miami or its follow-up meetings in Denver (June 1995) and Cartagena (March 1996). The Miami summit, which brought together delegates from over thirty countries in the Western Hemisphere to discuss plans to create a Free Trade Area of the Americas by 2005 (*New York Times* 1994d) generated virtually no positive reactions in Congress: Only Representatives Philip Crane and Bill Richardson, a Democrat from New Mexico, seemed to allude to it (*Congressional Record* 1995: E97, E118).

Above all, the post-NAFTA period saw a strong resurgence in opposition to the idea of economic regionalism in the Americas. There are three main reasons for this situation.

First, several Capitol Hill politicians felt that NAFTA had had a detrimental effect on the United States. Representative James Traficant of Ohio was one of the most virulent critics in this regard. As early as June 1994, the Democrat ironically commented that "after only 6 months of NAFTA . . . , trade is literally jumping across the border. That is the good news. Now, the bad news: Mexican trade is booming. Mexican imports have increased 10 percent. . . . NAFTA is working all right. It is working for Mexico" (*Congressional Record* 1994: H4296). Traficant, who was easily reelected in November 1994,[18] saw this worrying trend continue throughout 1995: "America has lost 250,000 jobs in 1995 alone. Lockheed laid off 15,000; . . . AT&T, 8500; Boeing, 12,000; . . . General Motors, 5000; Kodak, 4000" (*Congressional Record* 1995: H14026). The layoffs at the Boeing Seattle plant led the Ohio representative to chide his congressional colleagues: "The biggest export for NAFTA has been American jobs. Shame, Congress. Shame for turning your back on the American workers.

What will be left? A couple more McDonald's jobs" (*Congressional Record* 1995: H13941).

Not surprisingly, many members of Congress who were on record for their previous opposition to free trade shared Traficant's views. Representative Marcy Kaptur, for instance, proclaimed that "it is time to cancel NAFTA" (*Congressional Record* 1995: H8667), and Senator Byron Dorgan called the trade agreement "a lemon" and "a total disaster for our nation" (*Congressional Record* 1995: S17183). In April 1996 Democratic representative William Lipinski of Illinois reminded the House that polls were indicating that "55 percent of the [U.S.] people believed that NAFTA is causing jobs to go to foreign countries" (*Congressional Record* 1996: H3806). Some legislators even introduced bills to pull the United States out of NAFTA—bills such as H.R. 499, presented in 1995 by a delegation of representative led by Oregonian Peter DeFazio (*Congressional Record* 1995: H241), and S. 1417, initiated the same year by North Dakotan Byron Dorgan and several cosponsors (*Congressional Record* 1995: S17183).

Second, widespread concern in Congress over the Mexican peso crisis of December 1994 was hardly conducive to stimulating regionalism in the Americas, as political scientist Sidney Weintraub has pointed out: "The Mexican financial crisis is . . . affecting the potential expansion of free trade elsewhere in the Western Hemisphere" (Weintraub 1996: 235). Naturally, certain NAFTA opponents were quick to capitalize on the 35 percent devaluation of the peso (*New York Times* 1995a), which was called "a major embarrassment for supporters of NAFTA" by the *Chicago Tribune* (1995a). According to Marcy Kaptur, the effects of the Mexican financial crisis were obvious: "It will be cheaper for [Mexicans] to send more into our marketplace and it will be much harder for the United States to send goods down there because our goods will become more expensive in their market" (*Congressional Record* 1995: H211). Representative William Lipinski, convinced by the general dissatisfaction of public opinion regarding the December 1992 agreement, felt much the same: "Under NAFTA the peso's value has dropped fantastically. This represents a dramatic wage cut for Mexican workers. Consequently United States exports to Mexico will slow while Mexico's exports to the United States will rise, wiping out what little trade advantage we had" (*Congressional Record* 1995: H387). In short, the peso crisis, which U.S. immigration authorities feared could provoke a flood of illegal immigrants across the border (*New York Times* 1995a), was a key element in explaining NAFTA's decreasing appeal.

Third, many members of the 104th Congress (1995–1996) were first elected in 1990 or later, after the end of the Cold War. Indeed, more than half of the members of the House and 29 of the 100 members of the more stable Senate were first elected after the fall of the Berlin Wall (*Los Angeles Times* 1995a). This change in composition helps explain the rise of a certain isolationist mood on Capitol Hill. In the post–Cold War world, many of Congress's new Democratic and Republican members tended to believe "that solving the United States' domestic problems [was] the top priority and that the nation should spend less money and energy on foreign policy" (*Los Angeles Times* 1995a). Consequently, a good number of parliamentarians were less supportive of free trade. A *Los Angeles Times* article of February 1995 went so far as to suggest that "even without Mexico's recent financial problems, NAFTA might have a tough time winning approval if it came back to Congress for a vote today" (*Los Angeles Times* 1995a). Indeed, of the 102 pro-NAFTA Democrats in the House in 1993, only 68 were still in office two years later (*Los Angeles Times* 1995a).[19]

Although none of the bills to revoke NAFTA were successful, the Mexican peso crisis and perceptions that NAFTA results were inconclusive fueled a wave of congressional coolness with regard to regionalism in the Americas, best exemplified by Capitol Hill's attitude toward Chile. In 1994 President Bill Clinton invited Chile to join NAFTA. However, in the fall of 1995, the Republican-controlled Congress, to the great disappointment of the business community (*Los Angeles Times* 1995b), refused to renew President Clinton's fast-track authority (*Chicago Tribune* 1995c) to speed Chile's admission. Republican senator Robert Dole of Kansas was one of those who saw no urgency in concluding a free trade agreement with Chile. At the beginning of November 1995, he justified his position: "I believe it would be a mistake to extend new fast-track authority at this time. There are a number of good reasons, but in my view first and most important is President Clinton's complete failure to explain to the American people why we need yet another trade agreement at this time" (*Congressional Record* 1995: S16695). Dole added: "The fact is we recently concluded two major trade agreements, GATT and NAFTA. I believe it only makes good common sense to step back a little and assess the results. . . . We need a cooling-off period, a time to digest the results. We need to focus on our domestic house, on the actions we can take here at home that will improve our global competitiveness" (*Congressional Record* 1995: S16695).

This fight over fast-track authority—essentially a struggle to determine which branch of the U.S. government controlled the trade agenda (*Globe and Mail* 1995: B1)[20]—meant that the issue of NAFTA expansion was delayed until after the 1996 U.S. presidential election (*Chicago Tribune* 1995b). Commenting on this stalemate in free trade negotiations with Chile, managing director of the Council of the Americas G. Philip Hughes declared that "the momentum of the Miami Summit of the Americas is being lost" (*Wall Street Journal* 1995).

In addition to the issue of Chile's integration into NAFTA, the Cuban problem eloquently highlighted the difficulties surrounding the creation of a hemispheric free trade zone. In fact, the controversial Helms-Burton law signed by President Clinton in March 1996, which sought to discourage foreign investment in Cuba and to tighten the U.S. embargo on the Caribbean island (*Washington Post* 1996), aroused tremendous hostility in the Americas. Approved overwhelmingly by the U.S. Congress after a February 1996 incident in which Cuban air force pilots shot down two small civilian aircraft owned by Cuban exile groups (*New York Times* 1996c), the legislation met with fierce opposition from NAFTA partners. Canada, which has extensive trade links with Cuba, announced in March that it had lodged a protest with the Clinton administration over the law's potential violation of NAFTA provisions (*New York Times* 1996b).[21] Mexico showed similar misgivings and asked to join Canadian-U.S. talks on the issue (*New York Times* 1996b).

Even more important, the Helms-Burton measure, formally known as the Cuban Liberty and Democratic Solidarity Act (*New York Times* 1996a), gave rise to recriminations elsewhere in the hemisphere. Leaders of the Caribbean community voiced their opposition to the extraterritorial provisions of the law at a meeting in Grenada in March 1996 (*Los Angeles Times* 1996), and in a display of near unanimity, members of the Organization of American States passed a resolution in June 1996 rebuking the United States for this extension of the economic embargo against Cuba (*New York Times* 1996c). The resolution was directed against "all laws that 'obstruct international trade and investment' or 'the free movement of persons'"(*New York Times* 1996c).[22]

On the whole, the momentum toward NAFTA expansion appeared somewhat diminished on the eve of the U.S. presidential election of 1996.

Conclusion

The attitude of the U.S. Congress on hemispheric free trade, which has received scant attention from scholars, was ambivalent during the period 1988–1996. Prior to 1994, members of Congress, most of whom also seemed committed to multilateralism, tended to endorse regionalism in the Americas enthusiastically, as their bipartisan vote in favor of the 1988 Free Trade Agreement with Canada clearly demonstrated. Basically, this accord must be viewed in light of the special relationship between the two neighbors and the transformations taking place in the world system during the 1980s. Although congressional support for the North American Free Trade Agreement was less extensive in 1993—especially in the House, where several Democratic representatives from the older industrial states of the Northeast feared job losses for U.S. workers—the passage of this accord was not surprising. In fact, NAFTA was backed by many prominent and influential groups in U.S. society, as numerous Republican and Democratic members of Congress were well aware.

The congressional attitude toward free trade was less supportive during the post-NAFTA years. Indeed, in spite of some promising signs, the 1994–1996 period was not particularly favorable for the promotion of regionalism in the Western Hemisphere. The Miami summit and its follow-up meetings in Denver and Cartagena provoked little openly positive reaction in the legislative branch, and anti-NAFTA speeches, largely fueled by the Mexican peso crisis of December 1994, were frequent on Capitol Hill. Undoubtedly, Congress's refusal to renew President Clinton's fast-track authority concerning Chile is the best illustration of the wave of coolness observed during these years. This refusal also exemplifies the key role of Congress in the evolution of regionalism in the Americas.

In spite of the uncertainties of this period and the detrimental effects of the Helms-Burton law, I nonetheless believe that the momentum generated by the Miami summit is not seriously threatened for the future, at least as far as the United States and its legislative branch are concerned. In fact, the trend toward regionalism in the Western Hemisphere could even get a boost from the United States.

On the one hand, President Clinton has continued to announce his willingness to expand NAFTA in the near future. The president, who once stated that "the most powerful country in the world cannot escape the global economy" (*Public Papers of the Presidents of the United States* 1995b: 2160), repeated that "we must include more nations in our partnership" during a visit to Mexico in May 1997 (*New York Times* 1997). It also seems likely that both the business community and the influential newspapers (e.g., the *Wall Street Journal, New York Times, Boston Globe,* and *Los Angeles Times*) that warmly endorsed the December 1992 trade agreement (*Congressional Record* 1995: H4411) will remain committed to the ultimate goal of the Miami summit inasmuch as most economists have argued that NAFTA had little or nothing to do with the Mexican peso crisis (*New York Times* 1995c). Needless to say, Congress, whose composition is subject to change, will take note of this argument, as well as the fact that protectionist interest groups are not alone in pressing for governmental action: liberal trade groups, including producers of high-technology products like semiconductors, telecommunications, and machine tools, are increasingly active in the political arena (Destler 1986: 159). Congress will also take note of the fact that certain Latin American countries have begun talks with the European Union regarding the formation of a joint free trade area (Stern and Paretzky 1996: 221) and that allies such as Mexico and Canada already have free trade deals with Chile (Stern and Paretzky 1996: 216; *Globe and Mail* 1996).

On the other hand, considerations of U.S. presidential politics are less important now that President Clinton is serving his second term in office, an element that will certainly help the hemispheric free trade agenda over the next few years. Indeed, we must not overlook the fact that Congress's refusal to grant fast-track authority to President Clinton in 1995 concerning Chile was also related to a Republican strategy to deny the chief executive a "trade victory" on the eve of an election (*Wall Street Journal* 1995).

In short, I tend to agree with Senate Minority Leader Robert Dole's comment of November 1993 that "the battle for free trade . . . does not end with the passage of the North American Free-Trade Agreement. It is just the beginning" (*Congressional Record* 1993: S16703). Nevertheless, recent developments, such as the Clinton administration's withdrawal in November 1997 of a fast-track bill from a scheduled vote that augured its defeat and the defeat of fast-track trade legislation in the House of Representatives in September 1998 ("Barshefsky Foresees" 1998; "Few Trade Bills" 1998), suggest that some pitfalls are still ahead on the road to greater economic regionalism in the Western Hemisphere.

Notes

I would like to thank Isabelle Poulin, Alexandre Hébert, Annie Laliberté, and my colleagues Gordon Mace, Louis Bélanger, and Donald Fyson, from Laval University, for their invaluable help in preparing this chapter.

1. Interestingly enough, political scientist Ralph Carter has revealed that the U.S. Congress "plays an active role in 73 percent of the significant post–cold war trade cases and gets part of all of its desires reflected in 84 percent of the policy outputs" (Carter 1996: 15–16).

2. As Jerel Rosati has noted:

> Virtually every president has faced major foreign policy setbacks because of the reassertion of Congress. . . . Nixon had Watergate; the Nixon-Ford détente policies toward the Soviet Union were thwarted by congressional concern about Jewish immigration from the Soviet Union and a covert war in Angola; Carter could not get Senate approval for the second round of . . . [SALT II]; and Reagan could not escape the stigma of the Iran-Contra affair. Despite his ultimate triumph in the Persian Gulf War, President George Bush faced a considerable challenge to his policies within Congress before he took the country to war with Iraq in January 1991. (Rosati 1997: 308–309)

3. For instance, 300 protectionist bills were introduced in Congress in 1985 alone (Aho 1988: 181). In fact, several factors can explain the general protectionist sentiment in the 1980s, which was already perceptible during the 1970s. According to I. M. Destler:

> The 1970s and 1980s brought far-reaching changes to the world economy. U.S. firms and workers became much more exposed to foreign competition in both home and overseas markets. The relative position of the United States declined, as European rivals were joined by Asian ones. . . . The rules of the international trading regime, the General Agreement on Tariffs and Trade . . . , grew less effective.

The advanced industrial economies, buffeted by two "oil shocks," entered a period of stagflation, combining rapid price increases with sluggish growth. (Destler 1986: 37)

Interestingly enough, this period differed drastically from the climate of trade liberalization that characterized the two decades after World War II. Destler, incidentally, has noted that such a postwar regime of freer trade, which had strong domestic support, can be attributed to factors such as the Cold War imperative and the United States' economic predominance (Destler 1986: 4–6).

4. For his part, Democratic representative Jim Moody of Wisconsin regretted that the January 1988 accord excluded cultural industries (U.S. House 1988a: 705).

5. Essentially, the term "intermestic policy" is used to designate policy "with both important foreign and domestic ramifications" (Rourke, Carter, and Boyer 1996: 268).

6. Republican senator Ted Stevens of Alaska pointed out that the most important of these bureaucracies, the North American Free Trade Commission, will have twenty-four subbureaucracies (*Congressional Record* 1993: S16352).

7. Donald Riegle declared that

NAFTA, if it passes, will allow Mexican drivers to pick up a load at a Mexican factory and drive directly to their destination anywhere in the United States or Canada. . . . However, there are fundamental differences in the way Mexico regulates trucks and truck drivers and the way the United States regulates them. . . . Mexico doesn't require its trucks to have front brakes. Without them, trucks cannot stop as fast. . . . Mexican drivers can legally drive as long as they want. . . . By contrast, U.S. drivers can only drive up to 10 hours a day, greatly reducing the possibility of fatigue. (*Congressional Record* 1993: S10934)

8. Incidentally, the "neo-isolationism" whose resurgence was linked in part to the end of the Cold War and the neglect of urgent domestic problems in the 1980s largely took the form of an anti-UN campaign (Schlesinger Jr. 1996: 157–160).

9. For example, David Dreier declared that "Ronald Reagan recently wrote an editorial in the *Wall Street Journal* in strong support of the North American Free Trade Agreement, and former President Nixon, who is recognized as a paramount expert in international policy, has strongly supported [NAFTA]" (*Congressional Record* 1993: H6973).

10. Republican representative Joel Hefley of Colorado reported that no less than forty-two of fifty state governors supported NAFTA in mid-November 1993 (*Congressional Record* 1993: H9863).

11. As for the California and Arizona delegations, the vote in favor of NAFTA was respectively 31–21 and 6–0 (*New York Times* 1993a: A20).

12. Five of the 9 (56 percent) Senate opponents to the 1988 agreement were from this region, along with 11 of the 38 (29 percent) senators who had voted against NAFTA.

13. The 55 opponents included 10 representatives from Ohio, 10 from Michigan, 14 from Pennsylvania, and 21 from New York (*New York Times* 1993a: A20).

14. Scholar Peter Trubowitz has defined the "manufacturing belt" as the region comprising New England as well as the Middle Atlantic and Great Lakes regions (Trubowitz 1992: 174).

15. According to Trubowitz, the manufacturing belt's declining competitiveness, a reflection of the increasing mobility of capital and the spread of technology within the United States, is partly tied to the rise of Western Europe and Japan as industrial rivals (Trubowitz 1992: 184).

16. Conversely, the free trade idea seems to have rallied more supporters in the sunbelt since the 1960s. During the NAFTA debate, incidentally, "sunbelt senators" such as Harlan Mathews (Tennessee) and David Pryor (Arkansas) contended that many companies in their respective states supported the deal (*Congressional Record* 1993: S12059–S12060, S14584).

17. In essence, this concept, which is frequently opposed to bilateralism, "means a recognition that major world-wide problems . . . cannot be handled by individual countries making their own policies, but must be dealt with by coordinated efforts and policies developed collectively by many nations" (D. Robertson 1993: 327).

18. He obtained 77 percent of the vote in his district (*New York Times* 1994a: B19).

19. Pro-NAFTA Democratic representatives such as Dan Rostenkowski (Illinois), Peter Hoagland (Nebraska), David Price (North Carolina), and Maria Cantwell (Washington) were all defeated in the midterm elections of November 1994 (*New York Times* 1994a: B18–B19).

20. As journalist Drew Fagan explained, this political scrap revealed the different conceptions prevailing at the White House and on Capitol Hill: "The Clinton administration insists that the fast-track bill should be written broadly enough to include NAFTA labour and environmental side deals that all three NAFTA members want expanded to Chile. . . . However, Republican members of the House of Representatives are using the fast-track debate to press their philosophy that the side deals should not be part of the trade negotiations" (*Globe and Mail* 1995).

21. Canadian officials were particularly upset that the measure sponsored by Republican senator Jesse Helms of North Carolina and Republican representative Dan Burton of Indiana attempted to extend U.S. law to other jurisdictions where it "could interfere with companies engaged in legitimate business" (*New York Times* 1996b). In fact, the Helms-Burton law, among other things, "allows American citizens to sue foreigners and foreign companies that 'act to manage, lease, possess, use or hold an interest in' property confiscated by the Cuban Government from people who are now American citizens" (*New York Times* 1996b).

22. It is worth noting that the Helms-Burton act permits the United States "to bar entry to . . . foreign executives whose companies do business in Cuba" (*New York Times* 1996b).

7

Brazil's Alternative Vision

Maria Regina Soares de Lima

Is Brazil an exceptional case within the Americas? Throughout much of its history as an independent state, Brazil cultivated a special alliance with the United States and turned its back on the rest of Latin America. Negotiations to create a hemispheric free trade area have raised possibilities for change in the practice and foundations of Brazil's foreign policy. However, as in any process of economic integration, aside from its depth and degree of formalization, the exercise is marked by uncertainty. At stake are issues affecting society as a whole and affecting it in an uneven fashion. This uncertainty precludes any definitive conclusions as to the outcome of the process under way. However, the manner in which it has unfolded to date is suggestive of the limits and possibilities of regional foreign policy within the novel context of hemispheric regionalism.

In this chapter I focus on Brazilian foreign policy in relation to the process of hemispheric regionalism presently under way. In the first section I summarize the history of Brazil's efforts at regional cooperation and its relations with the United States. In the second I describe the current strategy for hemispheric regionalism. In the third I analyze the rationale for Brazil's current strategy. In the final section I discuss the limits and possibilities of Brazilian strategy and its consequences for the future of continental regionalism.

Brazilian Regional Cooperation and Relations with the United States: Historical Background

Historically, two distinct regionalist perspectives coexisted in the Americas: the Western Hemisphere Idea incarnating the U.S. vision of a regional

133

system, which is examined by Gordon Mace in Chapter 2 of this volume, and the Bolivarian Vision, which sought to integrate the continent without U.S. participation. After its independence from Portugal in 1822, Brazil expressed only mild interest in these two models of Pan-Americanism. Not only was the Brazilian monarchy's foreign policy oriented toward Europe during the nineteenth century, but Brazil's system of government was at variance with the republican standard enshrined in the rest of Latin America.

Under the republic, Brazil's foreign policy orientation shifted away from close relations with England to a new emphasis on ties with the United States. First conceived as a paradigm during Baron Rio Branco's term as minister of foreign affairs (1902–1912), the special alliance with the United States endured, with some variations in emphasis, into the early 1960s. Intended as a pragmatic means to defend Brazil's regional and world interests, this special relationship was predicated on the acceptance of the United States as a global hegemonic power in the Western Hemisphere and a focal point for Brazilian foreign policy. The United States was seen as a tacit ally that would enhance Brazil's bargaining power vis-à-vis its Hispanic neighbors.

Since the late 1960s, Brazil's relations with the United States and the Latin American countries have been influenced by economic and political variables. Politically, the size of the Brazilian economy compared with those of other countries in the region has been an inhibiting factor for regional cooperation. Hispanic countries perceived a potential threat in Brazil's massive geoeconomic dimensions, and Brazil's own elites seemed to sustain the belief that the country was destined to have its own independent future.

Economic factors also influenced the decision to abandon special relations with the United States when Brazil's military regime undertook its great power project in the 1970s. The expansion of industrial capacity, diversification of foreign economic relations, and the pursuit of military objectives such as the development of an indigenous armaments industry and the quest for self-sufficiency in sensitive technologies were the major motivations for Brazil's foreign policy reorientation in the 1970s. Nuclear nonproliferation, trade issues, population control, environmental protection, human rights violations, territorial waters, North-South issues, and nuclear energy figured among the more contentious items on its bilateral agenda with the United States during the 1970s.

The military nature of the Brazilian political regime also influenced Brazil's outlook on regional cooperation. Following the 1964 military coup, which marked Brazil's renewed participation in the hemispheric security system, Brazil came to be viewed by other Latin American countries as the region's subimperialist power and the preferential ally of the United States. Although Washington had initially welcomed Brazil's military regime, changes in U.S. foreign policy priorities ushered in by the Carter administration, which was manifestly concerned with human rights and nuclear nonproliferation, were matched by a more assertive Brazilian foreign policy. This led to changes in U.S. attitudes toward Brazil. Delinking domestic politics from foreign affairs, which were to be conducted according to a new globalist orientation, Brazil's military regime sought to explore a European option for the acquisition of sensitive technologies and as a market for raw materials and commodities exports. It also decided to target Latin America and Africa as potential customers for Brazilian manufactured products and approach the Middle East with an eye toward guaranteeing its oil supplies.

Brazil's transition from military to civilian rule and its increasing international economic vulnerability in the mid-1980s led to a change in this globalist orientation. Cooperation with the countries of the Southern Cone became a priority in Brazilian foreign policy after the 1986 Economic Integration and Cooperation Program with Argentina, which was followed by the creation of the Southern Cone Common Market (Mercosur) in 1991.[1] In addition, awareness of the growing costs of policy conflict with Washington led diplomatic, political, and business elites to a relative consensus on the undesirability of a permanent negative agenda with the United States. Brazilian authorities have sought to restore more positive relations by readjusting policies on economic and industrial issues such as trade liberalization, privatization, economic deregulation, computer technology, and intellectual property rights, as well as security matters and, last but not least, such global issues as human rights, nuclear nonproliferation, and the environment. Brazil, unlike Argentina, has not gone so far as to push for a sort of peripheral partnership with the United States. However, good relations with Washington have became a priority for the Fernando Henrique Cardoso administration, particularly since Brazil achieved economic stabilization. Although the desire to limit damages was important in fueling these initiatives, foreign policy priorities—chiefly Brazil's aspiration to obtain a permanent seat on the UN Security Council—also played a role.

In any case, Brazil's regional cooperation and relations with the United States now involve a much more diverse set of domestic actors representing new societal pressures and transnational alliances. Although the foreign ministry is responsible for conducting Brazil's external relations, economic liberalization and civilian rule have tended to expand the scope of the actors concerned, and international postures have become less homogeneous as a result (Hirst and Soares de Lima 1994). At the same time, internal convergence between foreign policy interests and domestic economic and political interests have tended to increase Brazil's bargaining power in international negotiations. Such convergence is present in the current debate over hemispheric regionalism.

Brazil's Current Strategy Toward Hemispheric Regionalism

As Gordon Mace notes in Chapter 2, the current U.S.-led project for hemispheric regionalism retains certain similarities to the original Western Hemisphere Idea. The same cannot be said for existing subregional experiments, which not only differ among themselves but also lack the political component of *latinidad* contained in the erstwhile Bolivarian Vision. However, with the renewed U.S. hemispheric initiative launched at the Miami summit, distinct positions reflecting divergent national interests in the United States and Brazil/Mercosur have begun to emerge.

Despite these differences, there is also a clear convergence between current arrangements. The subregional experiments share the logic of economic liberalization with the hemispheric proposal, a departure from state-led, inward-oriented models. A certain consensus also exists between the region's government and business elites, for whom the failure of Latin America's previous development model spawned the conditions for the new regionalism. However, this apparent similarity in viewpoints is not necessarily a precursor to the convergence and eventual disappearance of subregional arrangements and the subsequent hegemony of the hemispheric proposal under U.S. leadership. Indeed, this outcome represents everything Brazil would rather avoid. It is for this reason that negotiations between the United States and Brazil/Mercosur—the second largest subregional arrangement after the North American Free Trade Agreement (NAFTA)—constitute the most significant process for the definition of the course of regionalism in the Americas.

Brazilian strategy regarding regionalism in the Americas has been guided by two main principles: (1) a strong preference for multilateralism over regionalism on account of fairly diversified markets—notably, the relative importance of U.S., Latin American, and European Union involvement in Brazilian trade and investment—and concerns about possible trade deviations resulting from a regionalistic strategy; and (2) a preference for subregional integration—namely Mercosur—over any U.S.-led hemispheric arrangement.[2]

Brazil's preference for multilateralism, its decision to maintain policy-making autonomy in economic affairs, and the sheer volume of its economy in comparison with its Mercosur partners resulted in a number of unilateral economic policy steps that have bred resentment among other Mercosur member states. Nevertheless, Brazil's marked preference for Mercosur over a hemispheric arrangement has led to a positive linkage between processes at the subregional and hemispheric levels. Every U.S. move aimed at deepening or intensifying the hemispheric experiment has resulted in the reinforcement of Brazil's commitment to Mercosur and greater emphasis on cooperative strategies designed to replace unilateral ones. This pattern was set with the genesis of the Mercosur project itself, which can be viewed as a response to the anticipated effects of NAFTA on the Southern Cone economies. Brazil explicitly pursued foreign policy initiatives in view of strengthening regional cooperation after George Bush announced the Enterprise for the Americas Initiative. Brazil's efforts led to an institutional solution geared toward ensuring a unified Mercosur position, a solution that took the shape of a bilateral agreement between the United States and Mercosur known as the 4+1 Agreement (Nunes Amorim 1991).

Since 1994, when the Clinton administration once again set hemispheric integration as a priority, Brazil has reiterated similar concerns about the Free Trade Area of the Americas (FTAA), especially since FTAA negotiations happened to coincide with Bill Clinton's failure to secure fast-track authority from Congress to speed Chile's proposed adhesion to NAFTA.

Brazil's foreign policy actors tend to fear Argentina's opportunistic behavior each time the United States makes positive gestures toward hemispheric integration. Such behavior on Argentina's part is viewed as weakening the Argentinean commitment to Mercosur, thereby decreasing Brazil's bargaining power in hemispheric negotiations. At the same time, given that regionalism has not been an economic priority for Brazil, its diplomats are unable to avoid the fallout from unilateral economic policy decisions affecting regional partners. Economic policy, foreign as well as domestic, is not only set but also executed by the Ministry for the Economy and the Central Bank. Brazil's Ministry of Foreign Relations plays only a marginal role in this area, as does the Ministry for Industry and Commerce (MIC), which is sensitive to the interests of industrial sectors. The Ministry of Foreign Relations has led regional cooperation initiatives since their inception in the form of the Brazil-Argentina Economic Integration and Cooperation Program in the mid-1980s. More recently, the Ministry for Industry and Commerce has taken on a more active role as economic considerations become increasingly important in Southern Cone cooperation.

The foreign ministry still plays a significant role in conducting regional and trade negotiations. This role is enhanced by the MIC's lack of international experience, which can be attributed to the nature of Brazil's economy, which was relatively closed until quite recently. When positions converge, as they have with the FTAA, the influence and bargaining power of the foreign office are strengthened within the governmental decision-making apparatus. Unlike the Ministry for Industry and Commerce, the foreign ministry is an agency with few domestic clienteles. It is further removed from the business world than the more protectionist MIC, which has traditionally maintained close ties with industrial interests. Protectionist inclinations at the foreign ministry not only are weaker than they have been in the past but also tend to be motivated by ideology when they do manifest themselves. When an occasional protectionist policy decision conflicts with Brazil's obligations before the World Trade Organization (WTO), or when such policies give rise to problems with Mercosur partners—as was the case with recent trade restrictions on automobile imports—the foreign ministry tends to be less protectionist than the MIC. In such instances, the foreign ministry is more than likely to find allies within the Ministry for the Economy. Despite their fears of possible mercantilist and protectionist effects, Ministry for the Economy officials favor economic liberalization and regionalism because they help open up the Brazilian economy.

Brazil's strategy on hemispheric regionalism has remained virtually unchanged since President Bush announced the Enterprise for the Americas Initiative. At the time, two objectives were perceived as crucial: preventing Argentina's defection and guaranteeing a unified position among the four Mercosur partners—Brazil, Argentina, Uruguay, and Paraguay—to enhance bargaining power vis-à-vis Washington. Later, when proposals for the creation of a hemispheric free trade area were mooted—and especially after the establishment of NAFTA—it became clear that Brazil's position differed from that of most other countries in the region. Unlike its neighbors, Brazil did not envision Mercosur as a step in the direction of hemispheric integration.

Prior to the launch of the FTAA initiative in 1994, discussion in Brazil centered on the advantages and disadvantages of joining NAFTA. Brazilian diplomats, scholars, politicians, civil servants, and businesspeople tended to stress the disadvantages of such an arrangement. From an economic standpoint, they argued that Brazil should prioritize negotiations with Mercosur and other blocs such as the European Union, Brazil's largest trade partner. The idea was that Brazil should give priority to the consolidation of the subregional arrangement, a strategy that would leave it in a stronger bargaining position in future negotiations. In light of the multifaceted character of Brazil's integration in the global economy, they also raised arguments against the supposed inevitability of eventual membership in some of the existing megablocs along with questions about the liabilities Brazil would incur in joining regionalist initiatives.

From a political standpoint, these same sources argued that NAFTA membership would have the following negative effects on Brazilian interests: a considerable reduction in foreign policy autonomy on international initiatives that could affect U.S. interests; a drastic decrease in policymaking freedom on such contentious bilateral issues as intellectual property, services and investments, environmental protection, science and technology, and macroeconomic policy; and, finally, in light of the absence of institutional arrangements within the hemispheric integration model of the time, an asymmetric bargaining position favorable to the United States (Departamento de Integração Latino-Americana/MRE 1993).

The main difference between then and now is the change in tone in bilateral relations. In contrast to President Fernando Henrique Cardoso's current government, the Itamar Franco regime (1992–1994) saw relations with the United States hit their lowest point of the decade. The deteriorating relationship was marked in particular by the failure of U.S. policymakers to grasp the reasons for Brazil's reluctance to follow the example of other Latin American countries that were taking drastic measures to achieve economic stabilization and full political compliance with nuclear nonproliferation regimes. With the advent of economic stabilization under the Cardoso administration, bilateral relations shifted significantly. The Economic Stabilization Plan, or Real Plan, was implemented in three successive phases starting in June 1993 with the launching of a new currency—the real—in July 1994. Aiming to control inflation, it consisted of a monetary reform anchored in a stable exchange rate and efforts to reach fiscal equilibrium; to speed up privatization of state enterprises; to control domestic demand by means of high interest rates; and to keep prices low with trade liberalization. Not only did the Real Plan prove effective in eliminating a critical inflationary situation, but the Cardoso administration was also able to pursue successfully the economic reforms it had set for itself.[3]

The government also sought to reduce bilateral tensions, especially in the areas of intellectual property and sensitive technologies. It joined the Missile Technology Control Regime and, in mid-1997, announced its adhesion to the Nuclear Nonproliferation Treaty. In the theater of regional foreign policy, the project for the creation of a South American Free Trade Association (SAFTA) was shelved, at least in the form envisioned by the preceding administration. An irritant to the bilateral relationship, the original SAFTA project was viewed by the United States as a demonstration of Brazil's tendency to overestimate its international leverage.

It is curious that, in spite of the aforementioned changes in foreign policy, Brazil's posture in relation to hemispheric integration has remained unaltered. Changes in strategy may have occurred, not least in reaction to a process outside of Brazil's control, but the country's basic position has not shifted from the one set forth during the 1990s, when hemispheric integration became part of the Brazilian agenda for economic diplomacy. The fate of SAFTA provides a telling sign of the continuity of regional policies. The shelving of the political initiative to create a South American free trade area marked the beginning of the northward expansion of Mercosur, with the adhesion of Chile, Bolivia, and Venezuela. Likewise, the Mercosur–European Union framework agreement aimed outright at "maintaining equilibrium in the Americas" (Almeida-Medeiros 1995).

The main change in foreign policy was the assessment in official Brazilian circles that the FTAA process would prove largely irreversible provided the United States could muster the political will to see it through. At the Summit of the Americas in 1994, Brazil therefore agreed to work toward the creation of a hemispheric free trade area by the year 2005. This reversed an earlier and recurring attitude that the United States had perceived as a strategy to avoid negotiations and the concessions that would have to be made. Underlying Brazil's acceptance was the recognition that any attempts to obstruct the process at the time would leave it isolated. In practice, however, the strategy for negotiations has been to attempt to stall as much as possible the actual onset of tariff and nontariff negotiations.

From the Brazilian standpoint, uncertainty about the ability of the U.S. executive branch to move forward on the FTAA centers on the U.S. Congress, as evidenced by the White House's difficulties in obtaining congressional ratification for NAFTA and congressional refusal to grant fast-track authority for NAFTA expansion. Brazilian policymakers see U.S. congressional resistance as a factor that weakens Washington's negotiating position because, in the absence of fast-track authority, there are no assurances that official agreements entered into by international players will in fact be implemented.[4] It is curious that the erosion of Washington's bargaining capacity has been accompanied by a hardening of its negotiating stance in favor of a swifter and more encompassing timetable that fails to take existing integration initiatives into account. As a result, differences between the two countries' negotiating positions have become more visible and have favored Brazilian leadership by allowing for the agglutination of divergent positions.

Brazil's position differs from that set forth in the U.S. proposal on such issues as a timetable, the level of commitment, the format, and the scope of an agreement. Brazil's preference is for slower integration, with tariff reductions to begin in 2005. It has outlined a three-phase negotiation process: The first phase, extending until 2000, would basically consist of business facilitation measures, or measures designed to reduce transaction costs to economic agents; the second, to take place between 2001 and 2002, would deal with issues such as harmonizing rules and disciplines, the elimination of unjustified nontariff measures, and the definition of a dispute settlement mechanism; the third, to last until 2005, would cover market access, including liberalization of the service sector.[5]

Brazil favors negotiating the FTAA as a single undertaking using a building block methodology based on negotiations between blocs. The United States, for its part, prefers country-to-country negotiations, which effectively inverse the order of priority for the issues to be negotiated. Whereas Brazil/Mercosur favors initiating negotiations on such issues as agricultural subsidies, dispute settlement, and technical norms, the United States has prioritized issues such as market access for goods and services, intellectual property, and government procurement—issues that in the Brazilian view ought to be taken up at the end of the negotiations. In addition to promoting a swifter negotiating process, the United States has stated that it would like its priority issues settled by 2000. Generally speaking, the United States favors a "most comprehensive" agreement approach that would establish FTAA disciplinary norms along NAFTA lines, whereas the Mercosur proposal excludes such U.S. agenda items as environmental and labor relations standards (Abreu 1997).

Brazil's strategy in delaying the FTAA for as long as possible—or at least in pressing for a slower pace in negotiations—is eminently pragmatic. It seeks to gain time to complete its own market-oriented reforms first. This would allow it to upgrade its own industrial base and enhance its competitiveness in preparation for a vast, FTAA-scale trade liberalization without incurring major internal costs. The economic arguments invoked by Brazil to defer priority on the FTAA are similar to those raised in the past: The sheer volume of the Brazilian economy, in contrast with that of its smaller neighbors, would tend to flatten the benefits accruing from integration into a free trade zone. Moreover, given the diversification of its trade relations, it would be advisable for Brazil to stick to its policies of economic openness and extend eventual trade concessions to all partners rather than cast its lot with a regionally preferential agreement such as the FTAA. Politically, Brazil disagrees with the U.S. proposal casting the FTAA as an extension of NAFTA, a prospect that would entail setting disciplinary rules and standards for tariff and nontariff barriers at levels both more comprehensive and more restrictive than the prevailing WTO standards to which Brazil currently adheres.

Aside from the fundamental continuity in Brazilian strategy, what is particularly noteworthy is the consensus among diplomats, scholars, policymakers, the business community, and opinion leaders regarding Brazil's official position on FTAA negotiations. In a departure from past practice, Brazilian foreign policymakers have explicitly delinked bilateral Brazil-U.S. relations from regional negotiations. The prevailing orientation regarding bilateral relations is to develop a positive agenda with the United States despite differences over the FTAA. Although divergences with the United States are almost always politically charged, policymakers have sought to minimize differences so as not to enlarge the scope of conflict.[6] And unlike the situation prior to FTAA, Brazil's negotiating stance has become more consistent since it gained the support of its business community. Brazil has thus been able to buttress its diplomatic arguments with the concrete backing of private interests. This has proved to be a considerable asset at the bargaining table because in the past the United States regularly alleged that Brazilian foreign policy positions were based on ideological principles rather than on the concrete interests of the business sector.

Business interests in the most competitive sectors aside, Brazilian industrialists who support Brazil's negotiating position would rather play for time so as to shore up their affairs within Mercosur and adjust to the pressures of a more open market. Market access as well as nontariff barriers have been the issues most likely to mobilize the business community. Exporters are especially concerned with slow growth in exports to the United States, and they single out restrictions to access in sectors like steel as examples of U.S. trade policy outgrowths devised in reaction to Brazil's alleged dumping and export subsidy practices. In fact, the most immediate FTAA benefits for broad sectors of the Brazilian export community would be to minimize U.S. protectionism and promote the reasonable harmonization of industrial and incentives policies. Nevertheless, the prevailing consensus is that a more deliberate pace in establishing this arrangement would buy the time these sectors require to be able to compete on equal terms with their counterparts, particularly those in the United States and Canada. As for the already competitive producers in the agricultural sector, they stand to benefit directly from the FTAA because they are significantly penalized by U.S. protectionist practices.[7]

The same divergences observable between governments have been echoed in discussions between various national business communities. Just as Mercosur businesses, led by Brazil, prefer a gradual pace for negotiations, their Canadian, U.S., and Mexican counterparts would rather speed up the establishment of the FTAA and concurrent negotiations on all related topics. When the Business Forum failed to reach a consensus on these issues, the report drafted for assessment by the Ministries for Trade at the Belo Horizonte ministerial meeting in May 1997 ended up voicing both positions ("Divergências" 1997).

Although the Business Forum was convened as part of official FTAA negotiations, the creation of a similar mechanism for labor unions was rejected by certain participating governments, although the Brazilian foreign ministry supported the participation of organized labor in an effort to expand its domestic base of political support. As a result, labor union participation in the debate on FTAA negotiations has been considerably limited. Labor unions have been especially fearful of the FTAA, which they associate with a process of economic globalization that is likely to aggravate problems of unemployment and social exclusion. Moreover, for union leaders, the sharp social and economic disparities between the North and the rest of the Americas will not only make it difficult to reach a fair and balanced agreement but also prevent competition on equal terms. In addition, the exclusion of workers from the decisionmaking process is seen as an "absence of democracy" that will diminish the legitimacy of the decisions made ("Sindicatos" 1997; "Sindicalistas" 1997).

In their assessment of the U.S. negotiating position, Brazilian negotiators stress offensive and defensive elements. In offensive terms, the FTAA would amount to an extension of U.S. trade policy, albeit with a lesser degree of unilateralism, in the sense that it aims to establish de facto liberalization of trade, services, and investments in the region. In defensive terms, the United States would view Mercosur growth and its agreements with other entities such as the European Union as harmful to U.S. interests and the consolidation of bilateral agreements between blocs or countries on the South American continent as a threat to its primacy in the area. North American scholars agree with this assessment and have argued that the Clinton administration's focus on U.S. domestic issues has left the United States effectively absent from a region that currently constitutes one of the world's most promising emerging markets, particularly in the case of the southern republics. It is interesting that both U.S. and Brazilian observers attribute each other with self-interested economic objectives. Generally speaking, government elites in Brazil view NAFTA and the FTAA as mercantilist strategies devised by the United States in order to pursue its own economic interests. Among the informed public, few consider the hemispheric proposals advanced by the United States as a step in the direction of world trade liberalization.[8]

Explanations for Current Brazilian Strategy

Certain theories of regionalism may be used to evaluate the possible explanations for Brazil's current regional strategy. In a recent work, Andrew Hurrell (1995b) classifies these theories according to the level of analysis of their respective explanations: systemic, regional, or domestic. Although these approaches deal with the phenomenon of regionalism rather than foreign policy per se, they are useful in identifying the factors that can influence the regionalist strategy of any nation, which is why I shall employ them to discuss the case of Brazil.

In the case of regionalism, systemic theories promise a high analytical yield, since the simultaneity of regional cooperation processes at certain periods, including the one currently under way, highlights the weaknesses of explanations based on domestic variables. Systemic explanations aim to account for converging preferences among states and assume that the demand for regional cooperation is identical, regardless of a country's domestic characteristics. According to Hurrell, the two most frequent systemic explanations are neorealist arguments and hypotheses based on structural interdependence and globalization. When applied to foreign policy, they generate diametrically opposed explanations of each country's degree of freedom in regional cooperation.

The neorealist explanation of regionalism stresses the pressures and opportunities derived from geopolitical and geoeconomic transformations. Mindful of the assumption of self-help that is characteristic of this approach, it views regionalism as a neomercantilist strategy aimed at reducing eventual external constraints and obtaining more favorable conditions for international political and economic competition (Hurrell 1995b: 48). Whereas the neorealist explanation emphasizes the dimension of choice, however limited, in foreign policy, the globalist explanation is more deterministic in its emphasis on the compulsory nature of choice and the disciplinary changes regional arrangements impose upon domestic policy. From this standpoint, globalization exerts pressure toward homogenization and convergence around market-oriented policies. Regional cooperation policies are seen as attempts to effectively lock particular countries into an overall strategy of economic liberalization and deregulation, which, in the final analysis, serves to buttress neoliberal reforms.

If regionalist strategies imply a reduction in a state's freedom of action with regard to other states, the systemic approach has the merit of highlighting the changes in external parameters that explain why states choose to reduce their freedom to act. Surprisingly, the interpretation of systemic change is distinct, as are the implications derived regarding probable strategies. From the neorealist perspective, these implications are typically offensive; from the globalist perspective, defensive. Moreover, if systemic perspectives are useful for circumscribing moments of change in strategy, they are insufficient to indicate the direction of foreign policy change because this direction depends on the response of each state in question.

Brazil's current strategy toward hemispheric regionalism suggests the reach and limitations of systemic explanations, because it combines both offensive and defensive elements. The former are present in the view that the regionalist orientation constitutes a change to or adaptation of previous development strategies and international orientations but maintains connections to the past in the form of a strong autonomist orientation and aspirations to a greater international role in a world where economic competitiveness has become crucial. This orientation draws support from sectors of the state bureaucracy, especially the foreign ministry and the armed forces. It is also backed by industrial interests, especially those such as capital goods industries and industrial labor unions that emerged under the auspices of the protected, state-sponsored model.

The orientation toward deeper integration with the global economy draws support from the economic bureaucracy responsible for macroeconomic policy (and stewardship of economic stabilization), as well as from the financial community and highly competitive emerging sectors like agribusiness, which have grown and developed on the margins of state support. These advocates of deeper integration prefer hemispheric regionalism to subregional arrangements (namely, Mercosur, which is viewed as a second-rate alternative for achieving the true goals of economic and trade liberalization).

The theories that Hurrell classifies as regional analysis—neofunctionalism, neoliberal institutionalism, and constructivism—are less useful for foreign policy analysis because they are geared toward explaining the dynamics of existing regionalisms rather than their origins. However, current hemispheric regionalism does not represent the institutional continuation of preexisting subregional arrangements, whether as a functionalist spillover or the reinforcement of a preexisting regional identity or awareness. In the Brazilian case, motivations located at the regional level appear to have little explanatory power. For reasons already mentioned, regionalism is a second-best strategy for Brazil regarding the institutionalization of multilateral arenas and rules. Moreover, Brazil's identification with Latin America—or with the Americas as a whole, for that matter—is relatively fragile in the face of the inward-looking interests that have played such a powerful role in determining Brazilian behavior.

Neoliberal institutionalism appears to have some relevance for the case at hand, if only in elucidating the lesser priority accorded the regional arena than the multilateral arena. According to this perspective, regionalist strategies aim to solve dilemmas of collective action in the face of externalities and mutual interdependencies by reducing transactional costs, diminishing asymmetries of information, and facilitating intraregional linkages (Hurrell 1995b: 63; Keohane 1984). As Stephen Krasner (1993) has demonstrated, perspectives developed on the basis of dilemmas of cooperation (i.e., situations in which cooperation is difficult or nonexistent owing to opportunistic incentives for free-rider behavior) focus only on the benefits of cooperation and fail to account for the more problematic issue of the distributive aspects of cooperation.

From this perspective, Brazil—which, unlike the United States, is not a *demandeur* of stricter rules in international economic regimes—prefers that trade regimes be negotiated in arenas such as the WTO, where a larger membership prevents the adoption of more restrictive trade rules. This preference is why the United States has pursued the FTAA, an arrangement with fewer and weaker members, as a first step toward greater international regulation in areas of its own interest, such as environmental and labor standards and intellectual property rights. What matters for Brazil, and other countries as well, is the nature of the rules and negotiating arenas, because they have different distributive consequences.

Among the domestic perspectives mentioned by Hurrell, an analysis of regime type and democratization processes is the most germane to the case at hand. Democratization of Southern Cone political regimes eroded Brazil's previous "defensive positionalism" in relation to Argentina, opening the way for subregional cooperation (Soares de Lima 1996: 156). As for hemispheric regionalism, Latin American democratization appears to be more significant for the U.S. regionalist stance than for the stance of the Latin American countries. It is unlikely that the United States would lead the formation of a free trade area in the Americas if the region were ruled predominantly by military regimes. However, political democratization may be important in cases where there is opposition to government regional policies. In a context of democratic normality, opposition and divergence can play itself out in the partisan political arena.

The remaining perspectives—state coherence and policy convergence—are less useful for explaining Brazil's regionalist strategy. The former establishes certain conditions necessary for integration and is thus less capable of distinguishing between specific individual strategies. The latter posits a relationship between the dynamics of regional integration and the convergence of domestic policy preferences among states located in a given geographic area (Hurrell 1995b: 70).

One could therefore argue that Latin America's previous import-substitution development strategies hindered the deepening of regional integration by penalizing exports and eliminating intraregional economic complementarities. In this view, the crisis of the closed, state-sponsored economic model eventually led Latin American countries to converge and adopt the liberal economic policies driving the new regionalism in the Americas. Like the preceding argument, this line of reasoning fails to take into account domestic specificities and assumes that the convergence of national policies occurred in a homogeneous fashion. This approach resembles the predictions about the effects of globalization described earlier.

Situated at the domestic level, the argument emphasizes the use of a regionalist strategy by domestic actors who aim to consolidate market-oriented reforms implemented by governments seeking to change economic models. From this perspective, the importance of Mexico's NAFTA strategy would lie not so much in the resulting economic liberalization but rather in "the ways in which the treaty locks Mexico into the particular set of domestic economic policies and insulates its economic reforms from future domestic political interference" (Hurrell 1995b: 71). In the case of Brazil, as I have already observed, this explanation would be only partially true, because the sectors with the political initiative in this process prefer not to handcuff themselves to a well-defined strategy. However, the argument does have the merit of acknowledging the interests of political and economic actors who stand to benefit from systemic incentives (globalization).

On the basis of the foregoing discussion, it is possible to link the different levels of analysis in the explanation of Brazil's regionalist strategy. Systemic parameters are of fundamental importance because they constitute the economic constraints that led to the crisis of the previous economic model. Geopolitical transformations are also important because they generate uncertainty among actors about possible configurations in a new international order. Changes in economic parameters penalize domestic actors who benefited from the earlier model while rewarding other actors who, for a variety of reasons, are able to forgo (or no longer require) the incentives available under the previous development strategy. In the Brazilian case—the most successful experiment in state-led development among peripheral countries—the former actors have maintained their political clout independent of economic changes. It is the inclusion of political variables related to government policy orientations and winning coalitions that explains why Brazil's strategy possesses offensive and defensive characteristics, an outcome that a systemic explanation would be unable to account for.

Brazil's strategy is offensive because the politically dominant coalition was constituted in the shadows of the previous development strategy. The defensive component results from the acceptance by these same actors of the need to change the model in light of global economic and geopolitical transformations. Their preference, however, is for gradual change over a longer period. Those who advocate deeper and swifter economic change and who are more inclined to welcome the immediate acceptance of hemispheric regionalism are not the actors currently setting the initiative for Brazil's regionalist strategy.

From a political standpoint, Brazil's current strategy reflects the victory of the foreign ministry's position on regionalism. In fact, the ministry remains the chief government actor in the hemispheric policy field. Diplomats begin with the premise of U.S. power, especially within the hemisphere, a premise that calls for a nonconfrontational strategy. However, in their scenarios for a new world order, they stress multipolarity and the opportunities it affords for Brazil's international ascent.

A certain measure of autonomy in relation to the United States—something Mexico forfeited by joining NAFTA—is also seen as important insofar as it allows for the maintenance of an independent dialogue with extrahemispheric powers in Europe and Asia (especially Japan and China). One can speak, therefore, of a connection between Brazil's current stance on hemispheric issues and its aspiration to a permanent seat on the UN Security Council.

Brazilian diplomats justify this gradualist strategy as a pragmatic political way to ensure that Brazil is not limited exclusively to the FTAA theater while other processes of negotiation and cooperation are under way. They point in particular to Mercosur's movement in the direction of a common market arrangement, the creation of a South American free trade area through agreements between Mercosur and its regional neighbors, the establishment of closer economic ties between Mercosur and the European Union, progress in multilateral negotiations in the WTO, and Russia and China's recent adhesion to the WTO (Abdenur 1997: 67).[9]

Given that Brazil has already promoted a wide, unilateral opening of its markets, diplomatic representatives also believe it is not in Brazil's interest to negotiate new concessions with the United States in exchange for U.S. elimination of "anomalous" nontariff barriers targeting such Brazilian exports to the United States as orange juice, textiles, steel, and shoes. In their view, removal of these barriers ought to precede any future negotiations on access to the Brazilian market (Abdenur 1997: 68–69).

All of the factors examined in this section are important. Along with Brazil's continental dimensions, which tend to generate reduced incentives for regionalization because of its relative size and potential market, they explain why Brazil has adopted a foreign policy of restraint in the face of hemispheric regionalism. In this sense, albeit for different reasons, Brazil and the United States have both pursued the same objectives for strategic regionalism in the Americas.

Limits and Possibilities of Brazilian Foreign Policy and Future Consequences for Hemispheric Regionalism

The first consequence of the FTAA for Brazilian foreign policy has been to increase considerably the societal or interest-based component in foreign policy formation. As I discussed earlier, Brazilian strategy has relied on support from the business community, which actively participated in shaping the country's negotiating position.

Another consequence has been to increase political coordination between Brazil and other Mercosur members, especially Argentina, and, concurrently, to extend the degree of joint regional action. Following the Miami summit in 1994, Brazil helped lead efforts to develop a common platform through the formation of the Rio Group, thereby acknowledging the need for more time in establishing a free trade area. Brazil also advocated that Mercosur and other subregional agreements be accepted as building blocks for future hemispheric liberalization (Abdenur 1997: 63).

At the same time, the FTAA process has exposed some of the inconsistencies in Brazil's position toward the Southern Cone, allowing divergences to surface between it and its Mercosur partners. For instance, Brazil's demands for greater institutionalization within a future FTAA show the ambiguity of its opposition to pressures for institutionalization within Mercosur (Machado and Motta Veiga 1997: 4). And the implementation of a hemispheric free trade area will further expose Brazilian protectionism to Brazil's Mercosur partners, perhaps forcing it to make concessions (Abreu 1997).

Be that as it may, the new economic realities of Mercosur have been Brazil's main asset in negotiations. Without Mercosur, Brazil's position would be weakened. At the same time, the density of ties between partners provides an assurance that these economic realities will be taken into account when the partners design their respective continental negotiating strategies.[10]

Evidently, any speculation about the consequences of current foreign policy on the future of hemispheric regionalism must first take into account the existing power asymmetries between the United States and its future partners and the extremely attractive prospect of gaining access to the U.S. market. However, U.S. resource superiority and its asymmetric interdependence vis-à-vis its potential partners have yet to translate into greater U.S. bargaining power for domestic political reasons. Indeed, the potential impact of these factors has been virtually nullified by the Clinton administration's inability to define clearly its goals or strategy for FTAA negotiations.

In this context, Brazil does possess bargaining power and has been able to assume regional leadership in the process to date. Without fast-track approval, the U.S. administration is unable to push ahead with bilateral trade agreements like the one devised for Chile, which could lead to irresistible pressures to speed up FTAA negotiations. As long as the United States has so little to offer at the bargaining table, the initiative will remain with those interested in blocking negotiations. Because Brazil's inclusion is of vital importance in imparting greater economic density to an eventual hemispheric extension of NAFTA, Brazil can therefore momentarily assume the role of veto player in hemispheric regionalism.

From a domestic standpoint, the Brazilian situation is the opposite of that prevailing in the United States. Whereas the White House and Congress have frequently been at cross-purposes, the Brazilian government position enjoys the necessary political and economic support for the reasons spelled out earlier. The Brazilian government is also advantaged by the fact that talks have so far focused on the negotiating process and timetable rather than more substantive issues.

Were the White House and Congress to reach an understanding on the FTAA and make it a U.S. foreign policy priority, Brazil's role as veto player would vanish altogether (Machado and Motta Veiga 1997: 4). Brazil is incapable of blocking strong U.S. pressures for the FTAA if such pressures were ever to develop. In such a context, Brazil's bargaining power would hinge on its capacity to articulate, through Mercosur, an alternative to the FTAA model as proposed by the United States. The outcome of this scenario is highly uncertain. What does seem certain is that at some future stage in negotiations, Brazil's bargaining power will become increasingly dependent on its acceptance of the concept of qualified sovereignty with respect to Mercosur. This would represent a de facto "paradigm shift in the conceptual bases of Brazil's foreign relations" (Barbosa 1992: 122).

A somewhat different question is whether Brazil would be able to counterbalance an overwhelming U.S. presence in the region. Alone, the answer is no. None of the countries in the region has the power to single-handedly counterbalance the United States. However, an alliance between regional middle powers could make the difference, especially in light of growing interest in the region on the part of extrahemispheric powers in Europe and Asia.[11]

Hemispheric regionalism is a U.S. project, and in spite of profound changes in the international order over the past century, it retains a strong resemblance to its historical predecessor, the Western Hemisphere Idea. Political outcomes, however, are not determined solely by power structures. They are also the product of contingencies and unexpected consequences. Hemispheric regionalism is a telling example in this regard. Notwithstanding its hegemonic intention, the onset of this process not only has ushered in deeper cooperation in the Southern Cone but has also diminished the distance between the historically separate regions of the Americas. A more formalized articulation between the middle powers in North and South America would appear to be the most effective means of achieving a more balanced dialogue with the United States.

Notes

1. For the evolution of regionalism in Brazilian foreign policy, see Soares de Lima (1996).

2. There are significant economic reasons for Brazil's desire to consolidate Mercosur: "Brazil's exports to its Mercosur neighbors are characterized by substantial value-added by the Brazilian work force, in contrast to the predominance of raw materials and agricultural produce that usually predominate in the exports of so-called developing countries" (Purcell 1997: 94).

3. For an overall assessment of the Cardoso administration, see Purcell and Roett (1997).

4. For an evaluation of the current FTAA process from the standpoint of Brazilian economists, diplomats, and businesspeople, see "Perspectivas de Integração Hemisférica" (1997).

5. Brazil's negotiating posture is set forth in Lampreia (1997); see also Abreu (1997).

6. See interview with the Brazilian ambassador to the United States, Paulo Tarso Flecha de Lima, in *Jornal do Brasil* (1997).

7. For the business sector point of view, see, for example, "A ALCA e o Comércio" (1997); "A Importância do Setor Privado" (1997); "Empresários Ganham Espaço no Debate" (1997); "Ordem é Mobilizar o Empresariado" (1997); and "Os Empresários Ganham Força" (1997).

8. See interview with the Minister for Industry and Commerce, Dr. Francisco Dornelles, "Nossa" (1997); see also "Prazos" (1997); "Embaixador" (1997); and Dupas (1997).

9. Certain critics of the diplomatic handling of negotiations on continental integration have remarked on the prevalence of "properly diplomatic diplomacy." This approach prioritizes procedural issues at the expense of debate on substantive issues

and ultimately aims to defer measures geared toward promoting the competitiveness of Brazilian products (Guilhon Albuquerque 1997).

10. Trade between Mercosur partners increased from U.S.$4 billion in 1993 to an estimated U.S.$17 billion by the end of 1997.

11. For speculation along this line, see Mace and Thérien (1996a: 66). In the United States, supporters of a hemispheric free trade area fear that Brazil will opt out of a continental arrangement if it is successful in achieving formal agreements with South American countries and with the European Union. From their perspective, this would give Europe a comparative advantage over the United States in dealings with South America and thus be contrary to U.S. interests (Purcell 1997: 96).

8

Building Role and Region: Middle States and Regionalism in the Americas

Louis Bélanger & Gordon Mace

During the Cold War, a certain number of states defined themselves and were defined by others as middle powers. These states were said to possess certain characteristics: sufficient power, when skillfully used, to maintain a certain level of independence from their major or superpower allies; the leeway this independence provided to perform such stabilizing functions in the international system as peace mediation, institution building, and the denunciation of injustice; and the benefits of an international reputation based on a solid, ethical record in domestic and foreign policy. Clearly, this category and the status that goes with it are linked to much more than the classical attributes of power. That is why scholars increasingly prefer to use, as we have here, the term "middle state" instead of "middle power" to define this type of actor in the international system. Australia, Canada, Norway, and Sweden are frequently cited examples of middle states, but, depending on the period and the definition, Mexico, Nigeria, Turkey, Malaysia, and many others—even Algeria—may also fit the description (Cooper 1997).

The difficulty of determining which countries are middle states and which are not is largely due to the fact that, as Robert W. Cox has remarked, the role of middle states is inextricably linked to the configuration of the international system during a given period and to the conception of the international order that is dominant at the time (Cox 1989). In a world no longer characterized by the East-West divide but rather by increasing multipolarity and regionalization, middle-state roles and identities are inevitably changing. Inversely, as Cox points out, the choice made by states capable of embracing or rejecting middle stateness in a period of transformation also has an impact on the future world order. In this chapter we seek to evaluate this impact at the regional level within the inter-American system. Is there room in the Americas for middle states to act as such? Who are the candidates for middle statehood? And more important for this book, how does middle-state behavior affect the construction of regionalism?

Before addressing these questions, it is important to recognize that middle stateness and regionalism are both complex and problematic international realities, which makes them hard to study together. They don't have the same kind of empirical weight and conceptual clarity that scholars and practitioners have invested in other systemic- or unit-level features of the international system. Middle stateness, as we have said, is not characterized by a clearly determined position in the international hierarchy of power but by vague locational parameters—somewhere between the major powers and the small states—and role conceptions. And regionalism, as mentioned in Chapter 1 of this book, has yet to inscribe its logic in the deep structure of international society, especially outside Europe. This leaves us with two disputed realities that are highly dependent on state efforts for their very instantiation.

Viewed from this angle, the study of the relationship between middle states and the regionalist project in the Americas may appear adventurous. But rather than rejecting the concept of middle statehood or even regionalism as overly ambiguous, we have adopted the opposite attitude in this chapter and asked ourselves what these ambiguities can teach us about the interaction between the two phenomena. We will argue that for some states, middle stateness, like regionalism, is a policy option as well as a framework for action. It is therefore possible, using a foreign policy approach, to look at how the two phenomena influence each other.

Middle States as Parties to Regionalism

Laura Neack (1991, 1995) has empirically demonstrated that the countries political scientists have identified as middle states or middle powers do not share a clearly defined position within the international system in terms of their attributes or relative capacities. We are thus forced to deduce that states accorded the diplomatic and scientific status of middle state are those demonstrating not only the capacity but also the will to conform to the behavioral model associated with this category, that is, good international citizenship, multilateral activism, peacekeeping and peacemaking, institution building, and mediation. In fact, the very ability of middle states to do more than accommodate themselves to their structural position in the system seems to be characteristic of middle statehood (Cooper, Higgott, and Nossal 1993: 19–27). Such manifestations of autonomy toward structural positioning depend on state agents' perceptions of the international environment as a source of opportunities for action rather than as strictly a source of constraint (Breuning 1995: 237). They also depend on the intensity of societal and technical interactions in the system (Buzan, Jones, and Little 1993: 66–80), which give middle states opportunities to exercise a typical form of leadership that stems more from skills of a technical or entrepreneurial nature than from a structural or purely attributive order (Cooper, Higgott, and Nossal 1993: 19–27).

Andrew F. Cooper, Richard A. Higgott, and Kim Richard Nossal detail these skills—which they qualify as "diplomatic"—as a mixture of entrepreneurship, diplomatic know-how, and the ability to manage knowledge of sectorial issues that are the object of international cooperation or litigation. In the post–Cold War period, these skills may prove particularly significant as the weight of structural leadership diminishes and the international agenda is increasingly given over to political questions that accord middle states greater room to maneuver (Higgott, Cooper, and Nossal 1993: 21–22). This shift gives middle states the opportunity to exercise a particularly active form of leadership and exert influence at the systemic level by effectively contributing to coalition and institution building, agenda setting, and policy coordination (Cooper, Higgott, and Nossal 1993: 26). To the extent that these activities are significant to the construction of American regionalism, we can hypothesize that middle-state foreign policies not only are acted upon by regionalism but should also be acting regionalists.

If middle stateness, by definition, involves a certain degree of autonomy from superpowers and structural positioning, it is in turn a constraining model of behavior for the states adopting it. This is what foreign policy analysts refer to as a national role conception on the basis of which states define their interests and preferences (Holsti 1970; Breuning 1997; Chafetz, Abramson, and Guillot 1997). If certain states have acquired national role conceptions forged on the middle-state model, it is because they echo basic and closely interconnected external and internal strategic issues.

We argue that in acting upon and reacting to regionalism, middle states attempt to reproduce an existing middle-state status and role or develop a new model. This agent/structure kind of affirmation may seem simplistic and tautological in the sense that middle-state behavior is considered both a criterion to identify middle stateness and a predicted path of action. However, this approach takes on its full importance when the elective character of middle stateness and the sensitive nature of normative, cognitive, and functional dimensions inherent to each case become clear. For scholars studying the development of regionalism, the issue is to determine the impact that such primary middle-state goals—that is, producing or reproducing regional institutional forms of cooperation for their own status-seeking and position-seeking actions—will have on regionalism.

Because middle states must perform their role in the international system using specific attributes, we hypothesize that, to the extent that they attempt to reproduce or acquire middle-state status within the regional framework, the states studied here will seek to increase the social and technical capabilities of the regional system under construction. Here our agent/structure proposition takes a soft stand: We borrow from structural realism the idea of an interactional level of systemic attributes between structural and unit levels, and we make it the privileged locus of middle-state action on the system (Buzan, Jones, and Little 1993). In concrete terms, we posit that states will take action by initiating and supporting efforts aimed at institutionalizing regional cooperation, placing problems with high technical content on the cooperative agenda, and developing the normative content of the new regional reality. This proposition takes for granted that the regionalist projects, although often initiated and promoted by superpower action, must be studied not only as a source of constraint for middle states but also as a source of opportunity. In this respect, we echo the hypothesis of Cooper, Higgott, and Nossal: Even in cases where regionalism is imposed upon rather than initiated by a middle state, the middle state will try to orient regional construction in the direction of multilateral cooperation, a more appropriate terrain for middle-state activity. By acting to promote a higher level of societal interactive capability within the regional system, the middle state reproduces on a regional scale the level of systemic action that will allow it to put its particular capabilities to use.

One way to limit tautological reasoning about middle states is to bring in the domestic level of analysis. General literature on middle states assumes that in the absence of strong external determinants, domestic influences are a key element in explaining the willingness to shape foreign policy behavior in accordance with the middle-state model. This assumption explains why studies of Canadian foreign policy have been dominated by the idea that the idealism and mediatory efforts characteristic of Canada's foreign policy behavior are international projections of domestic culture and political experience (Hawes 1984). Marijke Breuning (1997) has also convincingly argued that middle-state role modeling can be explained by national political culture and shared cognition, as in the case of Dutch and Belgian foreign aid policy. Although previous studies clearly demonstrate the close link between domestic political culture and the pursuit of a foreign policy modeled on the middle-state ideal type, it cannot be concluded, as several authors have automatically done, that this relation is univocal. It is certainly legitimate to suppose that political culture is externalized through the role modeling adopted by agents of foreign policy. It is just as legitimate to suggest, as Neack does (Neack 1995: 226), that middle-state foreign policy is not just the external manifestation of domestic political culture and experience but an integral part of that culture and experience that is often internalized by foreign policy agents. It can easily be argued that in Canada, for example, international peacekeeping has forged political culture just as much as it has been forged by it.

In sum, we can hypothesize that middle-state foreign policy is particularly embedded in the political culture of the societies concerned. Moreover, foreign policy agents, by reproducing and orienting the typical external behavior of middle states, are at the same time agents of domestic political culture. Knowing this, we can posit that in behaving as middle states, diplomatic agents are simultaneously constrained and empowered by their specific domestic political identity and culture and by the links that bind that identity and culture to middle-state role conceptions and role modeling. In using the regional context to reproduce, transform, or acquire middle-state status, state agents draw upon symbols, practices, and modes of state intervention that have resonance on the domestic scene. This resonance may limit their external action, but it may also push them to develop regional policies for domestic consumption. In both cases, political culture and identity can explain how regionalist foreign policies may be affected by the local reappropriation of the initial regionalist project. Once again, the embeddedness of middle stateness in the political culture of the domestic society should be studied in strategic rather than deterministic terms.

At this point, we must add another identitary dimension to our analysis to take into account the fact that being a regional middle state is not exactly the same as being a middle state acting regionally. We want to consider how a regional identity can be superimposed on a middle-state identity. We argue that in developing a regionally oriented foreign policy, middle-state foreign policy agents attempt to act upon the identitary and functional dimensions of state legitimacy. This can be verified through the analysis of the function of the external reference to regionalism in state agent discourse. The regional dimension is not instrumental here. States taking an active role in the development of regional systems necessarily participate in what Alexander Wendt (1994) calls "collective identity formation." As Wendt notes, "social identities and interests are always in process during interaction" (Wendt 1994: 386). The regionalist project supposes a correlate evolution in state modes of identification and intervention. This has domestic implications and it can be presumed that the domestic political situation and even the strategic position of state agents themselves allow us to explain the particular direction that a regionalist foreign policy may take.

What we propose is to look at each of those domestic and external game levels simultaneously. The problematic character of middle stateness and its implications for the definition of political culture in middle-state societies result in a complex kind of double-edged diplomacy (Evans, Jacobson, and

Putnam 1993). It is a multilevel game in which the external and internal interests at stake in the perpetual process of nation building itself—and not just those at issue in specific negotiations—are interlocked.

The Candidates for Middle Stateness in the Americas

The preceding review of the literature confronts us with a certain number of methodological and analytical difficulties, not the least of which is distinguishing a middle state from another state. Attempts to classify states quantitatively on the basis of their attributes or power have not allowed scholars to isolate an objective position within the international system for states whose behavior is associated with middleness (Neack 1991, 1992). This has led Neack (1995: 225) to argue that middle states have "elected" themselves to this position, a level of international status that has more to do with role modeling than with objective criteria. Definition and identification based on behavior should thus be more useful than those based on position or function (Cooper, Higgott, and Nossal 1993), but this approach poses certain problems as well. Indeed, it is far from evident that behaviors such as the search for multilateral solutions to international conflicts, the search for compromise, or "good international citizenship" (Cooper, Higgott, and Nossal 1993: 19) are sufficient criteria to describe middle states or that they can easily be made operational.

For the moment, it appears preferable to characterize middle states according to three criteria dominating the literature: the first is positional, the second is relational, and the third is behavioral.

1. The middle state occupies a position in the hierarchy of power just next to that of the superpowers. There is considerable subjectivity involved in the quantitative measurement of power, but, as stated by Cooper, Higgott and Nossal, "attempts at measurement do satisfy the intuitive desire to differentiate between those states which clearly are not great powers but are not minor powers either" (1993: 17).
2. The middle state relates to the others in the international system by virtue of its societal and technical capabilities rather than its purely structural attributes.
3. The middle state models its behavior in accordance with a role conception that includes an inclination toward good international citizenship, multilateral activism, coalition and institution building, and mediation.

The three states we have chosen to study—Argentina, Canada, and Mexico—satisfy the first criterion. In the measurement of the hierarchy of power in the Americas presented in Chapter 3, Argentina, Canada, and

Mexico consistently appeared in the group of five states immediately following the United States and recording a decile rank superior to 1.[1] Argentina, Canada, and Mexico also commonly satisfy Carsten Holbraad's neorealist classification of middle powers (Neack 1991: 115–118) and figure among the more frequently listed middle states according to Neack's literature survey (Neack 1991: 119). Satisfying the positional criterion makes them at least candidates to middle stateness.

With regard to the second criterion, it is clear that, in the regional context, Brazil relates to the other states more by virtue of its structural (or counterstructural) leadership qualities than its societal or technical capabilities. Consequently, even if it qualifies for middle stateness on the basis of its position in the hierarchy of power, it cannot be treated as such here. To put it bluntly, Brazil is too powerful compared with other Latin American countries to consider itself or to be considered by these other countries a middle state (see Chapter 7 for a discussion of this issue).

We have also excluded Venezuela from our analysis. In the 1970s, Venezuela's foreign policy behavior closely resembled that of a middle state, although Caracas adopted a low profile in diplomatic affairs after the debt crisis. However, access to oil revenues rather than technical capacities may better explain the prominent role assumed by Caracas in Latin America in the 1970s. That is why we have chosen to concentrate on Argentina, Canada, and Mexico. Argentina is presented as a middle state in relation to the dominant Brazilian power in South America. Canada and Mexico are in a similar position in relation to the United States in North America.

The situation is more problematic regarding the behavioral criterion. This aspect of the classification should be part of our investigation and treated more as hypothesis than as fact. Whereas Canada appears to be the archetypal middle state in general terms (Cooper, Higgott, and Nossal 1993), although this remains to be verified in the hemispheric context, Argentina and Mexico have in the past shown little evidence of middle-state role modeling. However, it could be hypothesized that their more traditional and narrow-minded form of diplomacy has shifted to one based on a more liberal and activist international citizenship parallel to the development of the new post–Cold War regionalism. Thus, a good part of our investigation should focus on determining whether Argentina, Canada, and Mexico, three serious candidates for middle stateness in the Americas, effectively perform a middle-state role.

Argentina

The end of the Cold War and the launch of the contemporary regionalist project in the Americas corresponded with a radical change in the orientation of Argentine foreign policy. After attempting to play a leadership role in the nonaligned movement and acting as a challenger of the established international order during the first years of democratic government, Buenos Aires adapted its behavior to the more conformist middle-state model in the early 1990s. This new orientation also corresponded with the arrival of Carlos Menem at the head of the Argentine state. Menem adopted a clearly pro-U.S. and pro-Western foreign policy, which led to, among other things, the involvement of Argentine troops in the Gulf War and Washington's recent decision to grant the country major non–North Atlantic Treaty Organization (NATO) ally status.

The Argentine state then took on the task of propagating the values of the new international order on a continent traditionally attached to established principles of noninterventionism and the people's right to decide their own future. In 1992 it proposed and obtained the adoption by the Organization of American States (OAS) of the principles contained in the Protocol of Washington providing for the suspension of a member state that ceases to be democratically governed (Bloomfield 1994; Muñoz 1993a). Argentina also strove constantly for the reinforcement of OAS structures and normative obligations: it defended the idea of a convention on disappearances proposed by the Inter-American Commission on Human Rights (Human Rights Watch 1994: 73–74), was the most ardent advocate of an armed intervention in Haiti ("OAS Ministers" 1994: 1), and was responsible for the demand that resulted in Peru's suspension from the Rio Group in the aftermath of the 1992 *autogolpe* (Vaky 1993: 25).

In the area of trade liberalization, Argentina sought to mediate between the Southern Cone Common Market (Mercosur) partners grouped around Brazil and advocating a distinct approach to integration and the states that wanted to see the extension of the North American Free Trade Agreement (NAFTA) to the continent as a whole (Menem 1990: 149–157; Saccone 1994). At the Denver conference, Argentine representatives proposed a first step in the latter direction in the form of a continental free trade agreement covering the agricultural sector (Jellinek 1995). Argentina also declared itself favorable to OAS involvement in the leveling of legal obstacles to integration (Organization of American States 1993). Active on two fronts—NAFTA extension and further development of the Mercosur experience—Argentina sought from 1992 to 1995 to gradually transform Mercosur into an organization more compatible with NAFTA. Considered by the United States as a credible partner in both regional economic and political spheres but equally intent on conserving privileged relations with the giant Brazil, Argentina has positioned itself at the intersection of the two continental currents of integrationist logic. Furthermore, the country has every intention of taking advantage of the strategic role that it has in large measure given itself.

Argentina had thus positioned itself up to the mid-1990s as an unavoidable strategic interlocutor on the chessboard of regional construction with regard to the two strategic elements that drive the new regionalist logic in the Americas: trade and democratic stability. Through diplomatic activism, it pushed for increased institutionalization of the regional reality and the extension of its normative content, elements that in return reinforced Argentina's capacity for action as an emerging middle state. In sum, the new regional dynamic gave Argentina the opportunity to reshape its international role. Invested with the moral stature and diplomatic capacity of a middle state, Argentina in turn allowed regionalism to develop in a more liberal direction that would have been unimaginable without its participation. As we will discuss later, it was Argentina, and not Mexico, that tried to act as a diplomatic bridge builder of the new American regionalism.

This international role modeling on the part of the Argentine state corresponds with important changes in Argentine political culture. The defeat of Raul Alfonsín's radicals at the hands of Menem's neo-Peronists gave the signal for Argentina to align itself with the Western political and economic model. In Argentina, as in all countries of the southern part of the hemisphere, the democratic revolution took place on the basis of a shifting definition of democracy (Wiarda 1990, 1995b). Furthermore, references to the exterior—or the positioning of its own national experience in relation to external experiences—are both an instrument of legitimization for the government in power and an object of struggle over fundamental common values between different factions within political society. Although Argentina had stated its philosophical attachment to Western values under the Alfonsín government (Vacs 1989: 39), the diplomatic position adopted by Buenos Aires in favor of nonalignment and an independent course for nations of the South indicated a certain ambiguity in the foreign policy arena. The Menem regime continued to defend democracy but left the nonaligned movement and adopted a foreign policy that was more realistic and faithful to the principles of good international citizenship. This evolution can be understood as a search for external sources of legitimization in light of the Argentine state's move to reform the values of the political culture and the socioeconomic foundations on which it was to base its political legitimacy and power during the 1990s. The economic reforms undertaken by Argentine authorities proceeded from a liberal logic that signified a rupture with the traditional protectionist mentalities and practices that had structured Argentina's sociopolitical landscape in the past. By linking these domestic measures with the logic of international and regional integration through its new diplomatic orientation, the Menem regime effectively disqualified the alternative: a nationalist retreat inward associated with Argentine economic decline.

The Argentine case demonstrates that changes in diplomatic roles cannot simply be explained by the inevitably slow transformation of the national political culture. Instead, the rapidity with which Buenos Aires modified its international behavior suggests that the transformation of the

Argentine political profile was also an intervening variable in the process of shaping a new political identity and consciousness for Argentines. Through its actions, Argentina acquired a new international prestige that reflected positively on the regime in power as well as on its political programs.

The essential point is that Argentina's international role modeling is occurring through a new form of regional identification. At the same time that it was abandoning its position as a challenger of the established international order to defend the rules and institutions of the new international order, Argentina was actively redefining its exterior space: From membership in a peripheral world organized along a South-South axis, it took steps to become part of a space organized around a North-South axis of cooperation and trade. In doing so, it adopted a new region of reference, one no longer defined as essentially Latin American and opposed to North America but rather as hemispheric in scope.

This did not mean that Buenos Aires turned its back on the subregion of the Southern Cone. There again, the Argentine state did more than just follow the evolution of Argentine political culture. Relying on that culture for support, the state forced it beyond both its traditional, nationalist terms of reference and its rivalry with Brazil (Bartolome 1990; Child 1985), pushing it toward a more liberal form of nationalism. This form of nationalism was more favorable to the redeployment of the foundations of state legitimacy on the basis of the state's new role as agent of Argentina's insertion into the world economy and modernity (Roy 1995). By linking Argentine pride and self-identification to the state's new position as model and defender of both democratic action and liberalization in a regional context, Argentina's diplomacy contributed in turn to the consolidation of that new legitimacy.

The new regionalist impetus originating in the United States created an opportunity for the Argentine state. Buenos Aires took advantage of the new dynamic to redefine its international role to correspond with parallel domestic restructuring projects and to acquire the position of a middle state within the new international system. The strategic position Argentina acquired as a result of the new continental political dynamic allowed it to orient the development of regional cooperation in a direction favorable to its new role.

Since 1995, however, the Argentine government has been much less vocal in both its previous main fields of intervention, namely, democracy and free trade. Buenos Aires has said very little about the hemispheric regime for democracy, which is somewhat consistent with the level of attention given to the subject by the other countries in the region since that time. This low level of attention can probably be explained by the fact that, in contrast to the early 1990s, there have been no major occasions, like the coup in Haiti or the adoption of the Washington protocol, where the actors have had to articulate positions or engage in specific commitments. After the intense period of OAS-led region building in the field of democracy in the Americas, it seems that the second half of the 1990s is a period of more basic groundwork of policymaking and institution building. In such a context, governments like that of Argentina are probably still quite active but in a more discreet fashion.

Buenos Aires maintains a policy of strong support of the FTAA project but has not shown the kind of leadership that might have been expected. During the successive trade ministerials, the Argentine government has made propositions and pronouncements aimed above all at keeping the process on track, opposing maneuvers of dilution by Mexico and Brazil on the timetable and efficiency, but it has not suggested many original propositions.

Consequently, there is clearly a supportive but low-profile attitude on the part of Argentina toward the hemispheric regionalist project. This attitude is interesting, particularly when it is compared with that of Canada. This hemispheric foreign policy behavior of Buenos Aires and Ottawa were very similar during the first half of the 1990s. But Washington's congressional difficulties and apparent lack of a consistent hemispheric policy made Canada more determined to assume a leadership role in the continental regionalist project. These matters seemed to have an opposite effect on Argentina.

Argentina's domestic factors may provide a probable explanation. The years 1994–1999 have been a very intense political period in Argentina. President Menem sought and obtained a constitutional revision permitting his reelection in 1994. He tried the same procedure again for the 1999 presidential election, this time without success. Therefore, the domestic political maneuvering for the electoral deadline of 1999 and after may have turned the attention of the political elite in Argentina away from the foreign policy agenda.

But the most probable explanation of Argentina's lower profile is the state's perception of the fragility of the regionalist project. Continental integration increases Argentina's room to maneuver in relation to Brazil, and Buenos Aires was an active player in the hemispheric project when it was convinced that the project would materialize. But when the Menem government became less certain about the success of the FTAA and the regionalist project, an uncertainty due in good part to the inability of the U.S. executive to obtain fast-track legislation from Congress, it became less aggressive.

It is possible that this attitude of the Argentine government is only temporary. But in the absence of U.S. leadership in hemispheric affairs, Argentina will not take a leading role to sustain a process about which its principal ally, Brazil, has significant reservations. Brazil has already expressed some dissatisfaction toward certain Argentine positions—for example, its new status as a major U.S. non-NATO ally—and thus it is logical that Buenos Aires does not want to antagonize its neighbor regarding a project that might never become a reality. Should the project fail, Argentina would be left with its bilateral relation with Brazil as a major foreign policy constraint.

Mexico

Because of its participation in NAFTA, Mexico appears to be a key actor in the American regionalization process. For Mexico, however, NAFTA may have been more important for securing its bilateral relations with the United States than for supporting regional construction. Mexico's geopolitical situation suggests that it would be to the country's advantage to take on the role of diplomatic bridge builder between North America and Latin America. The evidence says otherwise: Mexico has resisted the regionalist project as much as its partnership with the United States allows. We argue that Mexico is resisting the development of the societal and technical capacities of the inter-American system because it cannot fill the role of middle state that it would have to occupy within such a system to conserve the equivalent level of international status it currently possesses for simple geostrategic reasons.

Let us first look at the direction in which Mexican foreign policy has taken the regionalization process. On the trade front, Mexico is not an ardent promoter of regional integration. Public declarations aside ("Zedillo" 1994: 1), the country appears cold to the idea of NAFTA expansion, a position confirmed in the spring of 1994 by the publication of a White House diplomatic report (González and Chabat 1996: 83–84). On a hemispheric scale, Mexico would rather look into much less restrictive liberalization measures, within the OAS framework, for example (Organization of American States 1993: 13).

The country's stance is much clearer on questions unrelated to trade. Mexico is fiercely opposed to an institutional and normative reinforcement of the inter-American system. This opposition is particularly evident with regard to the democratization process, an important element of the regionalization process envisaged at the Miami summit (Summit of the Americas 1994). In 1992 Mexico was the only state to vote against the Protocol of Washington, which allows the OAS to expel countries no longer conforming to the principles of representative democracy (González and Chabat 1996: 83). In the preceding year, heavy pressure was required to secure in extremis Mexico's vote in favor of OAS Resolution 1080, which obliges member states to consult each other when the democratic process is disrupted within the boundaries of a member country (Bloomfield 1994: 162ff). Mexico also opposed OAS interventions to reestablish democracy in Haiti (Brooke 1994), Peru ("Mexico Rejects" 1992), and Guatemala ("Guatemala" 1993) and rejected the creation of a multinational force to protect democracy (Cevallos 1995), all in the name of the principle of non-intervention in the internal affairs of a foreign country. In doing so, Mexico positioned itself alongside Brazil as one of the most conservative states in the hemisphere (Gosselin, Mace, and Bélanger 1995).

In contrast, Mexico has been prepared to support certain state groupings such as the Group of Eight—born in 1987 out of the fusion of the Contadora Group and the Contadora Support Group—and the Group of Three (Colombia, Mexico, and Venezuela). However, these groupings have so far served more as fora for the discussion of economic and political questions than as veritable tools for cooperation (González and Chabat 1996: 82).

This portrait clearly illustrates that Mexico has not adopted a foreign policy profile corresponding with the middle-state model. Unlike Argentina, it has not pushed its objective of reinsertion into the international order to the point of radically questioning traditional isolationism and its principles of noninterventionism and self-determination (Abella 1992: 69–70). Mexico's new foreign policy doctrine, which Guadalupe González and Jorge Chabat (1996) call "participative realism," aims to connect the Mexican economy to the poles of world development without modifying its diplomatic profile. The goal is first to increase Mexico's relative economic capabilities and to base its political power on future economic attributes rather than to seek political dividends through immediate diplomatic involvement in a regionalization process that would permit others to benefit from the comparative advantages it now enjoys. In other words, Mexico is not ready to share with its Latin American neighbors the current advantage given to it by privileged access to the U.S. market.

In the final analysis, this dichotomy between the economic and the political accurately reflects Mexico's internal evolution and the orientations of the Revolutionary Institutional Party (PRI) regime that controls the Mexican state. By pursuing its present policy and refusing the middle-state role that it has been offered, Mexico is not just responding to the constraints of a political culture that could perhaps be qualified as unconducive to the development of qualities attributed to this diplomatic role (idealism, pacifism, and liberalism). It constitutes, through its diplomacy, an important agent for the reproduction of the characteristics that distinguish the political culture in question.

Furthermore, Mexican foreign policy has always been a privileged instrument of legitimization for both the regime in power and what has proven to be a largely statist form of nationalism. More particularly, it has been put to the service of PRI nationalist and revolutionary ideology. This resulted in the exacerbation of a defensive policy orientation, especially toward the United States, and toward a certain isolationism. During the 1970s, this orientation expressed itself in a pro–Third World policy that challenged the international economic order. Mexico even attempted to take a leadership role among reform-minded states by proposing a Charter of State Economic Rights and Responsibilities (Chabat 1990). This doctrinaire line was intended to provide support for a form of strong state nationalism that found its justification in the hostile characterization of the external environment. In turn, this state nationalism permitted the reproduction of an authoritarian development model, based on protected national industry and a quasi one-party regime.

When Mexico decided to reorient its foreign economic policy in the wake of the 1982 financial crisis and the failure of the trade diversification policy (Villegas 1988), it had to do so without contradicting too openly the traditional diplomatic doctrine that helped legitimize the regime in power. Increased Mexican openness and a more participative diplomatic profile have been limited to the economic dimensions of Mexican foreign policy. Even so, the change is still major. By adopting a liberal form of discourse and practice, the Mexican state is attacking an entire political culture of domestic interventionism and calling into question some of its fundamental characteristics. These include state ownership and the state's subsidiary and protectionist roles; the sacred character of national sovereignty; traditional challenges to the dominant liberal economic order; and the characterization of the outside world as a source of threat (Abella 1992). In contrast, these unifying aspects of Mexican political culture and of the legitimizing action of the state are reaffirmed in the more political realm, particularly in Mexican regional policy. Therefore, although the United States is no longer viewed solely as a symbol of external threat, the Mexican state—trade aside—uses the regional diplomatic scene to affirm its independence with regard to its big northern neighbor and to revive revolutionary themes still important in Mexican political culture (E. Ferris 1984).

It is clear, then, that the ambivalence that prevents Mexico from behaving as a middle state has both an internal and external explanation. By positioning itself on the margins of the regionalist project with regard to a political issue as central as that of democratization, Mexico has reproduced the role modeling that legitimizes the maintenance of a still centralized and authoritarian domestic policy dominated by nationalist state discourse. This discourse flies in the face of the new international order embraced by the middle states. Mexico, thus, has not followed the Argentine course, which radically altered the material and ideological foundations on which the state bases its power. Clearly, the PRI elites who initiated the liberalization of both Mexican domestic and foreign policy encountered much greater internal resistance than their Argentine counterparts.

Mexico's actions have slowed the development of the societal capacities of the inter-American system and prevented states that have chosen the path of middle stateness from benefiting from the advantages they could otherwise expect. By reacting as it has to the regionalist project—that is to say, by maintaining a relatively conservative policy on regionalism—Mexico has revealed that it does not posit itself as a middle state within the inter-American system. This conservative attitude allows the reproduction of certain strategic features of both the internal and external political environments that might otherwise be threatened, but it gives the regionalization process a less ambitious orientation in terms of its societal and institutional capabilities.

Canada

The concept of middle power has long been associated with Canada's behavior as an international actor (King Gordon 1966; Holmes 1976; Pratt 1990; Wood 1990; Cooper, Higgott, and Nossal 1993). At its inception, it was more a political concept than an analytical one. Ideology for some (Painchaud 1966), doctrine for others (Mackay 1969), the notion was developed by the architects of Canadian foreign policy in the immediate post–World War II period.

Between 1945 and the mid-1960s, Canada played a far greater international role than it would normally have been expected to solely on the basis of economic power or diplomatic tradition. In effect, Ottawa partly filled a vacuum in international affairs resulting from the world conflict of 1939–1945 and in so doing achieved a position and status that it would not have obtained under normal circumstances.

For Lester Pearson, John Holmes, Escott Reid, and the other architects of Canada's foreign policy at the time, the use of the term "middle power" was to some extent a means of securing Canada's status on the world scene. It was also part of a vision of what Canada's conduct in world affairs should be. This vision or doctrine came to be known as the internationalist tradition of Canadian foreign policy. Middle-power internationalism essentially implied two basic elements: the promotion of the principle of functionalism—which meant constantly supporting the multilateral organizations seen as vital to the functioning of the world system—and the promotion of world peace through the collective security and, more recently, cooperative security frameworks within which Canada has developed considerable expertise in mediation and peacekeeping (Hawes 1984: 3–6). These elements contributed to molding a specific role for Canada as an "honest broker" and a "helpful fixer."

If Canada acts as a middle state in the context of the regional system of the Americas, we should be able to identify elements of behavior consistent with the doctrine of middle-power internationalism. As outlined in the first part of the chapter, the challenge for a middle state in the context of the regional system of the Americas is to develop or reproduce middle-state status in that context. The benefits are tangible and involve substantial participation in the process of agenda building so that the regional agenda will enable a country to advance its national interests. In the case of Canada, this takes two forms: multilateral institution building and peace and stability through cooperative security.

Historically, Canada was never a major actor in the Americas; it traditionally neglected the countries south of the Rio Grande in the conduct of its foreign policy. A period of discovery occurred in the 1970s (Ogelsby 1976; Mace 1989: 412–424; Rochlin 1993: 65–92), followed by several years of relative neglect that was due to the world economic crisis of 1981–1982 and the external debt crisis that affected Latin America for most of the 1980s. The turning point came with the 1989 announcement of a new Latin American strategy for Canada, a major component of which was the decision to seek formal membership in the Organization of American States (Clark 1989).

Up to now, what regional governance exists in the Americas occurs under the auspices of four organizations: the OAS, the Inter-American Development Bank (IDB), the Economic Commission for Latin America and the Caribbean (ECLAC), and the Rio Group. Although a longtime member of IDB and ECLAC, Canada and indeed most American countries seem to view the OAS as the main forum for discussing hemispheric affairs in the years to come despite its past shortcomings (Canadian Foundation for the Americas 1994: 19–20).

Consequently, it is in the OAS setting that Canada has been most active in promoting multilateral cooperation since the beginning of the 1990s. Under the able stewardship of Jean-Paul Hubert, Canada's first ambassador of and permanent representative to the organization, the Canadian government has been heavily involved in the process of OAS administrative and financial reform instituted prior to Canada's officially becoming a member. The Canadian delegation pressed for technical and administrative reforms so that the OAS could better respond to problems at hand and increase its credibility in the eyes of its members. This same rationale lay behind Canada's calls for payment of past and present membership dues.

From the beginning, Canada has been an OAS activist, regularly participating in various committees and commissions, such as the Inter-American Commission on Human Rights, to name but one. Canada was also instrumental in the adoption of the Santiago Commitment and played a central role in the establishment of the Unit for the Promotion of Democracy (Mackenzie 1994: 4–6; McKenna 1995). In fact, Canada was so proactive in the OAS that longtime observers such as Edgar Dosman, former director of the Canadian Foundation for the Americas, were afraid that such an attitude might be counterproductive. In Dosman's view, the Canadian delegation to the OAS was too aggressive in pursuing matters related mainly to Canada's interests to the detriment of issues with greater relevance to the other members of the organization (Dosman 1992: 546–547).

Evidently, Canada has not been afraid to reproduce its traditional middle-state behavior in the context of the Americas, particularly with regard to the promotion of multilateral cooperation. It has primarily done so in the OAS framework, where it has most recently been active on the Cuban issue. At the June 1994 OAS meeting in Brazil, Secretary of State for Latin America and Africa Christine Stewart made an indirect appeal for Cuban rapprochement with the OAS (Stewart 1994) by announcing that Canada would resume aid to Havana after a sixteen-year suspension (Vincent 1994). But Canada is also active in promoting regional cooperation outside the OAS, as witnessed by the recent joint declaration establishing high-level political consultations between Canada and the members of the Rio Group (Canada 1995).

Canada has also been quite active with regard to peace and stability, the second major component of middle-state internationalism. It promoted the concept of cooperative security involving multilateral and multidimensional cooperation to reduce or eliminate threats to stability originating outside and inside countries of the region (Gosselin, Mace, and Bélanger 1995: 800). Cooperative security, in the Canadian case, took essentially three forms: participation in the monitoring of electoral processes in Haiti, Nicaragua, and elsewhere to help promote democracy and internal stability; condemnation of antidemocratic conduct such as the 1992 *autogolpe* in Peru (Ottawa did not impose sanctions but suspended direct support to the Peruvian government) (Nash 1992); and mediation and peacekeeping in Central America and Haiti. Canada was an important actor in UN Observer Mission in Central America, the UN peacekeeping mission in Central America, and also agreed to lead the UN mission in Haiti ("Le Canada" 1994).

Mediation and peacekeeping have long been associated with Canada's conduct in international affairs. They are major components of the middle-state internationalist doctrine developed in Canada, and it is clear that this model will also be applied in the framework of the Americas, as the Haitian case indicates. Ottawa was one of the first governments to condemn the military coup in Haiti in September 1991. Canada suspended its bilateral cooperation program with Haiti after the coup and pushed for OAS mediation of the situation. After the failure of OAS diplomatic efforts, the Canadian government consistently supported UN resolutions demanding a return to democratic rule and finally agreed to participate in the United Nations Mission in Haiti (Mackenzie 1994: 6–9). Canada was closely associated with all developments in the Haitian crisis. Ottawa preferred sanctions to military intervention but was forced to recognize that sanctions were slow in bringing results. Although the Canadian government declined to take part in the U.S.-led military intervention in September 1994, it intervened in the reconstruction process and also agreed to lead the UN mission in Haiti.

In terms of the external issues, it is clear that Canada has applied to the Americas a foreign policy based on the main tenets of middle-state internationalism, namely, multilateral cooperation and promotion of peace and stability. Let us now examine the internal issues by looking at the relationship between foreign policy behavior and Canadian political culture and by trying to assess the impact of this relationship on the legitimacy and identity of the Canadian federation.

Because of its long tradition of middle-state behavior and recognition as a middle state by other actors in the international system, the Canadian government, unlike Argentina and, up to a point, Mexico, felt less pressure to adapt its behavior in the Americas for internal consumption or to reflect Canadian political culture. After all, this behavior has always been more or less a constant of Canadian foreign policy (Hockin 1978).

But Ottawa uses its foreign policy in the Americas as it does the rest of its foreign policy. Although the means employed are multilateral cooperation and cooperative security, the ends pursued are democracy, respect for human rights, promotion of women, social justice, equitable distribution of wealth in a framework of economic liberalism, and so on. These values are presented as key components of the Canadian social fabric and as representing a Canadian societal model that is more gentle, more accommodating, and more compassionate with regard to the disadvantaged. By promoting such values in the context of the regional system of the Americas, the Canadian government is naturally contributing to the development of an environment consistent with the Canadian vision of society and, in so doing, to a reinforcement of these values inside the Canadian community. In the present Canadian political context, a foreign policy of this nature also serves to legitimize the federal government as a central actor in the federation inasmuch as it is seen by the Canadian public as the main channel for Canada's action in the world, as well as the main filter through which external pressures affect Canadian society. Consequently, Canada's behavior as a middle state of the Americas is essentially oriented toward the reinforcement of regional multilateral institutions, behavior that is intimately linked with the promotion of Canadian culture and values at home.

Finally, in the Americas as elsewhere in the world, the federal government uses its foreign policy as much as possible to reinforce the Canadian identity. Considering the centrifugal forces at work in Canada and the fact that the country's survival depends on the continued coexistence of the two major linguistic groups that built it, Canadian foreign policy must reflect this reality and at the same time play a special role in this respect. The development of Canadian relations with Francophone Africa in the 1960s can be explained in large measure by Ottawa's desire to have its foreign policy more accurately reflect the reality of Canadian politics and simultaneously discourage the secessionist movement in Quebec (Sabourin 1976). Canada's involvement in the Haitian crisis and its constant preoccupation with Haiti plays a somewhat similar role. Canada without Quebec would certainly have been less preoccupied by the Haitian crisis and would have devoted fewer resources to its resolution. In this sense, Canada's involvement with Haiti exemplifies how, in the context of the Americas, Ottawa uses middle-state diplomacy to strengthen Canadian identity.

But Canadian identity is not just a reflection of the internal dynamics of the federation. It also has to do with Canada-U.S. relationships, which became that much closer with the signing of the Canada-U.S. Free Trade Agreement (FTA). Because of the FTA and the United States' enormous influence on inter-American affairs, Canada's consistent efforts to reinforce multilateral institutions in the Americas must also be seen as a means to strengthen the Canadian identity with regard to U.S. influence. This seems to be the attitude in the trade sector, where Ottawa is creating a web of trade agreements with countries such as Chile and with Mercosur, the rationale being to keep up regionalist momentum when the United States seems to hesitate.

In short, this brief presentation demonstrates that even though Canada is a newcomer to the regional system of the Americas, it has already adopted behavior consistent with its status as a middle state. We have tried to show that the Canadian government also seeks to strengthen Canadian political culture and the Canadian identity through its behavior as a middle state.

Conclusion

Until now, the literature on middle states or middle powers has been hampered by two essential shortcomings. Notwithstanding notable contributions by Neack and Cooper, Higgott, and Nossal, the literature has failed to propose an operational concept that could be used for the purpose of comparative analysis. Furthermore, the literature has focused almost exclusively on the behavior of industrialized middle states such as Australia, Canada, and Sweden in a Cold War context of global politics.

In our exploratory study we have sought to offer a modest contribution to the analysis of middle-state behavior in regional politics at a theoretical and empirical level. In the first instance, we propose to operationalize the concept of middle state by incorporating three main attributes referred to as positional, relational, and behavioral. We also suggest that middle-state foreign policy behavior, and indeed all foreign policy behavior, must not be seen exclusively as the result of an essentially outward-looking policy process. We accept the long-standing notion that foreign policy is both action and reaction, but we propose that the action component of the process has two specific functions. Externally oriented national role conceptions of middle stateness are social constructs that seek to mold or structure the external environments of states in a bilateral, multilateral, or, in this case, regional context. In the case of middle states, the privileged locus of such action on the system lies at the interaction level in the societal and technical capabilities of the system. But the foreign policy initiatives of middle states also fulfill a second, internally oriented function. They participate in structuring the internal milieu so as to reinforce national identity and sustain or develop the legitimacy of the state itself.

At the empirical level, we have tried to follow Cooper's suggestion (Hayes 1994: 11) that with the world system now shifting from a bipolar to a multipolar structure and the world agenda more focused on issues of low politics, scholars should examine the behavior of states that were not traditionally referred to as middle states but that may be called upon to play that role in the future.

Inside the American regional system, we have selected three countries that qualified or had the potential to act as middle states. The results of the exploratory study show that since the late 1980s, Canada has effectively reproduced at the regional level the middle-state behavior that Canadian governments have perfected on the world scene since the end of World War II. President Menem's Argentina also managed to behave in a manner surprisingly consistent with anticipated patterns of middle-state behavior, at least up to 1995. Such behavior was probably made possible by the tight control that President Menem maintains over the state apparatus and by Argentina's previous experience in middle-state diplomacy, such as its participation in the Cairns Group. Mexico, in contrast, has not behaved as a middle state at all. One possible reason for this behavior is that the Mexican government prefers to consolidate the economic gains from its participation in NAFTA before seeing NAFTA benefits extended to the rest of the region and before becoming involved in the promotion of a hemisphere-wide regional system. This explanation is consistent with neorealist expectations about the cooperative behavior of intermediate powers (see Chapter 3). Given Mexico's behavior, general middle-state theory should perhaps be readjusted to take into account the fact that states that are candidates for middle stateness on the basis of their position are less likely to adopt the cooperative attitudes one might expect from them if they find themselves in a competitive situation that renders them sensitive to relative gains competitors could make. This consideration should be added to the fact that Mexico may also face stronger internal political resistance than Argentina with regard to middle-state behavior in the present regional context and its consequences for the political system.

These preliminary results are extremely interesting for the study of the dynamics of regionalism and international relations in the Americas. A regional system like the one being developed in the Americas cannot be determined solely by the action or interplay of two major actors, such as the United States and Brazil. Middle states of the region must and will intervene to fashion a system not exclusively limited to free trade but also capable of managing more complex issues without which regional capability will remain an empty notion and an unfulfilled reality.

Notes

This chapter is part of a research project funded by the Fonds pour la formation des chercheurs et l'aide à la recherche of the government of Quebec and the Social Sciences and Humanities Research Council of Canada. We would like to thank Joël Monfils and Martin Roy for research assistance.
    1. Along with Brazil and Venezuela.

9

The Organization of
American States and
Hemispheric Regionalism

Guy Gosselin & Jean-Philippe Thérien

In this chapter we examine the role of the Organization of American States (OAS) in the current resurgence of regionalism in the Western Hemisphere. Although we recognize that the OAS is a multifunctional institution, our analysis focuses on the issue of democracy and human rights. As Heraldo Muñoz explains, "The promotion and preservation of democracy is now the principal issue that defines the public profile of the OAS, in effect, the one that will determine its destiny" (Muñoz 1993a: 70). In sum, what we argue in this chapter is that an examination of OAS activities in recent years, particularly in the area of democracy and human rights, makes possible a deeper understanding of the overall state of inter-American cooperation and a better assessment of the future of hemispheric regionalism.

By virtue of its functions and membership, the OAS is the most important regional organization in the Western Hemisphere. It is the only institution that brings together all the states of the region. In addition, the OAS's mandate covers political, economic, and social matters. Nevertheless, the explicit link established in this chapter between the study of regionalism and the study of regional organizations is hardly self-evident. In fact, for over a generation the role of regional organizations in the development of regionalism has been the subject of sharp debate. An overview of that debate will make it easier to set the rest of our analysis in its proper context.

The first studies of regionalism and integration placed considerable emphasis on the importance of regional institutions. Drawing on the European experience, many experts and politicians in the 1960s perceived a causal relationship between the vigor of regional organizations and the speed of integration. True to this line of thought, Joseph Nye defined regionalism as "the formation of interstate associations or groupings on the basis of regions" (Nye 1968b: vii). This definition, however, was never unanimously accepted. A number of observers noted, for example, that the plethora of regional organizations founded at the initiative of developing countries had not fostered the rapid growth of regionalism in the Third World. Contending that regional organizations represented only one among several types of instruments for promoting integration, other authors stressed the need to better distinguish the notions of regional cooperation, regional system, regional organization, and regionalism (Haas 1970: 607–610; Hansen 1969: 262–271).

Nearly thirty years later, at a time when references to a "new regionalism" are more and more frequent, the role of regional organizations remains hazy. In defining regionalism as "a state-led or states-led project designed to reorganise a particular regional space along defined economic and political lines," Anthony Payne and Andrew Gamble tend to underestimate the political leadership exercised by regional bodies (Payne and Gamble 1996: 2). Gary Gereffi foregrounds the fact that in East Asia regionalism has been shaped more by the behavior of multinational firms than by the creation of intergovernmental institutions. What characterizes East Asia, in his view, is "a market-induced, rather than policy-induced, form of economic integration" (Gereffi 1995: 138). In comparison with these positions, other analyses assign much more weight to regional organizations. For example, basing his analysis on the assumption that there are "varieties of regionalism," A. LeRoy Bennett views regional organizations as the institutional engines of regionalism (Bennett 1995: 229–264). Similarly, a recent study by Louise Fawcett notes that the new wave of regionalism has been accompanied by "a proliferation of new regional groupings" and "a revival of older regional bodies" (Fawcett 1995: 9).

Though as yet unresolved, the debate regarding the connection between regional organizations and regionalism has allowed several useful guideposts to emerge. Clearly, the sole existence of regional institutions cannot be seen as a necessary and adequate condition for the development of regionalism. Yet regional organizations can obviously lend stability and predictability to cooperation among states, to the extent that, like all multilateral forums, they accomplish functions of norm creation, socialization, legitimation, and provision of information (Jacobson 1984: 88–90; Archer 1992: 159–177). This, ultimately, is what justifies paying particular attention to bodies like the OAS within a comprehensive study of hemispheric regionalism.

The Miami summit of December 1994 did a great deal to elevate the prestige of the OAS. The Plan of Action put forward there affirms that "the OAS will have a paramount role in following up on the various decisions of this Summit meeting" (Rosenberg and Stein 1995: 26). A watershed event in the modern history of inter-American relations, the meeting in Miami plotted out an ambitious cooperation plan centered on two major objectives: (1) the establishment of a free trade zone in the Americas by 2005 and (2) the strengthening of democracy and human rights in the region. And though the Miami summit ultimately attributed no more than a supporting role to the OAS in the realm of trade liberalization, the organization was identified as the "principal hemispheric body for the defense of democratic values and institutions" (Rosenberg and Stein 1995: 13).

The assignment of such an important political mandate to the OAS is remarkable considering that in the early 1980s the organization appeared to be on its last legs. Historically, inter-American relations had always evolved in an atmosphere of conflict deriving from the asymmetrical distribution of power between the United States and the other countries of the region (Stoetzer 1993). Thus, from a traditional Latin American viewpoint, the OAS was considered a shield against U.S. intervention, whereas in the United States, the organization was perceived as a vehicle for its foreign policy interests. During the Cold War period, this perceptual difference was constantly exacerbated by the U.S. government's overriding concern with the struggle against communism. Moreover, even though the International Union of American Republics—the OAS's predecessor founded in 1890—was primarily concerned with commercial matters, the OAS itself has never managed to become a major player in the economic arena. Inter-American cooperation in that field has been continually hampered by notions of development bearing the deep imprint of the North-South divide. Against the background of this less than brilliant past, the rise of hemispheric regionalism in the 1990s allowed the OAS to make an unexpected comeback (Hurrell 1995a; Varas 1992: 52–53).

Our study emphasizes the problem of democracy and human rights because these issues tend more and more to overshadow other OAS preoccupations. The OAS does, of course, continue to carry out various functions regarding, for instance, trade liberalization, security, and the war on drugs. But in these areas of inter-American cooperation, the OAS's role remains relatively muted. The negotiations on regional commerce and security have taken place within ad hoc forums known as Trade Ministerial and Defense Ministerial (Inter-American Dialogue 1997a: 22–28). As far as the war on drugs is concerned, it is common knowledge that the U.S. government favors a bilateral rather than a regional approach (Klepak 1996). Consequently, democracy and human rights dominate the OAS agenda as never before.

Democracy and human rights have sometimes been regarded as separate items on the OAS agenda. The approach we have adopted is different, our assumption being that, because they constitute the core of liberal pluralism, democracy and human rights constantly overlap. This is the viewpoint implicit, for example, in the appraisal made by former UN Secretary-General Boutros Boutros-Ghali, when he observed that "the protection of [human rights] is closely linked to the process of democracy" (Boutros-Ghali 1995: 3). The same vision also informs the Miami summit's Plan of Action, according to which "a democracy is judged by the rights enjoyed by its least influential members" (Rosenberg and Stein 1995: 13). In this chapter, the questions of democracy and human rights will be discussed as complementary and indissociable issues of inter-American cooperation.

Our analysis builds on a body of literature that focuses on the OAS's increasing involvement in the promotion of democracy and human rights (Acevedo 1993; Acevedo and Grossman 1996; Bloomfield 1994; Farer 1993, 1996; Gosselin, Mace, and Bélanger 1995; Padilla 1993; Valenzuela 1997; Villagran de León 1992; Vivanco 1994). Our objective is to determine whether, on the basis of its work in the area of democracy, the OAS is contributing to the construction of hemispheric regionalism either as a forum or as a player. In the first section of the chapter we describe how the OAS has recently made it possible to institutionalize certain regional principles and norms regarding democracy and human rights. In the second section we examine what the OAS is doing in order to put those regional principles and norms into effect. Basing the third section on a critical analysis of the OAS's role as both forum and player, we assess the extent of inter-American consensus in matters of democracy and human rights. Finally, in the conclusion we locate the OAS's work on democracy in relation to the overall dynamics of inter-American cooperation.

A Changing Democracy Doctrine

As of the mid-1980s, once the dictatorships had begun to topple in the hemisphere, a new climate of cooperation started to take shape in inter-American relations. The new climate allowed the OAS to refine its definition of democracy and human rights and to undertake a host of new initiatives regarding these matters. A first step was the adoption of the Protocol of Cartagena in 1985. In this charter amendment, the OAS's commitment toward the promotion and strengthening of representative democracy was articulated more explicitly than ever before, and the need to uphold the sacrosanct principle of nonintervention was reaffirmed. In particular, the Protocol of Cartagena recognized representative democracy as "an indispensable condition for the stability, peace and development of the region." It also established a direct link between democracy and human rights by referring to the need to "consolidate, in the framework of democratic institutions, a regime of individual liberties and social justice, based on the respect of human rights" (Organization of American States 1989: 1).

In 1990, as a new member of the OAS, Canada provided the leadership for the creation of a Unit for the Promotion of Democracy (UPD). Within a few years the UPD became the institutional focal point for most of the OAS's efforts in the area of democracy. The main purpose of the UPD is to provide advisory services and technical assistance to help OAS members develop democratic institutions and procedures. At the time of its creation, three specific fields of endeavor were identified: electoral processes, legislative processes, and educational programs for promoting democracy. Electoral monitoring soon took precedence over other priorities, but the UPD is now seeking to enlarge its scope by emphasizing the global and integral nature of democracy. Increasingly, the UPD's discourse stresses the need to consolidate both civic practices and mechanisms of participation in the political process (Organization of American States 1997b: 5). As UPD head Elizabeth Spehar explains, "The premise behind the Unit's support is the need to develop the democratic political culture of the countries of the hemisphere, as the most fundamental way of ensuring that democracy will thrive and endure in the Americas" (Organization of American States 1996: 5).

In the wake of the establishment of the UPD, the OAS General Assembly in June 1991 took another decisive step regarding representative democracy. In the Santiago Commitment to Democracy and the Renewal of the Inter-American System adopted on that occasion, member states reaffirmed their "inescapable commitment" to the defense and promotion of democracy and human rights in the Western Hemisphere (Vaky and Muñoz 1993: 104). The Santiago meeting also led to the adoption of Resolution 1080, which is less rhetorical and contains more operational provisions than the Santiago Commitment. Resolution 1080 requires an immediate meeting of the OAS Permanent Council in the event of a sudden interruption of the democratic process within a member state. The resolution also provides for the convening of an ad hoc meeting of the ministers of foreign affairs or a special session of the General Assembly within a ten-day period in order to determine the measures to be taken. What makes Resolution 1080 innovative is, above all, the mandatory nature of the proposed procedure as well as the involvement of top-level representatives of the member states. Widely recognized as a major breakthrough in inter-American cooperation, Resolution 1080 was not easily adopted. The reservations expressed by Brazil, Colombia, and Mexico bespoke a major divide between noninterventionists and activists (Argentina, Canada, Chile, the United States, and Venezuela were among the latter). Mexico was the last to rally to the final compromise, but it did so with extreme reluctance (Bloomfield 1994).

The OAS's commitment to the collective defense of democracy advanced with the adoption of the Protocol of Washington at the Sixteenth Special Session of the General Assembly in December 1992. When this amendment to the OAS charter goes into effect, it will give the organization the authority, provided there is a two-thirds majority, to suspend a member state whose democratic government has been overthrown by force. As of mid-1998, the Protocol of Washington had been ratified by twenty states. Like Resolution 1080, the Protocol of Washington is meant to have a dissuasive effect on any group or faction that may be tempted to disrupt the functioning of democratic institutions in a member state. The Protocol of Washington was another instance of confrontation between activists and noninterventionists in the OAS. Isolated once again, Mexico finally voted against it. In its official statement appended to the protocol, the Mexican government insisted that "Mexico is opposed to the punitive character ascribed to the OAS" and that "it is unacceptable to give to regional organizations supra-national powers and instruments for intervening in the internal affairs of our states" (Organization of American States 1997c: 2)

The OAS doctrine of democracy was extended further with the Declaration of Managua for the Promotion of Democracy and Development, adopted at the 1993 OAS General Assembly. This declaration made clear that the OAS's mission was not "restricted to defending democracy wherever its fundamental values and principles have collapsed" and called for "a continuing effort to prevent and anticipate the very causes of the problems that work against democratic rule" (Vaky and Muñoz 1993: 111). In particular, the Declaration of Managua established a direct link between the development of democracy and the eradication of extreme poverty.

The relationship between democracy and development was readdressed in a more solemn and comprehensive manner at the Miami summit. From its very title, the Declaration of Principles adopted on that occasion linked the issues of democracy, free trade, and sustainable development. Besides the ritualistic commitments to preserve and strengthen democratic systems, the declaration affirmed that "democracy and development reinforce one another" and that "the fruits of democratic stability and economic growth must be accessible to all" (Rosenberg and Stein 1995: 9, 11). Complementing the Declaration of Principles, the Miami Plan of Action drew attention to new problems that could be considered threats to democracy, such as corruption, crime, and terrorism (Rosenberg and Stein 1995: 14–16). In a subsection of the document devoted to human rights, the governments of the hemisphere renewed their commitment to inter-American human rights bodies and furthermore agreed to promote greater coordination in that regard between the OAS and the Inter-American Development Bank. The Miami summit thus helped clarify and further legitimize the hemispheric democracy doctrine.

Early in 1995, the new secretary-general of the OAS, César Gaviria, strove to sustain the "spirit of Miami" in a major document titled "A New

Vision of the OAS." This document was submitted as "a navigational chart in the quest for true participatory democracy" (Organization of American States 1995: 5). On a symbolic level, Gaviria's "New Vision" was a confirmation of the OAS's repositioning thereafter as an international forum dedicated above all to the promotion and defense of democracy. On a substantive level, the distinguishing feature of this document was its effort to propose a people-centered, as opposed to a state-centered, definition of sovereignty. "An active citizen and a well-organized civil society," wrote the secretary-general, "are the guarantees of effective exercise of popular sovereignty" (Organization of American States 1995: 9). Built on the concept of equality of all citizens, the approach advocated by Gaviria reinforced the link between the promotion of democracy and respect for human rights. Yet on the eve of the year 2000, the realization of a more solid conjunction between these two objectives remains the most difficult challenge facing the OAS.

The foregoing summary of events demonstrates how, for more than a decade, the OAS has been seeking to better define its role in strengthening democracy in the region. In general terms, that role can be analyzed with reference to two horizons: the short term and the long term. In the short term, Resolution 1080 and the Washington protocol are the OAS's main instruments for responding in a concerted manner to any attempt at interrupting democracy. In the long term, the UPD emerges as the primary tool for the organization's ability to ensure the growth of democratic institutions in the hemisphere. Overall, the inter-American doctrine of democracy is founded on a set of legal and policy norms that are increasingly consistent.

Such consistency, however, takes on a completely different cast in light of the fact that neither financial nor human resources have kept pace with the broadening of the OAS's mandate. In 1997, the UPD's budget was less than U.S.$15 million. The Inter-American Commission on Human Rights (IACHR) has only thirteen lawyers to monitor human rights in the entire hemisphere. Clearly, a significant gap exists between the organization's ambitious goals and the paucity of the means at its disposal. And the gap does not seem to be narrowing. At present, only a handful of countries make a significant contribution to the OAS budget. The United States is the one country capable of leading the way toward financial soundness but sees no interest in doing so. The U.S. share of the OAS budget was officially reduced from 66 percent to 59.47 percent in 1990 after Washington unilaterally decided, as it had done at the UN, to pay only a fraction of its assessment (Vaky 1993: 39). In the final analysis, the OAS's chronic lack of resources betrays a lack of political will among the member states and constitutes the most concrete impediment to the achievement of the organization's goals with respect to democracy and human rights.

OAS Activities

OAS activities are commonly divided into those concerning the defense of democracy and those concerning the promotion of democracy. The attention of diplomats and the media has focused primarily on defense operations because of their immediate political impact. Since 1991 Resolution 1080 has conferred on the OAS unprecedented powers to prevent the overthrow of elected governments. So far, Resolution 1080 has been used on four occasions. In the first three cases, constitutional authority had been aborted outright by a military coup or an executive move to shut down the national legislature. These were the September 1991 military coup in Haiti and the *autogolpes* (self-coups) of the president of Peru in April 1992 and the president of Guatemala in May 1993. The fourth case, the Paraguayan crisis of April 1996, was different inasmuch as democratic institutions, though seriously threatened, were ultimately maintained.

In each of these four situations, a meeting of the OAS Permanent Council was convened as provided in Resolution 1080. Except in the case of Paraguay, there followed an ad hoc meeting of the ministers of foreign affairs to determine which collective measures would be taken. These diplomatic initiatives made it possible to adopt resolutions condemning the interruption of constitutional rule and to undertake mediation. In the cases of Peru, Guatemala, and Paraguay, these actions, in conjunction with international and domestic pressures, helped resolve the crisis rapidly. In Peru, President Alberto Fujimori agreed to a compromise, which, though considered by some a step back for democracy, was deemed satisfactory by the OAS. In Guatemala, President Jorge Serrano Elías, who had dissolved the Congress and the Supreme Court, was soon forced to step down. Finally, in Paraguay, President Juan Carlos Wasmosy emerged victorious from his confrontation with army commander General Limo César Oviedo.

The OAS's involvement in the Haitian crisis turned out to be more difficult. The overthrow of President Jean-Bertrand Aristide on September 30, 1991, entailed the first enforcement ever of Resolution 1080. Thus, considering that it was a precedent, the OAS's response at the time was remarkably swift and resolute. The Permanent Council condemned the coup d'état the very day it took place. In the first days of October, the ad hoc meeting of ministers of foreign affairs decided that the OAS would not recognize the representatives of the new government and that the IACHR would present a report on the human rights situation in the country. The ministers called for the diplomatic isolation of the new regime and asked member states of the OAS to suspend economic relations with Haiti. However, when the de facto Haitian government systematically refused to comply with the demands of the other governments of the hemisphere, the

OAS found itself at a loss and was unable to step up its political and economic sanctions. The OAS's lack of leadership eventually opened the door to a joint intervention by the UN and the United States. Indeed, it was on the basis of a UN Security Council resolution authorizing the use of all means necessary that the United States organized the deployment of military forces that allowed President Aristide to return to power in 1994. In short, the Haitian crisis "dramatically reveal[ed] the limits of OAS action" (Acevedo and Grossman 1996: 145).

Overall, recent history testifies to the growth of the OAS's capacity to defend democracy collectively. Through a series of unprecedented actions, the organization has contributed, albeit in ways that are not easily measured, to the maintenance of the rule of law in the region. Yet the Haitian episode argues against the temptation to overestimate the OAS's newly acquired influence. The OAS is not in a position, for example, to enforce an embargo, nor can it resort to military force. Furthermore, the OAS's low profile during Ecuador's constitutional crisis in February 1997 prompted a number of observers to cast doubts on the level of commitment of governments in the region to a truly credible system for defending democracy (Inter-American Dialogue 1997b: 7).

Regarding the OAS's role in the broader arena of the promotion of democracy and human rights, once again, the 1990s represent a turning point. Under this head, the OAS's most important activity consists in supporting and evaluating election processes. As of mid-1998, the UPD has participated in more than thirty-seven electoral observation missions (Organization of American States 1998). Most of the missions were organized to monitor presidential elections, but in some countries the UPD was also invited to support municipal electoral processes. OAS missions cover a broad range of issues, including "the organization and administration of the elections themselves, enforcement of the electoral laws, the registration of parties and candidates, the preparation of the voter rolls, the campaign, and citizen participation" (Organization of American States 1997d: 30). Electoral missions have done much to enhance the OAS's reputation and credibility in recent years, yet they have been the target of some serious criticism. It has been suggested that "the missions . . . generally try to settle electoral irregularities privately with the national electoral authorities rather than confront the host government directly" (Inter-American Dialogue 1996: 5). To the extent that the OAS avoids "being politically contentious," its actual contribution to the democratization of the countries where it intervenes remains moot (Inter-American Dialogue 1996: 5). The question arises whether the organization does not at times serve only to lend international legitimacy to governments wishing to maintain the status quo.

Another major component of OAS activities in favor of democracy and human rights was developed to address the specific needs of countries

ravaged by civil war. Assuming as a premise that peace is the first condition for the establishment of democracy, the OAS has been extremely active in what has been termed "post-conflict reconstruction." Activities of
this type have included demining operations, as well as the demobilization
of armed groups, the verification of the application of the peace accords,
the provision of social services, and the rebuilding of institutions. OAS
post-conflict reconstruction work has been most intensive in Nicaragua.
There the OAS has been involved in the peace process since 1989 through
the International Commission for Support and Verification (CIAV), constituted jointly with the UN. According to one expert, "The experience of coordinated United Nations–OAS operations in Nicaragua was not a very
positive one" (Baranyi 1995: 351). The CIAV was criticized most notably
for having been incapable of preventing renewed outbursts of violence
(Millet 1994). As Stephen Baranyi concludes, however, "It is worth noting
that it is the OAS which remained in Nicaragua to provide the required
longer-term peace-building services and that the OAS appears to be learning the importance of maintaining strict impartiality when dealing with
disputants in such conflicts" (Baranyi 1995: 351).

The OAS has furthermore been active in other parts of Central America, although in El Salvador and Guatemala the conflicting parties preferred to call on the UN rather than the OAS. Looking outside Central
America, the OAS also assisted the peace process in Surinam, where it
was instrumental in the signing and application of the 1992 peace accords.
It was assigned responsibility for tasks related to the disarmament of com-
batants, demining, and the supervision of elections. As shown by the convergence of these various cases, post-conflict reconstruction has now become a key element of the OAS's approach to democracy.

The OAS also promotes the strengthening of democracy and human
rights through a series of training, education, research, and information
initiatives. In Nicaragua, for example, the UPD has provided support to establish peace and human rights commissions and has organized workshops
for local political officers from conflict zones. In Haiti, it has set up human
rights educational programs (Organization of American States 1997d:
26–29). Currently the UPD is trying to act more as the catalyst rather than
the chief manager of such undertakings. It increasingly insists on the need
for an exchange of experiences among OAS members and for partnerships
with other institutions such as the Inter-American Development Bank. The
UPD's long-term approach to democracy has generally been viewed favorably. In particular, the UPD has provided expertise that would not otherwise have been available. Yet the work accomplished by this agency has
nevertheless given rise to all sorts of questions. For one thing, it has been
suggested that "the Unit has not developed an integrated strategy concerning what 'democracy promotion' is," an omission that engenders the risk

that projects may be subordinated to political criteria (Inter-American Dialogue 1997a: 14–15). More fundamentally, one may ask how the UPD, with its very limited budget, can hope to make a significant difference for the development of a hemispheric democratic culture.

Finally, the OAS has helped to promote democracy and human rights through initiatives of a normative nature. For example, two such initiatives stem directly from the Miami summit. First, in March 1996, the member states of the OAS signed the Inter-American Convention Against Corruption. One of the noteworthy innovations of this convention was a set of measures designed to facilitate interstate cooperation regarding bank secrecy. Second, in April 1996, the OAS made possible the adoption of the Declaration of Lima to Prevent, Combat, and Eliminate Terrorism, which defines terrorism as a crime that "impairs the rule of law and democracy." These new legal instruments do not broaden the judicial functions of the OAS as such. However, they clearly illustrate how the OAS is actively seeking to enlarge and deepen its role in the consolidation of democracy in the region.

Scope and Limits of the New Consensus on Democracy

The OAS's new commitment to democracy and human rights has substantially raised the credibility of the project of hemispheric regionalism. There is little doubt that regional cooperation is more readily accomplished among states sharing common political values, and the OAS has done much over the past decade to foster the growth of such common values in the Americas. There is now an unprecedented consensus among states regarding the understanding of the rules of governance applicable to either their own jurisdiction or to others in the region. At the same time, the OAS's goal of bringing about a distinct and truly Pan-American conception of democracy is not yet at hand.

The expansion of the OAS's ambit and activities in the area of democracy and human rights derives from profound attitudinal changes within the countries of Latin America. The most significant of these changes is that democracy is no longer seen as a strictly domestic issue. As Tom Farer observes, governments in the region are showing a "growing tolerance" toward external action aimed at defending democracy. "Even measures that would once have been widely condemned as impermissible intervention," he explains, "are acquiring a remarkable aura of legitimacy" (Farer 1996: 4–5). This new interpretation of the notion of sovereignty is all the more consequential in light of how ardently Latin American governments had always defended nonintervention as a fundamental principle of inter-American cooperation. Some countries, such as Mexico and Peru, have sought to downplay the meaning of the new norms adopted by the OAS, and their governments continue to affirm the primacy of national sovereignty. But despite any "jurisprudential controversy" that may arise from the ranking of the principles governing inter-American relations, the sovereignty of the state has clearly lost its former status of inviolable doctrine (Tesón 1996: 33).

The Paraguayan crisis of 1996 offers one of the most telling illustrations of the recent ascendancy of democratic values in the Americas. The involvement of the international community, added to domestic pressures, was decisive for the resolution of the standoff between President Wasmosy, representing constitutional order, and a faction of the military headed by General Oviedo. The OAS was an active player in this international response, but its role was not the most influential. Much more crucial were the actions of the foreign ministers of Brazil and Argentina, who went to Asunción and threatened to exclude Paraguay from the Southern Cone Common Market should that country renege on its democratic commitments. As noted by Richard Feinberg, "It is difficult to overstate the historical significance of this willingness of South America's largest economies to intervene—boldly and openly—in the domestic affairs of another Latin American state" (Feinberg 1997: 167). Thus, what emerges above all from the Paraguayan episode is the increasing internalization of democratic principles by the political elites of the hemisphere. Ironically, General Oviedo himself is reported to have declared that "with the OAS's adoption of Resolution 1080 in Santiago, the era of military coups in Latin America had come to an end" (Valenzuela 1997: 54).

There is no doubt that the OAS considers the electoral process the single most important institutional component of a democratic system. Hence, the charter highlights the notion of representative democracy, a notion defined in the Santiago Commitment as the "expression of the legitimate and free manifestation of the will of the people" (Organization of American States 1991). The new inter-American consensus nevertheless encompasses the idea that the requirements of democratic government go much beyond the mere holding of elections. Gradually, a more substantive understanding of democracy has gained authority within the OAS's discourse. First, it is acknowledged as never before that a democracy cannot enjoy full legitimacy if it does not include an independent legislative body, an effective judiciary, a transparent public administration, a dynamic party system, and the decentralization of state powers in favor of local jurisdictions. Second, the governments of Latin America now agree that democracy requires close civilian supervision of the armed forces. In this regard, the launching of programs to educate civilian leaders on security issues and military officials on the workings of democracy is a promising initiative (Inter-American Dialogue 1997a: 24). Finally, a new consensus has been achieved on the notion that democracy is linked to the economic environment. The United States now admits that extreme poverty undermines democracy, whereas Latin America has come to recognize that trade liberalization promotes democracy. On the whole, then, there has been an ideological convergence among governments in the hemisphere regarding some basic elements that should define a democratic culture.

Furthermore, the OAS has fostered a strengthening of regional common values through its efforts on human rights issues. It has long been recognized that the OAS has established the "second-best regional regime for human rights," after the European Union (Forsythe 1991: 87). In the 1990s the OAS has succeeded in further broadening the inter-American human rights regime. For the first time, the IACHR was invited to observe the human rights situation in Brazil (1995) and Mexico (1996). More fundamentally, the OAS has paid increasing attention to all forms of discrimination—social, sexual, ethnic, and racial. Given the position of women in traditional Latin American societies, the adoption of the Inter-American Convention on the Prevention, Punishment and Eradication of Violence Against Women in 1994 represents a major symbolic victory in the struggle for equal rights.

Current discussions within the IACHR aimed at advancing the rights of indigenous peoples, the disabled, and migrants are another indication of the new conception of justice that is gaining momentum throughout the Americas. Historically, it is the most mature democracies that have paid the greatest attention to the rights of vulnerable groups. Seen in that light, the OAS's recent work on human rights issues certainly helps consolidate the democratic commitment of the governments of the hemisphere. From a broader perspective, this work provides another example of how the political values of the various countries of the region are evolving through the setting of ever more ambitious shared objectives.

The new inter-American consensus on democracy and human rights issues was made possible by a unique combination of domestic and international factors. On the domestic level, every country in the hemisphere, with the exception of Cuba, is currently ruled by an elected government. Since 1980, Haiti has been the only country to experience the overthrow of a democratic government; even so, President Aristide was eventually reinstated (Inter-American Dialogue 1997b: 7). This wave of democratization has resulted largely from the exhaustion of the authoritarian regimes long considered typical of Latin America. The "lost decade" of the 1980s irrevocably sapped the legitimacy of the military governments that held power in a number of countries. Thereafter, "the economic failure of most of [the] dictatorships, their militarizing self-serving policies and the human rights horrors they had perpetrated could no longer be ignored" (Brachet-Marquez 1997: 19). Such economic and political conditions were conducive to the growth of a strong pro-democracy movement throughout the region. Once elected, the democratic governments felt it was in their interests to obtain international protection; by ensuring the maintenance of democracy in nearby states, they would be ensuring the maintenance of democracy within their own borders.

The democratization of Latin America has also been aided by a favorable international environment. To quote Mihaly Simai, the post–Cold War era is characterized "by an unprecedented spread of universal suffrage and by greater pluralism . . . than the world has ever seen" (Simai 1994: 346). In 1994, 114 countries could be considered democratic, a twofold increase over the previous ten years (Diamond 1995: 9). A major effect of the end of the Cold War was the resolution of the civil wars in Central America, which paved the way toward national reconciliation in this subregion. More generally, the end of the Cold War provided spectacular confirmation that the political choices made by the countries of Latin America as of the early 1980s coincided with major historical trends. With the fall of socialism, no credible alternative to the democratic model was left standing. As Boutros Boutros-Ghali has noted, "People in nations around the world have become more insistent in their demands for democracy" (Boutros-Ghali 1995: 5). Latin America has been particularly affected by this global movement.

But although there has been remarkable progress in recent years, the inter-American consensus on democratic values remains fragile (Thérien, Fortmann, and Gosselin 1996: 228–229; Wiarda 1997, 15–22). First, it may be extravagant to describe the Americas as a "community of democratic societies," as was done at the Miami summit (Rosenberg and Stein 1995: 9). The term "community" implies a certain homogeneity, whereas, in fact, the political regimes of the various countries of the hemisphere are highly disparate. To gauge this diversity properly, Larry Diamond proposes a distinction between "democracies" and "semi-democracies." In his estimation, in 1994 only nine of the twenty-two Latin American countries "stood within the conceptual threshold of democracy" (Diamond 1996: 61). Hence, the notion of a community of democracies is mistaken inasmuch as a number of governments are unable to enforce the rule of law or uphold civil liberties effectively.

In addition, the newness of the inter-American consensus on democracy makes it all the more tenuous. However avant-garde Resolution 1080 may be, it goes back to only 1991; it is therefore too soon to draw conclusions about the depth of the attitudinal changes associated with the resolution. At this juncture, there is no assurance that democracy in Latin America is irreversible. The lukewarm endorsement of democratic ideals by such countries as Mexico, Peru, and Colombia is one reason for caution. A second is that in several polities the military continues to play a leading role. The two attempted coups that in recent years shook an apparently well-established democracy like Venezuela are enough to give pause. To a large extent, the speed and magnitude of political change in Latin America during the 1990s explain why the roots of democracy there remain as shallow as they do (Brachet-Marquez 1997: 46).

In addition, the scope of the inter-American consensus on democracy is limited. For example, the OAS doctrine concerning the collective defense of democracy excludes the creation of instruments such as early-warning systems, mandatory sanctions whenever a government is toppled, or the establishment of peacekeeping forces. Moreover, the road toward the attainment of democracy remains unclear. Secretary-General Gaviria has chosen to obscure this problem further by affirming that although democracy is a common objective for governments in the region, not every country is obliged to apply "the same model" (Organization of American States 1995: 9). Such ambiguous diplomatic language has the advantage of leaving the door open to a multiplicity of traditions and experiences; it is thus perfectly consistent with the demand-driven, noncoercive approach preferred by the OAS. Its ambivalence, however, testifies to the inability of governments in the hemisphere to articulate the contents of their democratic aspirations.

Thus far, the OAS has had far more success producing agreements on abstract and long-term goals than promoting specific legislative initiatives in favor of land reforms, tax reforms, or reforms in education systems. As noted earlier, the positions of the United States and Latin America have of late undergone a remarkable rapprochement regarding the links between democracy and development. Yet major differences persist. A huge gap still separates the United States and the countries of Latin America over their respective interpretations of the assignment of responsibilities in the struggle against poverty. Simply put, the United States sees poverty as a domestic issue, whereas Latin Americans argue that it is a transnational problem. In a broader perspective, a number of Latin American observers remain suspicious of the fact that U.S. support for democratization is closely tied to Washington's bias in favor of market liberalization (Payne 1996: 112–113). They stress that the benefits that were to be derived from Latin America's recent economic reforms are still hard to discern (Inter-American Dialogue 1997b: 11–12). All in all, the economic parameters that ought to provide the framework for the OAS's democratic project clearly remain an ongoing source of tension in hemispheric relations.

As for the defense of human rights, again, the confluence of values among the countries of the hemisphere has limits that should not be underestimated. First, the inter-American human rights regime is a two-tiered system because barely half of the governments of the region have accepted the Inter-American Court's jurisdiction. Nonparticipants include the United

States, Canada, Brazil, and Mexico; thus it is apparent that only small and medium-size countries are fully integrated into this regional regime. Second, there is a persistent controversy over the management principles of the system. For example, certain IACHR and Inter-American Court nominations over the years suggest that some OAS members prefer a system subordinated to political aims rather than to criteria of professional competency.

Moreover, the very nature of the roles played by the commission and the court remains contentious. The debates are crystallizing in an environment radically different from the one that prevailed until the early 1990s. As the commission's latest annual report points out, "Paradoxically, the new situation in the Hemisphere [has] . . . generated more cases for the Commission because in democratic systems individuals actively seek to assert their rights." The report adds that "cases [have] grown legally more complex to reflect a shift from violations of basic rights to disputes over more complex legal interpretations typical of increasingly open societies" (Organization of American States 1997e: 805). Irritated by this new trend, some governments, in an attempt to weaken the commission, have tried to restrict its functions to promotion and education. Drawing on their newly acquired democratic legitimacy, they argue that with the disappearance of authoritarian regimes the commission has lost much of its raison d'être. Though still marginal, this point of view does betoken the shortcomings of the convergence of values regarding human rights in the Americas.

As Richard Feinberg has stressed, with the end of the 1980s "the hemisphere's intellectual climate changed dramatically" (Feinberg 1997: 34). The countries of the region are more united than ever in their conception of democracy and human rights, and this new context has largely contributed to the dynamics of hemispheric cooperation. Not only is a freer politics increasingly considered ethically superior, but it is also seen as the most appropriate road to economic growth. Undeniably, among the intertwined domestic and international factors that have made possible this conceptual transformation, the multilateral initiatives of the OAS have played a considerable part. But it would be easy—and tempting—to overestimate the OAS's accomplishments as well as the true state of the inter-American consensus on democracy. To borrow Howard Wiarda's image, "The glass of democracy in Latin America is still only half full" (Wiarda 1997: 15). Because of this situation, the political values that might compose the cement for hemispheric regionalism remain an important subject of debate.

Conclusion

Inter-American relations have undergone a substantial transformation in the 1990s. Although the depth of this transformation should not be exaggerated, hemispheric regionalism has benefited from an exceptional political thrust owing to the 1994 Miami summit. This context of renewal explains why the OAS currently enjoys an unprecedented legitimacy. As we suggest in this chapter, the resurgence of the OAS has been evident primarily in the areas of democracy and human rights. In most other fields of inter-American cooperation, particularly economic and security issues, the OAS has played a distinctly less consequential role.

In the economic arena, it is true that in recent years the OAS has attended to matters of commerce and integration as never before. Soon after the launching of the Enterprise for the Americas Initiative by U.S. president George Bush in 1990, the OAS established a working group to handle this project; then, in 1993, a Special Committee on Trade was created to promote dialogue on hemispheric trade liberalization. Yet it became clear through these developments that the OAS was not likely to serve as anything more than a forum for discussion and the exchange of information. That status was confirmed when the Miami summit set up the so-called Trade Ministerial, a political process basically independent of the OAS, to steer the negotiations on the creation of a Free Trade Area of the Americas. The OAS's functions in relation to this project are restricted essentially to technical support. Hence, the duties of the OAS Trade Unit, which was created in 1995, are centered on the preparation of specialized studies and the coordination of ministerial meetings (Inter-American Dialogue 1997a: 27–28). With regard to development financing, the OAS's contribution also appears to be slim. The OAS's resources are simply too modest in comparison with those available to other aid agencies, such as the Inter-American Development Bank and the World Bank.

With respect to security, there are a number of reasons that its priority on the OAS agenda has been on the decline. First, with the end of the Cold War, the relative weight of security matters has decreased in the Americas, as it has elsewhere around the world. Instead, attention has been focused on the new threats to security, such as drugs and migration. But on these issues the OAS remains sharply divided; moreover, it does not command any real authority to resolve these problems. Regarding more traditional armed conflicts, the end of the East-West confrontation has allowed the OAS to be more active, but it has also brought to light some of the organization's limitations. In many conflicts—for example, those in El Salvador and Haiti—the OAS has been obliged to yield political leadership of the peacekeeping operations to the United States or the UN. Furthermore, the OAS has been marginalized in terms of regional negotiation structures. The Committee on Hemispheric Security, established in 1992 within the OAS, was bypassed via the Defense Ministerial set up by the U.S. government's initiative soon after the Miami summit. Finally, a number of the security problems that recently arose in the hemisphere were related to domestic rather than international conflicts. Because the solutions they required were far more political than military, these conflicts helped cast a new light on security issues and heightened the importance of the OAS's concern for democratization.

This, then, is the backdrop against which democracy and human rights have today become the OAS's top priority. Concurrently, these are the areas where the OAS has best succeeded in affirming its relevance and authority. Admittedly, the OAS cannot be considered as the main determinant of the advancement of the region toward democracy. Nevertheless, the organization has made a noticeable contribution to this advancement by combining its initiatives with those of many other political forces. The OAS has been influential as both a forum, through the progressive broadening of the organization's mandate regarding democracy, and as a player, through the application of a series of concrete measures designed to defend and promote the rule of law in the region. As Andrew Hurrell has suggested, the strengthening of the OAS's role in the fields of democracy and human rights testifies to an unprecedented "ideological convergence" in the hemisphere (Hurrell 1995a: 273). This convergence has made it possible to lend a far more cooperative impetus to inter-American relations. By the same token, it has generated a political climate favorable to the development of hemispheric regionalism. Yet the progress achieved in recent years should not obscure the magnitude of the challenges that remain.

Some of those challenges are related to conjuncture; others are structural in nature. Since the Miami summit, hemispheric regionalism has lost the momentum of the early 1990s. Because this negative trend seems largely due to Washington's foreign policy choices (Inter-American Dialogue 1997b: 4), Latin American governments will no doubt be increasingly wary of accepting any measure, whether it concerns democracy, human rights, or any other issue, that might be interpreted as a concession to the United States. From a structural perspective, the overall dynamics of inter-American relations continues to be encumbered by the weight of past conflicts. As argued by Feinberg, "Mistrust of the United States still pervades many sectors of Latin American societies, including parts of the foreign policy establishments and bureaucracies" (Feinberg 1997: 38). The United States, for its part, often sees Latin America as a group of underdeveloped countries "roughly fifty years behind Canada and the United States in terms of the prosperity of its citizens and the solidity of its democratic institutions" (Harrison 1997: 18). Rooted in the wide gap that characterizes the distribution of wealth in the Americas, this atmosphere of mutual suspicion constitutes a powerful brake on any new cooperation initiatives. In the end, it is clear that the OAS is now in a better position to make a significant contribution to the growth of hemispheric regionalism.

Unfortunately, this unique situation does not in itself guarantee the success of the organization's future undertakings.

Note

The authors would like to thank research assistant Joël Monfils for his excellent work in collecting and organizing data.

10

Business and Integration in the Americas: Competing Points of View

Klaus Peter Fischer

The private sector is driving economic integration, and governments are responding in an appropriate manner.

Thomas "Mack" McLarty,
Mexico Chamber of Commerce, May 1996

International relations within Latin America and between Latin America and the United States are undergoing a revolution. After decades of effort in pursuit of economic integration and only limited success, a handful of new initiatives less than ten years old appear to have fundamentally modified the dynamics of the integration process in the Western Hemisphere. On one side, there is the U.S.-sponsored Free Trade Agreement of the Americas (FTAA), which seems to be progressing against all odds, and on the other, the remarkable case of the Southern Cone Common Market (Mercosur).

At a time when integration efforts had essentially ground to a halt in the face of accumulated failures, the launch of Mercosur in the early 1990s seemed a bold move, with more skeptics than believers. Since then, not only has Mercosur proved itself a remarkable success by any standards in achieving the economic integration of its member states, but it has also injected new energy into integration processes in the rest of the hemisphere, including those involving the United States itself. It has done this in two different ways: first, by rapidly assimilating neighboring states into the Mercosur alliance[1] and, second, by becoming the standard by which the success of other initiatives such as the Andean Pact/Andean Community, the Group of Three (G3), and the Central American and Caribbean integration processes are measured. In fact, Mercosur is so successful that it

195

has now become a pole of attraction for business and integration efforts throughout the whole Southern Cone,[2] much like the North American Free Trade Agreement (NAFTA) (albeit in a somewhat humbler fashion) in North America.

Mercosur's economic success should not come as a surprise. It is the second richest regional development pole in the Americas and the richest south of the Rio Grande, with a population of some 200 million and a gross regional product of over $600 billion.[3] It is also the fourth largest (in terms of gross regional product) and richest (in terms of per capita income) integrated market in the world after NAFTA, the European Economic Community, and Japan.[4] As a result, other Latin American integration experiments have initiated a dynamic process of restructuring and renewal while preparing to associate themselves with either Mercosur or NAFTA, or both. Starting in 1988, the Andean Pact, originally founded in 1969, initiated a far-reaching restructuring process that went public in March 1996 under the new name of the Andean Community.[5] The Caribbean Community and Common Market (CARICOM) undertook a similar course of action beginning in 1993.

The FTAA is tentatively scheduled to come into effect in 2005. Originally launched by President George Bush as the Enterprise for the Americas Initiative in late June 1990, the FTAA was formulated at the Summit of the Americas in December 1994 and enthusiastically adopted by President Bill Clinton. The 1990 Bush initiative came at virtually the same moment as the agreement in principle to launch the Mercosur initiative, which was signed by Brazil, Uruguay, Chile, and Argentina in Brasilia in early August of the same year. It is interesting to note that two of the three initiatives (the FTAA, Mercosur, and NAFTA) that are changing the economic landscape of the continent were born almost simultaneously.

Since 1994, President Clinton has taken to visiting Latin America (and particularly the Mercosur countries) to actively promote the FTAA. Although clearly a much more complex undertaking than either Mercosur or NAFTA, the FTAA has received an unambiguously positive and constructive response from Latin American governments. Negotiations are progressing remarkably quickly and with a smoothness astonishing to any reasonably well informed observer of the historically bumpy relationship between the United States and Latin America. In fact, opposition to the process is currently stronger in the United States—where Congress refused to grant fast-track approval for free trade negotiations to President Clinton in late 1997—than it is in Latin America.

The consolidation of regional integration processes (Mercosur, the Andean Community, NAFTA, etc.) and FTAA negotiations should be seen as two complementary and converging processes, one from below and the other from above. The simultaneity of this bipolar process is perhaps the best guarantee of the kind of results that have eluded all previous attempts at continental integration, including the U.S.-sponsored initiatives Latin American Free Trade Association (LAFTA) and the Latin American Integration Association (ALADI) as well as the anti-U.S. Latin American Economic System (SELA). By the time the FTAA becomes a reality in 2005 or later, something like a South American Free Trade Zone will most likely be in place, extending many of Mercosur's achievements to the entire Southern Cone. Signs of this happening are already starting to appear. In fact, certain countries see the creation of such a zone as a precondition for hemispheric integration with the United States through the FTAA.[6]

How can we explain this change in climate? What has been fueling this flurry of negotiations on regional and continental integration? Although a full accounting of this political process would require a chapter all its own, political will, government leadership and opportunity have all played important roles. But there is more to it than that. Current integration efforts could not succeed without strong coalitions of interests ready to support them politically, as well as corporate interests ready to carry them through by engaging in the actual trade that makes integration processes a reality.

Throughout this chapter, I will use the term "coalition" to refer to associations of social forces or groupings that agglutinate around a particular set of objectives or in opposition to some political or economic process. These coalitions may take on some formal institutional structure but are more often than not loose arrangements held together by a particular objective or opposition target. Coalition members may represent a variety of societal forces, including business groups, entrepreneurial syndicates, labor organizations, political parties, church factions, the military, and others.

For a coalition to exist and act coherently, there is no need for explicit agreement between the parties, even though such agreements may exist between some of the members. Nor do national coalitions need to be limited to national forces; they may find natural international allies prepared to join their cause and bring additional political resources to bear in support of specific coalition objectives. Like previous initiatives, recent integration initiatives would have eventually failed in the absence of such coalitions, either at the agreement design and negotiation stage or during the subsequent implementation phase.

The objective of this chapter is to provide a description of the role and attitudes of the Latin American business community[7] with regard to the integration efforts launched since 1985, particularly the FTAA and the earlier U.S. initiatives. I will analyze the positions adopted by the various coalitions of business interests that have dominated the Latin American scene since the late 1960s. This analysis will provide an opportunity to explain how various business groups supported or opposed integration efforts at different times over the period, the reasons for their positions, and the factors that have contributed to the shifts occurring today. Indeed, the importance of business participation in the integration process should not be underestimated, as a recent report released by the American Business Forum emphasized (1996).

Only a naive observer would attempt to use purely ideological or ethical arguments to explain how economic groups and interests position themselves with regard to the major economic and political developments in a nation. Similar reasoning applies when analyzing the attitudes of business interests toward issues such as international trade and economic and political integration. To introduce a measure of realism into the analysis of the motives underlying business group actions, it is essential to investigate the extent to which a particular process benefits or affects the economic interests of these same groups. The same holds true when examining how the Latin American business community regards modern-day efforts at regional integration.

To better understand contemporary business attitudes toward the integration process, we must look back at the origins and evolution of both the integration process and the Latin American business community itself.

The Latin American Business Community: A Heterogeneous Lot

The Latin American business community is a heterogeneous lot, and its members' origins, interests, and politics can and do vary substantially. A North American observer would undoubtedly be able to identify differences in business interests and political alignments within, say, the United States or Canada. However, these differences pale in comparison to those observed since the late 1940s in Latin America, where integration is one of the focal points of dispute.

The Latin American business community is much more politicized than its North American counterpart. I will not discuss the reasons for this distinction in detail here, but differences in the institutional structures framing economic life (North 1995; Kalmanovitz K. 1997) and the way economic rents are appropriated (Fischer, Ortiz, and Palasvirta 1994) in North and South America play a key role. Although a Latin American subsidiary of a multinational corporation may, under certain circumstances, ally itself with a major domestic industrial group, medium-sized manufacturer, or major grain exporter on certain matters of national interest, they are all more than likely to be in total disagreement on many others. In fact, different business interests often have their own separate organizations, adopt opposing positions on issues of national interest, and align themselves with different political parties.

The roots of these contradictions lie in the origins of these companies and the markets they serve. For the sake of clarity, let me propose this somewhat rough classification of Latin American businesses into three distinct categories:

1. Traditional exporters and merchants.
2. New industrialists.
3. Subsidiaries of multinational corporations (MNCs).

Although the third category is self-evident, it is useful to define the other two in more detail. The traditional exporters and merchants category refers to businesses involved in the export of raw materials and semiprocessed goods (mining, forest, and agricultural products) to the industrialized nations and the importation of manufactured goods from those same countries for local consumption. These importers and exporters have been classified in the same category because, although they play different economic roles, they represent two sides of the same coin. They are the agents of the neocolonial international division of labor under which Latin America, Africa, and Asia were assigned with the function of supplying raw materials and primary products, and the industrialized nations with the role of producing manufactured goods for the world economy.

The new industrialists are business interests that originally developed as suppliers of locally manufactured goods to Latin American markets, either because transportation costs or explicitly designed import barriers protected them from international competition. Companies in this category benefited considerably from the import substitution policies that dominated the developing world, and Latin America in particular, from the late 1940s through the 1980s.

Since the late 1970s, this group has evolved further into two subcategories that I have labeled (1) political rent or market segmentation-dependent national businesses and (2) Third World multinationals (TWMs) of Latin American origin. The first grouping is made up of companies that still depend on the exploitation of rents associated with barriers either of natural origin or imposed by the state for their survival, hence the name. These firms are largely incapable of operating in a competitive international environment because the cost and quality of the goods and services they produce are most often unacceptable for international markets. Their survival depends on the continued segmentation of national markets to exclude competing imports or the artificial inflation of import costs through tariffs and other barriers. The second category is composed of the more successful of these businesses, which in some countries (mostly those with a relatively large domestic economy) have become known as Third World multinationals. These corporations compete with MNCs in low-level or easily adaptable technology sectors such as transportation, agrifood (notably beverages), steel and glass production, and, more recently, the manufacture of highly standardized high-tech products (e.g., Acer Inc., Taiwan's largest maker of personal computers, has rapidly expanded production in Latin America). By and large these enterprises developed economies of scale during the protectionist era of import substitution and were then able to internationalize operations, usually either by exporting a substantial portion of their output or through foreign direct investment, joint ventures with First World multinationals, and so on. Examples of Latin American businesses that have achieved TWM status are Grupo Bunge & Borne of Argentina, Bavaria of Colombia, and Grupo Alfa of Mexico (Monterrey).

Arguably, the distinction between these various groups is somewhat artificial and there is frequent overlap. Indeed, licensing agreements, joint ventures, import-export contracts, and supply agreements, among other things, often mean that their interests do converge. However, the political reality is that these groups have all played an important role in Latin American economic and political life. In some cases, they have actually established separate organizations to actively promote their members' respective interests.

One of the most explicit institutional manifestations of such interest group activity occurred in Argentina. There, traditional exporters and merchants joined forces in the Industrial Union of Argentina (UIA), an organization that also became a formal voice for foreign MNCs, whose strategic interests often coincided with those of the UIA. In the meantime, Argentina's new industrialists, most of them medium-sized and large companies in the import substitution sector, set up the General Business Confederation (CGE).[8] Confrontations between these two national business organizations were not unusual, and sometimes strident.

Over the years, business interests in the three categories (four, if we consider the split in the new industrialists category) have taken different positions on issues of national interest and have often actively sought to influence the course of events. Their positions have frequently diverged, sometimes radically. Economic integration, like many other international issues, has been one area in which views have diverged sharply and different groups have aligned themselves with opposing political forces and parties. In the next section I will take a detailed look at the positions that businesses in the different categories have adopted with regard to international trade, as well as their primary economic motivation for doing so.

It could perhaps be argued that MNC subsidiaries are not a Latin American business group. However, in the last half of the nineteenth century their presence in Latin America—especially that of U.S.-based MNCs—has been very significant, in terms of both their share of regional gross domestic product (GDP) and the political influence they have exercised (usually with the full support of the U.S. government and its entire arsenal of pressure tactics).

Business Interests and International Trade

The origin of the different business categories has a significant bearing on the various positions that Latin American business interests have adopted with regard to international trade and regional economic integration. Understanding the role of trade in the economic activities of companies in each category helps us understand their posture with respect to various integration processes. Let us first look at the role trade has played for each of these groups over the last half of the nineteenth century. I will then complete the analysis with an examination of their ideological evolution during the globalization era, from the early 1980s to the present.

The Traditional Exporters and Merchants

The traditional exporters and merchants import manufactured goods for local consumption and exploit major natural and agricultural resources (mostly cash crops, livestock, and some mineral resources) for export to the industrialized world. They are the national producers of sugar, coffee, cocoa, wheat, beef, forest products, bananas, and other fruits. They are the landowners and, often, latifundists. They are often, albeit not always, both merchant and exporter at the same time. For them, international trade to and from the industrialized "center"[9] has always been essential for survival. Regional trade, however, is of no interest to them. Products from neighboring countries are at best of no use and at worst a source of competition for their own primary product exports to the industrialized economies. Their ideology is predominantly mercantilist and coincides largely with that of their business associates in the industrialized world. Their revenue is sensitive to the trade policies of local governments with respect to Europe and the United States, not with respect to neighboring countries.

Not surprisingly, merchants and traditional exporters greeted regional integration initiatives with everything from mild indifference to virulent opposition, depending upon the type of regional integration process proposed. They often enjoyed active support from economic and political powers in the industrialized world and made liberal use of the well-developed ideological arguments elaborated by free mercantilists and Western liberal economists to justify the division of labor on the principle of comparative advantage. In extreme cases, these groups would not hesitate to convert themselves, quite conveniently, into self-appointed defenders of "Western Judeo-Christian civilization," moving the economic battle onto moral and religious grounds in defense of their particular set of narrow interests, often with the support of the hierarchy of the Catholic church. A good Christian could not, after all, support high tariffs on foreign imports with a clear conscience!

Their principal objective, expressed and pursued through their political activities, was the integration of local markets into the world economy according to the international division of labor. Communication, transportation links, and political barriers to trade with regional neighbors were of no direct concern. Regional integration processes that did not impede the critical North-South flow of trade (such as LAFTA and ALADI initiatives) were met with benign neglect. But regional integration processes that sought to develop a local industrial base capable of competing with MNCs or industries in the developed countries (as was the intention of SELA and the original Andean Pact) were more than likely to be the target of active condemnation and virulent opposition.

The rapid globalization of the economy (with accelerated communications and financial flows) since the early 1980s and the extensive reductions in trade barriers that have followed have changed little the interests and objectives of the merchants and traditional exporters. On the contrary, they see globalization as a historical vindication of their position and do not hesitate to support political parties that were once their archenemies but are now staunch advocates of free trade. The current dominant model of integration, with its indiscriminate elimination of trade barriers between regional markets (e.g., Mercosur) and selected markets in the industrialized countries (like NAFTA or the future FTAA), does not conflict with their interests. Thus, their position as a group is one of benign tolerance.

The New Industrialists

In the past the new industrialists generally viewed international trade as at best an unavoidable nuisance. On the one hand, North-South trade was the source of much needed inputs into the productive process (technology, machines, technical personnel, specialized raw materials, etc.). On the other hand, it was also a source of dangerous competition for their often poor quality and expensive local manufactured goods. As for regional trade, it was of little or no interest to this group. Neighboring countries had no role to play in supplying inputs and were another potential source of competition for local manufacturers in the import-substitution business. The most successful firms in this category developed into large business conglomerates that sometimes dominated entire segments of a single country's economy. Notable Latin American examples of such conglomerates, better known as "industrial groups," are Mexico's Grupo Alfa, Argentina's Grupo Bunge & Born, and Colombia's Sindicato Antioquia and Grupo Santo Domingo, to mention just a few.[10] These groups dominated local business interests and often played a highly visible role in domestic politics and decisionmaking.

The new industrialists shared something of a Boston Tea Party ideology. In many cases their profitability—indeed their very survival—was dependent on trade barriers that kept foreign products out and ensured them an effective local monopoly. This group also formed the social base for the reformist economic programs proposed, perhaps most notably and coherently, by such people as Raúl Prebisch and Aldo Ferrer. Governments implementing these programs rejected the international division of labor and supported the development and protection of local industries with a pragmatism that often led them to seek trade relations with any economic block that suited their interests, even if it meant being labeled "pink" by the hawks at the U.S. State Department. Barriers to trade were essential to the economic health of the new industrialists, who actively lobbied for their imposition and conservation by the state in both North-South and regional trade. The anti-trade position of the new industrialists often led to confrontations with European and U.S.-based MNCs, as well as with the merchants and traditional exporters.

On the issue of regional integration, this group traditionally adopted a stance of qualified opposition. In their eyes, regional integration meant the elimination of national reserve markets and an end to state-protected monopolies. The potential for competition from industrial groups and manufacturers in neighboring countries was particularly feared. Barriers against imports from industrialized countries could easily be justified on the grounds that local industries needed protection to develop the economies of scale, research and development capacity, and technological excellence that allowed the industrial economies to produce superior products at a lower cost. But protection from competition originating in neighboring countries was not so easily justified. After all, manufacturers in neighboring countries were in the same predicament.

As a result, the new industrialists generally offered little support for regional integration. However, in cases where integration initiatives were politically inevitable—as they often were—they were ready to play a role in order to protect their local interests. They did so using two different strategies. The first of these was to insist on an integration process based on selective tariff reduction. This involved producing lists of selected goods with the purpose of restricting tariff reductions solely to those that would not compete with locally available products.[11] Obviously, this was a very efficient way to stop real integration in its tracks. The second strategy was much more elaborate and also more constructive. It required that regional integration be accompanied by regional planning for the development of capacity based on comparative advantage and taking into account preexisting capacities in each country involved.

The most notable and well-developed model of this type was the original Andean Pact, with its relatively sophisticated structure and ambitious regional planning objectives. The Andean Pact was designed to take advantage of member country complementarities to build a regional industrial powerhouse possessing the scope and economies of scale necessary to compete with foreign MNCs.[12] Here again, the objective was to identify complementarities and avoid direct competition between different national import substitution industries in the same market. As with the selected product list approach, however, the process was extremely difficult to put into practice and produced limited results.

Using these two strategies, the new industrialists consistently undermined attempts to establish a true integration process capable of encouraging competitive and efficient economic development. In fact, but for a few exceptions, they were the most consistent and relentless opponents of regional integration initiatives through the late 1990s. And in many cases, they have joined forces with trade unions and left-leaning political groupings to become the most strident opponents and critics of the integration model dominating Latin America today. The political dominance of this coalition in Colombia and Venezuela largely explains the limited success of the G3 initiative and, in particular, the reticence of the Colombian and Venezuelan governments to open their markets completely to Mexican goods.[13] The G3 has had enormous difficulties in shaking off the item-by-item bargaining approach characteristic of the oldtime integrationist/protectionist tradition.

Opening up markets is, of course, a two-way street. It is, as Jack Edwards and Werner Baer (1993) have correctly noted, a precondition for becoming competitive and efficient, and many companies are now successfully competing against other products in foreign markets or against foreign products in their own markets. However, others are not, and a deep restructuring of industry is taking place. Numerous firms are disappearing under the pressures of foreign competition, unable to restructure and ensure their viability under the new market conditions. The Argentine toy industry offers a particularly dramatic example of this situation. Between 1991 and 1996, the share of imported toys on the Argentine market rose from 6 percent to 80 percent. As a result, 170 out of the approximately 200 toy manufacturers in operation in the country in 1991 either went bankrupt or were forced to close manufacturing facilities by 1996.

Eventually, some of the larger corporations in the new industrialist category evolved into Third World multinationals. One example is the Grupo Alfa, which has become the largest manufacturer of glass products in the world since teaming up with Corning of the United States. In its domestic market, it remains a conglomerate of loosely knit companies covering a wide range of industries. Argentina's Grupo Bunge & Borne (B&B) outgrew its domestic market and expanded its investment interests, mainly into Brazil. It eventually grew into one of the world's major maritime grain transport companies. Domestically, B&B, like Alfa, remained a diversified conglomerate. It is only in the face of the drastic economic liberalization measures of recent years, including the virtual elimination of most trade barriers, that B&B has been forced to refocus on its domestic core business—food products—and rapidly divest itself of peripheral operations.

The relative success of national corporations in internationalizing their operations (that is, in overcoming their dependence on rents originating with state-created market segmentation) largely influences their attitude toward modern-day integration initiatives. As it turns out, TWMs are on the forefront of the new wave of integration efforts in Latin America. These successful corporations are going through the same historical transformation experienced by U.S. businesses when they gradually abandoned the Boston Tea Party mentality to become staunch worldwide advocates for free trade. In fact, it would be no exaggeration to state that the successful Mercosur venture is the brainchild of a quintessential Latin American TWM: Grupo Bunge & Borne, which was first based in Argentina, then Brazil.[14] Perhaps it is no coincidence that these two countries are the focal point for the Mercosur initiative.

Subsidiaries of Multinational Corporations

MNCs, by definition, depend heavily on international trade to conduct their business. However, they are also versatile and resourceful and often capable of adapting to different situations, from economies that are wide open to international investment and financial flows to environments that are hostile and unfriendly to MNCs. North-South and intraregional trade plays a completely different role for MNCs than for other businesses. To some extent, North-South trade is essential to the survival of MNC subsidiary operations in a developing country, either as a channel for exports (if the subsidiary's role is to extract raw materials for use or consumption in the industrialized world) or as the source of crucial inputs (if its role is to manufacture goods for the local market). Even so, many MNCs are capable of operating under the most adverse trade conditions by increasing or reducing local content—within the limits of technology and economies of scale—in their finished goods.[15] Those exploiting natural resources for consumption in the industrialized world must deal with a different set of difficulties altogether. They typically face trade restrictions in the form of export duties designed to procure the host country a greater share of resource revenues. The host country, however, is limited in its rent expropriation capacity by the existence of alternative sources of natural resources in other countries and the rent expropriation practices there.

The MNCs' dependence on North-South trade makes them logical and natural allies of businesses in the merchants and traditional exporters category. Despite occasional minor and generally circumstantial conflicts of interest between the two groups, MNCs together with merchants and traditional exporters have formed one of the most solid and stable political coalitions in Latin America, capable of wielding enormous power through the use of domestic and international political and financial resources. Regional trade is relevant only to MNCs whose goal is to supply local markets with some kind of manufactured good. MNCs involved in resource extraction have no need or use for it. For the first group, however, regional trade, which may be essential in a few cases where large economies of scale are desirable or even necessary, is a definitive advantage. It allows MNCs to plan their capacities more efficiently with the goal of serving a larger market (consisting of several countries) rather than operate a scattered group of smaller, less efficient plants. This is why MNCs have been the most active and enthusiastic supporters of regional integration processes. But the kind of integration MNCs had in mind was quite different from that envisaged by other national business groups, particularly the new industrialists.

Models of Integration and Their Historical Evolution

The Latin American integration process, like others elsewhere, has not been linear. Although it would be possible to analyze the forces shaping and influencing contemporary integration initiatives in the region looking only at current events, such an analysis would lack richness and historical perspective. It would also make the role of Latin America's business community less clear. That is why it is important to look at the roots of the integration efforts launched in the 1960s. In this section I will examine these roots and include specific information about the coalitions (including the specific business sectors) behind each of the initiatives and the role of business as both a force in and a beneficiary of the integration processes. The majority of these integration efforts—including ALADI, SELA, and the Andean Pact—could, by any objective measure of achievement, be considered failures, and therefore unworthy of further consideration. However, they represent the accumulated collective experience underlying current efforts and, as such, can help us better understand what is happening today.

There has been no shortage of philosophies and models for regional and international integration. In fact, three distinct currents can be identified, each distinguished by its approach and the particular form of integration desired. Business groups have played an important role in articulating these models and providing the necessary political support for their implementation. Although some models have endured in certain regions over longer periods of time, up to recently no single model has dominated, and both the first and the second model contributed to the failure of the third. This may explain, at least partially, the numerous and overlapping efforts at market integration that have coexisted on the Latin American political scene. The only potential exception to the scenario is the most recent model, which appears to have superseded all other integration currents. It also appears to have unprecedented, though not unanimous, support from the three business groups defined earlier. Obviously, this convergence is essential to the success of the most recent integration initiatives.

I have labeled the three currents as follows:

1. The "secessionist-protectionist" model.
2. The "integrationist-protectionist" model.
3. The "integrationist-competitive" model.

The first two models were in competition throughout much of the 1970s and the 1980s and were, for all intents and purposes, exhausted by the end of the 1980s. The third model was launched with the Mercosur initiative as the others were failing. It is unquestionably the dominant integration philosophy in Latin America today, and the only model that has yielded any significant progress.

The three apparently disparate and contradictory labels describe quite accurately the underlying motivations and objectives of the models they represent. Let us look at each one more closely: its objectives, the role of business and the other political forces supporting it (the coalitions), and its institutional manifestations in the region. Each model is presented in some detail in Tables 10.1–10.3, including the policy instruments that are associated with it. The purpose of the tables is to facilitate the rapid identification of differences and similarities between the three models. In the tables are embedded many details that help explain the functioning of the models. To avoid repetition in the text, I will simply emphasize a few central ideas.

Of course, none of these definitions, objectives, and policy instruments are explicitly identified in the charters of the various integration agreements. Rather, they reflect the fundamental ideological currents at the basis of the coalitions behind each model.

The "Secessionist-Protectionist" (S-P) Model

This model represents the implementation at a regional level of the import substitution and directed development model first popularized in the 1940s. Examples of this model are the Andean Pact (Bolivia, Colombia, Ecuador, Peru, Venezuela and, initially, Chile) and the Latin American Economic System, which now has twenty-seven members in Latin America and the Caribbean. SELA was created in October 1975 through the Panama

Table 10.1   Model: Secessionist-Protectionist

Examples
"Old" Andean Pact (Bolivia, Colombia, Ecuador, Peru, Venezuela, and, initially, Chile), SELA

Objectives
Strong regional integration (possibility of a customs union covering goods but excluding services, no attempt to harmonize labor, monetary, and fiscal policies) within Latin America and (temporary) disengagement from world (industrialized country) markets. The purpose of the strategy was to establish a strategic regional industrial and technology base to foster economic development and develop the capacity to compete, ultimately, with MNCs. Modeled on past Japanese and U.S. protectionist periods.

Policy Instruments
High common external tariffs and trade barriers (to protect local industries) accompanied by relatively low intraregional barriers to trade (to protect, in some cases, national interests)

Extensive industrial and development planning aimed at exploiting comparative advantages and regional complementarities and economies of scale

Strong state presence as a substitute to the private sector in two situations: strategic investments (including nationalization of foreign interests when necessary) and investments considered too big for the private domestic business sector

Subsidized project financing, with a strong role for development financing institutions (development banks and corporations)

Heavy taxation of the rent available to traditional sectors (agriculture, mining, etc.) in order to finance the development of nontraditional industries

Heavy financial restrictions to control the price and allocation of capital in the economy

Coalitions
Domestic: Nationalist political forces (political parties and portions of the military); new industrialists, mostly medium-sized and large companies in the import substitution sector; labor unions; workers and peasants
International: Nonaligned movement; regional and international development financing institutions

Role of Business
The model was supported by medium-sized and large companies in the emerging manufacturing sector that saw the protected market environment and cheap credit policy as an opportunity for growth. Both the barriers to trade and the credit policies provided a substantial rent to nontraditional industrial enterprises that facilitated growth.

Convention as a response to a call by then-president of Venezuela Carlos Perez to initiate a continent-wide effort at integration to compete with the U.S.-led LAFTA and the MNCs. After twenty-three years of ups and downs, SELA is now working to adapt the organization to changes in the region's dominant ideology and the new realities of the world economy.[16]

The central idea behind the S-P model was to disengage the region temporarily from integration into the world market in order to establish a strategic regional industrial and technology base, foster economic development, and, ultimately, compete with MNCs. Supporters of this model often pointed to protectionist periods in Japanese and U.S. history as successful examples of this strategy. In policy terms, these integration models essentially sought to block the importation of industrial goods that could be produced locally and to engage in a comprehensive planning process to develop a regional industrial base on the basis of local comparative advantages. The state was to play a leading role in this process by influencing resource allocation and subsidizing selected industries that were considered essential.

We have synthesized these ideas in the figures incorporated in Table 10.1. The figure labeled "Before Integration" represents the starting position in which individual Latin American countries (DC) trade predominantly with the block of industrial countries (IC). At the same time a high degree of segmentation exists between countries in the region. The figure labeled "After Integration" represents the objectives of the model: to increase barriers for imports from the industrialized countries with the clear objective of discouraging trade with industrialized countries and to encourage strong integration within the region. Table 10.1 also includes a list of the main policy instruments used for the implementation of the model, the characteristics of the coalition that supported it, and the role business played in the process.

The domestic coalitions favorable to this model were made up of nationalist political forces (political parties and portions of the military), new industrialists—mostly medium-size and large industries in the import substitution field—labor unions, and workers and peasants. The resulting political fronts included a diverse mix of entrepreneurs, workers, peasants, and intellectuals and were often confused with European fascist movements. At the international level, the movement received political support primarily from the nonaligned movement and institutions involved in regional and international development financing. Medium-sized and large companies in the emerging manufacturing sector supported the model because they saw a protected market environment and cheap credit policy as an opportunity for growth. Both the barriers to trade and the credit policies were a source of substantial rents to nontraditional industries that facilitated and financed growth.

In contrast, MNC subsidiaries and merchants and traditional exporters vehemently opposed the model. The major irritant for companies in these two categories was that supporters of this model for integration (and national development) were intent on expropriating a substantial portion of their rent through (1) taxes (on income, capital, land, and revenues from exports and imports) intended to finance the development of other industrial sectors and social infrastructure that would benefit the industrial working class and (2) tariffs and other barriers that would transfer rents to protected business sectors, help eliminate traditional imports, and explicitly exclude preferential credit policies. In the case of MNCs, the model explicitly attempted to exclude or expropriate their economic interests and develop a sector capable of competing with them directly.

This complicated mix of politics and entrepreneurial support made this model difficult to implement and vulnerable to circumstance. This was the case with the Andean Pact, which was founded at a time when like-minded nationalist coalitions held power in all the countries involved. The pact soon ran into trouble when one of its members—namely, Chile—withdrew (for reasons explained earlier) four years after its creation and later when opposing political forces came to power in member countries.

The "Integrationist-Protectionist" (I-P) Model

Initiatives based on this model enjoyed the blessing of the United States and were among the earliest regional ventures in economic integration. It is fair to say that the United States played a leading role in promoting economic integration in Latin America, although its efforts did not always produce the intended results. In fact, the alternative models of integration presented here (like the S-P model just described) were often a reaction on the part of Latin American leaders to the models promoted by the United States. The most important initiatives in the I-P model are the ALALC and ALADI at the continental level, and CARICOM and the Central American Common Market (CACM) in the Caribbean region and Central America, respectively.

The objective of the I-P model was to foster weak regional integration within Latin America and weak Latin American integration into the markets of the industrialized world. The model sought to exploit regional complementarities whenever possible and to facilitate regional market integration for products manufactured by MNCs, which had the resources to implement economies of scale at the regional level. Policy instruments were relatively moderate and designed to provide the emerging regional industrial base with a relatively protected environment. In terms of intraregional trade, the model focused primarily on eliminating barriers to the movement of industrial goods.

Table 10.2   Model: Integrationist-Protectionist

Examples
ALALC, ALADI, CACM

Objectives
Weak regional integration within Latin America and weak integration into world (industrialized country) markets. The main purpose of this strategy was to exploit regional complementarities whenever possible and facilitate market integration for the benefit of the MNCs and their products.

Policy Instruments
Relatively high external tariffs and trade barriers (but generally lower than in the S-P model) to protect local industries, relatively low intraregional trade barriers, selective reduction (through multilateral and bilateral negotiation) of barriers to take advantage of complementarities while protecting national industries. Low barriers to MNC products
Weak state presence in the economy to allow private sector to decide on resource allocation. Presence of the state in strategic economic sectors considered of military importance or where private capital was insufficient
Subsidized project financing with strong role for development financing institutions (development banks and corporations). Not directed by the state
Low taxation of the rent available to traditional sectors (agriculture, mining, etc.), with most financing coming from international development aid institutions and through foreign direct investment
Moderate financial restrictions to influence the price and allocation of capital in the economy

Before Integration

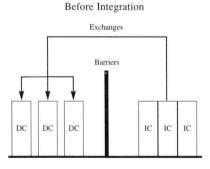

After Integration

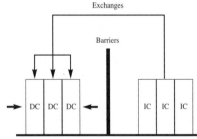

Coalitions
Domestic: Traditional, landowner-based political forces; frequent military support; merchants and traditional exporters; MNC subsidiaries
International: United States; multilateral development finance organizations (IFC, World Bank); the IMF

Role of Business
The model was supported by the merchants and traditional exporters (mining and agricultural products), who saw it as a means to maintain their land- and trade-based rents. MNCs viewed the model, with its provisions for unified regional markets, as fundamental to developing economies of scale and greater efficiency in their manufacturing operations.

The starting point shown in the figure labeled "Before Integration" in Table 10.2 is identical to the one described in the same figure in Table 10.1. The I-P model had some similarities to the S-P model in that its objective was a strong integration within the region. However, whereas the S-P had as an explicit objective to exclude MNCs, the I-P model was largely designed to create economies of scale for these corporations. It therefore should not be surprising that this sector was the most active supporter of the model. Barriers to North-South trade played less of a role in the I-P model than in the S-P model because the I-P model clearly preferred a lowering of these barriers. The versatility of the MNCs and their capacity to adapt (e.g., through local assembly lines and joint ventures) allowed many of them to circumvent a large number of these barriers. (Those MNCs extracting raw material were generally not affected by the barriers.) Table 10.2 includes a list of the main policy instruments used for the implementation of the model, the characteristics of the coalition that supported it, and the role business played in the process.

The domestic coalitions that supported the integrationist-protectionist model were predominantly made up of traditional landowner-based political forces, merchants and traditional exporters, MNC subsidiaries, and, quite often, the military. Internationally, the United States, multilateral development finance organizations (the International Finance Corporation [IFC], World Bank), and the International Monetary Fund (IMF) backed the model. Merchants and traditional exporters (mining and agricultural products) saw the model as a means to maintain their land- and trade-based rents. MNCs viewed it as fundamental to developing economies of scale and greater efficiency in manufacturing, notably through its provisions for unified markets. Not surprisingly, the model was strongly opposed by local industries, which stood to lose a substantial portion of the rents they derived from state-induced market segmentation.

The "Integrationist-Competitive" (I-C) Model

The main objective of the integrationist-competitive model, the current dominant model, is the extensive integration of national markets within Latin America (the possibility of a common market in products and services and the harmonization of labor, monetary, and fiscal policies) and strong integration into markets in the industrialized world. The main purpose of the strategy is to foster competition within the region and to exploit regional comparative advantages in international markets. To a large extent, this model was a response—promoted by the IMF, the United States, and the World Bank—to the exhaustion of earlier, inward-oriented development models.

The prime example of the I-C model is Mercosur, but other groupings such as the G-3, the new Andean Group (Andean Community), and the

Table 10.3 Model: Integrationist-Competitive

Examples
G3, Mercosur, Andean Community, the FTAA. CARICOM and the new CACM are also evolving toward an IC model.

Objectives
Extensive integration of national markets (possibility of a common market for goods and services and harmonization of labor, monetary, and fiscal policies) within the region and extensive Latin American integration into world (industrialized country) markets. The main purpose of the strategy is to foster competition within the region and to exploit regional comparative advantages in international markets.

Policy Instruments
Low common external tariffs and trade barriers (elimination of most protection for local industries) accompanied by low or nonexistent intraregional barriers to trade. Tariffs and barriers selectively maintained on certain products and services. Absence of discrimination between domestic industries and MNCs
Increasingly weak state presence in the economy to allow the private sector to decide on resource allocation. State disinvestment (privatization) of former strategic or priority economic sectors
Large-scale elimination of subsidized project financing. Role of development financing institutions (development banks and corporations) limited mostly to funding small and medium-sized private companies
Low taxation of the rent available to all sectors (traditional and nontraditional), with financing determined by international and domestic market forces
Financial liberalization with virtual elimination of controls over the price and allocation of capital in the economy

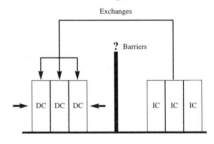

Before Integration | After Integration

Coalitions
Domestic: Progressive political forces with a broad social base; major industrial groups with international exposure in manufacturing and markets; MNC subsidiaries
International: United States; international investors; multilateral development finance organizations (IFC, World Bank, IDB); the IMF

Role of Business
This model is supported by new industrialists who have developed international operations as a result of their successful accumulation of capital in domestic markets and their subsequent need to diversify risks and markets internationally. MNCs are also strong supporters because of the opportunities the model provides for economies of scale and more efficient manufacturing operations.
Medium-sized and large companies in the emerging manufacturing sectors largely oppose the model. For them, the integration of national markets into the international economy spells the elimination of revenues derived from market segmentation and often the end of their business opportunities altogether.

new CACM and CARICOM are also evolving in this direction. The model is also the one most consistent with the FTAA. It has the backing of domestic coalitions dominated by the new intelligentsia, which increasingly controls both new and traditional political parties. This progressive political force has a wide social base, demonstrated by the successes of governments in Argentina, Bolivia, Brazil, and Peru. At the regional level, the model is supported by the TWMs, companies that have developed international operations as a result of their successful accumulation of capital in domestic markets and the subsequent need to diversify risks and markets internationally. MNCs also like the model because it provides them with the opportunity to develop regional economies of scale and improve efficiency in manufacturing. As for international support, it comes from the United States, international investors, multilateral development finance organizations (IFC, World Bank, and the Inter-American Development Bank [IDB]), and the IMF. As in the previous tables, in Table 10.3 many of the central ideas describing this model have been synthesized.

The model is widely opposed by medium-sized and large companies in emerging manufacturing sectors. For them, the integration of national markets into the international economy spells the elimination of rents derived from market segmentation and often the end of their business opportunities altogether. Traditional trade unions also vehemently oppose this model because their unionized employees absorb losses to domestic manufacturers. Traditional political forces with strongly nationalist economic policies are also opposed to the model.

Table 10.4 represents a classification of integration initiatives from the 1960s to Mercosur and the new Andean Community, as well as some comparative statistics.

Conclusion

Regional integration experiences in Latin America and the attitudes of business toward them are varied and complex. Since 1990, a wave of new initiatives distinct from earlier models of regional integration has shaken the region and introduced a new dynamic into the integration process, transforming the continental economic landscape. Since the late 1950s, the United States, Latin America's political elite, and the regional business community have promoted a variety of integration projects responding to three clearly distinct and sometimes strongly antagonistic models. Business attitudes toward these models have been equally varied, ranging from strong opposition and support to benign indifference. Business positions have largely been shaped by the sources of economic rents essential to company operations in various sectors of the economy.

Table 10.4 Integration Initiatives in Latin America

	Andean Pact	CACM	CARICOM	G3	Mercosur	ALALC, ALADI
Created	1969	1960	1973	1990	1991	1960 (ALALC)
Type of Agreement	common market	customs union	customs union	customs union	customs union	customs union
Model	secessionist-protectionist	integrationist-protectionist	secessionist-protectionist	integrationist-competitive	integrationist-competitive	integrationist-protectionist
Redefined	1988	1993	n.a.	n.a.	n.a.	1980 (ALADI)
Model	integrationist-competitive	tending toward I-C	tending toward I-C	n.a.	n.a.	integrationist-protectionist
Population	94.5 mil.	27.6 mil.	est. 6 mil.	138.6 mil.	194.6 mil.	425 mil.
International trade (billions of dollars)	1.6	n.a.	n.a.	n.a.	5.5	n.a.
GDP (billions of dollars) (% of U.S.)	149.8 (2.5%)	27.9 (0.4%)	est. 10.0 (0.1%)	438.7 (7.4%)	607 (10.3%)	1,178 (20%)

Note: n.a. indicates not applicable.

In this chapter, I have identified three integration models and three major business sectors. Integration models are defined on the basis of several criteria: their objectives with respect to local and international markets, the main policy instruments they employ to achieve the desired level of integration, the political and social coalitions that support them, and the reactions they foster among different segments of the business community.

Business sectors are defined on the basis of their main source of economic rents. Analysis reveals how changes to markets served by different business sectors affect business perspectives on regional and continental integration. This approach makes it possible to identify the underlying economic forces behind each of the integration projects and to explain the reactions each project provoked in the business community. It also allows us to identify some of the reasons for the failure of earlier integration experiences such as LAFTA, ALADI, and the Andean Pact, as well as factors explaining the current and somewhat surprising success of Mercosur. In addition, the analysis is optimistic about the future of a particularly challenging initiative—the Free Trade Agreement of the Americas—a project dependent not only on the political maturity of the United States but also on the readiness and willingness of the Latin American business community to face a challenge of this order.

Finally, the analysis also sheds light on the leading role the United States has played in promoting Latin American integration since the late 1950s, even though U.S. initiatives have not always produced the results their sponsors intended. In fact, the alternative models of integration presented in this chapter were often developed by Latin American leaders in reaction to the models promoted by the United States.

Notes

1. In June 1996, Chile signed a free trade agreement with Mercosur that became effective in October of that year. Chile's double membership (or quasi membership) in NAFTA and Mercosur puts it in a very good position compared with other Southern Cone countries. In September 1996, Mercosur began free trade talks with Mexico. By February 1997, Mercosur and Mexico had exchanged preliminary lists of goods on which tariffs would be eliminated. In December 1996, Mercosur signed a free trade agreement with Bolivia that became effective in February 1997. All trade between Bolivia and Chile and Mercosur will be duty-free by 2014. Mexico is negotiating a free trade agreement with Mercosur for the year 2001 or later based on a "four for one" formula.

2. For example, in fall 1996, the former Andean Pact—now the Andean Community (CA)—started two-phased free trade talks with Mercosur, first, to settle regulatory issues and, second, to discuss actual tariff reductions. The CA hoped to conclude an agreement by December 1997, but disagreements due in part to Mercosur's staunch pro–free trade stance and lingering CA protectionism have delayed

progress. Bringing Mercosur and the CA together would create a market of 306 million people.

3. The next richest grouping is the G3, which consists of Colombia, Mexico, and Venezuela. The G3 has a gross regional product of slightly over $400 billion, or 7.4 percent of the GDP of the United States. In June 1994, Presidents Carlos Salinas de Gortari of Mexico, Rafael Caldera of Venezuela, and César Gaviria of Colombia signed the Group of Three free trade agreement in Cartagena, Colombia, thus linking 150 million consumers in the three countries. The agreement, reached after three years of difficult negotiations, was expected to increase trade in sectors such as energy, petroleum, and transportation. When the G3 agreement was signed in 1994, it was considered one of the most comprehensive trade agreements in Latin America, with its sections covering services, investment, and intellectual property rights. Other countries in northern South America also expressed interest in joining the G3. For example, during the Cartagena summit that followed the signing of the G3 agreement, Ecuadoran president Sixto Durán Ballén reiterated his country's intention to join the group. Since then, however, protectionist sentiment, mostly in Colombia and Venezuela, has essentially put a halt to further progress.

4. This statement may raise some eyebrows. How did this regional basket of troubles suddenly become so successful? What about China and the Southeast Asian "tigers"? The fact is that there is no other regional economic unit with virtually no trade barriers that qualifies for the position, including China. Not that the Mercosur partners don't have any conflicts or unresolved issues between them. As of this writing, members have disputes pending over a range of hotly debated issues, including trade in sugar, local content rules, and regional investment incentives (for the automotive and other industries). However, these conflicts are common to every trading bloc or common market, including NAFTA and the EEC, and have not prevented Mercosur from moving ahead more or less on schedule to achieve common market status.

5. On June 4, 1987, the ever sharp *Christian Science Monitor* celebrated the original Andean Pact's turnaround with the headline "Yankee Come Back." This was an unveiled reference to the "Yankee, go home" philosophy that the pact's five founding members had espoused since the organization's establishment in 1969.

6. Brazil is one of them and made its position clear as early as 1994, when Jose Arturo Denot Medeiros, then economic integration and foreign trade undersecretary at the Foreign Relations Ministry, said, "Brazil would only look for a coming together of the continental trading systems once a South American bloc is in place" (Reuters News Service 1994).

7. I refer here to the complete spectrum of business interests, domestic and foreign, that are active in one way or another in the economic life of the continent.

8. The CGE was sponsored by the Peronist movement in the late 1940s and played a predominant role under the first two corporatist Peronist governments. After Juan Perón was deposed in a military coup, the organization's influence faded as the UIA gained favor during the years of military dictatorship and pseudo-democracy (1955–1973). The CGE regained its strength after democracy was restored in 1973 and was given responsibility for economic planning under the new democratic government regime, but it lost ground to the UIA again following the military coup of 1975. It would be naive and erroneous to discount the CGE as nothing more than a political tool of the Peronist governments. The organization crystallized a genuine set of business interests. As was the case with similar groups in other Latin American countries, the CGE represented the economic base of the

nationalist-protectionist movement, whose main objectives were import substitution and national industrialization.

9. An expression borrowed from the antineocolonialist literature, which actively condemned the international division of labor between the industrialized "center" and the underdeveloped "periphery" succinctly described here.

10. For a detailed analysis of the factors that contributed to the development of this form of corporate governance as well as its corporate strategy, see Fischer, Ortiz, and Palasvirta (1994).

11. Preparing the lists of eligible goods that were to benefit from the complicated scales of falling tariffs was extremely inefficient and slow. As a result, integration processes based on the list approach bogged down in bureaucratic haggling and had no real effect on regional trade. This was, in a nutshell, one of the main reasons that LAFTA and ALADI failed to foster a significant increase in regional trade.

12. This explains why Chile quickly withdrew from the pact after General Augusto Pinochet's military coup established a fundamentally pro–free trade government in Santiago.

13. Colombia and Venezuela have opposed the elimination of tariffs on a list of certain Mexican goods since September 1997, most notably products related to the automotive and petrochemical industry. One of the main arguments used by business representatives present at the G3 meeting in Medellín to justify this resistance was that "macroeconomic asymmetries" (including that of being the world's twelfth largest vehicle producer) meant Mexican business would be able to compete under favorable conditions with Colombian and Venezuelan suppliers. Around the same time, automotive and automotive parts manufacturers in the Mercosur countries were pushing their governments to accelerate the integration process and to reach an agreement on common external Mercosur tariffs and rules of foreign and local content.

14. B&B's chief financial officer was "borrowed" by President Carlos Menem and named the new administration's first minister of the economy. Although the minister died a few months later, the main thrust of the economic policies launched during his first few months in office never changed. Fine-tuning later was performed under the skillful direction of the hugely successful Domingo Cavallo, minister of the economy and a member of Argentina's Fundación Mediterranea.

15. MNCs engaging in international sourcing, such as Ford Motor Co., are a somewhat different case. They have large complementary manufacturing capacities in various regions of the world and their final products are assembled with components from several of these plants.

16. In 1996 the Latin American Council, the ministerial body of SELA, adopted a modernization and restructuring program. As part of this program, SELA is seeking to play a leading role in coordinating Latin America's position with respect to the FTAA and negotiations with the World Trade Organization. It also seeks to promote the convergence of the various integration processes under way in Latin America and the Caribbean.

11

Social Movements in the Americas: Regionalism from Below?

André C. Drainville

Whether functionalist, neofunctionalist, federalists, transactionalists, or dependentists, the first generation of integration theorists saw regional integration as a regionally bound process of harmonization responding to regionally specific exigencies and taking place in the largely unconstraining milieu of the world economy. In contrast, contemporary theorists of regional integration have emphasized that regionalism is also part and parcel of a global process and that regions are in many ways as much about the world economy as they are about themselves.

This concern for the relationship between regional integration and the construction of world orders has also defined the analysis of hemispheric integration in the Americas (Atkins 1993; Schott 1991; Urquidi 1993). Though the literature has made references to such American events as the Monroe (or Blaine) Doctrine, the Cold War Alliance for Progress, and Ronald Reagan's "Fortress America," more remarkable has been its attempt to situate the dynamics of integration in a global context.[1]

Such interest in the relationship between integration in the Americas and the management of the world economy contrasts sharply with contemporary analyses of social movements in the Americas. Indeed, with few exceptions, the literature on social movements in the Americas remains firmly anchored in the countries of the Americas themselves and emphasizes their national and regional specificity. Thus far, they have not been investigated in light of the increasingly transnational experience of other social movements elsewhere in the world economy.

There are, of course, good reasons for this. Generally speaking, social movements in the Americas (as elsewhere) have kept a primarily national focus, and their internationalist dimensions have not been readily obvious.

This is, as we shall see, especially true of social movements of the Americas that have arisen in opposition to contemporary neoliberal schemes for regional and hemispheric integration. Indeed, their opposition is built on a national variation of what Antonio Gramsci would have called an "economico-corporatist consciousness" of specific interest and specific, primarily national, position in an integrating market. Thus, for example, Canadian opponents, first of the Free Trade Agreement with the United States (FTA), then of the North American Free Trade Agreement (NAFTA), have spoken of "the betrayal of Canada" and of "taking back the nation" as they address themselves not to humanity in general but to that particular fraction of humanity that dwells in the Americas north of the forty-ninth parallel. Similarly, the Mexican Network for Action on Free Trade (Red Mexicana de Acción Frente al Libre Comercio, or RMALC) has organized primarily national events in defense of a specifically Mexican agenda.

Thus, notwithstanding overly internationalist claims that "the experience of the fight against NAFTA has given rise to the emergence of a new international solidarity" (Canadian Center for Policy Alternatives 1994), anti-integration movements in the Americas appear, if the literature is to be taken at face value, to have little to do with social processes and movements taking place in the world economy.

However, there may still be an important internationalist dimension to contemporary social movements in the Americas that has hitherto remained unexplored. Indeed, regionalist and hemispheric schemes of integration have, unwittingly, spawned growing transnational campaigns of resistance, animated by the defense of the imagined sovereignty of national communities yet situated by obligation on the terrain of the world economy, that look very much like an American variation on what Peter Waterman called the "new grass-roots internationalism of social movements" (Waterman 1988). In this chapter I attempt to explain contemporary social movements in the Americas in light of this new internationalism of social movements. As the new internationalism takes shape in reaction to world orders in the making, perhaps recent regional and hemispheric integration schemes will unwittingly give birth to regionalist or hemispherist social movements.

In the first part of the chapter, I draw a broad portrait of ostensibly American social movements in the context of regional integration. In keeping with the spirit of this book, I examine social movements situated within NAFTA and the Southern Cone Common Market (Mercosur) regions, the principal centers of gravity of a would-be hemispheric social formation, though I make occasional references to regions at the periphery of the integrationist policy initiatives. In the second part of the chapter, I use insights garnered in analyzing the broader experience of social movements elsewhere in the world economy to gain some political understanding of contemporary social movements in the Americas.

Social Movements in the Americas

Regional integration often appears as an incremental, almost managerial, process lacking the romantic internationalist appeal that André Malraux wrote of in *L'espoir*. Whereas antifascist brigades gave participants the sustaining illusion of a common humanity, opposition to regional integration takes difference and specificity as its starting points and turns them into stakes of struggle. This is an opposition that is at once a stand against the elimination of (for the most part international) difference and a struggle that in itself exacerbates differences. Depending on the place they occupy in the international division of labor and the social configurations they wish to protect from or secure through the process of integration, social forces mobilize differently and attempt to settle matters differently within national boundaries.

Thus, it is not surprising that regional and hemispheric integrationist schemes in the Americas have given birth in the first instance to national campaigns, coalitions, and networks of social movements. Beyond those, however, a regional internationalism of sorts has begun taking shape that has already transcended the level of the nation-state.

Nationally Structured Opposition
to Regional and Hemispheric Integration

That political mobilization against regional integration particularizes social struggles and reduces them, at least in the first instance, to nationally bounded skirmishes has been particularly evident in countries occupying a relatively peripheral or semiperipheral position within NAFTA and Mercosur clusters.

In NAFTA countries, from the time of the Canada-U.S. FTA in 1987 to the implementation of NAFTA in January 1994, social movements in opposition to integration have been shaped first and foremost as a collection of national or nationally centered movements. In Mexico, the most visible opposition to NAFTA was organized by the RMALC, a broad coalition of social movements assembled in April 1991. From its inception, the RMALC has discussed defining strategies to defend Mexican sovereignty against foreign capital, and it has organized a political movement that has taken distinctly Mexican realities as its starting point: the severity of the structural adjustment programs adopted by the Salinas government at the request of the International Monetary Fund (IMF); the social costs of export-led industrialization; institutionalized corporatism; and, most important, the entrenched position of the Revolutionary Institutional Party (PRI) as a governing party. Furthermore, Mexican opposition to NAFTA has objected not so much to hemispheric integration or themes common to the hemisphere as to the attempts by the National Solidarity Program (Pronasol) to capitalize small farms, the usurpation of Article 27 of the Mexican constitution (on agrarian reform) by the Salinas government, electoral fraud during the 1988 elections, and the undemocratic relationship between the PRI and Mexico's official unions such as the the Confederation of Mexican Workers and the Federation of Union Workers at the Service of the State.

RMALC opposition to NAFTA has been activated by national-corporatist appeals to an idealized notion of Mexican sovereignty, which imagines state regulation and state-led entrepreneurship as national barricades against transnational capital. More recent events such as the Liberty Referendum (Referéndum de la Libertad) (September 24–October 23, 1995), the People's Consultation (Consulta Ciudadana) (February 26, 1995), and the First National Day of Condemnation of the Government's Economic Policy (Primera Jordana Nacional de Condena a la Política Económica del Gobierno) (September 8, 1996) have also sought to promote national values and nationally defined social interests over regionalist initiatives. In the case of the Liberty Referendum, for example, this promotion took the form of a Keynesian Alternative Economic Strategy centered on fiscal reform, an expansionary monetary policy, an active industrial strategy, and measures designed to stimulate the growth of the domestic market (Alianza Cívicas 1995).

In the same spirit, Canadian opposition—first to the Free Trade Agreement with the United States and then to NAFTA—has taken the form of a "Campaign for Canada."[2] Though some of the issues raised by the anti-NAFTA campaign closely resemble themes animating the RMALC (anti-U.S. sentiments and stolen free trade elections, for example), the Council of Canadians (formed in 1985), the Pro-Canada Network (PCN) and the Action Canada Network (ACN) (respectively formed in 1987 and 1991), and the Quebec Coalition Against Free Trade (Coalition Québécoise Contre le Libre-Échange) have defined themselves in national and statist terms. They have kept watch over productivity and wage differentials between Canada and Mexico, Canadian jobs lost to the maquiladoras, and cultural differences between Canada and the United States and have generally attempted, as the nationalist Council of Canadians put it, to "Stand on Guard for Canada's Social Programs" by fetishizing state power.[3] Taken with the idea of state sovereignty, the Pro-Canada Network in 1991 went so far as to cast the Bank of Canada as a protector of the "general welfare of the country," this after a decade and a half of rigorous monetarism and zero-inflation policies (R. Robinson 1991: 6). Even when the Canadian opposition to NAFTA was linked with opposition to neoliberalism, as such opposition was in Mexico, it remained organized as a collection of national campaigns that supported fair taxes and opposed the goods and services tax, the weakening of the Canadian Health Act, and increases in patent protection for pharmaceutical companies operating in Canada.

To a lesser extent, opposition to regional integration in the United States has also been a national-centered movement (organized, if the Liberty Lobby is to be taken at its word, by "friends of American sovereignty"). Organized first by the farm lobby, which campaigned for a Fair Trade Caucus in the House of Representatives, the U.S. campaigns against the FTA and NAFTA have been guided (though with less coherence than in Mexico and Canada) by the Fair Trade Campaign (FTC) and, after 1992, the Citizens Trade Campaign (CIC), both loose federations of unions and social and religious groups that have only recently begun growing into RMALC-like coalitions of social forces. Since their creation, the FTC and the CTC, in coalition with pan-national groups (the Alliance for Responsible Trade and the Rainbow Coalition, for example) and local groups (the Federation for Industrial Retention and Renewal, Southerners for Economic Justice, Hometowns Against Shutdown, etc.), have continuously focused on corporations that have "run away" from the United States, job protection, labor rights, and the defense of U.S. environmental protection legislation.

Outside NAFTA, the Chilean Network in Favor of a Peoples' Initiative (Red Chile Para una Iniciativa de los Pueblos, or RECHIP) and Paraguayan Labor Movement on Mercosur (El Movimiento Sindical Paraguayo Frente al Mercosur), to mention two salient examples, have also assembled national coalitions of social movements that have taken a national stance against regional integration.

Thus, on the face of it, social movements born out of regional integration schemes in the Americas appear to have been structured as a collection of principally national and often statist groups that have little to do either with regional cooperation between social movements or with a broader internationalization of civil society. These movements appear to speak neither of the common struggle of the people of the Americas nor, more broadly, of fighting against regional zoning in the world economy. National coalitions united by their shared appeal to state sovereignty do not, however, tell the whole story of the politics of social movements in the context of regional and hemispheric integration. Indeed, both above and below the level at which the PCN, the ACN, the RMALC, the FTC, the CTC, and RECHIP speak of protecting the imagined sovereignty of national states, local and hemisphere-wide coalitions of social movements have also begun taking shape. These emerging coalitions are thought of by some, precipitously perhaps, as building blocks of an emerging civil society of the Americas.

Beyond Nationally Structured Social Movements:
The Double Process of Regionalism in Social Movements

The emergence of regional and hemispheric coalitions and networks of social movements beyond nationally centered coalitions is a double process.
Indeed, it is not simply a question of coalitions of social movements tran-
scending their national point of departure but a more dialectical process
whereby transnational networks emerge from regionalist organizations and
networks proper, as well as from episodic contacts and tactical alliances
between nationally centered movements that, once regularized and solidi-
fied, help transform social movement politics within distinct national
realms. To ignore one of these processes would lead to either an unwar-
ranted celebration of a regional civil society or a submission to nationally
centered politics. Instead, both processes must be understood as closely together as possible.

At the regional level, social movements in the Americas have begun
assembling themselves outside and somewhat above the realm of state and
statist politics. They are a collection of rather loose and sometimes rival
gatherings of regional and hemispheric social movements.

At the core of these gatherings are nongovernmental organizations
gravitating around interstate organizations that may be viewed as regional
affiliates of the nebula or organization managing the world economy. Just
as such organizations as the Organization for Economic Cooperation and
Development, the World Bank, and the IMF have set up an "architecture of
collaboration" with chosen nongovernmental organizations (NGOs) and
other representatives of an ostensibly "global civil society" in an effort to
solidify the social foundations of world orders (Drainville forthcoming),
such regional organizations as the Inter-American Development Bank
(IDB) and the Organization of American States (OAS) have set up a variety of outreach, consultation, and direct support programs that have encouraged a recentering of NGOs and social movements.

In the same spirit, regional offices of nebula organizations have sometimes set up NGO programs and policy consultations that have facilitated
the building of regional coalitions. Thus, for example, the World Bank
opened its Caribbean Public Information Center in Kingston, Jamaica, in
September 1994 just as the World Bank-NGO Committee was deciding to
restructure itself as a collection of regional groupings (Participation and
NGO Group 1996), which set the stage for the formation of the Latin
American Association of Promotional Organizations (Asociación Latinoamericana de Organizaciones de Promoción) (Nelson 1996).

Also at the regional level are NGOs and social movements that are
representatives of movements and organizations operating on a global
scale. In some cases, this second cluster of regionalist organizations is

made up of regional groups parachuted into the Americas by organizations fighting global battles on many regionalist fronts. The American Institute for Free Labor Development, for example, was created as a Cold War venture by the Department of International Affairs of the American Federation of Labor and Congress of Industrial Organizations, with funding from the U.S. Agency for International Development and the U.S. Information Agency (Garver 1989: 67). In the same spirit, the International Confederation of Free Trade Unions (ICFTU) sponsored the creation of the Coordination Agency of the Labor Unions of the Southern Cone (Coordinadora de Centrales Sindicales del Cono Sur) (1986), which later attached itself to the Mercosur apparatus (via a working subgroup on labor relations, employment, and social security) and became a regional anchoring point for national labor federations from Argentina, Brazil, Paraguay, and Uruguay.

In the same spirit, the International Metal Workers Federation has recently taken a position vis-à-vis the three most important schemes for regional integration in the Americas (Federación Internacional de Trabajadores de las Industrias Metalúrgicas 1995) and has organized a series of regional conferences in an attempt to facilitate the emergence of regional networks of civic NGOs and civil society organizations.[4]

Once removed from these top-down regionalist organizations is an assortment of networks, coalitions, and organizations that have been assembled by the aforementioned national coalitions largely in reaction to integrationist schemes. At this level, we find organizations such as Common Frontiers (Fronteras Comunes), the Ecumenical Coalition for Economic Justice, Woman to Woman (Mujer a Mujer), the Working Woman (La Mujer Obrera), Women to Women Global Strategies, the International Coordinating Committee of Solidarity Amongst Sugar Workers, the Coalition for Justice in the Maquiladoras (formed in February 1991), the North American Worker to Worker Network, the Caribbean Feminist Network (Red Feminista en el Caribe), the Maquila's Workers' Network (Red de Trabajadores de la Maquila), the Women's Network Against Structural Adjustments (Red de Mujer y Ajustes Estructurales), and the Hemispheric Network for Sustainable Development and Equitable Trade (Red Hemisférica para el Desarrollo Sustentable y el Comercio Justo).

National coalitions assembled in opposition to regionalist and hemispherical integrationist schemes have also organized a series of international meetings and exchanges that have, to a certain extent, nurtured a sense of common purpose among distinct, often national-centered organizations. Thus, NAFTA negotiations precipitated frequent transborder summits between the ACN, the RMALC, and the FTC (an explosion, according to one analyst). The first of these summits, the ANC-RMALC Meeting, took place in October 1990. On January 15, 1991, a conference titled "Agricultural, Environmental, and Labor Dimensions of North American

Integration" was held in Washington, D.C. Organized by a broad coalition of U.S.-based agricultural producers and labor and environmental groups, the conference also included representatives of Mexican and Canadian groups (Thorup 1991). An important meeting of the ANC, the RMALC, and the U.S. Fair Trade campaign, which resulted in a call for a more social and democratic NAFTA, took place in Mexico on April 12, 1991. Half a year later (October 25–27, 1991), the RMALC hosted an international forum in Zacatecas, Mexico, which issued the first trinational plan for the democratic and sustainable development of the NAFTA region (Red Mexicana de Acción Frente al Libre Comercio 1992). With some variations, this call was reissued in February 1992 at the Valle de Bravo Conference and on October 2, 1993, at the trinational cross-border meeting at Niagara Falls of representatives from the ACN, the RMALC, the CTC, and the American Alliance for Responsible Trade. This was the last trinational summit held before NAFTA came into effect in January 1994.

Beyond NAFTA, there has been an "unprecedented dialogue" between unions and social movements that has taken the form of occasional meetings between a wide variety of workers: "agro-industrial workers, rubber tappers, papermakers, milk producers, building and wood workers, steelworkers, automobile workers, metalworkers, professionals, government workers and bank workers" (Smith and Healy 1994). These alternative, popular, transnational summits have been sponsored by enduring organizations such as Mercosur's Coordination Agency, as well as by shorter-lived institutions such as the Movement for the Integration of Poor People of the Southern Cone (Movimeto pela Integração dos Povos de Cone Sul).

Of late, national organizations born out of opposition to the FTA, NAFTA, and Mercosur have extended their efforts to the whole of the continent, keeping pace with the increasingly hemispherical scope of integrationist schemes. Thus, in March 1994, the RMALC organized a meeting in Oaxtepec, Mexico, that included representatives of unions and popular organizations from South and Central America, Mexico, Canada, and the United States and called for a continental social pact of sustainable development. This call was reissued at the July 1994 International Gathering for Integration, Democracy, and Development (Encuentro Internacional Integración, Democracia y Desarrollo), also organized by the RMALC (Red Mexicana de Acción Frente al Libre Comercio 1994).

This geographical broadening of international points of contacts between heretofore nationally centered social movements and organizations has also been accompanied by the emergence of thematic and sectoral regional conferences that have gone beyond bringing together groups and organizations with essentially national centers of gravity. Thus, many conferences—for example, the Gathering of the Women of the Americas (Encuentro entre las Mujeres de las Americas) (Nicaragua 1995); the three

Regional Gatherings of Maquilas Working Women (Taller Regional de Trabajadoras de la Maquila), organized by the Center for Working Women (Centro de Atención a la Mujer Trabajadora A.C);[5] and the forums organized by the Association of Central American Peasants' Organizations for Integration and Development (Asociación de Organizaciones Campesinas Centroamericanas para la Cooperación y el Desarrollo), Unión de Pequeños y Medianos Productores de Café de México, Centroamérica Y el Caribe, and the Confederación de Cooperativas de Centroamérica y el Caribe—have brought together groups and organizations of the hemisphere that have taken as their starting point not distinct national realities, but common problems (health and safety issues, job security, crop prices, the "maquilization" of Central America). Sectoral transborder cooperation ventures (between teachers and health-care, sugar, garment, and auto workers) have increasingly become commonplace, within NAFTA countries as well as those outside.

Still further removed from the regional nebula are a multiplicity of fleeting actions, gestures of solidarity, short-lived and narrowly focused campaigns, and self-contained protests inspired less by a particularly developed regionalist or hemispherist consciousness than by the necessities to struggle against a regionally constructed disciplining cadre. This movement involves resistance communities fighting locally and regionally for jobs, land, family, and community and operating in the prepolitical dimension of everyday life. I will say more later in this chapter about the political importance of this movement. For the moment, it is sufficient to emphasize that these erstwhile local and national social movements that are far removed from the core of regionalist and hemispherical institutions have begun to assemble themselves into transnational communities that have challenged the ability of state and state-centered actors to make the Americas a continent in their image.

Thus, from the a priori regionalism of groups and organizations either gravitating around the regional nebula or recasting global agendas to fit the realities of the Americas to the reluctant regionalism of resistance communities, a first family of social movements and institutions has taken shape either alongside or against contemporary schemes for regional and continental integration. As significant as this "transnationalization of civic participation" (Thorup 1991) is, it is but the first of two intimately related social processes linked to contemporary regionalism in the Americas. The second involves groups and social movements that do not transcend national politics as much as they seek to transform it.

The current projects for regional integration have put in motion a double process—most evident in Mexico and Canada—that transforms national-centered politics as much as it stimulates the growth of a wide variety of cross-border coalitions and networks and international and transnational social movements and institutions. By virtue of their membership in NAFTA and their proximity to the U.S. epicenter of the current push for continental integration, these two countries are at once at the center of the movement for continental integration in the Americas and, by their national political mythology as well as by the self-interest of social groups most urgently interpellated by regionalism, rebuffed by it. In a word, social movements, especially in Canada and Mexico, are simultaneously driven by the emerging regional context to forge international and transnational strategic links and pushed inward and encouraged to broaden the social basis of opposition to integration. The latter effort has brought such networks as the RMALC and the ANC, which were the principal driving forces behind the creation of international and transnational coalitions of social movements in the Americas, to the forefront of national-centered struggles to broaden the democratic process.

In Canada the ACN has increasingly positioned itself as an assistant to coalition politics, and the national case against integration has increasingly adopted a broader, and somewhat idealized, notion of community sovereignty. This situation presents Canadian popular sovereignty, defined by the Canadian Center for Policy Alternatives as "our ability as a nation to determine our own destiny," as a necessary barrier to transnational neoliberalism (Canadian Center for Policy Alternatives 1992a).[6] What Tony Clarke calls a "new nationalism" begets such programs as the Council of Canadians' "Citizens' Agenda," the Roving People's Commission of the People Solidarity Quebec (Commission Populaire Itinérante de Solidarité Populaire Québec), and the "People's Agenda," launched by the Canadian Labour Congress in December 1991 after two years of consultation with anti-NAFTA groups (Canadian Center for Policy Alternatives 1992b). If, as Alain Touraine put it, political struggles are struggles over historicity— that is to say, struggles over "the set of cultural, cognitive, economic, and ethical models by means of which a collectivity sets up relations with its environment"—then Canadian opposition to integration in the Americas appears to be as much about constructing a national collectivity as it is about assembling international and transnational coalitions of social movements (Canel 1992: 28).

In Mexico there has also been an intimate connection between the growth of regional and hemispheric coalitions and networks of social movements and the transformation of national political relationships (Osorio 1996). Indeed, campaigns against NAFTA, the Enterprise for the Americas Initiative, and, more broadly, the maquiladorization of Central America have served as anchoring points for the current movement for democratization, as have other crucial episodes such as the 1988 and 1991 elections, the 1994 devaluation of the peso, and the Chiapas uprising and subsequent peace process. This connection has been especially evident of late, in such landmark episodes in the development of grassroots democratic politics in Mexico as the Liberty Referendum (September 24–October 23, 1995), the Citizens' Consultation (February 26, 1995), and the First Day of Condemnation of the Economic Policy of the Government (September 8, 1996). Other important episodes include events in which the RMALC played a central coordinating role alongside other newly formed social groups and networks of social movements: the Pacto de Grupos Écologistas, La Convergencia de Organismos Civiles por la Democracia, El Foro de Apoyo Mutuo, Ganando Espacio, Mujeres Punto, Entre Mujeres, and the Red Nacional de Organismos Civiles de Derechos Humanos.

Even in the United States, where coalition politics has not been stimulated by the intuitive anti-Americanism (in the U.S. sense of the term) energizing popular coalitions in Canada and Mexico, the struggle against regional and hemispheric integration has also spawned broad coalitions of unions and environmental and women's groups that are historically unprecedented. In Mercosur countries, schemes for hemispheric and regional integration have created a context that appears favorable to the widening and broadening of links between different segments of national social movements. In Chile, this broadening has brought RECHIP to the forefront of a broad coalition of social movements—unions and women's, peasants', and human rights groups—that has argued for a Carta de Derechos Económicos, Sociales, Culturales y Ambientales y de Derechos Ciudadanas (Red Chile de Acción por una Iniciativa de los Pueblos 1996). To a lesser extent, Paraguayan social forces have also broadened links in response to Mercosur (Céspedes 1994).

Contemporary initiatives for regional and hemispherical integration, then, have seemingly created a context that has both obliged social movements and groups to begin organizing defensive transnational networks, coalitions, and campaigns and moved them to foment the growth of nationally based social movements of opposition. It is important to note that the two processes—building at the regional level transnational strategic and tactical relationships that attempt to meet neoliberal regionalism on its increasingly regional terrain *and* weaving the fabric of a national-based civil society in opposition to plans for neoliberal integration—have gone hand in hand. They are dialectical moments of struggles intimately related by both the groups and social forces involved and the political agendas put forth.

On this basis, I will explore the relationship between contemporary social movements in the Americas and the ostensibly new internationalism of social movements, assembled from below by locally bound social forces resisting the transnational restructuring of capital.

Cosmopolitanism and Internationalism in the Americas

In many ways, the process at work in social movements in the Americas is the local expression of a broader phenomenon, "social movement internationalism" (Drainville 1995). This is the internationalism of fused groups united by their immediate circumstances and by the exigencies of the moment. It is made up of local, national, and regional social forces grounded in the specificity of locally lived situations inside the general framework of the world economy and defined in opposition to neoliberal internationalism. Furthermore, this modest internationalism takes on different appearances according to local and conjunctural specificities: food riots in Caracas or Warsaw, Buenos Aires, Abidjan, or Libreville; demonstrations for work safety in Trinidad and Tobago; campaigns against sex tourism in Southeast Asia or against poor working conditions and health standards in maquiladora factories.

Increasingly, this modest internationalism has taken shape beneath the cosmopolitan grand designs of global governance. Whereas the cosmopolitan grand designs have offered a collection of master plans, global social contracts, and reformist blueprint and humanist agendas for sustainable development, the modest internationalism has begun dragging what Anthony Giddens called "emancipatory life politics" into the realm of the world economy, not on the back of universal collective actors and not on behalf of grand plans, but through site-specific coalitions assembled.

Thus, side by side on the terrain of the world economy coexist two quite distinct movements, both attempting to clarify the relationship between locality and globality. The cosmopolitan movement is most readily visible. It starts from humanity in general and interpellates locally bound actors as members of a greater overdetermining whole. As I have emphasized elsewhere (Drainville forthcoming), this first movement is intimately linked with global governance's efforts to "bring more orderly and reliable responses to social and political issues that go beyond capacities of states to address individually" (Gordenker and Weiss 1996). Social movement internationalism, for its part, takes humanity to be a continuously unfinished project that comes into view only through contingent, contextualized, and purposeful struggles. It is not surprising that this modest, protean internationalism has not left artifacts as eloquent as the aforementioned cosmopolitan schemes. Rather, it has taken shape as a variegated collection of punctual, distinct campaigns and events, cemented not by appeals to common programs but, more materially, by the increasingly shared social and historical experience of everyday life in the world economy.

So it is in the Americas, where the recent push for hemispheric integration has spawned two distinct political postures. First and most visible are the cosmopolitan-like efforts to negotiate hemispheric grand plans and

comprehensive social contracts. In terms of political positions, these efforts have come from the core as well as the periphery of the loose collection of regional and hemispheric social movements discussed in the first
section of this chapter. At the core, organizations brought together by the
IDB, the OAS, and the ICFTU, for example, have echoed cosmopolitan
calls for a global order by presenting draft plans of their own: the Oaxaca
Initiative, the Social Charter of Integration, the Latin American Social
Charter, the Social Contract of the Americas. In this same spirit as well,
federations brought together by Mercosur's Coordination Agency have argued for a "Charter of fundamental rights" (Smith and Healy 1994).

Moving toward the periphery, cosmopolitan grand plans have also
come from occasional international gatherings of national coalitions.
Groups present at the Zacatecas summit, for example, produced a hemispheric plan that called for the protection of the environment and human
rights, the renegotiation of the Mexican debt, and democratic control over
economic policies (Red Mexicana de Acción Frente al Libre Comercio
1992: 83–89; Canadian Center for Policy Alternatives 1992c).[7] Similarly,
the Women's Plan of Action produced at the Valle de Bravo Conference
called for a Continental Charter of Rights for Women that would guarantee "basic rights to adequate education, health care, food, nutrition, hous-
ing, stability of employment, living salaries and training, voluntary mater-
nity, and peace."[8] In the same spirit, Cuauhtémoc Cárdenas, leader of the
Revolutionary Democratic Party (PRD) and a Mexican presidential candi-
date in 1988, together with Bob White, Monique Simard, Jesse Jackson,
and Ifigenia Martinez (also of the PRD), spoke of alternative visions of
sustainable development in the hemisphere and "an ambitious negotiation
for a coherent, integrated, global approach conducive to a broad, long-term
continental free trade and development pact" that would incorporate trade
and investment guidelines and a social charter setting norms for work-site
conditions, collective bargaining, consumer protection, and labor mobility.[9]

Moving still further from the core of regionalist and hemispherical organizations, participants at the Oaxtepec summit, who represented eleven
countries of the hemisphere, spoke on behalf of "The People of the American Continent" about "joint strategies and alternative policies for a popular model of integration and sustainable development" (Mujer a Mujer
1994).[10] More recently, the Encuentro Internacional: Integración, Democracia y Desarrollo (Mexico City, July 1994), the largest continental meeting of popular organizations, with over 300 people from 185 community-
based organizations throughout the Americas, produced a final declaration
titled "Integration, Democracy and Development: Towards a Continental
Social Agenda," which addressed the need "to advance the construction of
a Continental Social and Environmental Agenda that contributes to the development of an alternative proposal on integration that favors sustainable

development" (Canadian Center for Policy Alternatives 1994; Red Mexicana de Acción Frente al Libre Comercio 1992).

Thus, the recent push for regional integration in the Americas has created a context favorable to a certain regionalist cum cosmopolitan imagination and the setting of explicit regionalist agendas—this from organizations at the center of integration projects as well as from movements and organizations either peripheral to the process or critical of it, wholly or in part. Inasmuch as there is an increasing congruence between grand plans coming from the center as well as the periphery of the regional nebula of the Americas, one might anticipate that the double movement outlined in the second part of this chapter will beget elements of a hemispheric social contract resulting from compromises drawn between regionalist grand plans from below and above. Already, such initiatives as the IDB's Small Project Programme and the Fund for Women's Leadership and Representation, and such bureaus as the IDB's State and Civil Society Unit and the Sustainable Development Department have begun putting in place elements essential to such a hemisphere-wide compromise. They have done so by selecting NGOs and social movements worthy of being considered relevant interlocutors and responsible stakeholders and by circumscribing and mapping the political grounds on which these would-be citizens of the Americas will meet with institutions of the nebula (Inter-American Development Bank 1994).

Yet regardless of the conspicuousness of regionalist-cosmopolitan proposals and the political momentum of hemisphere-wide social pacts, they do not tell the whole story of American social movements in a context of regional integration. As we have already seen, part of the missing story is told in the manner in which international opposition to schemes of regional and hemispheric integration has begun to transform national politics, especially in Canada and Mexico and, to a lesser extent, Chile.

Furthermore, focusing exclusively on the making of regional and hemispheric grand plans would risk missing the fleeting actions, gestures of solidarity, and the evanescent and narrowly focused campaigns organized not on behalf of the people of the Americas in general by transnational organizations but by human beings living their lives somewhere in the Americas and forced by the exigencies of continental restructuring to bring their politics to new regional and hemispheric levels. Though actors involved in these reluctantly regionalist activities have not worn their regionalism on their sleeves, and though they are explicitly not offering a cosmopolitan alternative to cosmopolitan grand plans, they are nonetheless part of what is perhaps the most consequential political by-product of the recent push for integration in the Americas.

On occasions, these punctual actions have spawned enduring institutions and contributed to the making of what Barry Carr calls "a complex web of cross-border coalitions" (Carr 1994: 1), which in turn has added to the broader organization of transborder solidarity. A well-known example is the support given by Local 879 of the United Auto Workers (UAW) from St. Paul, Minnesota, and by the Mexico-U.S. Labor Coalition (formed for the occasion) to Ford workers in Cuautitlán, Mexico, after the murder of labor activist Cleto Ningo in January 1990 (a cause célèbre of inter-American labor cooperation), which led to the creation of the North American Ford Workers' Solidarity Network (Carr 1994). Similarly, the U.S. campaign (June–August 1987) organized by the Amalgamated Clothing and Textile Workers Union, the International Ladies' Garment Workers Union, the Teamsters, and the UAW on behalf of Lunafil workers in Amatitlán, Guatemala, was central to the formation of the U.S./Guatemala Labor Education Project, which in turn played a central role in organizing further labor protests in Guatemala, most notably for Petrosteel and Confecciones Transcontinentales workers (Hogness 1989). Likewise, the 1992 Strategic Organizing Alliance between the United Electrical Workers in the United States and the Mexican Workers' Authentic Front (Frente Auténtico de Trabajadores or FAT) led to the creation in 1992 of the North American Worker to Worker Network, which has had a considerable impact on specific unionizing drives (for example, the 1993 campaigns at General Electric and Honeywell plants in the maquilas of Chihuahua and Ciudad Juárez) and on the formation of a core of "committed activists [capable of organizing] rapid-response solidarity action to support workers and organizers who are victims of firing, threats, violence."[11]

More often than not, however, international and transnational campaigns and solidarity actions have remained more self-contained. To borrow a distinction made by Baldemar Velasquez, president of the U.S. Farm Labor Organizing Committee, they have presented "more of an *organizing response* to projects of continental integration than a *political response*" (Alexander and Gilmore 1994: 46). Gestures of solidarity and declarations of intent—such episodes as visits paid by workers of the United Electrical, Radio and Machine Workers of America (Locals 506, 731, and 1010) to their General Electric counterparts in Mexico; the common declaration of solidarity signed between the National Confederation of Unions (Confédération des Syndicats Nationaux) and FAT in Montréal on April 1991; the working relationship established between the Canadian Environmental Law Association and PACO (a Mexican network) and between the Canadian Catholic Organization for Peace and the FAT; and exchange projects between antipoverty activists in Toronto and Mexico City launched at Valle de Bravo—have not led directly to any enduring regional or hemispheric institutions. Nor have increasingly common (indeed innumerable) episodes of solidarity tourism given birth to anything resembling a set of regionalist institutions.[12] Still, taken together and studied in light of recent work on the new internationalism of social movements, these episodes acquire some significance. They point to the rise of an American civil society that is assembling itself from below against an emerging neoliberal conditioning framework.

Thus, from the descriptive compendium presented in the first part of this chapter, two quite distinct political postures can be discerned: an explicitly regionalist posture akin to an American variation on a cosmopolitan theme and a more modest, reluctant regionalism echoing the new internationalism of social movements. It is, of course, well beyond the scope of this chapter to assess the political limits and possibilities of each posture. Suffice it to say, then, that the relationship between the two has already taken the form of a political struggle, which I have elsewhere categorized as a struggle between bounded reformist attempts to settle social relations and an open-ended, potentially radical reinvention of civil society in the Americas (Drainville 1997).

Conclusion

Undoubtedly, this chapter has presented a thin slice of social movements in the Americas. I have concentrated on social forces occupying relatively exogenous positions vis-à-vis state policy. Thus, missing from my analysis is a sense of the impact contemporary projects of integration have on the more intimate relationship between state and different factions of capital in countries of the Americas. Furthermore, I have investigated neither the possible recomposition of capital along continental lines nor the potential impact of such meeting points as the Miami summit and the Bolivar program, which aspire to play for capital in the Americas the role that Bilderberg meetings played in transnational bourgeois class formation in the Atlantic area during the postwar years (van der Pijl 1979).[13]

Also missing from this chapter is a sense of historical continuity between the ostensibly new internationalism of social movements in the Americas and previous episodes of cross-border activism. International and transnational social movements, cross-border coalitions, and popular summits, of course, did not begin with the recent push for regional integration. The U.S.-Mexican border, to take but one active site of contemporary cross-border activism, was an important center of activism in the post–World War I period as well, when Industrial Workers of the World and Communist Party activists sought to structure internationalism from above (Carr 1994). Similarly, in the post–World War II period, the AFL-CIO attempted to frame labor internationalism through its dirigiste policies—nicknamed *monroismo obrero* by Latin American labor activists (Carr 1994). More recently, in the 1970s, the Latin American left constituted itself in a truly regionalist movement:

The Central American insurgent organizations cooperated closely among themselves. . . . So did some organizations of the Andean region. They collaborated with each other, and received guidance, training and advice from Cuba, a nation that they regarded as a tropical beacon on the hill. Eventually they also cooperated with loosely defined extracontinental allies, from Vietnam to the PLO. (Gorritti 1994)

What I have done in this chapter is highlight an important social dynamic accompanying the recent push for regional integration in the Americas and, obliquely, raise consequent political issues. Empirically, I can conclude by emphasizing the double movement of social forces in the Americas, which are beginning to transcend nationally bound politics and whose continuing efforts to transform national and local sites of politics are being energized by their growing embeddedness in international networks of social movements.

In the short term, the first of these movements will have a clearer impact on the contours of hemispheric integration. Indeed, the hemisphere is at a moment when global governance is attempting to put in place the social and political infrastructure of a new and sustainable transnational order, assembled in consultation with selected nongovernmental organizations, government-organized nongovernmental organizations, and quasi-nongovernmental organizations said to represent a global civil sociey in the making. Both the state-led push for regional integration in the Americas and social movements' efforts to resist it seem most likely to yield elements of a hemispheric social pact that would qualify, validate, and socialize what Ricardo Grinspun and Robert Kreklewich (1994) called (in relation to the FTA and NAFTA) a "neo-liberal conditioning framework." In the longer term, as I have argued elsewhere, the second movement, leading back from hemisphere-wide coalitions of issue-bound social movements to nationally and locally grounded coalitions, looks to be more open-ended (Drainville 1997).

Thus, rather than ending this chapter by drawing boundaries of the future shape of social movements in the Americas, I will instead surmise that the process of regional integration will further sharpen the divergences between two dialectically related but distinct movements. The former leads to the kind of social compact envisioned by agencies of global governance. The point of arrival of the later movement is indeterminate, perhaps radically so.

Notes

I wish to thank Jean-Pierre Carrier, Hossein Pouramahdi-Meibodi, and Simon Thibault for their research assistance and the following people, who have generously shared their insights with me or one of the aforementioned research assistants:

Alberto Arroyo, Peter Bleyer, Paul Brown, Bruce Campbell, Tony Clarke, Carlos Heredia, Patricia Hernandez, Andrew Jackson, Anne-Marie Jackson, Lorraine Michael, Ignacio Péon, Kerianne Piester, Estrella Rueda, Ken Traynor.

1. U.S. Secretary of State James G. Blaine "was the original advocate of hemispheric integration" who sought to create a hemispheric free trade zone (Grunwald 1993).

2. The Council of Canadians' "Campaign for Canada" was launched in the spring of 1993, in preparation for a federal election in the fall ("Trials" 1994).

3. On the issues of Canadian jobs lost to free trade, see, for example, the inaugural issue of the French publication of the Action Canada Network. The warning on the cover page ("Danger Maquiladora Express") is followed by a listing of companies that have moved Canadian jobs lost to the maquiladora. The magazine ends with an article from Bruce Campbell about the 226,000 jobs lost in Canada between November 1990 and April 1991 (Réseau canadien d'action 1991a). On this subject, see also Stanford (1991); Stanford, Elwell, and Sinclair (1993); Support Committee for Maquiladora Workers (1995); Council of Canadians (1994).

4. CIVICUS, the World Alliance for Citizens Participation, was founded and officially launched in Barcelona in May 1993 with the first meeting of the board of directors. It held its first world assembly on January 10–13, 1995, in Mexico and constituted regional groups in six regions (Asia Pacific, Latin America and the Caribbean, Africa, the Arab region, North America, and Eastern and Western Europe). In Mexico, it is represented by Philos.

5. The first meeting took place in Chihuahua, Mexico, on December 11–13, 1992. The second meeting took place in Torreón, Mexico, in July 1993, and the third in Ciudad Juárez a year later. On the first two workshops, see Centro de Atención a la Mujer Trabajadora (1992, 1993). On the three, see also Yanz (1994).

6. On community sovereignty, see Cavanagh (1992: 6). In the same spirit, see Clarke (1993: 1). The fetishism of Canadian popular sovereignty went so far during the anti-NAFTA campaign that even the Quebec Network Against Free Trade (Coalition Québécoise Contre le Libre-Échange), made up of such Quebec sovereignist organizations as the Quebec Workers' Federation (Fédération des Travailleurs du Québec), the Confederation of National Workers Union (Centrale des Syndicats Nationaux), and Quebec's Farmers Union (Union des Producteurs Agricoles), spoke in defense of Canadian federalism, which it presented as a "right to difference." See Coalition Québécoise d'Opposition au Libre-Échange (1987) and Hébert (1991).

7. The Zacatecas declaration calls for a pact of continental development. On the Canadian position going into the Zacatecas conference, see Réseau canadien d'action (1991b).

8. The Valle de Bravo Conference of February 5–8, 1992, was organized jointly by Mujer a Mujer and Mujeres en Acción Sindical. The Women's Plan of Action is quoted from Women to Women Global Strategies (1993). On the Valle de Bravo Conference, see also Yanz (1992).

9. On Cárdenas's "democratic continental pact," see Réseau canadien d'action (1991a: 15); and Cárdenas (1991; 1992: 96). For a more recent variation on the theme, see Alliance for Responsible Trade (1993). This document was prepared by the Alliance for Responsible Trade, the CTC, and the RMALC and was endorsed by the Action Canada Network. On the idea of an American social charter, see also Clarke (1991a: 3; 1991b: 6). For a Quebec variation on the theme of the social charter from Monique Simard, vice-president of the Confédération des Syndicats Nationaux, see Simard (1991).

10. The text of the Oaxtepec declaration as well as a complete list of the organizations that endorsed it can be found in Mujer a Mujer (1994).

11. "Proposal for Action: U.S.-Mexico-Canada Labor Solidarity Network," submitted by United Electrical Workers (UE) of U.S. and the Frente Auténtico del Trabajo of Mexico, quoted in Carr (1994).

12. In the NAFTA period, solidarity tourism was principally concentrated on the border region: In May 1991 the Canadian Federation of Labour, which had until then taken a neutral stance in NAFTA debates, sent a delegation to Monterrey and Matamoros, Mexico, and in August 1991 declared its opposition to NAFTA. In June 1992 the Canadian Catholic Organisation for Development and Peace put together a "Solidarity Visitor Programme" to help build awareness of living conditions in Mexico. Also in June 1992 the Canadian Federation of Students sent two representatives to a conference of the U.S.-based International Student Trade Environment and Development Program to meet with their U.S. and Mexican counterparts, whom they saw again at the U.S.-Canada-Mexico student conference in Mexico City in the fall of 1992. In that year as well, the Support Committee for Maquiladora Workers began organizing "Border Experience Tours," offering "a chance for groups and individuals to meet with workers leading the struggle for justice in Tijuana's maquiladora (Support Committee for Maquiladora Workers 1995).

More recently, as projects for regional and hemispheric integration begin taking a more concrete shape, solidarity tourists have broadened their horizons beyond NAFTA countries. In April 1994, for example, representatives of Mujer a Mujer went on an Andean tour (Correspondencia 1994). In November 1994, representatives of Common Frontiers and the Action Canada Network went on their own Andean tour, which was sponsored by the Instituto Latinoamericano de Servicios Legales Alternativos in Colombia and by RECHIP in Chile. For more episodes of hemispheric solidarity tourism, see Alexander and Gilmore (1994); Hogness (1989); Garver (1989); and Leclerc (1992).

13. On the Bolivar program, a regionwide political and social network of business alliances with links to globalized financial capital, see Silva (1995).

Part 3

Conclusion

12

A Provisional Assessment

Gordon Mace & Louis Bélanger

In this book we have tried to paint a picture of hemispheric regionalism in the Americas as it now stands. In a sense, continental regionalization has been in the making since the early 1980s, and the decisive thrust came at the end of that decade.

The acute worldwide economic recession of the early 1980s was a significant landmark in the management of contemporary international relations. In addition to fundamentally changing the nature of North-South relations as they had evolved since the mid-1960s, it forced each state, big or small, to reassess its situation and to rethink how it would relate to its external environment in the years to come.

In the case of the United States, the 1980–1982 world economic crisis was an occasion to reflect on its position—in particular its foreign economic policy—in the world economic system. These questions led to a reappraisal of Washington's traditional support for the multilateral trading system centered on the General Agreement on Tariffs and Trade (GATT) of which the United States was a leading advocate at the end of World War II. In U.S. political and economic circles, the view of GATT was that it did not serve the country's interests well and that some other organizational form of external trade policy should be explored. Multilateralism was now challenged by bilateralism, reciprocity, and even regional arrangements as possible alternative frameworks for U.S. trade policy (Destler 1986; W. Cline 1982; Bhagwati and Irwin 1987). This reappraisal led to the signing of free trade agreements with Israel and Canada, allowed for the establishment of the North American Free Trade Agreement (NAFTA), and opened the door to an eventual Free Trade Area of the Americas (FTAA).

In the case of Latin American and Caribbean countries, the world economic crisis was accompanied by a shattering external debt crisis that brought about a period of intense soul-searching. The effect was as psychological as it was economic for the political and economic elites of the region. Evidently, new attitudes and new ways of doing things would be necessary so that national governments would not completely lose credibility with both the outside world and their own populations. These economic and psychological shocks help explain the embrace of democracy and the adoption of market-oriented economic policies throughout the region during the 1980s. They also explain an apparent new receptivity to some U.S. proposals for increased cooperation.

The second set of intervening factors arose from the strategic changes that occurred in the last years of the 1980s, which are symbolized by the fall of the Berlin Wall in 1989. The passage from a tight, constraining bipolar international system to a more open but still imprecise world environment had many implications for all the actors involved. Each country had to assess the new situation and determine what course of action was most appropriate for positioning itself advantageously in the new world order.

This was true even for the United States, the only remaining superpower, which had to take advantage of the situation not only to maintain but also to try to increase its global influence. There appeared to be an emergence of commercial and economic blocs in Europe and Asia and therefore a new geoeconomic power configuration different from that of the Cold War period. As a result, the United States had to reevaluate its power base starting with the Americas, its own geographical region. This view was reinforced by the belief within Washington's decisionmaking apparatus that political and economic changes in Latin America and the Caribbean had created a particular convergence of values offering opportunities that had to be seized.

For the other medium and small countries of the world, like those of the Americas, the need for adaptation was no less evident. In Latin America and the Caribbean, the perception that the emerging world order was being structured around three powerhouses—the United States, European Union, and Japan—in the industrialized world fostered an acute fear of marginalization. There was also fear that the attention and moneys of international lending agencies and private banks would be diverted away from the developing countries to those in Eastern Europe. Fear of exclusion was a powerful incentive for Latin American and Caribbean governments to respond favorably, at least initially, to U.S. overtures concerning hemispheric regionalism.

Consequently, these two sets of events of the early and late 1980s essentially paved the way for U.S. proposals concerning continental integration, and they conditioned the initially positive response given by Latin America and the Caribbean. As shown in Chapter 2, this third attempt at hemispheric regionalism was based on two diplomatic initiatives. President George Bush's Enterprise for the Americas Initiative of June 27, 1990, focused exclusively on the economic dimension of continental integration. Its basic element, as perceived by most observers, was the proposal to establish a Free Trade Area of the Americas. The December 1994 Summit of the Americas extended hemispheric regionalism to other dimensions of integration, including political life, security matters, education, health, and the environment. Hemispheric regionalism, as conceived at the Miami summit, therefore implied a diversified process of cooperation and integration in all of the Americas.

As is the case with integration and regionalism everywhere in the world, this kind of process does not evolve and cannot be studied in isolation from its immediate environment. In Chapter 3 we demonstrated that the structural context in which hemispheric regionalism evolves in the Americas does not automatically lead to a deeper and more extensive continental integration, particularly as it relates to the initial conception of the U.S.-sponsored project.

Such integration might have been possible if the evolution of regional integration depended exclusively on the power relationship between the countries involved. As illustrated in Chapter 3, the huge advantage of the United States in terms of power distribution in the Americas has remained almost constant over the past thirty years. And as the example of the German-French axis in Europe has shown, a strong power base can provide considerable leverage for steering an integration process in one direction or another. But power alone is not sufficient; it can be limited by other considerations.

In the Americas, as we have seen in Chapter 3, important political and economic differences exist between the industrialized countries of the North and the Caribbean and South American countries. These differences results in disparate and sometimes opposing views concerning issues of inter-American affairs. This opposition is reinforced by the weight of the historical relationship between the United States and Latin America, which today shapes Latin American attitudes of apprehension and mistrust regarding U.S. intentions in the region. A certain convergence of values may have started to develop in the second half of the 1980s, but a profound and extensive compatibility of values remains a long-term goal.

Opposing views concerning key issues related to the governance of the Americas naturally constitute a significant structural constraint for the progress of continental integration. It is a handicap that is further reinforced, in a sense, by the existence of another particular situation. The large disparity in levels of economic development between the countries of the Americas poses a considerable challenge to the type of economic integration envisaged by the United States and implied, to a certain extent, by the Southern Cone Common Market (Mercosur) model of integration. The apparently dominant vision of an economic integration process wherein all countries are treated on an equal footing without any form of special treatment for the less developed countries of the region may prove unattainable and eventually counterproductive. It is understandable that the region's larger economies want to move quickly and not be burdened by measures that may not have been completely satisfactory in the past. But there is a very real danger that a "take it or leave it" attitude will bring the governments of the smaller countries to adopt adjustment policies that will place an extremely heavy burden on their own populations. It is not unrealistic to believe that such an outcome could generate Chiapas-type rebellions in many parts of the Americas, thereby creating region-wide instability. That is why the attention given to the situation of the smaller economies both at the San José ministerial and at the Santiago summit must be seen as a positive development.

The most immediately significant structural context for hemispheric regionalism may be that of trade patterns. As the study in Chapter 3 demonstrates, the evolution in the structure of trade in the Americas since the late 1970s reveals a growing concentration of commercial relations around two main centers. In the northern part of the hemisphere, Canada, Mexico, and the countries of Central America and the Caribbean are coalescing around the United States, which acts as the central magnet. A similar situation is developing in South America around the Brazil-Argentina axis, particularly since the creation of Mercosur. It is now possible to foresee that the future evolution of economic integration in the Americas will be determined by the nature of the interrelationship between the NAFTA and Mercosur subregions, given that the two commercial groupings represent 90 percent of intrahemispheric trade.

This is where the comparative analysis of both the NAFTA and Mercosur economic integration models, found in Chapter 4, becomes extremely relevant. Most observations currently emphasize that the nature and scope of the eventual economic integration scheme of the Americas will depend on how the NAFTA and Mercosur frameworks converge. As Ivan Bernier and Martin Roy illustrate, arriving at this convergence will not be easy because NAFTA and Mercosur represent two very different models of economic integration.

Consequently, the Enterprise for the Americas Initiative and the two Summits of the Americas represent significant diplomatic initiatives for launching a complex and diverse continental integration process. Despite an apparently favorable climate for such an endeavor at the start of the 1990s, a careful examination of the realities reveals that the structural context surrounding hemispheric regionalism is not automatically conducive to long-lasting region building in the Americas. All will depend on how the actors cope with the situation. A global assessment of hemispheric regionalism therefore needs to examine actors' strategies and responses, the focus of the second part of the book.

The Actors' Perspective

Our decision to use an actors' perspective in our analysis led us to identify three main categories of actors whose roles can influence the integration process by steering it in one direction or another. These actors are the state, multilateral regional organizations, and civil society. Depending on what perception they have of how the integration process fulfills or opposes their interests, they can either collaborate or try to oppose each other's strategies in one or all dimensions of the regionalist project. According to the situation, integration can make progress, stagnate, or regress.

The actors involved in the hemispheric regionalism process had different responses to the initial project as presented at the Summit of the Americas in December 1994. As a result, the various actors positioned themselves differently within the dynamics of the integration process.

Civil society can be viewed as being composed of two nebulae animated by various groups, associations, and, sometimes, individual actors. One nebula is centered on business interests and its main actors are individual companies or business associations in the field of industry (automobiles) or those with a wider, more diversified mandate (chambers of commerce). The other nebula is more loosely organized and more varied. It is more socially oriented and composed of a wide array of associations, social and political movements, and various types of other groups with a wide variety of concerns, ranging from acid rain to human rights to labor conditions. Chapters 10 and 11 examine this category of actors.

Firms and business representatives have always been strategic actors in most integration processes worldwide. The reason for this is simple: Firms usually make investments, produce goods, and sell these goods in national or international markets, thereby providing jobs for the workforce and revenues for governments. In doing so, they also determine whether a particular member country of an integration scheme will register economic gains or losses from its participation in the project. Because deliverance of economic benefits to member countries is one of the first requirements for an integration process to succeed, the attitudes and roles of the business community are important elements to take into consideration.

The business sector in Latin America is not and has never been homogeneous, as Klaus Peter Fischer aptly points out in Chapter 10. His own classification, based on how rents are appropriated, identifies three major categories of business actors: the merchant and traditional exporters, the "new industrialists," and the subsidiaries of multinational corporations. In Latin America all three categories of business actors appear to be favorable to the contemporary, open market form of integration in the Americas, a form that Fischer calls the integrationist-competitive model, which is exemplified by Mercosur and the proposed FTAA. The only exception is the emerging manufacturing sector, which fears that "open regionalism" will put an end to market segmentation based on rents and might even jeopardize its own existence. This sector of the Latin American business community will not directly oppose integration per se nor the integrationist-competitive model. But it will probably pressure Latin American governments, particularly in the context of the establishment of an eventual FTAA, to adopt measures of limited duration that would enable firms of this sector to be reasonably competitive in a hemisphere-wide market.

It has been shown that in North America the business community was involved in a regionalization process even before the signing of the Free Trade Agreement (FTA) and NAFTA. In fact, as Stephen Blank asserts, NAFTA and the FTA were essentially a recognition by national governments that economic integration was occurring in North America. The agreements represented "less an effort to stimulate new trade than to stabilize an emerging environment" (Blank 1993: 1). Furthermore, it appears that in the wake of NAFTA's implementation, more than half of the large firms in the United States are adopting or considering a North America-as-a-whole strategy and even considering structuring their production network on a continental basis (Blank, Krajewski, and Fry 1993: 10).

Not only does the business community have important stakes in hemispheric regionalism, it is also a central actor in the process. Business sectors are mostly supportive of efforts at continental integration and they have been given an important role to play in the establishment of the FTAA, both by being involved in the process of national consultations and by being active participants in the various working groups. By necessity, the business community will continue to be heavily involved in the development of continental integration in close association with national governments. But opposing points of view and even clashes between U.S. and some Latin American business representatives (in the pharmaceutical industry, for example) reveal that the business community of the Americas is not a homogeneous entity and that even limited accommodation to the business community will sometimes be difficult to achieve.

As for the other part of civil society, André Drainville illustrates clearly in Chapter 11 that social movements are acutely aware of the stakes involved in subcontinental integration projects such as NAFTA or the larger continental project. Their style of bottom-up regionalism aims to put various issues related to sustainable development, human rights, women's participation in society, health and labor regulations, and so on, on the hemispheric regionalism agenda. Social movements constitute a much looser and more diverse coalition of ecologists, churches, human rights activists, women's associations, labor unions, and native and peasant movements that are opposed to a corporate type of model of integration led by a government-business alliance. They fear that such a model of integration would benefit mostly large, multinational firms, threaten national sovereignty, and worsen the already difficult living conditions of large, vulnerable sectors of the populations of the Americas.

Until now, these groups have been more effective in national settings, where they have managed to build large coalitions and influence public opinion, as was the case in Canada on the FTA issue and in the United States and Canada on the NAFTA issue. But coalition building on a continental basis has been more difficult to achieve, although progress is slowly being made. Among the reasons that social movements have had difficulties organizing on a continental scale may be the fact that issues related to hemispheric governance may still appear abstract for grassroots organizations working at a local level. Differences in cultural background and levels of economic development may also play a role. But progress is being made as input from social movements is sought in national consultations. More important, social movements have tried to structure regional actions by holding a parallel summit in Miami and parallel forums like the one held in Belo Horizonte in May 1997. Three hundred representatives from various nongovernmental organizations, associations, and grassroots movements met in Belo Horizonte, at the same time that a hemispheric trade ministerial was being held, to discuss democratic participation and social and economic rights. They also demanded that civil society be given a seat at the discussion table at the Summit of the Americas in Santiago. Institutional participation of civil society did not materialize at the Santiago summit, but there was a positive outcome in this sense. Following developments at the San José ministerial, the participating governments decided in Santiago to establish the Consultative Committee on Civil Society. Although the impact of such a committee is still unclear, the Plan of Action of the Santiago summit sends a clear message that civil society will be welcome as a participant in the shaping of the regional agenda.

The business community has already taken an active role in the early stages of continental integration, though other components of civil society have remained on the fringes. It is clear, however, that if hemispheric regionalism is to develop and deepen, space must be made and channels put in place to allow the active participation of all sectors of civil society. These channels are what link the integration process to the national and local levels, whose support and follow-up are so essential to the long-term success of a regionalist project. Hemispheric regionalism will need to set up a framework, most likely within the Organization of American States (OAS), similar to those established by the European Union or the former Andean Group. This framework will provide firms, groups, and associations an opportunity to meet regularly to discuss problems and propose measures that hemispheric governments and regional organizations will need to take into account.

The second category of actors is the multilateral regional organizations, the most important of which is the OAS in the context of hemispheric regionalism. As described in Chapter 2, the OAS experienced an uphill struggle after losing most of its influence in inter-American affairs by the mid-1980s. Latin American political elites saw the organization as a U.S. invention and not the most appropriate institution to manage hemispheric affairs.

However, beginning in the early 1990s, the OAS's situation improved somewhat on account of the arrival of new members such as Canada. The image of the organization, with its traditional U.S.–Latin American focus, started to change. As Guy Gosselin and Jean-Philippe Thérien show, a new dynamic emerged wherein the OAS began to actively promote democracy in the Americas, even though the OAS has been less successful in preserving existing democratic regimes. Enduring Latin American mistrust of U.S. motives and intentions has made it difficult for the OAS to intervene in difficult political situations, as exemplified by the case of Haiti.

All in all, OAS pro-democracy measures implemented through its Unit for the Promotion of Democracy or other channels have had a positive impact in promoting a convergence of values that is essential to region-building efforts. But a lot more will have to be done if the OAS is to contribute effectively as a forum and as an active participant in the construction of hemispheric regionalism. It remains to be seen whether the organization will succeed in other areas of hemispheric cooperation, particularly in relation to the specific mandates given to the OAS in the Miami Plan of Action. Will the OAS be given enough resources and acquire sufficient legitimacy to do more than fulfil the mandates it is assigned? Will it reach the point where it is proposing measures to national governments and devising policies? It is still too early to judge the performance of the "new" OAS with regard to its contribution to hemispheric regionalism. The organization was neither an initiator nor a major actor in the first phase of continental integration, but if it can standardize democratic conduct in the region, it could play a positive role in sustaining and deepening the hemispheric regionalist project.

National governments, strategic participants in the first phase of current efforts to structure hemispheric regionalism, are the third category of actors. Historical evidence from integration experiences elsewhere in the world indicates that their role is a common one. Indeed, region building at an institutional level is difficult to imagine without the input and participation of national governments.

In the Americas of the 1990s, hemispheric regionalism would have been unimaginable without the initial push from the United States in its capacity as regional hegemon. Impressed by political and economic changes in Latin America and the Caribbean throughout the 1980s, the U.S. administration felt that values in the region had converged, creating opportunities that were not to be missed. This belief moved President Bush to propose the June 1990 Enterprise for the Americas Initiative, which was followed by the signing of NAFTA in 1992. Both events created the momentum that led to the December 1994 Summit of the Americas.

In Chapter 5, Louis Bélanger shows that hemispheric regionalism is one option in current U.S. foreign policy, where there is a lack of effective policy building. As a world power with an enormous domestic market, the United States has many points of interests and a wide range of choices with respect to its position in the world system. In matters of trade, security, and other areas of international relations, the United States can choose among multilateral, bilateral, or regional options and even combine these options on occasion. Hemispheric regionalism is clearly a regional option. However, it is an option that is not firmly entrenched and has not translated into a planned course of action with a well-constructed policy. This point is extremely difficult for non-American observers to understand. After all, hemispheric regionalism should benefit all the countries of the Americas but especially the United States. Large U.S. firms would be the first to profit from an open regional market. Moreover, as the regional hegemon, the U.S. would extend its power base, thereby increasing its global influence.

How can such apparently irrational behavior be explained? The lack of a clearly defined policy regarding the future of hemispheric regionalism—ironically, a lack most apparent since the Miami summit—may be explained by the fact that U.S. policymakers understand that a commitment to a multidimensional process such as hemispheric regionalism will entail specific obligations. The United States, perhaps even more so than other large countries, does not want to be constrained by an international structure, such as an integration scheme, if it is not absolutely necessary or if it thinks it can reap the rewards without incurring the obligations. Another reason may be that there is no strong domestic constituency to support hemispheric regionalism in the United States. Finally, in Chapter 6, Bernard Lemelin's examination of congressional conduct identifies increasing protectionist sentiment and growing antiregionalism in Congress since 1994 as a result of the Mexican peso crisis and negative perceptions of the effects of NAFTA on the U.S. labor market.

Although the United States took a somewhat erratic wait-and-see attitude toward hemispheric regionalism, Brazil, another major player, had a
well-focused policy. Brazilian governments have always sought to block
any U.S.-sponsored form of hemispheric regionalism exclusively designed
to suit U.S. interests. As Maria Regina Soares de Lima's analysis in Chapter 7 illustrates, Brazil's strategy has been to patiently construct an alternative to the U.S.-sponsored project of continental integration. Because the
Brazilian government could not single-handedly counteract U.S. initiatives
in favor of hemispheric regionalism, it had to build a coalition and a larger
power base. This first meant a rapprochement with Argentina and then,
more important, the creation of Mercosur. As Bernier and Roy discuss in
Chapter 4, Mercosur is a Brazilian-led effort intended to offer an alternative integration model for the construction of hemispheric regionalism.
Mercosur's success is therefore of utmost importance for Brazilian foreign
policy in the hemisphere because its smooth operation will keep the
Brazil-Argentina axis healthy and attract neighbors such as Chile, Bolivia,
and Peru.

The future of hemispheric regionalism may well be influenced by
Brazil-U.S. relations, but that does not mean that other countries of the region, particularly those we have called the middle states, will not have a
role to play. In Chapter 8 we examine the role of three middle states—Argentina, Canada, and Mexico—and reveal a few surprises in their performance in relation to the hemispheric regionalist project.

Despite its economic dependence on the United States, Mexico previously managed to pursue an active foreign policy that was in line with
Third World concerns and often in opposition to U.S. positions, particularly in inter-American affairs (in its policy toward Cuba, for example).
But Mexico has adopted a relatively low profile on hemispheric regionalism and has even developed a critical approach toward certain hemispheric
initiatives, particularly in the areas of cooperative security and the promotion of democracy. Mexico's traditional mistrust toward U.S. policies in
the Americas may partially explain this approach. However, the principal
reason for this wait-and-see attitude is that Mexico wants to maintain its
status as the sole Latin American country with preferential access to the
U.S. market. As a NAFTA member, Mexico finds itself in the enviable position of being the obligatory economic bridge between Latin America and
the United States. The success of hemispheric regionalism, and particularly the FTAA, could undermine Mexico's current position, because with
that success, Mexico would become a player among others.

Canada, for its part, took on a more positive role when it entered the
inter-American scene faithful to its reputation as an intermediary and honest
broker. Canada's economic dependency on the United States, like Mexico's,
has limited its room to maneuver. Nonetheless, the Canadian government

has managed to play a role by developing an interventionist policy that proposes middle-ground positions supporting region building. By applying its traditional middle-power diplomacy to the Americas, Canada seeks to contribute to the emergence of a regional multilateral order. This is the only way to dilute the restrictive bilateral relationship with the United States that the Canadian government agreed to when it signed NAFTA and the FTA.

Argentina is a less predictable and more interesting case study despite its similarities with Canada. Although Argentina had a more limited tradition of middle-power diplomacy at the start of the 1990s, the arrival of the new Menem government in 1990 led to a foreign policy realignment that has brought the country closer to the United States. Like Canada, Argentina also redirected its diplomatic efforts by becoming more interventionist and more supportive of initiatives to develop hemispheric regionalism. At the time, of course, Argentina had high hopes of becoming a NAFTA member itself. Like Canada in its relationship with the United States, the Argentine government was strongly attracted to hemispheric regionalism as a means to reduce the weight of its bilateral relationship with Brazil. But Mercosur's success, the U.S. administration's failure to obtain fast-track authority, and Chile's and Bolivia's decisions to seek a closer partnership with Mercosur have complicated the situation for Argentina. The Argentine government must now reevaluate its position as it becomes more difficult to resist the Mercosur bloc. With a presidential election looming, Argentina's strategy in relation to hemispheric regionalism will unquestionably be the most interesting to watch among the middle states of the Americas.

The Dyamics of Hemispheric Regionalism

We have circumscribed the continental integration project, situated it within its immediate structural environment, and analyzed the conduct of actors involved in the integration process. Now how can we evaluate the current dynamics of hemispheric regionalism? Regardless of the optimism surrounding the Miami summit, things are not proceeding as well as expected. But is there enough evidence to conclude, as some have done (i.e., refusal by the U.S. Congress to adopt fast-track legislation), that hemispheric regionalism is at a standstill and that this third attempt at continental integration will be as unsuccessful as the efforts of 1889 and 1948?

It is essential when answering these questions to remember that integration is a long-term process with ups and downs that require frequent adjustment from the actors involved. In the case of hemispheric regionalism, the early years were characterized by the momentum that began with the

Enterprise for the Americas Initiative and led to the Miami summit. This momentum was made possible by the presence of certain perceptions and beliefs, such as the acute perception throughout the region that the reorganization of the industrialized world into economic blocs, particularly in Europe, would result in the marginalization of other parts of the world, including the Latin American and Caribbean subregions. At a time when the United States was reevaluating its foreign policy options, the administration's belief that values had converged to a point that made the option of hemispheric regionalism conceivable was also an important factor.

A combination of events and perceptions at the end of the 1980s therefore prompted the U.S. government to propose a plan for the reorganization of inter-American affairs in an effort to strengthen continental integration. At issue was a political and economic development model that would bring political and economic conduct in the Americas in line with the U.S. vision of liberal democracy and market economics. Also at issue was U.S. leadership in the hemisphere and its global influence in the new world order.

It appears, however, that the early momentum of the regionalist project has been lost and that hemispheric regionalism is now in jeopardy. What has happened to explain this turn of events? Has hemispheric regionalism really ended? Our contention is that initial U.S. designs for continental integration are in difficulty and may have reached a dead end. Furthermore, hemispheric regionalism, as distinguished from the U.S. model, which is only one interpretation of continental integration, has essentially entered a new phase. This new phase is an attempt to redefine the contours of hemispheric regionalism in the face of the change in regional dynamics that occurred almost immediately after the Miami summit.

Ironically, it is the United States—the country that would apparently gain the most from the regionalist project—that is at the root of the changing dynamic. In the wake of the first Summit of the Americas, congressional representatives were influenced by new protectionist-minded members, the Mexican peso crisis, and the view that NAFTA was having negative effects on the U.S. economy and the labor market. They began to perceive NAFTA-style integration arrangements as detrimental to the U.S. workforce and economy. Even though experts had different opinions about the precise impact of both NAFTA and the peso crisis on the U.S. economy, Congress had become skeptical about the benefits of extending NAFTA to the rest of the hemisphere. This situation, aggravated by what appeared to be a weaker commitment to hemispheric regionalism on the part of the Clinton administration, led directly to the fast-track authority episode. This major policy fiasco in turn resulted in a significant loss of U.S. credibility concerning its ability to provide the necessary leadership to move continental integration forward.

This negative turn of events in the United States gave other actors involved in the regionalist project more political leeway. The most significant input came from Brazil. Bolstered by the success and geographical extension of Mercosur, Brazil led the movement to try to redefine and redirect the continental integration process. Rather than reject hemispheric regionalism per se, countries such as Brazil question the form that integration will take. Issues include the choice of topics in discussions leading to the FTAA, their order of priority, the timetable to be adopted, and larger questions such as the role of the state in the economy. In addition, many of the region's smaller countries are afraid that the extension of a NAFTA-style model throughout the entire hemisphere will place an unbearable burden on them by imposing adjustment measures unacceptable to local populations.

Now that there is more political space to move about in, many civil society actors have the opportunity to voice their concerns, propose alternative measures, and insist on participation in discussions to establish the parameters of an eventual integration scheme. The Miami experience has opened the door to civil society interventions, a development worth considering in the current process of redefining hemispheric regionalism.

The second Summit of the Americas, held in Santiago, Chile, in April 1998, left many options open in terms of redefining continental integration. Given the state of domestic affairs in the United States, it was difficult to imagine beforehand that the summit would result in major engagements on the part of the participating governments in relation to hemispheric regionalism. On the contrary, one would have expected immobilism or even a step back on the road toward integration.

But the worst fears did not materialize and the Santiago summit did achieve some successes. The most notable success was the decision to launch FTAA negotiations formally and to adopt a timetable and select the countries presiding over the various stages of the negotiations. The objective is to conclude the FTAA negotiations no later than 2005, with tangible progress made toward this goal by 2000. This decision was a compromise between the North Americans, who want to be able to sign interim agreements before all measures are agreed upon, and Brazilian-led Latin Americans, who insisted on negotiating on the basis of the single undertaking principle. By introducing education as a central theme of hemispheric regionalism, the Santiago Plan of Action also draws attention to other dimensions of integration, namely, the social and cultural aspect so important for the long-term success of the regional project. The importance given to civil society actors by the Santiago summit is also a positive development in the sense that it indicates a recognition of the significance of such actors for the legitimacy of the whole process. Finally, the attention given to the problem of the smaller economies as they try to become part of the integration process could be an important step forward if it is translated into concrete mechanisms enabling these countries to join the process without unbearable adjustment costs.

For the rest, the Santiago Plan of Action is essentially a follow-up of the measures included in the Miami Plan of Action. How the actors involved in the process will be able to translate these measures into specific realizations will depend on the outcome of the new dynamics at work in the integration process since 1995.

It is still too early to predict what this process of redefinition will mean for the future of hemispheric regionalism. But it is quite clear that the domestic situation in the United States since the mid-1990s has had a significant impact on the dynamics of continental integration. It has made room for other actors and created opportunities for them to redefine the agenda for hemispheric regionalism. It is evident that the outcome of the current redefinition phase will be influenced by the relationship between the United States and the Brazil-led coalition. Compromises must be made that are acceptable to both the United States and its neighbors; this is particularly true for the United States. If eventual compromises do not appear to take U.S. interests sufficiently into consideration, then Washington will be reluctant to get involved, and hemispheric regionalism will have little meaning in the absence of the regional hegemon. Finally, it is obvious that regional organizations such as the OAS, middle states such as Argentina and Canada, business community representatives, and the broader civil society have a crucial role to play in proposing compromises and solutions capable of generating large support.

Hemispheric regionalism is a complex, long-term process of which this book can offer nothing more than a provisional assessment. The current move toward continental integration—made possible by the particular configuration of the world order in the 1980s—is part of a larger historical process in the Americas that is still unfolding. As with all social and political constructs, hemispheric regionalism is influenced by the perceptions, values and behavior of the actors involved in its construction. Scholars must try to fully understand these elements if we are to more adequately assess a phenomenon that has begun to modify the landscape of the Americas in a profound way.

Acronyms and Abbreviations

ACN	Action Canada Network
ALADI	Latin American Integration Association
ASEAN	Association of Southeast Asian Nations
CACM	Central American Common Market
CARICOM	Caribbean Community and Common Market
CET	common external tariff
CGE	General Business Confederation
CIAV	International Commission for Support and Verification
CMC	Common Market Council
CMG	Common Market Group
CTC	Citizens Trade Campaign
EAI	Enterprise for the Americas Initiative
ECLAC/ECLA	Economic Commission for Latin America and the Caribbean (often referred to as CEPAL)
ECSC	European Coal and Steel Community
EEC	European Economic Community
FAT	Workers' Authentic Front
FTA	Free Trade Agreement
FTAA	Free Trade Area of the Americas
FTC	Fair Trade Campaign
EZLN	Zapatista National Liberation Army
G3	Group of Three
GATT	General Agreement on Tariffs and Trade
GDP	gross domestic product
IACHR	Inter-American Commission on Human Rights

IADB	Inter-American Defense Board
IAS	Inter-American System
ICFTU	International Confederation of Free Trade Unions
IDB	Inter-American Development Bank
IFC	International Finance Corporation
IMF	International Monetary Fund
LAFTA	Latin American Free Trade Association
Mercosur	Southern Cone Common Market
MIC	Ministry for Industry and Commerce
MNC	multinational corporation
NAFTA	North American Free Trade Agreement
NATO	North Atlantic Treaty Organization
NGOs	nongovernmental organizations
OAS	Organization of American States
PCN	Pro-Canada Network
PRD	Revolutionary Democratic Party
PRI	Revolutionary Institutional Party
RECHIP	Chilean Network in Favor of People's Initiative
RMALC	Mexican Network for Action on Free Trade
SAFTA	South American Free Trade Association
SELA	Latin American Economic System
TC	Trade Commission
TWM	Third World multinationals
UAW	United Auto Workers
UIA	Industrial Union of Argentina
UN	United Nations
UPD	Unit for the Promotion of Democracy
WTO	World Trade Organization

Bibliography

"A ALCA e o Comércio" (1997) *Sumário Econômico*, National Confederation of Trade, Rio de Janeiro, March 7, pp. 1–3.

"A Importância do Setor Privado" (1997) *Gazeta Mercantil Latino-Americana*, May 12–18, p. 9.

Abdenur, Roberto (1997) "Mercosul, Alca, União Européia—Reflexões Para Uma Estratégia Brasileira," *Política Externa* 6 (September): 62–70.

Abel, R. H., R. Taras, and James D. Cochrane (1991) *Political Culture and Foreign Policy in Latin America* (Albany: State University of New York Press).

Abella, Gloria (1992) "La política exterior de México en el gobierno de Carlos Salinas: ¿una nueva concepción?" *Revista Mexicana de Ciencias Políticas y Sociales* 37, no. 148 (April–June): 63–76.

Abreu, Marcelo (1997) "O Brasil e a Alca: Interesses e Alternativas," paper presented at the Ninth National Forum, Panel 5, Instituto de Aperfeiçoamento de Executivos (INAE), Rio de Janeiro, May 21.

Acevedo, Domingo E. (1993) "The Haitian Crisis and the OAS Response: A Test of Effectiveness in Protecting Democracy," in L. F. Domrasch (ed.), *Enforcing Restraint: Collective Intervention in Internal Politics* (New York: Council on Foreign Relations Press), pp. 119–155.

Acevedo, Domingo E., and Claudio Grossman (1996) "The Organization of American States and the Protection of Democracy," in Tom Farer (ed.), *Beyond Sovereignty: Collectively Defending Democracy in the Americas* (Baltimore: Johns Hopkins University Press), pp. 133–149.

Aguilar, A. (1968) *Pan-Americanism from Monroe to the Present: A View from the Other Side* (New York: Monthly Review Press).

Aho, C. Michael (1988) "A U.S. Perspective," in John Crispo (ed.), *Free Trade: The Real Story* (Toronto: Gage Educational Publishing), pp. 180–187.

"Al final, hay un acuerdo con Brasil" (1997) *La Nación on Line*, Wednesday, April 2. www.lanacion.com.ar.

Alexander, Robin, and Peter Gilmore (1994) "The Emergence of Cross-Border Labor Solidarity," *NACLA, Report on the Americas: Mexico in Crisis* 28, no. 1 (July–August): 42–48.

Alianza Cívicas (1995) "Vamos al Referéndum de la Libertad del 21 de septiembre al 21 de octubre," information document (document in possession of the author).

Alliance for Responsible Trade, Citizens' Trade Campaign, The Mexican Action Network on Free Trade (1993) *A Just and Sustainable Trade and Development Initiative for North America*, September 28.

Almeida-Medeiros, Marcelo de (1995) "Relações Externas do MERCOSUL: Uma Abordagem Brasileira," *Revista Brasileira de Política Internacional* 38, no. 2: 31–58.

American Business Forum (1996) "The Role of the Private Sector in the Creation of FTAA by 2005," March 18–21.

Anderson, Kym, and Richard Blackburst (eds.) (1993) *Regional Integration and the Global Trading System* (New York: Harvester/Wheatsheaf).

Appleton, Barry (1994) *Navigating NAFTA. A Concise User's Guide to the North American Free Trade Agreement* (Scarborough, Ontario: Carswell).

Archer, Clive (1992) *International Organizations*, 2nd ed. (London: Routledge).

Arocena, Martín (1997) "Common Market of the Southern Cone (MERCOSUR)," in A. J. Jatar and S. Weintraub (eds.), *Integrating the Hemisphere. Perspectives from Latin America and the Caribbean* (Washington, DC: Inter-American Dialogue), pp. 152–176.

Aronson, Bernard W. (assistant secretary of state for inter-American affairs) (1996) "Our Vision of the Hemisphere," *U.S. Department of State Dispatch*, October 15, pp. 184–185.

Arroyo, Alberto P., and Mario B. Monroy (1996) *Red Mexicana de Acción Frente al Libre Comercio: 5 años de lucha (1991–1996)* (Mexico: RMLAC).

Atkins, G. Pope (1977) *Latin America in the International Political System* (New York: Hill and Wang).

——— (1992) "Reorienting U.S. Policies in the New Era," in G. P. Atkins (ed.), *The United States and Latin America: Redefining U.S. Purposes in the Post–Cold War Era* (Austin, Texas: Lyndon B. Johnson School of Public Affairs), pp. 1–18.

——— (1993) "Institutional Arrangements for Hemispheric Free Trade," *Annals of the AAPSS* 526 (March): 183–194.

Axline, W. Andrew (1977) "Underdevelopment, Dependence, and Integration. The Politics of Regionalism in the Third World," *International Organization* 31: 83–105.

——— (1979) *Caribbean Integration: The Politics of Regionalism* (London: Pinter Publishers).

——— (1995) *Globalization, Marginalization and Integration: The New Regionalism and Developing Countries*, Department of Political Science Working Paper no. 9501P (Ottawa: University of Ottawa).

——— (1996) "External Forces, State Strategies, and Regionalism in the Americas," in G. Mace and J.-P. Thérien (eds.), *Foreign Policy and Regionalism in the Americas* (Boulder, CO: Lynne Rienner Publishers), pp. 199–218.

Badie, Bertrand (1995) *La fin des territoires* (Paris: Fayard).

Badie, Bertrand, and Marie-Claude Smouts (1992) *Le retournement du monde. Sociologie de la scène internationale* (Paris: Presses de la Fondation nationale des sciences politiques/Dalloz).

Baer, Delal M. (1994) "New Pattern of Conflict and Cooperation," in M. D. Baer and S. Weintraub (eds.), *The NAFTA Debate: Grappling with Unconventional Trade Issues* (Boulder, CO: Lynne Rienner Publishers), pp. 183–192.

Baer, Werner (1962) "The Economics of Prebisch and ECLA," *Economic Development and Cultural Change* 10 (January): 169–182.

Baranyi, Stephen (1995) "Peace Missions and Subsidiarity in the Americas: Conflict Management in the Western Hemisphere," *International Journal* 50, no. 2 (Spring): 343–369.

Barbosa, Mariela, et al. (n.d.) "Introduction: Women and Economic Integration," in P. Duggan and H. Dashner (eds.), *Women's Lives in the New Global Economy*, Notebooks for Study and Research no. 22 (Amsterdam: International Institute for Research and Education), pp. 7–11.

Barbosa, Rubens Antonio (1992) "A Integração Regional e o Mercosul," Proceedings of the International Colloquium Regional Economic Integration, Universidad de São Paulo, São Paulo, July, pp. 121–128.

Barry, Donald (1995) "The Road to NAFTA," in D. Barry, M. O. Dickerson, and J. D. Gaisford (eds.), *Toward a North American Community? Canada, the United States, and Mexico* (Boulder, CO: Westview Press), pp. 3–14.

"Barshefsky Foresees Problems from Likely Fast Track Defeat" (1998) *USIS Washington File*, September 24. http://www.usia.gov/products/washfile.htm.

Bartolome, Mariano C. (1990) "Las relaciones Argentina-Brasil: del conflicto a la cooperación," *Geopolítica* 15, no. 39: 30–38.

Belous, Richard. S., and Rebecca S. Hartley (eds.) (1990) *The Growth of Regional Trading Blocs in the Global Economy* (Washington, DC: National Planning Association).

Benn, Jim (1992) "The U.S. and the Global Economy," in J. Sinclair (ed.), *Crossing the Line: Canada and Free Trade with Mexico* (Vancouver: New Star Books), pp. 38–49.

Bennett, A. LeRoy (1995) *International Organizations: Principles and Issues,* 6th ed. (Englewood Cliffs, NJ: Prentice-Hall).

Benzécri, F. (1986) "Introduction à l'analyse des correspondances d'après l'analyse du commerce mondial des phosphates," in J.-P. Benzécri (ed.), *Pratique de l'analyse des données,* vol. 5: *Économie* (Paris: Dunod), pp. 3–47.

Benzécri, J.-P. (1992) *Correspondence Analysis Handbook,* Statistics, Textbooks and Monographs no. 125 (New York: Marcel Dekker).

Bhagwati, Jagdish, and Douglas A. Irwin (1987) "The Return of the Reciprocitarians: U.S. Trade Policy Today," *The World Economy* 10, no. 2: 109–130.

Blank, Stephen (1993) "The Emerging Architecture of North America," The North-South Agenda, Paper no. 1, Miami, North-South Center, March.

Blank, Stephen, Stephen Krajewski, and Earl H. Fry (1993) "Toward a 'New' Architecture of North America: NAFTA's Impact on Corporate Restructuring," paper read at the 34th annual convention of the International Studies Association and the Asociación Mexicana de Estudios Internacionales, Acapulco, March 23–27.

Bloomfield, Richard J. (1994) "Making the Western Hemisphere Safe for Democracy? The OAS Defense-of-Democracy Regime," *The Washington Quarterly* 17, no. 2: 157–169.

Bordet, J.-P., and A. Kokosowski (1982) *Analyse multidimensionnelle et typologie,* coll. Sciences sociales et analyse des données (Issy-les-Moulineaux: EAP/Publications de l'Université de Rouen).

Boutros-Ghali, Boutros (1995) "Democracy: A Newly Recognized Imperative," *Global Governance* 1, no. 1: 3–11.

Bouzas, Roberto (1992) "Un acuerdo de libre comercio entre Estados Unidos y MERCOSUR: una evaluación preliminar," in R. Bouzas and N. Lustig (eds.),

Liberalización comercial e integración regional: de NAFTA a MERCOSUR (Buenos Aires: Facultad Latinoamericana de Ciencias), pp. 165–195.

―――― (1996) "La agenda económica del MERCOSUR: desafíos de política a corto y mediano plaz," *Integración & Comercio* 1, no. 0 (January–April): 64–87.

―――― (1997) "MERCOSUR and Preferential Trade Liberalization in South America: Record, Issues and Prospects," in R. G. Lipsey and P. Meller (eds.), *Western Hemisphere Trade Integration: A Canadian-Latin American Dialogue,* International Political Economy Series (New York: St. Martin's Press), pp. 58–89.

Brachet-Marquez, Viviane (1997) "Democratic Transition and Consolidation in Latin America: Steps Toward a New Theory of Democratization," *Current Sociology* 45, no. 1 (January): 15–53.

Brand, Diana (1992) "Regional Bloc Formation and World Trade," *Intereconomics* (November–December): 274–281.

"Brasil defendió el MERCOSUR ante Clinton" (1997) *La Nación on Line,* Tuesday, October 14. http://lanacionline.com.ar. Translation by author.

Breuning, Marijke (1995) "Words and Deeds: Foreign Assistance Rethoric and Policy Behavior in the Netherlands, Belgium, and the United Kingdom," *International Studies Quarterly* 39, no. 2 (June): 235–254.

―――― (1997) "Culture, History, Role: Belgian and Dutch Axioms and Foreign Assistance Policy," in Valerie M. Hudson (ed.), *Culture and Foreign Policy* (Boulder, CO: Lynne Rienner Publishers), pp. 99–123.

Brewer, Thomas L., and Lorne Teitelbaum (1997) *American Foreign Policy: A Contemporary Introduction,* 4th ed. (Upper Saddle River, NJ: Prentice-Hall).

Brinkley, Douglas (1997) "Democratic Enlargement: The Clinton Doctrine," *Foreign Policy* 106 (Spring): 110–127.

Brooke, James (1994) "Latins Join in New Effort to Get Haitian Leaders to Step Down," *New York Times,* August 15, p. A-2.

Buelens, Frans (1992) "The Creation of Regional Blocs in the World Economy," *Intereconomics* (May–June): 124–132.

Bush, George (1989) "Remarks to the Council of the Americas," *Public Papers of the President of the United States,* vol. 1 (Washington, DC: U.S. Government Printing Office), pp. 504–507.

―――― (1990) "Remarks Announcing the Enterprise for the Americas Initiative," *Public Papers of the President of the United States,* vol. 1 (Washington, DC: U.S. Government Printing Office), pp. 873–877.

―――― (1991) "Written Responses to Questions Submitted by the South American Press," *Public Papers of the President of the United States: 1990,* vol. 2 (Washington, DC: U.S. Government Printing Office), pp. 1731–1737.

Buxedas, Martín (1994) *MERCOSUR y TLC: convergencias, divergencias y negociación* (Montevideo: Fondad-Uruguay).

Buzan, Barry, Charles Jones, and Richard Little (1993) *The Logic of Anarchy: Neorealism to Structural Realism* (New York: Columbia University Press).

"Campbell: 'Se debe cambiar la relación con Brasil'" (1997) *La Nación on Line,* Sunday, April 13. http://lanacionline.com.ar.

Canada, Ministère des Affaires étrangères et du Commerce international (1995) "Déclaration conjointe du Canada et du Groupe de Rio, 15 décembre 1995," *Communiqué* 233: 1–2.

Canadian Center for Policy Alternatives (1992a) *Which Way for the Americas: Analysis of NAFTA Proposals and the Impact on Canada* (Ottawa: CCPA).

—— (1992b) "Document 14" (Selected Documents), *Popular Sector Organizations and Trade: A Report to the Ministry of Industry, Trade and Technology, Government of Ontario* (Ottawa: CCPA).

—— (1992c) "Zacatecas Declaration: Towards an Alternative Approach to North American Development and Trade," *Popular Sector Organizations and Trade: A Report to the Ministry of Industry, Trade and Technology, Government of Ontario* (Ottawa: CCPA), C-10, C-17.

—— (1994) "Integration, Democracy and Development: Towards a Continental Social Agenda (Mexico City, July 22–23, 1994)," *Monitor: Reporting on Business, Labour and Government* 1, no. 5 (October).

Canadian Foundation for the Americas (1994) *Toward a New World Strategy: Canadian Policy in the Americas into the Twenty-first Century*, Focal Paper no. 1 (Ottawa: The Canadian Foundation for the Americas).

Canel, Eduardo (1992) "New Social Movement Theory," in W. Carroll (ed.), *Organizing Dissent: Contemporary Social Movements in Theory and in Practice* (Toronto: Garamond), pp. 22–51.

Cárdenas, C. (1991) "Our Goal Is to Join Forces with You," in Pro-Canada Network, *The Pro-Canada Dossier* 29 (January–February): 35.

—— (1992) "The Continental Development and Trade Initiative," in John Cavanagh (ed.), *Trading Freedom: How Free Trade Affects Our Lives, Work, and Environment* (San Francisco: Institute for Food and Developmental Policy), pp. 95–99.

"Caricom: ECLAC RIF Study Does Not Go Far Enough" (1997), *AmericasTrade* 4, no. 22 (October 30): 17–18.

Carlsnaes, Walter (1992) "The Agent-Structure Problem in Foreign Policy Analysis," *International Studies Quarterly* 36, no. 3 (September): 245–270.

Carr, Barry (1994) "Labor Internationalism in the Era of NAFTA: Past and Present," paper read at conference, Labor, Free Trade and Economic Integration in the Americas: National Labor Union Responses to a Transnational World, Duke University Program in Latin American Studies, Durham, North Carolina, August 25–27.

Carter, Ralph G. (1996) *Congressional Trade Politics in the Post–Cold War Era*, paper presented at the annual meeting of the International Studies Association, San Diego, April 16–20.

Cavanagh, John (1992) "Free Trade as Opportunity," in J. Cavanagh (ed.), *Trading Freedom: How Free Trade Affects Our Lives, Work, and Environment* (San Francisco: Institute for Food and Development Policy), pp. 1–14.

Centro de Atención a la Mujer Trabajadora (1992) "Una respuesta desde las mujeres ante el proceso de integración económica," in *Taller Regional de Trabajadoras de la Maquila* (Chihuahua, Mexico: SEDEPAC/CAMT).

—— (1993) *II Taller Regional de Trabajadoras de la Maquila* (Torreón, Mexico: SEDEPAC/CAMT).

Céspedes, Roberto (1994) "El Movimiento Sindical Paraguayo Frente al Mercosur," *Labor, Free Trade and Economic Integration in the Americas: National Labor Union Responses to a Transnational World* (Durham, NC: Duke–University of North Carolina Program in Latin American Studies).

Cevallos, Diego (1995) "Democracy, Free Trade: Main Topics at the OAS Meeting," *Inter Press Service*, June 5.

Chabat, Jorge (1990) "Los instrumentos de la política exterior de Miguel de la Madrid," *Foro Internacional* 30, no. 3 (January–March): 399–418.

Chafetz, Glenn, Hillel Abramson, and Suzette Guillot (1997) "Culture and National Role Conceptions: Belarussian and Ukrainian Compliance with the Nuclear

Non-Proliferation Regime," in Valerie M. Hudson (ed.), *Culture and Foreign Policy* (Boulder, CO: Lynne Rienner Publishers), pp. 169–200.

Chase-Dunn, Christopher (1989) *Global Formation* (London: Blackwell).

Chicago Tribune (1995a) January 13, p. 1.

—— (1995b) November 8, p. 2.

—— (1995c) November 10, p. 28.

Child, Jack (1985) *Geopolitics and Conflict in South America: Quarrels Among Neighbors* (New York: Praeger Special Studies).

Christopher, Warren (1993) "A Bridge to a Better Future for the United States and the Hemisphere," *U.S. Department of State Dispatch* 4, no. 37 (September 13): 625–626.

—— (1995a) "Embracing a New Consensus of the Americas," *U.S. Department of State Dispatch* 6, no. 21 (May 22): 417–418.

—— (1995b) "The OAS: Playing an Essential Role in the Western Hemisphere," *U.S. Department of State Dispatch* 6, no. 24 (June 12): 491.

Clark, Joe (1989) *Notes for Remarks by the Right Honourable Joe Clark, P.C., M.P., Secretary of State for External Affairs, at the Meeting of the General Assembly of the Organization of American States, Washington, November 13, 1989* (Ottawa: Department of Foreign Affairs).

Clarke, Tony (1991a) "Challenging the Fortress," Pro-Canada Network, *The Pro-Canada Dossier* 29 (January–February): 3.

—— (1991b) "International Forum Highlights," Pro-Canada Network, *Action Canada Dossier* 34 (November–December): 6.

—— (1993) "Yes We Do have Alternatives," Pro-Canada Network, *Action Canada Dossiers* 39 (Autumn): 6.

Cline, Ray (1980) *World Power Trends and U.S. Foreign Policy for the 1980s* (Boulder, CO: Westview Press).

Cline, William B. (1982) *"Reciprocity": A New Approach to World Trade Policy?* (Washington, DC: Institute of International Economics).

"Clinton-MERCOSUR: cambio de frente" (1997) *Sucesos*, October 24. www.mercosur.com.

Coalition Québécoise d'Opposition au Libre-Échange: CEQ, CSN, FTQ, UPA (1987) *Danger: libre-échange* (Montréal: CQOLE).

Connell-Smith, Gordon (1974) *The United States and Latin America, An Historical Analysis of Inter-American Relations* (London: Heinemann Educational Books).

Congressional Quarterly Almanac vol. 44: *1988* (1989) (Washington, DC: Congressional Quarterly).

—— vol. 49: *1993* (1994) (Washington, DC: Congressional Quarterly).

Congressional Record (Washington, DC) (1988) August 9 and September 19.

—— (1993) April 5, May 13, July 14, July 20, July 28, July 29, August 6, September 8, September 15, September 21, September 23, September 30, October 6, October 21, October 28, November 4, November 10, November 15, November 17, November 18, November 19, November 20, November 22.

—— (1994) June 10, June 30, October 7.

—— (1995) January 11, January 13, January 18, January 19, April 6, September 7, October 10, October 25, November 3, November 16, December 5, December 6, December 19.

—— (1996) April 24, June 19.

Cooper, Andrew F. (ed.) (1997) *Niche Diplomacy: Middle Powers After the Cold War* (London: Macmillan).

Cooper, Andrew F., Richard A. Higgot, and Kim Richard Nossal (1993) *Relocating Middle Powers: Australia and Canada in a Changing World* (Vancouver: University of British Columbia Press).

Cooper, Robert (1996) *The Post-Modern State and the World Order* (London: Demos).

Correspondencia (1994) 16 (May).

Cottam, Martha L. (1994) *Images and Intervention: U.S. Policies in Latin America* (Pittsburgh: University of Pittsburgh Press).

Council of Canadians (1994) *Canadian Perspectives* (Autumn).

Cox, Robert W. (1987) *Production, Power and World Order: Social Forces in the Making of History* (New York: Columbia University Press).

———. (1989) "Middlepowermanship, Japan, and Future World Order," *International Journal* 44, no. 4 (Autumn): 823–862.

Daby, Justine (1994) "Has Mexico Crossed the Border on State Responsibility for Economic Injury to Aliens? Foreign Investment and the Calvo Clause in Mexico After NAFTA," *St. Mary's Law Journal* 25: 1147.

Davidow, Jeffrey (assistant decretary for inter-American affairs) (1997) *Testimony Before the House of International Relations Committee, Subcommittee on the Western Hemisphere*, Washington, DC, March 19. www.state.gov/www/regions/ara/970314–davidow.html.

Davis, Bob (1992) "U.S. Grassroots Coalitions Unites Against NAFTA," *Globe and Mail* (Toronto), December 26, p. B1.

De la Torre, Augusto, and Margaret R. Kelly (1992) *Regional Trade Arrangements* (Washington, DC: International Monetary Fund).

De Vree, J. K. (1972) *Political Integration. The Formation of Theory and Its Problems* (Paris: Mouton).

Del Castillo V., Gustavo (1995) "The NAFTA: A Mexican Search for Development," in R. S. Belous and J. Lemco (eds.), *NAFTA as a Model of Development* (Albany: State University of New York Press), pp. 113–128.

Departamento de Integração Latino-Americana/MRE (1993) "MERCOSUR-NAFTA: Perspectivas de Relacionamento," *Boletim de Integração Latino-Americana* 8 (January–March): 58–72.

Destler, I. M. (1986) *American Trade Politics: System Under Stress* (Washington, DC: Institute of International Economics).

——— (1994) "Delegating Trade Policy," in Paul E. Peterson (ed.), *The President, the Congress, and the Making of Foreign Policy* (Norman: University of Oklahoma Press), pp. 228–245.

Deutsch, Karl W. (1952) "On Communication Models in the Social Sciences," *Public Opinion Quarterly* 16, no. 3: 356–380.

——— (1954) *Political Community at the International Level* (New York: Doubleday).

——— (1964) "Communication Theory and Political Integration," in Philip E. Jacob and James V. Toscane (eds.), *The Integration of Political Communities* (Philadelphia: Lippincott), pp. 46–74.

Deutsch, Karl W., Sidney A. Burrell, Robert A. Kann, Maurice Lee Jr., Martin Lichterman, Raymond E. Lindgren, Francis L. Loewenheim, and Richard W. Van Wagenen (1957) *Political Community and the North Atlantic Area* (Princeton, NJ: Princeton University Press).

Di Marco, Luis Eugenio (1995) "Las relaciones MERCOSUR-NAFTA," in L. E. Di Marco (ed.), *Verdad y Mitos del MERCOSUR: Un análisis interdisciplinario* (Córdoba, Argentina: Editorial Atenea), pp. 11–31.

Diamond, Larry (1995) *Promoting Democracy in the 1990s: Actors and Instruments, Issues and Imperatives* (Washington, DC: Carnegie Commission on Preventing Deadly Conflict).

———— (1996) "Democracy in Latin America: Degrees, Illusions, and Directions for Consolidation," in T. Farer (ed.), *Beyond Sovereignty: Collectively Defending Democracy in the Americas* (Baltimore: Johns Hopkins University Press), pp. 52–104.

"Divergências Entre Empresários Provocam Impasse na Questão do Acesso a Mercados" (1997) *O Globo* (May 15): 3.

Dixon, William J., and Bruce E. Moon (1993) "Political Similarity and American Foreign Trade Patterns," *Political Research Quarterly* 46, no. 1 (March): 5–25.

Doran, Charles F. (1991) *Systems in Crisis—New Imperatives of High Politics at Century's End* (Cambridge: Cambridge University Press).

Dosman, Edgar J. (1992) "Canada and Latin America: The New Look," *International Journal* 47, no. 3 (Summer): 529–554.

Drainville, André C. (1995) "Left Internationalism and the Politics of Resistance in the New World Order," in D. Smith and J. Böröcz (eds.), *A New World Order: Global Transformations in the Late Twentieth Century* (Westport, CT: Praeger), pp. 217–238.

———— (1997) "Continental Integration and Civil Society in the Americas," *Social Justice* 24, no. 1 (Spring): 120–148.

———— (forthcoming) "The Fetishism of Global Civil Society: Global Governance, Transnational Urbanism and Sustainable Capitalism in the World Economy," *Comparative Urban and Community Research.*

Dupas, Gilberto (1997) "A Questão da Alca e os Interesses do Brasil," *O Estado de São Paulo*, Working Paper 2, São Paulo, April 13, pp. D1–D5.

Economic Commission for Latin America (ECLA) (1950) *The Economic Development of Latin America* (New York: United Nations).

Economic Commission for Latin America and the Caribbean (1992) *A Western Hemisphere Trade Area: An Overview of the Issues* (Santiago: ECLAC).

———— (1994) *Open Regionalism in Latin America and the Caribbean* (Santiago: ECLAC).

Economist (1997) December 20, pp. 32–33.

Edwards, Jack K., and Werner Baer (1993) "The State of the Private Sector in Latin America: Reflections on the Past, the Present and the Future," *Quarterly Review of Economics and Finance* 33: 9–19.

Eggleton, Art (1996) *Intervention by the Honourable Art Eggleton*, Second Western Hemisphere Trade Ministerial and Business Forum, Cartagena, Colombia, March. www.sice.oas.org/FTAA/carta_e.stm.

"El Banco Mundial insistió con sus advertencias sobre el MERCOSUR" (1997) *Sucesos*, July 11. www.mercosur.com.

"Embaixador Acha Prematura ALCA em 2005" (1997) *O Globo,* May 22, p. 3.

"Empresários Ganham Espaço no Debate" (1997) *Gazeta Mercantil*, May 17–18, pp. A–5.

Etzioni, Amitai (1968) *The Active Society: A Theory of Societal and Political Processes* (New York: Free Press).

Evans, Peter B., Harold Jacobson, and Robert D. Putnam (eds.) (1993) *Double-Edged Diplomacy: International Bargaining and Domestic Politics* (Berkeley: University of California Press).

The Europa World Yearbook (1966–1995) (London: Europa Publications).

Farer, Tom (1993) "Collectively Defending Democracy in a World of Sovereign States: The Western Hemisphere's Prospect," *Human Rights Quarterly* 15: 716–750.

——— (1996) "Collectively Defending Democracy in the Western Hemisphere: Introduction and Overview," in T. Farer (ed.), *Beyond Sovereignty: Collectively Defending Democracy in the Americas* (Baltimore: Johns Hopkins University Press), pp. 1–25.

Fawcett, Louise (1995) "Regionalism in Historical Perspective," in L. Fawcett and A. Hurrell (eds.), *Regionalism in World Politics: Regional Organization and International Order* (Oxford: Oxford University Press), pp. 9–36.

Fawcett, Louise, and Andrew Hurrell (eds.) (1995) *Regionalism in World Politics: Regional Organization and International Order* (Oxford: Oxford University Press).

Federación Internacional de Trabajadores de las Industrias Metalúrgicas (1995) *Los Sindicatos en el Proceso de la Integración Andina* (Geneva: FITIM).

Feinberg, Richard E. (1997) *Summitry in the Americas: A Progress Report* (Washington, DC: Institute for International Economics).

Fernández, Wilson (1997) "El MERCOSUR ante el Nuevo Siglo: Tendencias y Perspectivas," paper read at the annual meeting of the Latin American Studies Association, Guadalajara, April 17.

Ferris, Elizabeth G. (1984) "Mexico's Foreign Policies: A Study in Contradictions," in Jennie K. Lincoln and Elizabeth G. Ferris (eds.), *The Dynamics of Latin American Foreign Policies: Challenge for the 1980s* (Boulder, CO: Westview Press), pp. 213–227.

Ferris, Wayne (1973) *The Power Capabilities of Nation-States* (Lexington, MA: Lexington Books).

"Few Trade Bills Seem Likely to Pass After Fast Track Defeat" (1998) *USIS Washington File*, September 28. http://www.usia.gov/products/washfile.htm.

Fischer, Klaus P., E. Ortiz, and A. P. Palasvirta (1994) "Risk Management and Corporate Governance in Imperfect Capital Markets," reprinted in D. K. Ghosh and E. Ortiz (eds.), *The Changing Environment of International Financial Markets: Issues and Analysis* (London: Macmillan Press).

Fischer, William E. (1969) "An Analysis of the Deutsch Sociocausal Paradigm of Political Integration," *International Organization* 23, no. 2: 254–290.

Fishlow, Albert, and Stephan Haggard (1992) *The United States and the Regionalisation of the World Economy* (Paris: Organization for Economic Cooperation and Development).

Fontaine, Roger W. (1977) *The Andean Pact: A Political Analysis* (Beverly Hills: Sage Publications).

Forsythe, David (1991) *The Internationalization of Human Rights* (Lexington, MA: Lexington Books).

Foweraker, Joe (1996) "From NAFTA to WHFTA? Prospects for Hemispheric Free Trade," in S. Nishijima and P. H. Smith (eds.), *Cooperation or Rivalry? Regional Integration in the Americas and the Pacific Rim* (Boulder, CO: Westview Press), pp. 150–169.

Freedom House (1991) *Freedom at Issue* 22: 1.

Galtung, Johan (1968) "A Structural Theory of Integration," *Journal of Peace Research* 4: 440–458.

Gamble, Andrew, and Anthony Payne (eds.) (1996) *Regionalism and World Order* (New York: St. Martin's Press).

Gamio, José Ma (1995) "Ordenamiento jurídico del MERCOSUR," *Revista Uruguaya de Derecho Constitucional y Político* 11: 73–94.

Garreton, Manuel Antonio (1994) "Human Rights and Processes of Democratisation," *Journal of Latin American Studies* 26: 221–234.

Garver, Paul (1989) "Beyond the Cold War: New Directions for Labor Internationalism," in Labor Research Review, *Solidarity Across Borders* (Chicago: Midwest Center for Labor Research), pp. 61–71.

Gelbard, Robert S. (deputy assistant secretary for inter-American affairs) (1992) "Security in the Americas: Challenges and Opportunities," *U.S. Department of State Dispatch* 3, no. 45 (November 9): 809–811.

Gereffi, Gary (1995) "Global Production Systems and Third World Development," in B. Stallings (ed.), *Global Change, Regional Response: The New International Context of Development* (Cambridge, MA: Cambridge University Press), pp. 100–142.

Giddens, Anthony (1991) *Modernity and Self-Identity: Self and Society in the Late Modern Age* (Stanford, CA: Stanford University Press).

Gill, Stephen, and David Law (1988) *The Global Political Economy* (Baltimore: Johns Hopkins University Press).

Gilpin, Robert (1981) *War and Change in World Politics* (Cambridge: Cambridge University Press).

Globe and Mail (Toronto) (1995) August 7, p. B1.

——— (1996) November 19, p. B9.

Gmardellis, H. (1986) "Commerce par produits au sein de l'OCDE de 1970 à 1979: comparaison avec le commerce entre l'OCDE et l'OPEP," in J.-P. Benzécri (ed.), *Pratique de l'analyse des données*, vol. 5: *Économie* (Paris: Dunod), pp. 281–310.

González, Guadalupe, and Jorge Chabat (1996) "Mexico's Hemispheric Options in the Post–Cold War Era," in Gordon Mace and Jean-Philippe Thérien (eds.), *Foreign Policy and Regionalism in the Americas* (Boulder, CO: Lynne Rienner Publishers), pp. 39–51.

Gordenker, Leon, and Thomas G. Weiss (1996) "Pluralizing Global Governance: Analytical Approaches and Dimensions," in T. G. Weiss and L. Gordenker (eds.), *NGOs, the UN, and Global Governance* (Boulder, CO: Lynne Rienner Publishers), pp. 17–50.

Gore, Albert, Jr. (1994) "The OAS and the Summit of the Americas," *U.S. Department of State Dispatch* 5, no. 48 (November 28): 785–789.

Gorritti, Gustavo (1994) "Utopia Unarmed: The Latin American Left After the Cold War," *The New Republic*, May 9, p. 34.

Gosselin, Guy, Gordon Mace, and Louis Bélanger (1995) "La sécurité coopérative régionale dans les Amériques: le cas des institutions démocratiques," *Études internationales* 26, no. 4 (December): 799–817.

Gowa, Joanne (1994) *Allies, Adversaries, and International Trade* (Princeton, NJ: Princeton University Press).

Grieco, Joseph M. (1990) *Cooperation Among Nations: Europe, America, and Non-Tariff Barriers to Trade* (Ithaca, NY: Cornell University Press).

——— (1996) *Realism and Regionalism: American Power and German and Japanese Institutional Strategies During and After the Cold War*, paper presented at the annual meeting of the International Studies Association, San Diego, April 16–20.

Griffin Cohen, Marjorie (1992) "The Lunacy of Free Trade," in J. Sinclair (ed.), *Crossing the Line: Canada and Free Trade with Mexico* (Vancouver: New Star Books), pp. 14–25.

Grinspun, Ricardo, and Robert Kreklewich (1994) "Consolidating Neoliberal Reforms: 'Free Trade' as a Conditioning Framework," *Studies in Political Economy* 43 (Spring): 33–61.

Grugel, Jean (1996) "Latin America and the Remaking of the Americas," in Andrew Gamble and Anthony Payne (eds.), *Regionalism and World Order* (New York: St. Martin's Press), pp. 131–167.

Grunwald, Joseph (1993) "Hemispheric Economic Integration? Some Reflections," *Annals of the AAPSS* 526 (March): 135–150.

"Guatemala: Concerns Over OAS Response to Latest Coup" (1993) *Inter Press Service*, May 26.

Guilhon Albuquerque, José Augusto (1997) "Em Marcha Lenta," *Carta Internacional* 50 (April): 16.

Haas, Ernst B. (1958) *The Uniting of Europe: Political, Economic and Social Forces, 1950–1957* (London: Stevens and Sons).

———— (1961) "International Integration: The European and the Universal Process," *International Organization* 15, no. 3: 336–392.

———— (1964) *Beyond the Nation-State: Functionalism and International Organization* (Stanford, CA: Stanford University Press).

———— (1970) "The Study of Regional Integration: Reflections on the Joy and Anguish of Pretheorizing," *International Organization* 24, no. 4 (Autumn): 607–646.

———— (1975a) "Is there a Hole in the Whole?" *International Organization* 29, no. 3 (Summer): 827–876.

———— (1975b) *The Obsolescence of Regional Integration Theory* (Berkeley, CA: Institute of International Studies).

———— (1976) "Turbulent Fields and the Theory of Regional Integration," *International Organization* 30, no. 2 (Spring): 173–212.

Haas, Ernst B., and Philippe C. Schmitter (1964) "Economics and Differential Patterns of Political Integration: Projections About Unity in Latin America," *International Organization* 18, no. 3: 705–737.

Haass, Richard N. (1995) "Paradigm Lost," *Foreign Affairs* 74, no. 1: 43–58.

Habermas, Jürgen (1981) "New Social Movements," *Telos* 49 (Fall): 33–37.

Haggard, Stephen (1995) *Developing Nations and the Politics of Global Integration* (Washington, DC: The Brookings Institution).

Haines-Ferrari, Marta (1998) "MERCOSUR: Individual Access and the Dispute Settlement Mechanism," in James Cameron and Karen Campbell (eds.), *Dispute Resolution in the World Trade Organisation* (London: Cameron May), pp. 270–285.

Halperin, Marcelo (1992) "El reto de la nueva integración: objetivos e instrumentos para la consolidación del MERCOSUR," *Integración latinoamericana* 175 (January–February): 32–40.

Hansen, R. D. (1969) "Regional Integration, Reflections on a Decade of Theoretical Efforts," *World Politics* 21, no. 2: 242–271.

Harrison, Lawrence E. (1997) *The Pan-American Dream: Do Latin America's Cultural Values Discourage True Partnership with the United States and Canada?* (New York: Basic Books).

Hawes, Michael K. (1984) *Principal Power, Middle Power, or Satellite? Competing Perspectives in the Study of Canadian Foreign Policy* (Toronto: York Research Programme in Strategic Studies).

Hayes, Geoffrey (1994) "Middle Powers in the New World Order," *Behind the Headlines* 51, no. 2 (Winter): 1–14.

Hébert, Chantal (1991) "La CSN et la CEQ redeviennent 'canadiennes' le temps de faire la guerre aux politiques fédérales," *Le Devoir*, April 5, p. A2.

Heredia, Carlos (1994) "NAFTA and Democratization in Mexico," *Journal of International Affairs* 48, no. 1: 13–38.

——— (1996) "The Oaxaca Initiative: A Framework for Equitable and Sustainable Development in the Americas," in Inter-American Development Bank (ed.), *Forum on Democratic Alternatives to Structural Adjustment in the Americas* (Washington, DC: IADB), pp. 1–11.

Hettne, Björn (1994) "The New Regionalism: Implications for Development and Peace," in B. Hettne and A. Inotai (eds.), *The New Regionalism: Implications for Global Development and International Security* (Helsinki: UNU World Institute for Development Economics Research), pp. 1–49.

Hirst, Monica, and Maria Regina Soares de Lima (1994) "Between Neo-Alignment and Neo-Autonomy: Is There a Third Way in U.S.-Brazilian Relations?" *Documentos de Investigación* 164 Working Paper, Buenos Aires, FLACSO (July).

Hirst, Paul, and Graham Thompson (1992) "The Problem of 'Globalization': International Economic Relations, National Economic Management and the Formation of Trading Blocs," *Economy and Society* 21 (November): 357–396.

Hockin, Thomas (1978) "Foreign Affairs: Canada Abroad as a Measure of Canada at Home," in J. Redekop (ed.), *Approaches to Canadian Politics* (Scarborough, Ontario: Prentice-Hall), pp. 83–102.

Hogness, Peter (1989) "One More Hole in the Wall: The Lunafil Strikers on Guatemala," in Labor Research Review, *Solidarity Across Borders* (Chicago: Midwest Center for Labor Research), pp. 1–17.

Hollis, Martin, and Steve Smith (1992) *Explaining and Understanding International Relations* (Oxford: Clarendon Press).

Holm, Hans Henrik, and Georg Sorensen (eds.) (1995) *Uneven Globalization and the End of the Cold War* (Boulder, CO: Westview Press).

Holmes, John W. (1976) *Canada: A Middle-Aged Power* (Toronto: McClelland & Stewart).

Holsti, Kalevi J. (1970) "National Role Conception in the Study of Foreign Policy," *International Studies Quarterly* 14, no. 3: 233–309.

Hudson, Valerie (ed.) (1997) *Culture and Foreign Policy* (Boulder, CO: Lynne Rienner Publishers).

Hufbauer, Gary Clyde, and Jeffrey J. Schott (1993) *NAFTA: An Assessment* (Washington, DC: Institute for International Economics).

Human Rights Watch (1994) *Human Rights Watch Report 1994* (New York: HRW).

Huntington, Samuel P. (1996) *The Clash of Civilizations and the Remaking of World Order* (New York: Simon and Schuster).

Hurrell, Andrew (1992) "Latin America in the New World Order: A Regional Bloc of the Americas?" *International Affairs* 68, no. 1: 121–139.

——— (1994) "Regionalism in the Americas," in A. F. Lowenthal and G. T. Treverton (eds.), *Latin America in a New World* (Boulder, CO: Westview Press), pp. 167–190.

——— (1995a) "Regionalism in the Americas," in L. Fawcett and A. Hurrell (eds.), *Regionalism in World Politics: Regional Organization and International Order* (Oxford: Oxford University Press), pp. 250–282.

——— (1995b) "Regionalism in Theoretical Perspective," in L. Fawcett and A. Hurrell (eds.), *Regionalism in World Politics: Regional Organization and International Order* (Oxford: Oxford University Press), pp. 37–73.

Inglehart, Ronald (1967) "An End to European Integration?" *American Political Science Review* 61, no. 1: 91–105.

Instituto de Relaciones Europeo-Latinoamericanas (IRELA) (1997) *El MERCO-SUR: Perspectivas de un bloque emergente* (Madrid: IRELA).

Inter-American Development Bank (1994) "From Grassroots to Government," *The IDB Extra*: 8–9.

Inter-American Dialogue (1996) *Multilateralism and the Promotion and Defense of Democracy and Human Rights: An Interim Report* (Washington, DC: Inter-American Dialogue).

――――― (1997a) *The Inter-American Agenda and Multilateral Governance: The Organization of American States* (Washington, DC: Inter-American Dialogue).

――――― (1997b) *The Americas in 1997: Making Cooperation Work* (Washington, DC: Inter-American Dialogue).

International Institute of Strategic Studies (1995) *Military Balance 1995–1996* (London: Oxford University Press).

International Monetary Fund (1990) *International Financial Statistics* (Washington, DC: IMF).

――――― (1995a) *Direction of Trade Statistics Yearbook* (Washington, DC: IMF).

――――― (1995b) *Government Finance Statistics Yearbook* (Washington, DC: IMF).

――――― (1995c) *International Financial Statistics* (Washington, DC: IMF).

Jacobson, Harold K. (1984) *Networks of Interdependence: International Organizations and the Global Political System*, 2nd ed. (New York: A. A. Knopf).

Jellinek, Sergio (1995) "America: Regional Meeting Adopts Roadmap Towards Free Trade Area," *Inter Press Service*, June 30.

Johnson, Jon R. (1994) *The North American Free Trade Agreement: A Comprehensive Guide* (Aurora, Ontario: Canada Law Book).

Jornal do Brasil (1997) March 17, p. 4.

Kalmanovitz K., Salomon (1997) "Las Instituciones, La ley y el desarrollo económico," *Revista del Banco de L.A. República* (Colombia) 70, no. 83: 28–47.

Katzenstein, Peter J. (ed.) (1996) *The Culture of National Security: Norms and Identity in World Politics* (New York: Columbia University Press).

Kennedy, Paul (1989) *The Rise and Fall of the Great Powers* (New York: Vintage Books).

Keohane, Robert O. (1984) *After Hegemony: Cooperation and Discord in the World Political Economy* (Princeton, NJ: Princeton University Press).

――――― (1993) "Institutional Theory and Realist Challenge After the Cold War," in David A. Baldwin (ed.), *Neorealism and Neoliberalism: The Contemporary Debate* (New York: Columbia University Press), pp. 269–300.

Keohane, Robert O., and Joseph S. Nye (1977) *Power and Interdependence: World Politics in Transition* (Boston: Little, Brown and Company).

――――― (eds.) (1971) *Transnational Relations and World Politics* (Cambridge: Harvard University Press).

Keohane, Robert O., Joseph S. Nye, and Stanley Hoffmann (eds.) (1993) *After the Cold War: International Institutions and State Strategies in Europe, 1989–1991* (Cambridge: Harvard University Press).

Kindleberger, Charles P. (1973) *The World in Depression, 1929–1939* (Berkeley: University of California Press).

King Gordon, J. (ed.) (1966) *Canada's Role as a Middle Power* (Toronto: Canadian Institute of International Affairs).

Klepak, Harold P. (1996) "Le multilatéralisme, le régionalisme et la coopération en matière de répression du trafic international de narcotiques dans les deux Amériques," in M. Fortmann, S. N. MacFarlane and S. Roussel (eds.), *Tous pour un ou chacun pour soi: Promesses et limites de la coopération régionale en matière de sécurité* (Quebec: Institut québécois des hautes études internationales), pp. 317–336.

Krasner, Stephen D. (ed.) (1983a) *International Regimes* (Ithaca, NY: Cornell University Press).

—— (1983b) "Structural Causes and Regime Consequences: Regime as Intervening Variables," in S. D. Krasner (ed.), *International Regimes* (Ithaca, NY: Cornell University Press), pp. 1–22.

—— (1993) "Global Communications and National Power: Life on the Pareto Frontier," in D. A. Baldwin (ed.), *Neorealism and Neoliberalism* (New York: Columbia University Press), pp. 234–249.

Laïdi, Zaki (1994) *Un monde privé de sens* (Paris: Fayard).

Laird, Sam (1997) *MERCOSUR: Objectives and Achievements*, TPRD-97-002 (Geneva: World Trade Organization).

Lampreia, Luiz Felipe (1997) "O Consenso Brasileiro em Torno da ALCA," *Política Externa* 5–6 (March–August): 3–16.

Lapid, Y., and F. Kratochwil (eds.) (1996) *The Return of Culture and Identity in IR Theory* (Boulder, CO: Lynne Rienner Publishers).

"Le Canada dirigera la mission de paix en Haïti" (1994) *Le Soleil* (Quebec), March 1, p. A-12.

Leclerc, André (1992) "La solidarité internationale: les syndicats s'ajoutent-ils à la liste des quémandeurs?" *Dossiers, RCA* 2, no. 1 (February): 10–11.

Lee, Thea (1993) "Happily Never NAFTA," in R. Nader, William Greider, Margaret Atwood, David Philips, and Pat Choate (eds.), *The Case Against Free Trade: GATT, NAFTA and the Globalization of Corporate Power* (San Francisco: Earth Island Press), pp. 70–77.

Lindberg, Leon N. (1963) *The Political Dynamics of European Economic Integration* (Stanford, CA: Stanford University Press).

—— (1967) "The European Community as a Political System: Notes Toward the Construction of a Model," *Journal of Common Market Studies* 5, no. 4: 344–387.

—— (1970) "Political Integration as a Multidimensional Phenomenon Requiring Multivariate Measurement," *International Organization* 24, no. 4: 649–731.

Lindberg, Leon N., and Stuart A. Scheingold (1970) *Europe's Would-Be Polity: Patterns of Change in the European Community* (Englewood Cliffs, NJ: Prentice-Hall).

Lipsey, Richard G., Daniel Schwanen, and Ronald J. Wonnacott (1994) *The NAFTA: What's In, What's Out, What's Next* (Toronto: C. D. Howe Institute).

Los Angeles Times (1995a) February 14, p. A1.

—— (1995b) November 4, p. D2.

—— (1996) March 6, p. A1.

Mace, Gordon (1981) *Intégration régionale et pluralisme idéologique au sein du groupe andin* (Quebec: Centre québécois de relations internationales).

—— (1989) "Les relations du Canada avec l'Amérique latine et les Antilles," in P. Painchaud (ed.), *From Mackenzie King to Pierre Trudeau. Forty Years of Canadian Diplomacy, 1945–1985* (Quebec: Les Presses de l'Université Laval), pp. 401–432.

Mace, Gordon, and Jean-Philippe Thérien (1996a) "Canada in the Americas: The Impact of Regionalism on a New Foreign Policy," in Gordon Mace and Jean-Philippe Thérien (eds.), *Foreign Policy and Regionalism in the Americas* (Boulder, CO: Lynne Rienner Publishers), pp. 53–67.

—— (eds.) (1996b) *Foreign Policy and Regionalism in the Americas* (Boulder, CO: Lynne Rienner Publishers).

Mace, Gordon, Louis Bélanger, and Jean-Philippe Thérien (1993) "Regionalism in the Americas and the Hierarchy of Power," *Journal of Interamerican Studies and World Affairs* 35, no. 2 (Summer): 115–157.

Machado, João Bosco, and Pedro Motta Veiga (1997) "A Evolução da ALCA Pede Uma Nova Estratégia," *Carta Internacional* 50 (April): 4.

Mackay, R. A. (1969) "The Canadian Doctrine of the Middle Power," in H. L. Dyck and H. P. Krosby (eds.), *Empire and Nations: Essays in Honour of Frederic H. Soward* (Toronto: University of Toronto Press), pp. 133–143.

Mackenzie, David (1994) *Canada in the Organization of American States: The First Five Years* (Toronto: Canadian Institute of International Affairs).

Mandelbaum, Michael (1996) "Foreign Policy as Social Work," *Foreign Affairs* 75, no. 1 (January–February): 16–32.

Martz, John D. (1992) "Democracy and Human Rights," in G. P. Atkins (ed.), *The United States and Latin America: Redefining U.S. Purposes in the Post–Cold War Era* (Austin, TX: Lyndon B. Johnson School of Public Affairs), pp. 43–55.

Mastanduno, Michael, and G. John Ikenberry (eds.) (1988) *The State and American Economic Policy* (Ithaca, NY: Cornell University Press).

"Matrix Comparing Proposals for Launching FTAA Talks" (1997) *AmericasTrade*, May 12, pp. 8–16.

McGaughey, William, Jr. (1992) *A U.S.-Mexico-Canada Free-Trade Agreement: Do We Just Say No?* (Minneapolis: Thistlerose).

McKenna, Peter (1995) *Canada and the OAS: From Dilettante to Full Partner* (Ottawa: Carleton University Press).

Menem, Carlos (1990) *Estados Unidos, Argentina y Carlos Menem* (Belgrano, Argentina: Editorial Ceyne).

"Mexico Rejects Intervention in Peruvian Crisis" (1992) *Foreign Broadcast Information Service*, FBIS-LAT-92–072, April 14, p. 14.

Millet, Richard L. (1994) "Beyond Sovereignty: International Efforts to Support Latin-American Democracy," *Journal of Interamerican Studies and World Affairs* 36, no. 3 (Fall): 1–23.

Mitchell, C. (1967) "The Role of Technocrats in Latin American Integration," *InterAmerican Economic Affairs* 21, no. 1: 3–39.

Mittelman, James H. (ed.) (1996a) *Globalization: Critical Reflections* (Boulder, CO: Lynne Rienner Publishers).

Mittelman, James H. (1996b) "Rethinking the 'New Regionalism' in the Context of Globalization," *Global Governance* 2, no. 2 (May–August): 189–213.

Molineu, Harold (1986) *U.S. Policy Toward Latin America: From Regionalism to Globalism* (Boulder, CO: Westview Press).

Mujer a Mujer (1994) "Popular Alternatives & Continental Alliances," *Correspondencia* 16 (May): 20, 22.

Muñoz, Heraldo (1993a) "A New OAS for the New Times," in Viron P. Vaky and Heraldo Muñoz (eds.), *The Future of the Organization of American States* (New York: The Twentieth Century Fund Press), pp. 67–95.

——— (1993b) "The OAS and Democratic Governance," *Journal of Democracy* 4, no. 3 (July): 29–38.

Muñoz, Heraldo, and Robin Rosenberg (eds.) (1993) *Difficult Liaison: Trade and the Environment in the Americas* (Boulder, CO: Lynne Rienner Publishers).

Mutimer, David (1989) "1992 and the Political Integration of Europe: Neofunctionalism Reconsidered," *Revue d'intégration européenne* 13, no. 1 (Fall): 75–101.

Mytelka, Lynn K. (1979) *Regional Development in a Global Economy. The Multinational Corporation, Technology and Andean Integration* (New Haven, CT: Yale University Press).

Nash, Nathaniel (1992) "Peru Chief Orders New Mass Arrests," *New York Times*, April 8, p. A12.

Neack, Laura (1991) "Beyond the Rhetoric of Peacekeeping and Peacemaking: Middle States and International Politics," Ph.D. diss., University of Kentucky.

―――― (1992) "Empirical Observations on 'Middle State' Behavior at the Start of a New International System," *Pacific Focus* 7, no. 1: 5–21.

―――― (1995) "Linking State Type with Foreign Policy Behavior," in Laura Neack, Jeanne A. K. Hey, and Patrick J. Haney, *Foreign Policy Analysis: Continuity and Change in Its Second Generation* (Englewood Cliffs, NJ: Prentice-Hall), pp. 215–228.

Nelson, Paul J. (1996) "Transnational NGO Networks in Global Governance: Promoting 'Participation' at the World Bank," paper read at the International Studies Association annual meeting, San Diego, April 16–20.

New York Times (1993a) November 18: A1, A20.

―――― (1993b) November 21, p. A22.

―――― (1994a) November 10, pp. B18–B19.

―――― (1994b) November 30, p. A1.

―――― (1994c) December 2, p. A1.

―――― (1994d) December 8, p. A14.

―――― (1995a) January 13, p. A1.

―――― (1995b) February 1, p. A1.

―――― (1995c) October 10, p. A10.

―――― (1996a) February 29, p. A1.

―――― (1996b) March 14, p. A7.

―――― (1996c) June 6, p. A6.

―――― (1997) May 8, p. A6.

Nishijima, Shoji, and Peter H. Smith (eds.) (1996) *Cooperation or Rivalry: Regional Integration in the Americas and the Pacific Rim* (Boulder, CO: Westview Press).

Nivola, Pietro S. (1990) "Trade Policy: Refereeing the Playing Field," in Thomas E. Mann (ed.), *A Question of Balance: The President, the Congress, and Foreign Policy* (Washington, DC: Brookings Institution), pp. 201–253.

Nofal, María Beatriz (1995) "The Economic Integration of Argentina and Brazil, MERCOSUR, and the Regionalization of the Southern Cone," in E. Echeverri-Carroll (ed.), *NAFTA and Trade Liberalization in the Americas* (Austin, TX: Bureau of Business Research), pp. 202–231.

North, Douglass C. (1995) *Instituciones, cambios institucionales y comportamiento económico*, México, Fondo de Cultura Económica.

"Nossa Economia Precisa de Mais Tempo" (1997) *O Globo*, May 18, p. 8.

Nunes Amorim, Celso L. (1991) "O Pano de Fundo Regional e Global," in J. P. dos Reis Velloso (ed.), *O Brasil e o Plano Bush: Oportunidades e Riscos Numa Futura Integração das Américas* (São Paulo: Nobel).

Nye, Joseph S. (ed.) (1968a) *International Regionalism* (Boston: Little, Brown and Company).

Nye, Joseph S. (1968b) "Introduction," in Joseph S. Nye (ed.), *International Regionalism* (Boston: Little Brown and Company), pp. v–xvi.

―――― (1970) "Comparing Common Markets: A Revised Neo-Functional Model," *International Organization* 14, no. 4: 796–835.

―――― (1990) *Bound to Lead: The Changing Nature of American Power* (New York: Basic Books).

"OAS Ministers Oppose Armed Intervention in Haiti," (1994) *Foreign Broadcast Information Service*, FBIS-LAT-94-108, June 8.

Observatoire de l'information (1989) *L'information dans le monde: 206 pays au microscope* (Paris: Seuil).

Ogelsby, J. C. M. (1976) *Gringos from the Far North: Essays in the History of Canadian–Latin American Relations, 1866–1968* (Toronto: Macmillan).

Oman, Charles (1994) *Globalization and Regionalization: The Challenge for Developing Countries* (Paris: Organisation for Economic Co-operation and Development).

"Ordem é Mobilizar o Empresariado" (1997) *Gazeta Mercantil Latino-Americana*, May 19–25, p. 24.

Organisation de coopération et de développement économiques (1993) *Intégration régionale et pays en développement* (Paris: OCDE).

Organization of American States (1989) *Charter of the Organization of American States*, Treaty Series No. 1–D (Washington, DC: Organization of American States).

———— (1991) "Santiago Commitment to Democracy and the Renewal of the Inter-American System," OAS/Ser. P, AG/doc 2734/91, twenty-first session, Santiago, June 4.

———— (1993) "Conseil permanent, Rapport du Président du Groupe de travail sur les obstacles juridiques à l'intégration," OAS/Ser. G., CP/doc 2373/93 rev. 1, Washington, DC, May 23.

———— (1995) *A New Vision of the OAS: Working Paper of the General Secretariat for the Permanent Council* (Washington, DC: Organization of American States).

———— (1996) "The Organization of American States and its Role in Democracy," speech delivered by Elizabeth Spehar, executive coordinator of the Unit for the Promotion of Democracy, October 28.

————. Trade Unit (1997a) *Trade and Integration Arrangements in the Americas. An Analytical Compendium* (Washington, DC: Organization of American States).

———— (1997b) *Work Plan of the Unit for the Promotion of Democracy* (Washington, DC: Organization of American States).

———— (1997c) *Protocol of Amendments to the Charter of the Organization of American States, "Protocol of Washington,"* internal document of the Department of Development and Codification of International Law, Secretariat for Legal Affairs (Washington, DC: Organization of American States).

———— (1997d) *Representative Democracy in the Americas: Proposed Framework for Action for the Inter-American System* (Washington, DC: Organization of American States).

———— (1997e) Annual Report of the Inter-American Commission on Human Rights 1996 (Washington, DC: Organization of American States).

————. Unit for the Promotion of Democracy (1998) Electoral Observation Missions. http://www.oas.org/EN/PROG/UPD/specprog.htm.

"Os Empresários Ganham Força" (1997) *Gazeta Mercantil Latino-Americana*, May 19–25, p. 15.

Osorio, Victor (1996) "RMLAC: Five Years of Citizen Action," *Nuestra America* (Summer), February 11. www.igc.apc.org/dgap.

Padilla, David J. (1993) "The Inter-American Commission on Human Rights of the Organization of American States: A Case Study," *American University Journal of International Law and Policy* 9, no. 1 (Autumn): 95–115.

Painchaud, Paul (1966) "Middlepowermanship as an Ideology," in J. King Gordon (ed.), *Canada's Role as a Middle Power* (Toronto: Canadian Institute of International Affairs), pp. 13–36.

"Papa Noel Viene de China" (1996) *Clarin*, December 16, p. 1.

Participation and NGO Group (1996) *The World Bank's Partnership with Non-governmental Organizations* (Washington, DC: Poverty and Social Policy Department/World Bank).

Pastor, Robert A. (1992) *Whirlpool: U.S. Foreign Policy Toward Latin America and the Caribbean* (Princeton, NJ: Princeton University Press).

Payne, Anthony J. (1996) "The United States and Its Enterprise for the Americas," in A. Gamble and A. J. Payne (eds.), *Regionalism and World Order* (New York: St. Martin's Press), pp. 93–129.

Payne, Anthony J., and Andrew Gamble (1996) "Introduction: The Political Economy of Regionalism and World Order," in A. Gamble and A. J. Payne (eds.), *Regionalism and World Order* (New York: St. Martin's Press), pp. 1–20.

Pentland, Charles (1973) *International Theory and European Integration* (London: Faber and Faber).

"Perspectivas de Integração Hemisférica" (1997) *Política Externa* 5–6 (March–August): 25–74.

Peschel, Karen (1990) "Spacial Structures in World Trade," in Arie Shachar and Sture Oberg (eds.), *The World Economy and the Spatial Organization of Power* (Brookfield, VT: Aldershot), pp. 71–89.

Petrash, Vilma E. (1997) "From Subregionalism to Inter-American Regionalism: NAFTA, MERCOSUR and the 'Spirit of Miami,'" paper presented at virtual conference, Power and Integration, March 17–April 21.

Piening, Christopher (1997) *Global Europe: The European Union in World Affairs* (Boulder, CO: Lynne Rienner Publishers).

Polachek, Soloman W. (1980) "Conflict and Trade," *Journal of Conflict Resolution* 24, no. 1: 55–78.

Pollins, Brian M. (1989a) "Conflict, Cooperation, and Commerce: The Effect of International Political Interactions on Bilateral Trade Flows," *American Journal of Political Science* 33, no. 3 (August): 737–761.

——— (1989b) "Does Trade Still Follow the Flag?" *American Political Science Review* 33, no. 2 (June): 465–480.

Pratt, Cranford (1990) *Middle Power Internationalism: The North-South Dimension* (Kingston, Ontario: McGill-Queen's University Press).

"Prazos Devem Ser Dilatados" (1997) *Gazeta Mercantil Latino-Americana*, May 5–11, p. 19.

Public Papers of the Presidents of the United States (1990) *Ronald Reagan, 1988, Book 1: January 1 to July 1, 1988* (Washington, DC: U.S. Government Printing Office).

——— (1991) *Ronald Reagan, 1988–1989, Book 2: July 2, 1988 to January 19, 1989* (Washington, DC: U.S. Government Printing Office).

——— (1994) *William J. Clinton, 1993, Book 2: August 1 to December 31, 1993* (Washington, DC: U.S. Government Printing Office).

——— (1995a) *William J. Clinton, 1994, Book 1: January 1 to July 31, 1994* (Washington, DC: U.S. Government Printing Office).

——— (1995b) *William J. Clinton, 1994, Book 2: August 1 to December 31, 1994* (Washington, DC: U.S. Government Printing Office).

Puchala, Donald (1970) "International Transactions and Regional Integration," *International Organization* 24, no. 4: 732–763.

——— (1972) "Of Blind Man, Elephants and International Integration," *Journal of Common Market Studies* 10, no. 3: 267–284.

Purcell, Susan Kaufman (1997) "The New U.S.-Brazil Relationship," in S. K. Purcell and R. Roett (eds.), *Brazil Under Cardoso* (Boulder, CO: Lynne Rienner Publishers), pp. 89–102.

Purcell, Susan Kaufman, and Riordan Roett (eds.) (1997) *Brazil Under Cardoso* (Boulder, CO: Lynne Rienner Publishers).

Rangel, Carlos (1977) *The Latin Americans: Their Love-Hate Relationship with the United States* (New York: Harcourt Brace Jovanovich).

Red Chile de Acción por una Iniciativa de los Pueblos (1996) "Encuentro Sindical: Los trabajadores frente al NAFTA," *Nuestra America* (Summer), February 11. www.igc.apc.org/dgap.

Red Mexicana de Acción Frente al Libre Comercio (1992) *Memoria de Zacatecas: La opinión pública y las Negociaciones del Tratado de Libre Comercio: Alternativas Ciudadanas* (Mexico City: RMAFLC).

———— (1994) *Memoria de Encuentro Internacional "Integración, Democracia y Desarrollo"* (Mexico City: RMAFLC).

Reporters sans frontières (1994) *Rapport 1994: la liberté de presse dans le monde* (Montpellier, France: Reporters sans frontières).

Réseau canadien d'action (1991a) *Dossier (Dossier spécial libre-échange Canada-É-U, Mexique)* 1, no. 1 (March–April).

———— (1991b) *Document de travail pour le* [sic] *rencontre "Zacatecas,"* October.

Reuters News Service (1994) Central and South America, April 26.

Rhodes, Carolyn (ed.) (1998) *The European Union in the World Community* (Boulder, CO: Lynne Rienner Publishers).

Risse-Kapen, Thomas (ed.) (1995) *Bringing Transnational Relations Back In* (New York: Cambridge University Press).

Rittberger, Volker (ed.) (1993) *Regime Theory and International Relations* (Oxford: Oxford University Press).

Robertson, David (1993) *A Dictionary of Modern Politics* (London: Europa Publications Limited).

Robertson, Roland (1990) "Mapping the Global Condition: Globalization as a Central Concept," in M. Featherstone (ed.), *Global Culture, Nationalism, Globalization and Modernity* (London: Sage), pp. 15–30.

Robinson, C. William (1995) *Le Mercosud: ce qu'il est, ce qu'il fait*, document prepared for the Canadian Embassy in Brazil and the Canadian consulate general in São Paulo, January 23.

Robinson, Randy (1991) "Des groupes réclament des négociations publiques," *Dossier, RAC* 1, no. 4 (September–October): 6.

Robson, Peter (1993) "The New Regionalism and the Developing Countries," *Journal of Common Market Studies* 31, no. 3: 329–348.

Rochlin, James (1993) *Discovering the Americas: The Evolution of Canadian Foreign Policy Towards Latin America* (Vancouver: University of British Columbia Press).

Rogers, K. S. (1995) "Rivers of Discontent—Rivers of Peace: Environmental Cooperation and Integration Theory," *International Studies Notes* 20, no. 2 (Spring): 10–21.

Rosati, Jerel A. (1984) "Congressional Influence in American Foreign Policy: Addressing the Controversy," *Journal of Political and Military Sociology* 12, no. 2 (Fall): 311–333.

———— (1997) "United States Leadership into the Next Millennium: A Question of Politics," *International Journal* 52, no. 2 (Spring): 297–315.

Rosenau, James (1990) *Turbulence in World Politics: A Theory of Change and Continuity* (Princeton, NJ: Princeton University Press).

Rosenberg, R., and S. Stein (eds.) (1995) *Advancing the Miami Process: Civil Society and the Summit of the Americas* (Boulder, CO: Lynne Rienner Publishers).

Rourke, John T., Ralph G. Carter, and Mark A. Boyer (1996) *Making American Foreign Policy* (Dubuque, IA: Brown & Benchmark Publishers).

Roy, Martin (1995) *Les paradoxes de l'intégration économique dans le cône sud-américain: PICE, TICD et MERCOSUR sous l'angle des stratégies internationales de l'Argentine*, Les Cahiers de l'Institut no. 2 (Quebec: Institut québécois des hautes études internationales).

Ruggiero, Renato (1997) "Address to the XII Meeting of the Common Market Council," paper read at the Twelfth Meeting of the Common Market Council, Asunción, June 19. See *World Trade Organization* Press/74, June 19, 1997.

Rupert, Mark (1995) *Producing Hegemony: The Politics of Mass Production and American Global Power* (Cambridge: Cambridge University Press).

Sabourin, Louis (1976) "Canada and Francophone Africa," in Peyton V. Lyon and Tareq Y. Ismael (eds.), *Canada and the Third World* (Toronto: Macmillan), pp. 133–161.

Saccone, María Alejandra (1994) "Aspectos político-diplomaticos de una nueva prioridad en la política exterior argentina: el MERCOSUR," *La política exterior del gobierno Menem: Seguimientos, reflexiones al promedio de su mandato* (Rosario, Argentina: Ediciones CERIR), p. 115.

San José Ministerial Joint Declaration (1998) San José, Costa Rica, Summit of the Americas, Fourth Trade Ministerial, March 19. Quotes are from website www.ftaa-alca.org.

Sánchez Bajo, Claudia B. (1992) *Argentine-Brazilian Integration in a Historical Perspective* (Boston: Institute of Social Studies).

Schlesinger, Arthur M., Jr. (1996) "America and the World: Isolationism Resurgent?" *Ethics and International Affairs* 10: 149–163.

Schott, Jeffrey J. (1991) "Trading Blocs and the World Trading System," *The World Economy* 14, no. 1 (March): 1–17.

"Se complica la situación en Brasil" (1997) *La Nación on Line*, Tuesday, April 1. www.lanacion.com.ar.

Silva, Samuel (1995) "A Network of Networks: Bolívar Fosters Alliances," *The IDB Extra*.

Simai, Mihaly (1994) *The Future of Global Governance: Managing Risk and Change in the International System* (Washington, DC: United States Institute of Peace).

Simard, Monique (1991) "Libre-échange à trois : les syndicats inquiets," *Journal de Québec*, February 11, p. 21.

"Sindicalistas Protestam Hoje Contra Veto à Participação de Centrais no Debate da ALCA" (1997) *O Globo*, May 14.

"Sindicatos Fazem Manifestações em Belo Horizonte" (1997) *Gazeta Mercantil*, May 17–18, p. A-4.

Smith, Gaddis (1994) *The Last Years of the Monroe Doctrine 1945–1993* (New York: Hill and Wang).

Smith, Peter H. (ed.) (1993a) *The Challenge of Integration: Europe and the Americas* (New Brunswick, NJ: Transaction Publishers).

Smith, Peter H. (1993b) "Introduction: The Politics of Integration: Concepts and Themes," in P. H. Smith (ed.), *The Challenge of Integration: Europe and the Americas* (New Brunswick, NJ: Transaction Publishers), pp. 1–14.

—— (1996a) *Talons of the Eagle: Dynamics of U.S.–Latin American Relations* (New York: Oxford University Press).

—— (1996b) "The United States, Regional Integration and the Reshaping of the International Order," in S. Nishijima and P. H. Smith (eds.), *Cooperation or Rivalry? Regional Integration in the Americas and the Pacific Rim* (Boulder, CO: Westview Press), pp. 27–51.

Smith, Russel E., and Mark A. Healy (1994) "Labor and Mercosur: A Briefing Book," paper read at conference, Labor, Free Trade and Economic Integration in the Americas: National Labor Union Responses to a Transnational World, Durham, North Carolina, Duke–University of North Carolina Program in Latin American Studies, August 25–27.

Soares de Lima, Maria Regina (1996) "Brazil's Response to the 'New Regionalism,' in G. Mace and J.-P. Thérien (eds.), *Foreign Policy and Regionalism in the Americas* (Boulder, CO: Lynne Rienner Publishers), pp. 137–158.

Soldatos, Panayotis (ed.) (1989) *Le système institutionnel et politique des communautés européennes dans un monde en mutation: théorie et pratique* (Brussels: Bruylant).

Stanford, Jim (1991) *Going South: Cheap Labour as an Unfair Subsidy in North American Free Trade* (Ottawa: Canadian Center for Policy Alternatives).

Stanford, Jim, Christine Elwell, and Scott Sinclair (1993) *Social Dumping Under North American Free Trade* (Ottawa: Canadian Center for Policy Alternatives).

Stark, Jeffrey (1996) "Globalization and Democratic Governance in the Americas," paper read at International Studies Association annual meeting, San Diego, April 16–20.

Stein, Stanley, and Barbara Stein (1970) *The Colonial Heritage of Latin America: Essays on Economic Dependence in Perspective* (New York: Oxford University Press).

Stern, Paula, and Raymond Paretzky (1996) "Engineering Regional Trade Pacts to Keep Trade and U.S. Prosperity on a Fast Track," *Washington Quarterly* 19, no. 1 (Winter): 211–222.

Stewart, Christine (1994) "An Address by the Honourable Christine Stewart, Secretary of State (Latin America and Africa), to the 24th General Assembly of the Organization of American States, Belem, Brazil, 7 June," in Government of Canada, *Statement 94/28.*

Stockholm International Peace Research Institute (various years) *SIPRI Yearbook* (New York: Humanities Press).

Stoetzer, O. Carlos (1993) *The Organization of American States*, 2nd ed. (New York: Praeger Publishers).

Stoll, Richard, and Michael D. Ward (eds.) (1988) *Power in World Politics* (Boulder, CO: Lynne Rienner Publishers).

Summit of the Americas (1994) *Declaration of Principles*, Miami, Florida, December 9–11.

Summit of the Americas Trade Ministerial (1995) *The Denver Joint Ministerial Declaration*, Denver, Colorado, June 30. www.ftaa-alca.org/englishversion/denver_e.htm.

Support Committee for Maquiladora Workers (1995) *Cross-Border Connection* (Fall).

Taylor, Philip (1984) *Nonstate Actors in International Politics: From Transregional to Substate Organizations* (Boulder, CO: Westview Press).

Tesón, Fernando R. (1996) "Changing Perceptions of Domestic Jurisdiction and Intervention," in Tom Farer (ed.), *Beyond Sovereignty: Collectively Defending Democracy in the Americas* (Baltimore, MD: Johns Hopkins University Press), pp. 29–51.

Thérien, Jean-Philippe, Michel Fortmann, and Guy Gosselin (1996) "The Organization of American States: Restructuring Inter-American Multilateralism," *Global Governance* 2, no. 2: 215–240.

Thompson, John Herd, and Stephen J. Randall (1994) *Canada and the United States: Ambivalent Allies* (Montreal: McGill-Queen's University Press).

Thorup, Cathryn L. (1991) "The Politics of Free Trade and the Dynamics of Cross-Borders Coalitions in U.S.-Mexican Relations," *Columbia Journal of World Business* 22 (June): 12–27.

"Trials, Tribulations and Triumphs: The History of the Council of Canadians," (1994) *Canadian Perspectives* (Winter): 14–15.

Trubowitz, Peter (1992) "Sectionalism and American Foreign Policy: The Political Geography of Consensus and Conflict," *International Studies Quarterly* 36, no. 2 (June): 173–190.

Tulchin, Joseph S. (1993) "The Enterprise for the Americas Initiative: Empty Gesture, Shrewd Strategic Gambit, or Remarkable Shift in Hemispheric Relations?" in R. E. Green (ed.), *The Enterprise for the Americas Initiative: Issues and Prospects for a Free Trade Agreement in the Hemisphere* (Westport, CT: Praeger), pp. 143–158.

Urquidi, Victor L. (1993) "Free Trade Experience in Latin America and the Caribbean," *Annals of the AAPSS* 526 (March): 59–60.

"U.S. Drops Demands for Two-Stage FTAA Talks, Isolating MERCOSUR" (1997) *AmericasTrade* 4, no. 8 (April): 131.94.20.45/inside.

U.S. House (1988a) *United States–Canada Free Trade Agreement: Hearings Before the Subcommittee on Trade of the Committee on Ways and Means,* 100th Congress, 2nd session, February 9, February 29, March 11, March 25.

——— (1988b) *United States–Canada Free Trade Agreement: Impact on the Domestic Plywood Industry: Hearing Before the Subcommittee on Regulation and Business Opportunities of the Committee on Small Business,* 100th Congress, 2nd session, March 8.

U.S. Senate (1988) *United States–Canada Free Trade Agreement—Hearing Before the Committee on Finance,* 100th Congress, 2nd session, March 17 (Part 1 of 3).

——— (1993) *Environmental Aspects of the North American Free Trade Agreement: Hearing Before the Committee on Environment and Public Works,* 103rd Congress, 1st session, March 16.

Vacs, Aldo C. (1989) "A Delicate Balance: Confrontation and Cooperation Between Argentina and the United States in the 1980s," *Journal of Interamerican Studies* 31, no. 4 (Winter): 23–60.

Vaky, Viron P. (1993) "The Organization of American States and Multilateralism in the Americas" in V. P. Vaky and H. Muñoz (eds.), *The Future of the Organization of American States* (New York: The Twentieth Century Fund Press), pp. 3–65.

Vaky, Viron P., and Heraldo Muñoz (eds.) (1993) *The Future of the Organization of American States* (New York: The Twentieth Century Fund Press).

Valenzuela, Arturo (1997) "Paraguay: The Coup that Didn't Happen," *Journal of Democracy* 8, no. 1 (January): 43–55.

van der Pijl, Kees (1979) "Class Formation at the International Level: Reflections on the Political Economy of Atlantic Unity," *Capital and Class* 9 (Autumn): 1–21.

Varas, Augusto (1992) "From Coercion to Partnership: A New Paradigm for Security Cooperation in the Western Hemisphere?" in J. Hartlyn, L. Schoultz, and A. Varas (eds.), *The United States and Latin America in the 1990s: Beyond the Cold War* (Chapel Hill: University of North Carolina Press), pp. 46–63.

Villagran de León, Francisco (1992) *The OAS and Democratic Development* (Washington, DC: United States Institute of Peace).

Villegas, Francisco Gil (1988) "Opciones de política exterior: México entre el Atlántico y el Pacifico," *Foro Internacional* 29, no. 2 (October–December): 263–288.

Vincent, Isabel (1994) "Canada Calls for End to Cuban Isolation," *Globe and Mail*, June 8, p. A12.

Vivanco, José Miguel (1994) "International Human Rights Litigation in Latin America: The OAS Human Rights System," in C. Kaysen (ed.), *Collective Responses to Regional Problems: The Case of Latin America and the Caribbean* (Cambridge: American Academy of Arts and Science), pp. 73–91.

Volk, Steven (1997) "'Democracy' Versus 'Democracy,'" *Report on the Americas* 30, no. 4 (January–February): 6–12.

Wall Street Journal (1995) December 29, p. A11.

Wallace, Michael D. (1973) *War and Rank Among Nations* (Lexington, MA: Lexington Books).

Wallerstein, Immanuel (1974) *The Modern World-System, vol. 1* (New York: Academic Press).

"Washington apoya los bloques regionales, en especial al MERCOSUR" (1997) *Sucesos*, October 17. www.mercosur.com/.

Washington Post (1996) March 7, p. A28.

Waterman, Peter (1988) "The New Internationalism: A More Real Thing Than a Big, Big Coke?" *Review: Fernand Braudel Center* 10, no. 3: 289–328.

Watson, Alexander F. (1994a) "Key Issues in Inter-American Relations," *U.S. Department of State Dispatch* 5, no. 3 (January 17): 21–26.

——— (1994b) "U.S.–Latin America Relations in the 1990s: Toward a Mature Partnership," *U.S. Department of State Dispatch* 5, no. 11 (March 14): 153–157.

——— (1995) "Toward a New Relationship of Western Hemisphere Democracies," remarks by Alexander F. Watson, Assistant Secretary of State for Inter-American Affairs, to the Advisory Committee of the David Rockefeller Center for Latin American Studies, Cambridge, Massachusetts, April 28, 1995, U.S. Department of State dispatch, pp. 1–5.

Weintraub, Sidney (ed.) (1994a) *Integrating the Americas: Shaping Future Trade Policy* (Miami: Transaction Publishers).

Weintraub, Sidney (1994b) *NAFTA: What Comes Next?* (Westport, CT/Washington, DC: Prager/Center for Strategic and International Studies.

——— (1996) "The Depth of Economic Integration between Mexico and the United States," in Brad Roberts (ed.), *New Forces in the World Economy* (Cambridge: MIT Press), pp. 227–238.

——— (1997) "U.S.–Latin American Economic Relations," *Journal of Interamerican Studies and World Affairs* 39, no. 1: 59–69.

Wendt, Alexander (1987) "The Agent-Structure Problem in International Relations Theory," *International Organization* 41: 335–370.

——— (1994) "Collective Identity Formation and the International State," *American Political Science Review* 88, no. 2 (June): 384–396.

Weston, Ann (1995) "The Development Impact of the NAFTA: A Canadian Perspective," in R. S. Belous and J. Lemco (eds.), *NAFTA as a Model of Development* (Albany: State University of New York Press), pp. 145–158.

Wiarda, Howard J. (1990) *The Democratic Revolution in Latin America: History, Politics and U.S. Policy* (New York: Holmes and Meier), pp. 47–48.

——— (1994) "The U.S. Domestic Politics of the U.S.-Mexico Free Trade Agreement," in M. Delal Baer and Sidney Weintraub (eds.), *The NAFTA Debate:*

Grappling with Unconventional Trade Issues (Boulder, CO: Lynne Rienner Publishers), pp. 117–143.

—— (1995a) "After Miami: The Summit, the Peso Crisis, and the Future of U.S.–Latin American Relations," *Journal of Interamerican Studies and World Affairs* 37, no. 1: 43–68.

—— (1995b) "The Future of Political Reform in the Southern Cone: Can Democracy Be Sustained?" *Washington Quarterly* 18, no. 3 (Summer): 91–102.

—— (1997) "Consensus Found, Consensus Lost: Disjunctures in U.S. Policy Toward Latin America at the Turn of the Century," *Journal of Interamerican Studies and World Affairs* 39, no. 1 (Spring): 13–51.

Winham, Gilbert R., and Heather A. Grant (1995) "NAFTA: An Overview," in Donald Barry, Mark O. Dickerson, and James D. Gainsford (eds.), *Toward a North American Community? Canada, the United States, and Mexico* (Boulder, CO: Westview Press), pp. 15–31.

Women to Women Global Strategies (1993) *Changing Economies: Free Trade and the Global Agenda* (Toronto: Women to Women Global Strategies).

Wood, Bernard (1990) *Middle Powers and the General Interest* (Ottawa: North-South Institute).

World Bank (1997) Annual Bank Conference on Development in Latin America and the Caribbean. Trade: Towards Open Regionalism, Montevideo, Uruguay, June 29–July 1.

Yanz, Linda (1992) "Learning Solidarity: Women Make the Links," and "Setting a Course for Action," *ACN/Dossier* 36 (March–April): 7–9.

—— (1994) "Women's Maquila Network—Mexico to Central America," *Correspondencia* 16 (May): 2–5.

Yeats, Alexander (1997) *Does MERCOSUR's Trade Performance Raise Concerns About the Effects of Regional Trade Arrangements?* Working Paper 1729 (Washington, DC: The World Bank, International Economic Development).

Zakaria, Fareed (1998) "Our Hollow Hegemony: Why Foreign Policy Can't Be Left to the Market," *New York Times Magazine*, November 1, pp. 44–47, 74, 80.

"Zedillo Assesses Results of Summit" (1994) *Foreign Broadcast Information Service*, FBIS-LAT-94-231, December 1, p. 17.

Zoellik, Robert B. (1992) "The North American FTA: The New World Order Takes Shape in the Western Hemisphere," *U.S. Department of State Dispatch* 3, no. 15 (April 13): 290–295.

The Contributors

Louis Bélanger has been assistant professor in the Department of Political Science at Laval University since 1996. Formerly, he was research associate at Laval's Graduate Institute of International Studies. He is coauthor (with Louis Balthazar and Gordon Mace) of *Trente ans de politique extérieure du Québec, 1960–1990* and has published articles in journals such as *Études internationales, American Review of Canadian Studies, Politique et sociétés,* and *Journal of Interamerican Studies and World Affairs.*

Ivan Bernier is professor and former dean of the law faculty at Laval University. He was a research director for the Royal Commission on the Economic Union and Development Prospects for Canada and a former director-general of the Quebec Center for International Relations. Recent publications include *Souveraineté et protectionnisme en matière culturelle* (with David Atkinson and Florian Sauvageau), *Développement culturel et mondialisation de l'économie: un enjeu démocratique* (with Marc Raboy, David Atkinson, and Florian Sauvageau), and articles in journals such as *Études internationales, Les Cahiers de droit,* and *Annuaire canadien de droit international.*

André C. Drainville is associate professor in the Department of Political Science at Laval University. A specialist in international political economy, he has developed an expertise on international financial relations and social movements' strategies with regard to globalization. His articles have appeared in *Social Justice, Comparative Urban and Community Review, Studies in Political Economy, Alternatives,* and *Review of International Economy.*

281

Klaus Peter Fischer is associate professor in the Department of Finance and Insurance and codirector of the Centre de recherche en économie et finance appliquée (CREFA), both at Laval University. He has published in a number of journals, including the *Journal of International Finance, Problemas del Desarrollo: Revista Latinoamericana de Economía, Global Finance Journal*, and *Quarterly Review of Economics* and *Finance*. He has also compiled books and special journal issues on financial management in developing countries.

Guy Gosselin is professor of political science at Laval University. A specialist of international organizations, particularly the UN and the OAS, he has published articles in journals such as *Global Governance, Études internationales*, and *Revue québécoise de science politique*.

Bernard Lemelin is assistant professor in the Department of History at Laval University. A specialist of contemporary history of U.S. politics and foreign policy, his research focuses mostly on the Truman period and the internal dynamics of foreign policy making in the United States. His articles have been published in *SHAFR Newsletter, Bulletin d'histoire politique*, and *Canadian Review of American Studies*, among others.

Gordon Mace is professor in the Department of Political Science and at the Graduate Institute of International Studies at Laval University. The former editor of the newsletter of the Canadian Political Science Association, he is also director of the Research Group on International Relations at Laval. Recent publications include *Foreign Policy and Regionalism in the Americas* (edited with Jean-Philippe Thérien), *Trente ans de politique extérieure du* Québec, *1960–1990* (with Louis Balthazar, Louis Bélanger, and contributors), and pieces in journals such as *International Journal, Canadian Public Policy, Études internationales, Canadian Journal of Latin American and Caribbean Studies, International Journal of Canadian Studies*, and *Journal of Interamerican Studies and World Affairs*.

Martin Roy is a policy analyst at the Canadian Foundation for the Americas (FOCAL) and a former research associate at the Graduate Institute of International Studies at Laval University. Recent publications include *Les paradoxes de l'intégration économique dans le cône sud-américain: PICE, TICD et MERCOSUR sous l'angle des stratégies internationales de l'Argentine* and *Les conséquences de l'ALÉNA sur les relations du Canada avec le Mexique* (with Ivan Bernier).

Maria Regina Soares de Lima is professor in the Political Science Graduate Program of the Instituto Universitário de Pesquisas do Rio de Janeiro and also teaches at the Institute of International Relations of the Catholic University of Rio de Janeiro. Recent articles include "Between Neo-Alignment and Neo-Autonomy: Is There a Third Way in U.S.-Brazilian Relations?" (with Monica Hirst), "Brazil's Response to the 'New Regionalism,'" and "Teses Equivocadas sobre a Ordem Mundial Pos-Guerra Fria."

Jean-Philippe Thérien is associate professor in the Department of Political Science at Université de Montréal, where he is also director of the undergraduate studies program. He has published articles in journals such as *Global Governance, International Journal, International Organization, Canadian Journal of Political Science, International Social Science Journal,* and *Journal of Interamerican Studies and World Affairs.* He is co-editor of *Foreign Policy and Regionalism in the Americas* (with Gordon Mace).

Index

Acer, Inc., 200
Action Canada Network (ACN), 222, 225–226, 228, 236n3
Act of Chapultepec, 25
Act of Havana (1940), 24
Africa, 3, 103, 135, 171
African Americans, 119
After Hegemony (Keohane), 99
Agrarian reform, 222
Agricultural subsidies, 80, 114–115
ALADI. *See* Latin American Integration Association
Alfonsin, Raul, 161
Allende, Salvador, 27
Alliance for Progress, 5, 27, 28, 101, 219
Alliance for Responsible Trade, 223, 226
Amalgamated Clothing and Textile Workers Union, 233
American Business Conference, 115
American Business Forum, 198
American Coalition for Trade Expansion with Canada, 115
American Federation of Labor and Congress of Industrial Organizations (AFL-CIO), 122, 225, 234
American Institute for Free Labor Development, 225
American Treaty on Pacific Settlement, 26

Andean Community (CA), 7; creation of, 4; dissolution of, 52; Mercosur influence on, 195, 196
Andean Group. *See* Andean Community
Andean Initiative, 105
Andean Pact, 195; Chilean withdrawal from, 5, 207, 218n12; exporter/merchant view of, 202; failure of, 210, 216, 217n5; as model of integration, 206, 207, 208tab, 215tab; new industrialist view of, 203–204; restructuring of, 196
Antidumping, 76
Appleton, Barry, 84
Arbitration, 78, 86
Argentina: Brazilian relations with, 90n5, 148, 162, 163–164; business sector, 200, 204; Economic Integration and Cooperation Program (1986), 135; Free Trade Area of the Americas, 163; government procurement, 87; human rights, 55; as "maker" in integration process, 39; Mercosur role of, 42, 77, 160, 251; Mexican relations with, 43; as middle state, 158–164, 172; NAFTA, 160; opposition to U.S. hegemony, 23; Organization of American States, 160; political reform in, 55; as power pole in hemispheric regionalism, 42,

285

position, 163; Congressional attitude
toward, 129, 252; environmental
elements, 35; future of, 36; Latin
American commitment to, 95–96;
Mexican position, 164; NAFTA as
model for, 69, 70–71, 244; OAS role
in, 192–193; power distribution as
factor in, 38–43; sociocultural
elements, 35; structural contexts of,
37–38, 58; trade as pillar of, 44–53;
U.S. commitment to, 95–97; as U.S.
initiative, 19–20, 36*n1*, 150. *See also*
Integration; Regionalism
Hettne, Björn, 9–10, 12
Hierarchy of power, 38–43
Higgott, Richard A., 155, 156
Hispanics, 121
Hoekstra, Peter, 117
Holmes, John, 167
Hometowns Against Shutdowns, 223
Honeywell, 233
Horn, Steve, 117
House of Commons, Canadian, 116
House of Representatives, U.S.: Fair
Trade Caucus, 223; FTA passage,
115; NAFTA passage, 111, 121. *See
also* Congress
Hubert, Jean-Paul, 168
Hufbauer, Gary, 123
Hughes, G. Philip, 127
Human rights: in Brazil, 135, 187, 190;
Canadian support for, 190; in Chile,
55; in Colombia, 55; by country,
56*tab;* during transition to
democracy, 55; in El Salvador, 55; in
the European Union, 187; in Mexico,
120, 187, 190; in Nicaragua, 55;
north-south divide in, 54; OAS
declaration on, 180, 187; in Peru,
55; violations, 103. *See also*
Democracy
Hurrell, Andrew, 1, 10–12, 19, 112,
143–145, 191

Iacocca, Lee, 119
Immigration, 103, 118, 120, 126
Import-substitution, 146, 199
Indigenous peoples, 187
Industrial centers of gravity, 51
Industrialists, 199
Industrial Union of Argentina (UIA),

200, 217*n8*
Industrial Workers of the World
(IWW), 234
Institutional Revolutionary Party (PRI),
120
Integration: cores of strength in process
of, 38; integrationist-competitive
model, 207, 212–214; integrationist-
protectionist model, 207, 210–212;
political, 2–3, 15*n1*, 53–57;
secessionist-protectionist model,
207–210; varieties of, 4, 206. *See
also* Hemispheric regionalism;
Regionalism
Intellectual property, 140
Inter-American Commission on Human
Rights (IACHR): Canadian role in,
168; disappearances, 160;
discrimination, 187; Haitian crisis,
182; lack of support for, 181
Inter-American Conference for the
Maintenance of Continental Peace
and Security (Rio de Janeiro, 1947),
25
Inter-American Conference on
Problems of War and Peace (Mexico
City, 1945), 25
Inter-American Convention Against
Corruption, 185
Inter-American Convention on the
Prevention, Punishment, and
Eradication of Violence Against
Women, 187
Inter-American Court, 189–190
Inter-American Defense Board, 24,
35
Inter-American Development Bank,
90*n8*, 168, 191; creation of, 5; EAI
investment package, 32; human
rights, 180; outreach programs, 224;
role of, 34, 35, 107, 108; Small
Project Programme, 232; social
movements and, 231; State and Civil
Society Unit, 232; UPD partnership
with, 184
Inter-American System (IAS), 107
Inter-American Treaty of Reciprocal
Assistance (Rio Treaty, 1947), 5,
25–26, 107
International Commission for Support
and Verification (CIAV), 184

About the Book

The FTA, Mercosur, the Enterprise for the Americas Initiative, NAFTA, the Summit of the Americas—do these constitute building blocks in the construction of a new regional system? This book explores that question, offering an assessment of the state of regionalism in the Americas.

The authors first outline the regionalist project—which they view as essentially a U.S. initiative—and analyze the environment in which it has evolved. They then focus on the reactions and strategies of the various actors involved.

The final chapter of the book seeks to articulate the present contours of regionalism in the Americas and to identify future trends.

Gordon Mace is professor in the Department of Political Science and at the Graduate Institute of International Studies at Laval University. He is also director of the Research Group on International Relations at Laval. His recent publications include *Foreign Policy and Regionalism in the Americas* (coedited with Jean-Philippe Thérien). **Louis Bélanger** is assistant professor of political science at Laval. He is coauthor (with Louis Balthazar and Gordon Mace) of *Trente ans de politique extérieure du Québec, 1960–1990.*

E 18·85 MAC